# Assembly Language for Pascal Programmers

Steven Holzner

BRADY

New York London Toronto Sydney Tokyo Singapore

Copyright © 1990 by Steven Holzner
All rights reserved
including the right of reproduction
in whole or in part in any form.

BRADY

Simon & Schuster, Inc.
15 Columbus Circle
New York, NY 10023

DISTRIBUTED BY PRENTICE HALL TRADE

Manufactured in the United States of America

10 9 8 7 6 5 4 3 2 1

**Library of Congress Cataloging-in-Publication Data**

Holzner, Steven.
Assembly language for Pascal programmers / Steven Holzner
p. cm.
1. Assembler language (Computer program language) I. Title
QA76.73.A8H64 1990
005.13'3—dc20 89–71165
ISBN 0–13–652975–5 CIP

## Dedication

To the hard-working people at Brady Books, especially Marjorie Gursky, Jennifer Boynton, and Tom Dillon.

## Limits of Liability and Disclaimer of Warranty

The author and publisher of this book have used their best efforts in preparing this book and the programs contained in it. These efforts include the development, research, and testing of theories and programs to determine their effectiveness. The author and publisher shall not be liable in any event for incidental or consequential damages in connection with, or arising out of, the furnishing, performance, or use of these programs.

## Registered Trademarks

Microsoft C, Microsoft Assembler, and Microsoft OS/2 are registered trademarks of Microsoft Corporation.

Turbo C and Turbo Assembler are trademarks of Borland International Corporation.

IBM, IBM PC and IBM PS/2 are registered trademarks of International Business Machines Corporation.

Intel is a registered trademark of Intel Corporation.

Apple and Macintosh are registered trademarks of Apple Computer, Inc.

# Contents

# Introduction

Welcome to assembly language. This book will be your guide as we tour many areas: input and output, file handling, graphics, databases, indirect addressing, debugging, and interfacing Pascal to assembly language.

This last topic is an important one because this book is specially designed to be an assembly language primer for Pascal programmers. Pascal is one of the most popular programming languages today. However, there are times when you need more—more speed, more control over the computer, or more control over your data. At such times, you need assembly language.

Mixing assembly language with high-level languages like Pascal has become a popular practice. It's a potent combination; you get the raw power of assembly language and all the advantages of Pascal. However, before you can mix the two, you have to understand what's going on in assembly language. For that reason, you'll get a good background in assembly language before we connect it to Pascal.

## The Details

The first chapter of this book is dedicated to welcoming you to assembly language. Here we begin by noticing the similarity between a program written in Pascal and one written in assembly language, both of which do the same thing. As programmers, you are already familiar with much of the introductory matter usually described in assembly language texts, so we can skip that (i.e., what a byte is, how computers work) and start directly by putting together a working program that produces output.

In this book, the emphasis is on short, working examples. There's nothing like an example to make a point clear, and you'll see some of them right here, as you learn what an assembler does and the basics of our own assembly language programs.

The next chapter deals with accepting input from the keyboard. We accept data from the keyboard and work with it, using assembly language's equivalent of readln().

You'll find that much of the hard work in assembly language has already been done for us in DOS; we'll use many of the low-level system resources available to us. In fact, assembly language programming on the PC is really a mix of assembly language instructions and the system services, which provide many pre-written routines, ready to use.

These routines include ones to write to the screen, handle disks, or accept input from the keyboard. Many of them are dedicated to working with files, and we will investigate that in Chapter 3.

File handling, which is extraordinarily quick in assembly language, gives you complete control over your data. If you want to read 32117 bytes from a file and place it at a given address in memory, now you can do it. In assembly language, we remove the layers buffering you from your data often found in Pascal. We'll learn about the many file-handling options under DOS and how to use files to our advantage. We'll continue on to more advanced topics like the file position pointer and use of file records.

In Chapter 4, we explore another popular part of assembly language programming: screen control and graphics. Again, assembly language is frequently used here for its speed and compactness. We'll see how to write directly to the screen buffer for the ultimate in speed.

Before we interface Pascal and assembly language, we'll investigate one more very popular assembly language use—pop-up programs. Pop-up programs are usually written mostly in assembly language to save space. Here, you'll see how they work, how to send data to the screen, and how to intercept keystrokes.

There is much to say about assembly language when it comes to speed and precision, of course. However, it is difficult to write full-scale programs in assembly language. Instead, it is often used with Pascal to form composite programs—you can accelerate those tight loops, speed any graphics, or shorten critical code when you need to. Chapter 6 is where we connect assembly language and Pascal together. We see how to use in-line machine code first. You have the option of including machine code directly in your program in Pascal and that's often very useful.

However, it is also very limited, and you'll see that this practice isn't up to complicated tasks. For larger applications, we'll have to link assembly language modules directly to Pascal programs. You'll see how to work with Pascal data from an assembly language module, how to emulate a Pascal function, and how to use the new assembler directives that make the whole process easy.

As you get more comfortable with that interface, we will be able to put it to work—and we do, with many examples.

Now that you know how to connect assembly language into Pascal programs, you will see why it's worthwhile to do so. The next two chapters deal with fast math (a frequent use of assembly language), and the math coprocessors. We'll find that the 80x87 chips have an instruction set all their own and that they work quite differently from the 80x86.

Up to this point, we've been dealing only with DOS. But there is a new operating system on the horizon—OS/2. Now that the Presentation Manager has appeared,

OS/2 is rapidly becoming more popular. For that reason, the final two chapters, Chapters 9 and 10, are devoted to it.

The microprocessor's assembly language instructions don't change when we switch to OS/2, but the way we use the system resources certainly does. We'll find most of the system routines we've been using under DOS also available under OS/2 but with different names. And they must be accessed differently. We spend one chapter getting down the fundamentals of OS/2 (including multitasking) and one chapter on the Presentation Manager. However, the Presentation Manager, a complex topic, should be treated as advanced material.

# What You'll Need

Throughout the book, we will use both Turbo Pascal and Quick Pascal. These compilers are similar enough so that the differences will rarely be important in this book—you can use either one. However, you will need a recent assembler: MASM (the Microsoft Macro Assembler) 5.1 or later; or TASM (the Turbo assembler) 1.0 or later. The "simplified segment directives" used throughout this book are supported only in recent assembler versions.

Also, if you want to work with OS/2, you need to use the Microsoft software—Borland's products don't yet produce programs that run under OS/2. To do any Presentation Manager work, you'll need either a recent OS/2 Software Development Kit or the Microsoft Presentation Manager Toolkit. While all the other parts of OS/2 are available for anyone to work with, the Presentation Manager requires a file named OS2.LIB, available only from these sources.

You'll also need an editor to type in the programs we develop. Almost any editor will do (particularly the built-in editors in Quick Pascal and Turbo Pascal): If it can print out intelligible English, the compilers and assemblers can read it. Word processors that store text in their proprietary format may not work.

The reason we'll use an editor is that this book is filled with examples, which are often omitted in assembly language books. But leaving out examples is like learning to fly by reading a catalog of plane parts. Too often books on programming are just like catalogs: long lists of "classes" of commands and impenetrable discussions of every available option for each instruction—without any coherent means of tying it all together.

But the easiest way to learn is just by seeing it work. To a reader earnestly making his or her way through this material, one simple example is worth a thousand descriptions.

You'll find that assembly language is much like Pascal in many ways—you already have a leg up. Taking a look at assembly language from the Pascal programmer's point of view will be a fruitful approach for us. Let's begin immediately with Chapter 1, "Welcome to Assembly Language."

# 1

# Welcome to Assembly Language

Take a look at this program:

```
program calculator;
var
   a,b,c : integer;
begin
     a := 5;
     b := 3;
     a := a + b;
     c := a - b;
end.
```

It looks pretty simple. We declare three integer variables, a, b, and c. In the program itself, we place 5 in a and 3 in b, then do a little math, adding and subtracting a and b.

Now, take a look at this program:

```
        .CODE
        ORG     100H
BEGIN:
        MOV     AX,5
        MOV     BX,3
        ADD     AX,BX
        SUB     CX,BX
END     BEGIN
```

This one looks less familiar, but not more complex. The actions here are similar: We place 5 into a variable named AX and 3 in BX. Then we do a little math, adding and subtracting AX and BX.

This program is written in assembly language, and that's what assembly language looks like. It's different than Pascal, but knowing Pascal is going to give you a huge advantage in learning assembly language.

# What a Compiler Does

Here's another Pascal program, sort_ab.pas:

```
program sort_ab;
var
   a, b, c : integer;
begin
     a := 3;
     b := 5;
     if a > b then begin
c := a;
a := b;
b := c;
     end;
end.
```

This program does some work internally, but it doesn't produce any visible result. It simply moves some data around and sorts the data in a and b so that b holds the higher value.

As you know, the PC cannot run sort_ab.pas as it stands. You need a *compiler* like Turbo Pascal or Quick Pascal to translate it into *machine language*.

## Machine Language

To get a computer to do something, you have to supply machine language instructions, and these bytes are really comprehensible only to the processor. Often, only part of the machine language instruction will be used to tell the computer what to do. The rest of the instruction is made up of data. For example, you can write an instruction to put the byte FFH (the H means it's in hex, just as the $ symbol does in Pascal) into a certain memory location. Part of the instruction tells the microprocessor that you want to store a number, part tells it where in memory you want to store the number, and part is the number itself, FFH.

Although machine language instructions can be many bytes long, data and the instruction code itself never mix across byte boundaries. For example, one machine language instruction may be all instruction to the microprocessor:

```
01010101

Instruction
```

And some will be a mix of instruction and data:

```
10101010   10111010

Instruction   Data used by the instruction.
```

or even mostly data:

```
01010101   10111010 10010101 001010100

Instruction   Data used by the instruction.
```

The data used by the instruction is either memory address(es) or immediate data, like the FFH we wanted to store in a memory location earlier.

Reading this binary code is extremely difficult. Imagine yourself confronted with a page of numbers, all 0's or 1's. Even if such instructions were converted to hex, you'd have to look up the meaning of each byte before understanding what was going on (there are tables in the manuals that accompany assemblers spelling out binary instructions). Mostly, what means everything to the microprocessor means nothing to us.

For example, take another look at sort_ab.pas:

```
program sort_ab;
var
   a, b, c : integer;
begin
     a := 3;
     b := 5;
     if a > b then begin
        c := a;
        a := b;
        b := c;
     end;
end.
```

These statements are translated into machine language instructions, which just look like a string of bytes to us. Here they are (all values are hexadecimal):

```
C7 06 3E 00 03 00 C7 06 40 00 05 00 A1 3E 00 3B 06 40 00 7E
12 A1 3E 00 A3 42 00 A1 40 00 A3 3E 00 A1 42 00 A3 40 00
```

Each of these bytes has its own meaning to the PC but not much to us. We can even group these machine language bytes into machine language instructions (again, all in hexadecimal):

```
C7063E000300
C70640000500
A13E00
3B064000
7E12
A13E00
A34200
A14000
A33E00
A14200
A34000
```

But that is not much more help.

# What Assembly Language Is

This is where assembly language comes in. For *each* machine language instruction, there is a corresponding assembly language instruction.

In Pascal, each statement may be translated into many, even dozens, of machine language instructions. In assembly language, there is only one. The statements of sort_ab.pas can be translated from machine language into assembly language like this:

```
C7063E000300  →  MOV    WORD PTR [003E],0003
C70640000500  →  MOV    WORD PTR [0040],0005
A13E00        →  MOV    AX,[003E]
3B064000      →  CMP    AX,[0040]
7E12          →  JLE    0135
A13E00        →  MOV    AX,[003E]
A34200        →  MOV    [0042],AX
A14000        →  MOV    AX,[0040]
A33E00        →  MOV    [003E],AX
A14200        →  MOV    AX,[0042]
A34000        →  MOV    [0040],AX
```

Each number in brackets above, like [003E], stands for a memory reference. If we put in the name of the corresponding one-word variables instead, we get this:

```
        MOV     a,3
        MOV     b,5
        MOV     AX,a
        CMP     AX,b
        JLE     OK
        MOV     AX,a
        MOV     c,AX
        MOV     AX,b
        MOV     a,AX
        MOV     AX,c
        MOV     b,AX
OK:
```

If you have some familiarity with assembly language, you can probably see what's going on here already. If not, then welcome to assembly language. This is what our assembly language programs will look like in this book.

The statements you can use in Pascal are defined by people like Nickolaus Wirth; the statements you can use in assembly language are defined by the instruction set of the 80x86 microprocessor. In other words, for each machine language command, there is one, and only one, assembly language instruction (keep in mind that a single Pascal statement might translate into dozens of machine language commands).

## What an Assembler Does

In this book, we'll learn the built-in instructions of the 80x86 (and, in Chapter 8, of the 80x87). We can use each of those instructions in assembly language. When you want to produce machine language from an assembly language program, you use an assembler instead of a compiler.

An assembler does the reverse of the preceding process: It takes our assembly language instructions and produces machine language:

```
    MOV    a,3       →       C7063E000300
    MOV    b,5       →       C70640000500
    MOV    AX,a      →       A13E00
    CMP    AX,b      →       3B064000
    JLE    OK        →       7E12
    MOV    AX,a      →       A13E00
    MOV    c,AX      →       A34200
    MOV    AX,b      →       A14000
    MOV    a,AX      →       A33E00
    MOV    AX,c      →       A14200
    MOV    b,AX      →       A34000
OK:
```

This book is about instructions on the left. Let's start by deciphering some of them. To do that, we need to know more about the insides of the computer.

## Registers in Your Microprocessor

The 80x86 is built with a number of internal *registers*, called *general-purpose* registers, and we may think of them as predefined variables. Each one of these registers holds exactly one word, 16 bits.

The four general purpose registers are AX, BX, CX, and DX. If you've worked with the Intr() procedure, you already know about these registers. They are always there inside the 80x86, and it's hard to think of an assembly language program that could get along without them. They'll hold our data, one word at a time (or two words in the 80386), while we work with it.

Operations that involve moving data around (except for some options with the 80x86's useful string moving instructions, which we'll see later) always use these registers in some way. This moving operation will be our introduction to assembly language in action.

# The MOV Instruction

The most fundamental assembly language instruction is MOV, the instruction that moves data between registers and memory or between register and registers. It is assembly language's version of the assignment operator, :=.

The MOV format is this: MOV Destination, Source. The microprocessor moves the data from the source into the destination. If you have something stored in memory and want to work with it, you can use MOV. Here's how it works:

```
MOV     AX,0FFFFH
```

Here we are putting the number 0FFFFH (65535) into AX. This is the biggest number any register (except for the 80386, all are 16 bits) can hold: 0FFFFH.

> Note the leading 0, which is added to let the assembler know that we intend 0FFFFH to be taken as a number and not an English word.

We can take the value 0FFFFH in the register AX and move it into the register DX:

```
MOV     DX,AX    (Move the data from AX into DX)
```

And now DX and AX hold the same value.

Data can also be moved into these registers from memory. Let's say we have a memory location with 0 in it: This value can be moved into, say, CX, this way:

```
MOV     CX,[Memory Location]
```

or we can move whatever is in DX into the memory location this way:

```
MOV     [Memory Location],DX
```

However, data cannot be moved from memory to memory in one step. This is one of the peculiarities of the 80x86. Data cannot go directly from memory location to memory location in one instruction. If we wanted to, we could move data from a memory location labeled COUNTER to a general purpose register and then to a memory location named INDEX like this:

```
MOV AX, COUNTER
MOV INDEX, AX
```

But we cannot do this:

```
MOV COUNTER, INDEX
```

> This is why there were twice as many MOV instructions in the assembly language translation of sort_ab as there were assignment operators to begin with.

# Seeing It Work

It's all very well to talk in the abstract, but it's always better to see an example. There is an excellent program named DEBUG that comes with all DOS versions. DEBUG can assemble on the spot small programs that you write—a mini-assembler is built into the program. We'll use this mini-assembler to convert the instruction MOV AX,5 into machine language and then run it, watching the value stored in AX change from 0 to 5.

If you want to follow along on your computer, start the DEBUG program; it gives you its hyphen prompt:

```
A>DEBUG
-
```

The command R in DEBUG stands for Register and lets you see the contents of all the 80x86's registers. You can readily pick out the general purpose registers AX, BX, CX, and DX (note: All numbers displayed in DEBUG are in hexadecimal, which is standard for assembly language debuggers):

```
A>DEBUG
-R
AX=0000  BX=0000  CX=0000  DX=0000  SP=FFEE  BP=0000  SI=0000  DI=0000
DS=0EF1  ES=0EF1  SS=0EF1  CS=0EF1  IP=0100   NV UP EI PL NZ NA PO NC
0EF1:0100 9AEC04020F    CALL    0F02:04EC
```

In addition to the registers shown:

```
A>DEBUG
-R
AX=0000  BX=0000  CX=0000  DX=0000  SP=FFEE  BP=0000  SI=0000  DI=0000
DS=0EF1  ES=0EF1  SS=0EF1  CS=0EF1  IP=0100   NV UP EI PL NZ NA PO NC
0EF1:0100 9AEC04020F    CALL    0F02:04EC
```

The settings of the internal *flags* of the 80x86 are shown (there are eight flags; later microprocessors have more):

```
A>DEBUG
-R
AX=0000  BX=0000  CX=0000  DX=0000  SP=FFEE  BP=0000  SI=0000  DI=0000
DS=0EF1  ES=0EF1  SS=0EF1  CS=0EF1  IP=0100   NV UP EI PL NZ NA PO NC
0EF1:0100 9AEC04020F    CALL    0F02:04EC
```

Flags are used in conditional jumps, and we'll work with them in the next chapter. When you execute an instruction—a comparison, for example, between two integers—the flags are set in a way that indicates the result. You can then execute a conditional jump, which will do different things depending on how the flags have been set. DEBUG also tells you the current memory location. Here, we are at memory location 0EF1:0100 (the location will probably be different on your computer):

```
A>DEBUG
-R
AX=0000  BX=0000  CX=0000  DX=0000  SP=FFEE  BP=0000  SI=0000  DI=0000
DS=0EF1  ES=0EF1  SS=0EF1  CS=0EF1  IP=0100   NV UP EI PL NZ NA PO NC
0EF1:0100 9AEC04020F     CALL     0F02:04EC
```

Addresses in the PC are always given in this format—two hexadecimal numbers separated by a colon. You'll see how they work in a few pages.

The final part of the DEBUG R display indicates what is to be found at the current memory location. In our case, those are the bytes following the address in the R display.

```
A>DEBUG
-R
AX=0000  BX=0000  CX=0000  DX=0000  SP=FFEE  BP=0000  SI=0000  DI=0000
DS=0EF1  ES=0EF1  SS=0EF1  CS=0EF1  IP=0100   NV UP EI PL NZ NA PO NC
0EF1:0100 9AEC04020F     CALL     0F02:04EC
```

DEBUG tries to group bytes together, starting at the current memory location (which only holds one byte), into what would be a valid machine-language instruction. It then provides us with an assembly language translation of the machine-language instruction that begins at our present location.

When there is in reality no machine language instruction there, as there often is not, the translation is meaningless. This is the case here: having just started up DEBUG, there is as yet no program to look at. It is just taking leftover bytes in the computer's memory and trying to make sense of them; in fact, DEBUG's supplied translation means nothing:

```
A>DEBUG
-R
AX=0000  BX=0000  CX=0000  DX=0000  SP=FFEE  BP=0000  SI=0000  DI=0000
DS=0EF1  ES=0EF1  SS=0EF1  CS=0EF1  IP=0100   NV UP EI PL NZ NA PO NC
0EF1:0100 9AEC04020F     CALL     0F02:04EC
```

We'll use the A (for Assemble) command to put in our own program, which consists of only one line: MOV AX,5. The A command requires an address at which to start depositing the machine language instructions it will generate in memory. Our current address is EF1:0100, and we will tell it to assemble the machine language right there, using the shorthand A100:

```
A>DEBUG
-R
AX=0000  BX=0000  CX=0000  DX=0000  SP=FFEE  BP=0000  SI=0000  DI=0000
DS=0EF1  ES=0EF1  SS=0EF1  CS=0EF1  IP=0100   NV UP EI PL NZ NA PO NC
0EF1:0100 9AEC04020F    CALL    0F02:04EC
-A100                          ← Here is the A100 command.
0EF1:0100                      ← DEBUG's response.
```

Following the A100 command, DEBUG returns with the line:

```
0EF1:0100
```

showing the current address at which it will deposit assembled code. We simply type

```
MOV AX,5
```

and then a carriage return.

```
A>DEBUG
-R
AX=0000  BX=0000  CX=0000  DX=0000  SP=FFEE  BP=0000  SI=0000  DI=0000
DS=0EF1  ES=0EF1  SS=0EF1  CS=0EF1  IP=0100   NV UP EI PL NZ NA PO NC
0EF1:0100 9AEC04020F    CALL    0F02:04EC
-A100
0EF1:0100 MOV     AX,5            ← Type "MOV AX,5<cr>"
0EF1:0103
```

DEBUG then prompts us for the next instruction we wish to give by displaying the address

```
0EF1:0103.
```

There are no more instructions to assemble at this time, so we give DEBUG a carriage return: DEBUG interprets the blank line to mean that we are through assembling and returns to its normal prompt.

That's all there is to it. We've just assembled our first line of assembly language. To see what occurred, remember that the R command displays the current memory location and instruction. Since we assembled

```
MOV AX,5
```

at the current memory location, let's give the R command and take a look:

```
A>DEBUG
-R
AX=0000  BX=0000  CX=0000  DX=0000  SP=FFEE  BP=0000  SI=0000  DI=0000
```

```
DS=0EF1   ES=0EF1   SS=0EF1   CS=0EF1   IP=0100    NV UP EI PL NZ NA PO NC
0EF1:0100 9AEC04020F     CALL     0F02:04EC
-A100
0EF1:0100 MOV      AX,5
0EF1:0103
-R
AX=0000   BX=0000   CX=0000   DX=0000   SP=FFEE   BP=0000   SI=0000   DI=0000
DS=0EF1   ES=0EF1   SS=0EF1   CS=0EF1   IP=0100    NV UP EI PL NZ NA PO NC
0EF1:0100 B80500          MOV     AX,0005
```

We can see the instruction (note the machine language instruction B8H 05H 00H corresponding to MOV AX,5 in DEBUG's display). Executing the instruction is simple; DEBUG has a trace command. If you have debugged Pascal programs, then you're familiar with the idea of tracing through programs. Typing T once will execute the current instruction, and increment us to the next memory location:

```
A>DEBUG
-R
AX=0000   BX=0000   CX=0000   DX=0000   SP=FFEE   BP=0000   SI=0000   DI=0000
DS=0EF1   ES=0EF1   SS=0EF1   CS=0EF1   IP=0100    NV UP EI PL NZ NA PO NC
0EF1:0100 9AEC04020F     CALL     0F02:04EC
-A100
0EF1:0100 MOV      AX,5
0EF1:0103
-R
AX=0000   BX=0000   CX=0000   DX=0000   SP=FFEE   BP=0000   SI=0000   DI=0000
DS=0EF1   ES=0EF1   SS=0EF1   CS=0EF1   IP=0100    NV UP EI PL NZ NA PO NC
0EF1:0100 B80500          MOV     AX,0005
-T                        ← This will execute our MOV instruction.

AX=0005   BX=0000   CX=0000   DX=0000   SP=FFEE   BP=0000   SI=0000   DI=0000
DS=0EF1   ES=0EF1   SS=0EF1   CS=0EF1   IP=0103    NV UP EI PL NZ NA PO NC
0EF1:0103 020F            ADD     CL,[BX]                           DS:0000=CD
```

After the T command, DEBUG gives its usual display, indicating what the register contents and flags are now. AX now holds 5.

All the flags remain unchanged. On the other hand, the memory location *has* changed, from 0EF1:0100 to 0EF1:0103. 0EF1:0103 is three bytes past the address 0EF1:0100. This is because the machine language instruction corresponding to MOV AX,5 is three bytes long in memory (B8H 05H 00H). The instruction following it will begin three bytes later: Therefore the 100 has changed to 103.

# A Program

DEBUG not only allows you to assemble programs but to write them out to the disk as well. Let's use DEBUG to assemble our first assembly language progam. It will simply type the letter Z and exit.

We'll start with the A command; as before, we will put our machine language code starting at location 0100H:

```
A>DEBUG
-A100          ←
0EF1:0100
```

Just type in the following assembly language instructions verbatim, followed by a carriage return after the prompt 0EF1:010A to stop assembling:

```
A>DEBUG
-A100
0EF1:0100 MOV      AX,0200        ←
0EF1:0103 MOV      DX,005A        ←
0EF1:0106 INT      21             ←
0EF1:0108 INT      20             ←
0EF1:010A        ← Just type a <cr> here.
-
```

Our program is loading the registers AX and DX by using the MOV instruction. This is the preparation for having the program print the character Z.

What happens next is that two INT instructions are given, INT 21H, and INT 20H. These instructions will be important ones for us—they are the way programs can interface with DOS and BIOS. Later we'll discuss the exact nature of these instructions in our program. The way we have loaded the registers AX and DX here will make the instruction INT 21H print a Z; at the end we use the INT 20H instruction to end the program.

We will write our program to the disk by naming the program first with the N (for name) command. Let's call the program PRINTZ.COM, following its function. We name it this way:

```
A>DEBUG
-A100
0EF1:0100 MOV      AX,0200
0EF1:0103 MOV      DX,005A
0EF1:0106 INT      21
0EF1:0108 INT      20
0EF1:010A
-NPRINTZ.COM     ←
```

And now we can write it out (DEBUG will write this file in the current directory). DEBUG needs the number of bytes to write out, and in our case, the program goes from locations 0100H to 0109H. Each memory location holds a byte, so that makes 10 bytes. DEBUG is expecting hex, so we will give it a value of 0AH.

The DEBUG W command, Write, reads the number of bytes to write as a file directly out of the CX register. This means that to write our 10-byte program PRINTZ.COM, we will have to load the CX register with 0AH and then give the W command.

## Loading a Register in DEBUG

To move 0AH into CX, we can use the R (Register) command again. If you use the R command without any arguments, DEBUG gives you its standard register display. On the other hand, giving the command RCX tells DEBUG that you wish to change the value in CX (this works with any register). DEBUG displays the current value in CX (which will be 0000) and gives us a colon prompt, after which we will type our new value for CX, A (for 0AH), and a carriage return. Then we can write PRINTZ.COM by giving the W command:

```
A>DEBUG
-A100
0EF1:0100 MOV     AX,0200
0EF1:0103 MOV     DX,005A
0EF1:0106 INT     21
0EF1:0108 INT     20
0EF1:010A
-U100 109
0EF1:0100 B80002          MOV    AX,0200
0EF1:0103 BA5A00          MOV    DX,005A
0EF1:0106 CD21            INT    21
0EF1:0108 CD20            INT    20
-NPRINTZ.COM
-RCX
CX 0000
:A
-W                 ← The W command
Writing 000A bytes
-Q
```

Let's run it PRINTZ.COM:

```
F:\>printz
Z
F:\>
```

And PRINTZ does what it's supposed to do: types Z and exits.

## The High and Low Bytes of General Purpose Registers

In the 80x86 microprocessors, there is a way of splitting the general purpose registers—AX, BX, CX, and DX—into their high and low bytes, and using them independently. Only the general purpose registers can be split up. For example, the top half of AX can be referred to as AH (H for High byte) and the bottom byte can be referred to as AL (L for low byte). We could say:

```
MOV     AH,5          or          MOV     AL,3AH H
```

> Note that the single instruction MOV AX,053AH does the same thing as using both instructions MOV AH,5 and MOV AL,3AH.

The high and low registers that can be used as separate registers are AH, AL, BH, BL, CH, CL, DH, and DL. Very often, when we pass information to DOS or BIOS, we will have to use these one-byte registers.

The INT 21H instruction, which we can use to print our character and do many more things, needs information to be passed to it in the AH and DL registers. Our program could have been shortened to:

```
MOV     AH,02H ←
MOV     DL,5AH ←
INT     21H
INT     20H
```

This version of PRINTZ works just as our old one did, because this printing service of INT 21H requires information only in the one-byte registers AH and DL. Let's take a closer look at the INT instruction now.

# Interrupts

Maybe you are already familiar with interrupts from using the Intr() procedure. Interrupts are given numbers; you might have seen a call to, say, INT $13 this way:

```
Intr($13, regs)
```

where regs is the Pascal structure that holds values passed to the 80x86 registers. Intr() is a popular procedure, but if interrupts are are useful in Pascal, they are indispensable in assembly language.

When you give an INT instruction, a pre-written program—already in memory—is run. For example, one of these programs prints out characters on the screen. The programs that are run are parts of DOS or BIOS, and the instructions are stored in reserved parts of memory.

These pre-written programs were just written themselves in assembly language, they do all the hard work of actually handing the disk drive controllers or the screen controller chips by having the microprocessor send signals to them. That's not something we should have to do in our programs—every time we want to print on the screen, we don't want to have to check the video controller rescan register and the dozens of other necessary things—and with software *interrupts*, all the work can be condensed into one instruction.

The 80x86 has the ability to use 256 possible interrupts, from INT 00 to INT FFH. Some of these interrupts are used by DOS, some by BIOS, and some by BASIC. Here are all the interrupts the PC or PS/2 is capable of, and what part of the operating system they are used by:

| *Interrupt Number (Hex)* | *Used By* |
|---|---|
| 00 - 1F | BIOS |
| 18 | Starts ROM BASIC |
| 19 | BOOTSTRAP (Boots PC) |
| 1A - 1F | BIOS |
| 20 - 3F | DOS |
| 40 - 5F | BIOS (PC XT and Later) |
| 60 - 66 | Free |
| 67 | LIM/EMS Support |
| 68 - 7F | BIOS (PC XT and Later) |
| 80 - F0 | BASIC |
| F0 - FF | Free |

You can see that a group of interrupts, INTs 20H-3FH, have been set aside for DOS. The DOS interrupts do many things, from printing on the screen to opening and closing files, from putting keyboard input into a buffer in memory for you to printing out many characters at once if you so decide. Among the DOS interrupts, numbers 20H to 3FH, there is a giant that we will come to know well, INT 21H.

## INT 21H

IBM decided to group almost all of DOS's capabilities into INT 21H (see the listing of all the interrupts in the appendix). From Pascal, you can reach INT 21H with either Intr($21,regs) or MsDos(regs).

For example, to work with files on the PS/2 or PC, a program calls INT 21H at a low level. You can be sure that the executable code that a Pascal compiler produces is full of INT 21H instructions. To get a quick overview of what is available with software interrupts, take a look now at the Appendix.

These capabilities of DOS are open to us, since we are programming in its home language, assembly language. For example, our program PRINTZ has been typing characters on the screen the same way DOS itself does it, using INT 21H, service 2.

INT 21H is divided into numerous services, and the number of services grows with each DOS version. The INT 21H printing service is service number 2. To select an INT 21H service, we have to load its number in the AH register before our INT 21H instruction, as we have done in PRINTZ.

```
MOV     AH,02H ←
MOV     DL,5AH
INT     21H
INT     20H
```

In addition, service 2 expects us to supply it with the ASCII code of the letter it is to type. In this case, Z is equal to ASCII 90, or 5AH. Then we can execute the INT 21H instruction and Z appears on the screen.

Here are some popular services that can be used in INT 21H: this list is just to get us started, we will add more services later. To use these INT 21H services, just load the registers as shown and execute an INT 21H instruction:

| *Service #* | *Name* | *Set These* | *What Happens* |
|---|---|---|---|
| 1 | Keyboard Input | AH = 1 | ASCII code of typed key returned in AL |
| 2 | Character Output | AH = 2<br>DL = ASCII Code | The character corresponding to the ASCII CODE in DL is put on the screen |
| 9 | String Output | AH=9<br>DS:DX = Address of string of characters to print | Prints a string of bytes from memory on the screen (we will use this service in this chapter) |

In particular, service 9, String Output, is the writeln() of assembly language. We will make frequent use of it. Other INT 21H services create files or subdirectories, delete files, load programs, allocate memory, and many other things.

INT 20H, the last instruction in PRINTZ, lets DOS know that we are done—DOS will exit from the program and we return to the command prompt like C:\>. Most of the programs we write will end with INT 20H, the standard last instruction for assembly language programs.

Now that we have some experience, we can start putting together assembly language programs without using DEBUG.

To do that, we'll have to review the way memory is accessed by the 80x86 chips—memory usage is even more important in assembly language than it is in Pascal. When you write an assembly language program, you have to specify everything about how it should be set up in memory, so memory is the first thing we'll cover.

# Memory Usage

You may recall that when we were using DEBUG, we saw addresses like 0EF1:0100. That address is made up of two hex numbers, each 16 bits long. This is usual for addresses—two words are involved for a full address. The 0EF1H in 0EF1:0100 is the *segment* address of that particular memory location, and 0100H is the *offset* address:

```
A Typical Address

        0EF1:0100
        |    └──────────── Offset Address
        └───────────────── Segment Address
```

There are actually 20 address *lines* in the 80x86 CPUs (in real mode), which means that addresses are 20 bits long. Binary numbers 20 bits long can range from 0 to $2^{20} - 1$, so you give a unique number to each of $2^{20}$ memory locations, or 1 Megabyte. The way a 20-bit address is generated from two 16-bit words (segment:offset) is to shift the segment over one hexadecimal place and then to add the offset, like this:

```
  0EF1   ← Note: Segment shifted over one place
+ 0100
 -----
 0F010
```

The resulting answer is 5 hex digits long. Every hex digit is made up of 4 binary digits, so this number is 20 bits long. In other words, 0EF1:0100 corresponds to the memory location 0F010H. Another way of looking at it is that the segment address 0EF1 corresponds to the memory location 0EF10H, and that 0EF1:0100 is 100H bytes after that point.

Using these 20-bit addresses, we can refer to 1 Megabyte, 1024K:

| Segmented Address | | Real Address | |
|---|---|---|---|
| F000:FFFF | 1 Byte | FFFFFH | ← The top of memory |
| F000:FFFE | 1 Byte | FFFFEH | (FFFFFH = 1 MByte - 1) |
| F000:FFFD | 1 Byte | FFFFDH | |
| F000:FFFC | 1 Byte | FFFFCH | |
| | : | | |
| C000:AAAA | 1 Byte | CAAAAH | |
| C000:AAA9 | 1 Byte | CAAA9H | |
| C000:AAA8 | 1 Byte | CAAA8H | |
| C000:AAA7 | 1 Byte | CAAA7H | |
| | : | | |
| 0000:0003 | 1 Byte | 00003H | |
| 0000:0002 | 1 Byte | 00002H | |
| 0000:0001 | 1 Byte | 00001H | |
| 0000:0000 | 1 Byte | 00000H | ← The bottom of memory |

Pascal offers you many ways of examining segments. For example, if you can use the Seg() and Ofs() functions like this:

```
program MemLocs;
uses
    crt;
var
   a : integer;
procedure Hello(w:string);
       begin
       writeln("Hello",w);
       end;
begin
→  writeln ("Address of procedure Hello is",
Seg(Hello):6,":",Ofs(Hello):6);
end.
```

Here we find the segment and offset of a procedure named Hello(). It produces this output:

```
Address of procedure Hello is  9827:     6
```

(Note that these numbers are in decimal). Every single byte stored in memory, data or microprocessor instructions has an address attached to it. In assembly language, it will be easy to refer to individual memory locations.

You can do the same in Pascal with the mem[] "array" to reference memory values. For example, the current screen mode is stored internally at location 0040:0049; we can make this change to our program:

```
program MemLocs;
uses
    crt;
var
   a : integer;
procedure Hello(w:string);
       begin
       writeln("Hello",w);
       end;
begin
writeln ("Address of procedure Hello is", Seg(Hello):6,":",Ofs(Hello):6);
→  writeln ("The screen mode is", mem[$0040:$0049]:4);
end.
```

And this is the result:

```
Address of procedure Hello is  9827:     6
The screen mode is   3←
```

Let's spend a little more time understanding segments, since they are crucial throughout the rest of the book.

## Segments In Memory

A segment is the memory space that can be addressed with one particular segment address. That space can go from xxxx:0000 to xxxx:FFFF, which makes it 64K long. For example, the segment that starts at the bottom of memory, segment 0000, can extend from 0000:0000 to 0000:FFFF (keeping the segment address, 0000, unchanged). Once you choose a segment address, like 0000, you have a 64K workspace you can use without having to change the segment address again.

On the other hand, even though segments can describe such a large area, they can overlap. The next possible segment is segment 0001. This segment extends from 0001:0000 to 0001:FFFF. Converting these numbers to 20-bit addresses gives 00010 to 1000F.

Segment 0001 starts just 16 bytes (called a *paragraph*) after segment 0000. Segment 0002 starts just 16 bytes after segment 0001. Choosing a segment gives you a 64K work space: but that 64K work space overlaps with many other segments too:

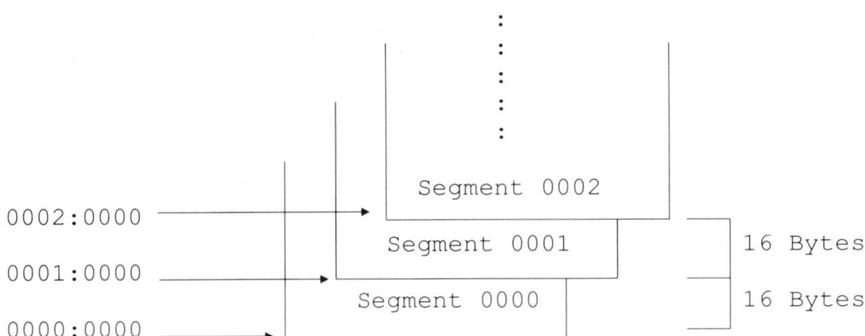


To let you set the segment that you want to choose as your work area, the 80x86 provides four *segment registers*. Typically you set these segment registers at the beginning of a program or let them be set automatically for you. Keep in mind, however, that they define only a 64K area. If you want something outside that area, you'll have to take care of setting them as required.

The four segment registers—CS, DS, ES, and SS—stand for code segment, data segment, extra segment, and stack segment:

| *Segment Register* | *Means* | *Used With* |
|---|---|---|
| CS | Code Segment | Your program's Instructions. |
| DS | Data Segment | The data you want to work on. |
| ES | Extra Segment | Auxilary data segment register. |
| SS | Stack Segment | Set by DOS; holds the "stack." |

The code segment is where the instructions of your program will be stored. When your program is loaded, the code segment is chosen for it by the program loader.

You will not have to set this segment register, CS, for the things we are going to do in this book. If however, a program wants to know where it was placed in memory (i.e., what the segment address of the code is), it can read the value in CS at any time.

```
              CS
         Code Segment
        ______________
       |              |
       |  MOV AX,5    |     ← CS holds the segment
       |  MOV DX,0    |       address of your
       |              |       program's code. It
       |       :      |       is set for you.
               :
```

We can modify the program MemLocs to let us take a look at its code segment. We do that with the Cseg function:

```
program MemLocs;
uses
    crt;
var
   a : integer;
procedure Hello(w:string);
       begin
       writeln("Hello",w);
       end;
begin
    writeln ("Address of procedure Hello is", Seg(Hello):6,":",Ofs(Hello):6);
    writeln ("The screen mode is", mem[$0040:$0049]:4);
→   writeln ("Code segment is", CSeg:6);
end.
```

When we run it, we find (not surprisingly) that the code segment is the same as the segment address of the procedure Hello:

```
Address of procedure Hello is  9827:     6
The screen mode is   3
Code segment is   9827  ←
```

The DS register holds the value of the data segment. Anything that you want to store as data and not have the computer execute (cell entries in a spreadsheet, for example, or text in a word processor), can be stored here.

We usually set DS, the data segment register, if ever (DOS usually does it for us), at the beginning of the program and then leave it alone. If, however, we want to read bytes from far-away places in memory—to examine the screen buffer or the keyboard buffer, for example—we'll have to set DS before we can address them. Using DS as the high word of our addresses, we can reach and read (or write) any byte in memory.

Let's say that our program code is in the segment 2000H, and data in the segment at 3000H:

Now let's say that we wanted to change data in the video buffer (i.e., the letters that appear on the screen), which is at segment B000H for a monochrome monitor. We'd have to change the data segment that we're using, in DS, to B000H:

And then we could reference any data there with our instructions.

We can modify the program MemLocs to give us a look its data segment, as well as the segment address of its dummy variable, a:

```
program MemLocs;
uses
    crt;
var
   a : integer;
procedure Hello(w:string);
       begin
       writeln("Hello",w);
       end;
begin
    writeln ("Address of procedure Hello is", Seg(Hello):6,":",Ofs(Hello):6);
    writeln ("The screen mode is", mem[$0040:$0049]:4);
    writeln ("Code segment is", CSeg:6);
→   writeln ("Data segment is", DSeg:6);
→   writeln ("Address of variable a is", Seg(a):6,":",Ofs(a));
end.
```

That change results in this:

```
Address of procedure Hello is  9827:      6
The screen mode is   3
Code segment is  9827
Data segment is 10123                  ←
Address of variable a is 10123:62      ←
```

We can see that space has been set aside for the variable a in the data segment.

Keep Pace with Today's Microcomputer Technology with:

**Brady Books** and **Software**

Brady Books and software are always up-to-the-minute and geared to meet your needs:

- Using major applications
- Beginning, intermediate, and advanced programming
- Covering MS-DOS and Macintosh systems
- Business applications software
- Star Trek™ games
- Typing Tutor

Available at your local book or computer store or order by telephone: (800) 624-0023

# BradyLine

Insights into tomorrow's technology from the authors and editors of Brady Books

FREE

You rely on Brady's bestselling computer books for up-to-date information about high technology. Now turn to *BradyLine* for the details behind the titles.

Find out what new trends in technology spark Brady's authors and editors. Read about what they're working on, and predicting, for the future. Get to know the authors through interviews and profiles, and get to know each other through your questions and comments.

*BradyLine* keeps you ahead of the trends with the stories behind the latest computer developments. Informative previews of forthcoming books and excerpts from new titles keep you apprised of what's going on in the fields that interest you most.

- Peter Norton on operating systems
- Winn Rosch on hardware
- Jerry Daniels, Mary Jane Mara, Robert Eckhardt, and Cynthia Harriman on Macintosh development, productivity, and connectivity

**Get the Spark. Get *BradyLine*.**

Published quarterly, beginning with the Summer 1990 issue. Free exclusively to our customers. Just fill out and mail this card to begin your subscription.

Name ______________________________

Address ______________________________

City ____________ State ________ Zip ________

Name of Book Purchased ______________________________

Date of Purchase ______________________________

Where was this book purchased? *(circle one)*

Retail Store    Computer Store    Mail Order

*Mail this card for your free subscription to BradyLine*

67-65297

Place First Class
Postage Here
Post Office
Will Not Deliver
Without Postage

**Brady Books**
15 Columbus Circle
New York, NY 10023

ATT: J. Padlad

The extra segment can be used as another data segment. For example, the 80x86 has a number of fast string instructions—instructions that can move strings of bytes from one location in memory to another extremely quickly. If the location we are sending bytes to is far away, we cannot point to both source and destination with the same segment register, DS. Instead, we can use ES as a second segment register for that far destination. The string instructions in the 80x86 require that you use ES as well as DS (although they may be set to the same segment).

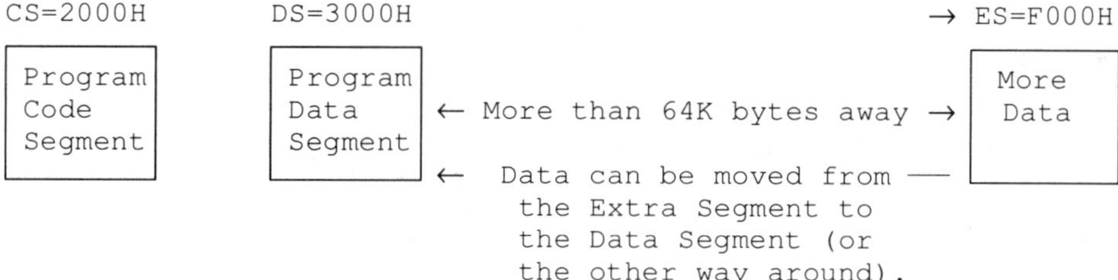


Finally, DOS stores the address for function calls on the stack, an area of memory put aside for this purpose. Since DOS maintains it, we will pay little attention to the stack until later. We can take a look at the stack segment in MemLocs, however, using Sseg:

```
program MemLocs;
uses
    crt;
var
   a : integer;
procedure Hello(w:string);
       begin
       writeln("Hello",w);
       end;
begin
    writeln ("Address of procedure Hello is", Seg(Hello):6,":",Ofs(Hello):6);
    writeln ("The screen mode is", mem[$0040:$0049]:4);
    writeln ("Code segment is", CSeg:6);
    writeln ("Data segment is", DSeg:6);
    writeln ("Address of variable a is", Seg(a):6,":",Ofs(a));
    writeln ("Stack segment is", SSeg:6);
end.
```

This change gives us a result different from either of the other segments:

```
Address of procedure Hello is  9827:     6
The screen mode is   3
Code segment is  9827
Data segment is 10123
Address of variable a is 10123:62
Stack segment is 10165          ←
```

## Segment Registers in Use: .COM Files

The first programs we write will be .COM files, and the default for .COM files is to set all four segment registers to the same value, the code segment.

We will do this expressly so that we do not have to worry about the segment registers just at the time when we are being introduced to our first programs.

Everything that goes on in a .COM file will be limited to one 64K workspace. And when the program is loaded, DOS sets that segment address for us. That means in practice that we will not have to be careful about how the segment registers are set for .COM files until later. Here, CS = DS = ES = SS.

A .COM file is the simplest working program you can write on the PC or PS/2. This file consists of just machine language instructions, ready to be executed.

# Directives

Assembly language source files have the extension .ASM, just as Pascal source files have the extension .PAS. When you write an assembly language program, you are responsible for setting up segments and placing your code and data in them. In other words, you have to tell the assembler what part of the program is to be loaded into the code segment (and where in it), what part into the data segment if there is one, and so on. The way you set up your segments is by using assembler directives.

Directives give directions to the assembler—they do not generate any machine language instructions.

You can set up either code or data segments when you are writing a program and you use directives to do it. If you are setting up a code segment, your program instructions themselves will go there. If you are setting up a data segment, you are predefining some variables or constants that your program will use later—or you are just setting aside some blank space that the program will use. The assembler will make sure that this information is loaded into the correct segments in memory if you specify them with directives.

## The .CODE Directive

We will convert our earlier program PRINTZ into PRINTZ.ASM. Here's the way those instructions looked earlier:

```
MOV     AH,2
MOV     DL,5AH
INT     21H
INT     20H
```

Now we have to surround them with directives to make them into a .ASM file. To begin writing the code, we have to label the code segment with the .CODE directive:

```
.CODE   ←
MOV     AH,2
MOV     DL,5AH
INT     21H
INT     20H
```

We define a segment name with a directive like .CODE, .DATA, or .STACK. In a .COM file, everything goes into the code segment. The assembler will translate the .CODE directive into the standard name for code segments.

That name depends on the *memory model* which determines whether the code or data areas of a program are limited by 64K. We'll have much more to say about memory models later, but because .COM files are limited to less than 64K total in any case, we will use the *SMALL* memory model here and not worry about it:

```
.MODEL  SMALL←
.CODE
MOV     AH,2
MOV     DL,5AH
INT     21H
INT     20H
```

> You must set the memory model before using the segment directives like .CODE.

## Labeling

Labels are also directives. We can label our data byte by byte or word by word, if we wish to. Similarly, we can label an instruction in our program itself so that we can jump from the current instruction to the labeled one, which may be some distance away (just as we can in Pascal).

When MOV AH,2 is translated into machine language, it will be three bytes. We can give a label to that instruction: Let's call it START, and we can also give a label to the last instruction (INT 20H)—let's call it EXIT:

```
        .MODEL  SMALL
        .CODE

START:  MOV     AH,2    ←
        MOV     DL,5AH
        INT     21H
EXIT:   INT     20H     ←
```

A label is just a name followed by a colon, just as it is in Pascal. If, during our program, we wanted to leave quickly, we could just go the label EXIT, and the INT 20H instruction would be executed, causing us to finish and quit. If we did decide to go there, the assembler would have to know the address of the EXIT instruction, and it finds this by counting the number of machine language bytes it has produced from the beginning of the code segment (what we have labeled START).

What the assembler does is to translate all these labels into offsets—that is, 16-bit words holding the distance in bytes of the label from the beginning of the appropriate segment—when it assembles the code. If we are dealing with a data label, the label is translated into the offset—in other words, a pointer—from the beginning of what we have called the data segment (the segment address of the data segment will be in DS at run time).

For labels given to instructions, the assembler uses the offset from the beginning of the code segment. It is the offsets of the labels that are actually stored in the machine language program, not the labels themselves. Labels will come in very handy when we write programs: Anything that gets more English into the program can help.

> You may make labels as long as you want. However, only the first 31 characters count—that's all the assembler reads.

## Positioning the Code in the Code Segment

There are two types of executable files—.COM files and .EXE files. When .EXE files are loaded, they are put at the beginning of the code segment they have been given, at CS:0000. Their first instruction can start right there. .COM files, on the other hand, are supplied with a header that is loaded in before they are, and it is the header that is put at CS:0000, not the first instruction of the .COM file.

This header is 100H—256 decimal—bytes long. The header thus runs from CS:0000 to CS:00FF, and the .COM file, now loaded into memory, starts exactly at CS:0100:

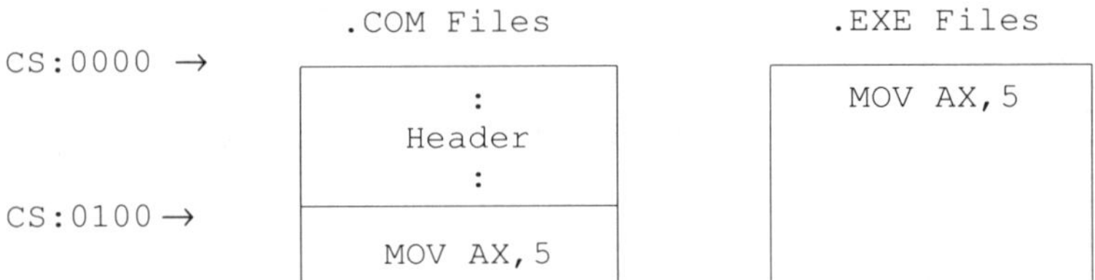


This means that we are going to have to start the code in PRINTZ.ASM at offset 0100H in the code segment.

> This is why we started assembling at 0100H in our DEBUG example (using A100): In a .COM file, machine language instructions must start at offset 0100H inside the program.

## The ORG Directive

We set our location in the code segment with the directive ORG:

```
         .MODEL   SMALL
         .CODE
         ORG      100H    ←
START:   MOV      AH,2
         MOV      DL,5AH
         INT      21H
EXIT:    INT      20H
```

This tells the assembler to make the offset of START (the line immediately after the ORG Directive) into 0100H. The assembler now treats the instruction MOV AH,2 as though it will be placed at CS:0100 and not at CS:0000, and everything to follow gets treated as though it were placed after this instruction. This will be very important when we use labels, because they are translated into offsets from the beginning of the segment. Now we have made the correct allowance for the .COM file header that is automatically loaded.

## The END Directive

The final thing that is required is to set an entry point for the program. In Pascal, the entry point is set when you define the main procedure with begin and end—control is always passed there. In assembly language, you can set the entry point anywhere in your program.

Here we set the entry point with the END directive. Every .ASM file needs to end with END so the assembler knows when to stop. This is exactly like the end. you place at the end of Pascal programs. At the same time, you can set the entry point by adding its label after END.

In our case, we want the entry point to be at 0100H in the code segment. We have labeled that instruction already, and called it START. So our final Directive will be END START —

```
         .MODEL   SMALL
         .CODE
         ORG      100H
START:   MOV      AH,2
         MOV      DL,5AH
         INT      21H
EXIT:    INT      20H

         END      START   ←
```

END also informs the compiler that the code segment, which began after the .CODE directive, is finished. The other way of ending the code segment definition is with another segment directive, such as .DATA—the statements that follow go into the data segment.

## The Instruction Pointer

When the .COM file is loaded into memory for the first time, we know that the value chosen by DOS for the code segment will be placed into CS. But there is also a special register that will hold the offset address in the code segment of the instruction about to be executed. This register is called IP, the Instruction Pointer.

When the program is loaded and CS is set, IP is loaded with 0100H (for a .COM file). The next instruction about to be executed is always at CS:IP; here that will be CS:0100. When .COM files begin, IP is automatically given a value of 0100H—in .EXE files, however, the offset address of the first instruction to execute can be anywhere in the code segment—so IP is loaded from a value stored in the .EXE file's header.

# Assembling PRINTZ.ASM

If you have a word processor or editor, use it to type our program into a file that you name PRINTZ.ASM. We are ready to use an assembler. If you have the Microsoft assembler (we will be using Microsoft MASM version 5.1), type this command:

```
A>masm printz;
```

And the macro assembler will do this:

```
A>masm printz;
Microsoft (R) Macro Assembler Version 5.10
Copyright (C) Microsoft Corp 1981, 1988.  All rights reserved.


  50144 + 31277 Bytes symbol space free

      0 Warning Errors
      0 Severe  Errors
```

If you are using the Turbo assembler (we will be using TASM version 1.0), type this:

```
A>tasm printz;
```

And TASM prints this:

```
Turbo Assembler  Version 1.0  Copyright (c) 1988 by Borland International
Assembling file:   PRINTZ.ASM
Error messages:    None
Warning messages:  None
Remaining memory:  381k   H
```

We've assembled the program, but, so far, all we have is an .OBJ file. The next step is to strip off some information left by the assembler in the .OBJ file. Although the linker is normally used for combining .OBJ files into big executable files, even single .OBJ files have to go through the linker before becoming .COM files.

The linker checks all segments, among other things. Since this is going to be a .COM file, there is only one segment. In particular, it is our code segment. Programs that are not .COM files need all segments to be explicitly spelled out—and the linker is going to give us a warning here that we have no STACK segment. This is the normal warning you receive when you are producing .COM files. If you are using the Microsoft assembler, use LINK:

```
A>link printz;
Microsoft (R) Overlay Linker  Version 3.64
Copyright (C) Microsoft Corp 1983-1988.  All rights reserved.

LINK : warning L4021: no stack segment
```

If you are using the Turbo Assembler, use TLINK:

```
A>tlink printz;
Turbo Link  Version 2.0  Copyright (c) 1987, 1988 Borland International
Warning: no stack
```

The warning is there, and we are now almost ready: The linker has taken the .OBJ file, PRINTZ.OBJ, and produced an .EXE file, PRINTZ.EXE. However, we did not set this program up as a .EXE file—it is a .COM file. For the final step, stripping off the header that the linker left in the .EXE file, we run a DOS program called EXE2BIN. Run this on output from either LINK or TLINK.

The last program that we need to run, this converts the .EXE file to .COM format:

```
exe2bin printz printz.com
```

Finally, our .COM file is there, ready to go. Try running it to confirm that it prints out the Z. Give PRINTZ.COM a try—you will see that it prints out Z, just as our DEBUG version did. Now we've got a working .ASM file.

Even so, this is really only half the story—as it stands, PRINTZ.ASM is a working program, but it is not very representative. In almost all .COM files, some data will be stored.

Every variable used in a program is data, like the variable VALUE, which we might set to 5. We might want to read in a file from the disk and store it in the data area, treating it as data. Or we might have program messages like "Hello, world." in the data area.

Let's look at an example. Here we will show how you can use variables in assembly language, just like Pascal. In fact, later in the book, we'll have our assembly language procedures read data directly from Pascal code when we link the two together. In assembly language, you use data directives, like the DB, or Define Byte directive, instead of the var keyword to set aside space for data.

# Using Data

The way that we define bytes like VALUE in the data segment is with special instructions in the part of your program that you have set aside as the data segment. To define a byte named VALUE, use DB in a data segment definition like this:

```
VALUE DB 5
```

In your program, the code might look like this:

```
.MODEL SMALL
.CODE
MOV      AX,VALUE
         :
         :
.DATA
VALUE    DB 5    ←
         :
         :
END
```

And in memory, the code and data segments might then look something like this:

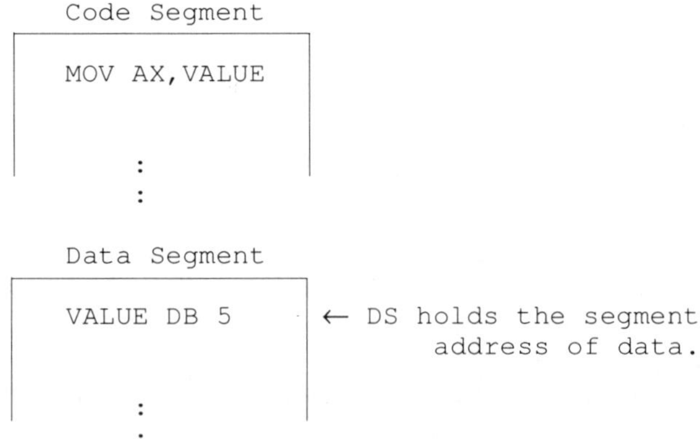


Now we are free to read the data in VALUE in the program:

```
MOV AX, VALUE
```

This is the way to use memory in assembly language; set up storage for it in the part of your program that you will label the data segment (or the common segment in a .COM file) and give names of variables to all the bytes you set aside (with DB or, as we will see, similar directives). Then, you can use these names just like variables in Pascal.

Let's add some data to PRINTZ.ASM. About the only data we have is the character we're going to print out, Z, so let's store that in memory:

```
         .MODEL   SMALL
         .CODE
         ORG      100H
         Our_Character   DB "Z" ←
START:   MOV      AH,2
         MOV      DL,5AH
         INT      21H
EXIT:    INT      20H

         END      START
```

DB tells the assembler that the data that follows is to be put in the program without interpretation: It is data. We have set aside a location, one byte, that we've called Our_Character and initialized it by putting the character Z in it. The assembler will translate the Z for us into the ASCII code that the machine needs: 5AH (or we could have said Our_Character DB 5AH—it is the same thing to the assembler). Here are some DB examples:

```
Flag     DB 0
  Char_Z  DB "Z"
  Numbers DB 1,2,3,4,5,0    ← 6 bytes are put aside.
  Prompt  DB "How long has it been since you called "
          DB "your mother?"
```

When we refer to the names Flag, Char_Z, Numbers, or Prompt, we are actually referring to the first byte in what follows DB. Labels like these are actually pointers. For example, if we were to say:

```
MOV      AH,Numbers
```

The 1, that is, the first number after DB, would be loaded into AH.

In PRINTZ.ASM, here is how we load our character into DL, just before printing it out:

```
         .MODEL   SMALL
         .CODE
         ORG      100H
         Our_Character   DB "Z"
START:   MOV      AH,2
         MOV      DL,Our_Character ←
         INT      21H
EXIT:    INT      20H

         END      START
```

That is how we define and use variables in assembly language. We've been able to label and use a memory location now.

On the other hand, we've left ourselves with a problem. The label START is supposed to be at 100H in the code segment, and now that we've added one byte of memory space just before it, it will be at the wrong location (specifically, 101H). To solve this problem, we do what most .COM files that use data do. We set aside a data area at the beginning of the program and add a *jump* command, so that when things start up at 100H, the first thing the microprocessor will do is jump *over* the data area and to the first instruction. It looks like this:

```
        .MODEL SMALL
        .CODE
        ORG     100H
START:  JMP     PRINTZ ←
        Our_Character   DB "Z"
PRINTZ: MOV     AH,2
        MOV     DL,Our_Character
        INT     21H
EXIT:   INT     20H

        END     START
```

We've moved the label START to point to an instruction that is at 100H, but that instruction is JMP PRINTZ, which means the microprocessor will jump to the label PRINTZ and then continue.

## The JMP Instruction

JMP, an assembly language command—is like goto in Pascal. All that happens is that control jumps to wherever you tell it and starts executing code there. To use JMP, just provide it with a label to jump to, as we have done here (JMP PRINTZ).

The goto instruction in Pascal is not held in high esteem. Pascal is a very structured language that makes use of strong typing and strict declarations. On the other hand, the JMP instruction is essential in assembly language. In fact, there are many variations of JMP, called *conditional jumps*, that we will see in the next chapter. Because assembly language does not have Pascal's if...then...else statement, we will often have to put our own together out of jumps.

# A .COM File Shell

In general, this is how a .COM file shell looks:

```
        .MODEL  SMALL
        .CODE
        ORG     100H
START:  JMP     PROG
```

```
                    :
```

This the data area. Use DB here.

```
                    :
PROG:
```

And this is where the program goes.

```
                    :
EXIT:    INT        20H

         END        START
```

There is an area set aside for data (using DB) and a part for the program (use this shell for your own programs). Now we've updated PRINTZ.ASM to include data and a data area.

# Strings in Memory

We still have not resolved how to store character strings in memory, or for that matter, how to store whole 16-bit words (DB only stores byte by byte). A character string in Pascal is made up of a single byte that holds the length of the string, followed by the bytes of the string itself, like this:

> Because the byte at the beginning can hold values only up to 255, in Pascal strings are limited to 255 characters.

It makes sense to us but not to the computer. We want to keep them together: The computer sees only a number of bytes with no apparent relation.

Strings in assembly language are just stored as bytes, as they are in Pascal. Usually, assembly language strings end with 0 (in what is called ASCIIZ format):

But this is not always the case. Strings are stored like PROMPT above, and if you want the string to end with a 0 byte, it is your responsibilty to put it in:

```
Prompt  DB "How long has it been since you called "
          DB "your mother?",0
```

The assembler lets you store strings this way—using the quotation marks as shorthand (otherwise, you'd have to use DB for each letter).

## INT 21H Service 9—Print a String

The string printing service, service 9, of INT 21H prints out strings. As mentioned, it is the writeln() of assembly language. Service 9 has no way of knowing when it has come to the end of the string. This is a case where a string is not ended with a 0; to terminate the string for this service, a "$" character is added as the last character. This is an indication to service 9 to stop printing. Here's how it might look if we were to change our program to PRINTXYZ:

```
        .MODEL SMALL
        .CODE
        ORG     100H
START:  JMP     PRINTZ
        Our_Characters  DB "XYZ$" ←
PRINTZ: MOV     AH,2
        MOV     DL,Our_Character
        INT     21H
EXIT:   INT     20H

        END     START
```

Note that the $ character is the last byte in the string. We have to tell service 9 where to find the string it should print, and change the call from service 2 to service 9. What service 9 requires is the address at which the string to print begins in memory. You pass the segment of Our_Characters in DS and the offset in DX. If the address was 0EF1:0105, for example, we'd have to load 0EF1H into DS, and 0105H into DX.

Since we are dealing with a .COM file, the value of DS never changes, so DS is already set for service 9: When the program runs, DS will be pointing at the data segment, the only segment. To get the offset address of Our_Characters, we use the *OFFSET* directive like this:

```
CODE_SEG        SEGMENT

        ASSUME  CS:CODE_SEG,DS:CODE_SEG,ES:CODE_SEG
        ORG     100H
START:  JMP     PRINTZ
        Our_Characters  DB "XYZ$"
PRINTZ: MOV     AH,9
        MOV     DX, OFFSET Our_Characters      ←
        INT     21H
EXIT:   INT     20H

CODE_SEG        ENDS
        END     START
```

The OFFSET Directive is just like Ofs(). It gives you a label's offset value from the beginning of the data segment. For example, the line:

```
MOV     DX, OFFSET Our_Characters
```

loads the offset of Our_Characters into DX. OFFSET is a handy directive that we'll use often, since many interrupt services require that we pass them the address of data.

That's all there is to it; we now have a new working .ASM file that prints out XYZ instead of just Z.

## Using Comments

The final topic of this chapter is the use of comments. Comments are important in Pascal, and they are important here too. They can be added in assembly language by preceding them with a semi-colon, (;) like this for PRINTXYZ:

```
        .MODEL SMALL
        .CODE
        ORG     100H   ;Set up for a .COM file.
START:  JMP     PRINTZ ;JMP over data area.
        Our_Characters  DB "XYZ$"       ;We will print out this string.
PRINTZ: MOV     AH,9   ;Request INT 21H service 9.
        MOV     DX, OFFSET Our_Characters       ;Point to our string.
        INT     21H    ;And print it out here.
EXIT:   INT     20H    ;End the program.

        END     START  ;Set entry point to label START.
```

The assembler doesn't read anything on a line after the semicolon. Just by reading down the side of the program, you can see what was intended by each line. Now that we have the fundamentals of program-writing, let's broaden our library of instructions.

# 2

# Accepting and Handling Data

## Accepting Input

Now we'll start using assembly language in earnest. To start, our programs will have to accept input.

The most basic of the DOS services is service number 1, which reads keyboard input. This is a primary input service. You request service 1 from INT 21H by setting AH to 1 and executing an INT 21H instruction. When a key is typed, it is echoed on the screen and its ASCII code is returned in the AL register.

Not all character input services echo the typed character—there is more than one way of reading a single character. Besides INT 21H service 1, there are also services 6, 7, and 8. They all return the ASCII code of the key that was typed in AL. Of them, only service 1 echoes the typed character on the screen. Some of them will quit when a Control-Break is typed, some won't. Service 6 won't wait until a key is struck—it returns a character immediately if one is in the keyboard buffer, and it returns without waiting. Here is a list of how DOS single-character input services work:

| *INT 21H Service* | *Will Wait* | *^Break Seen* | *Will Echo* |
|---|---|---|---|
| 1 | X | X | X |
| 6 | | | |
| 7 | X | | |
| 8 | X | X | |

Besides these single-character services, we will see a program in this chapter that accepts buffered input, which can read a character string—the assembly language version of readln(). Let's start with an example that accepts character input to put all this to work.

## The Program CAP.COM

The example program that we'll develop here will accept a letter that you type, capitalize it, and print it on the screen. For the first time, we will get our assembly language program to accept input from us. Let's start with the .COM file shell:

```
        .MODEL SMALL
        .CODE
        ORG 100H
START:  JMP CAP
        ;Data Area
CAP:
        ;Program will go here.

EXIT:   INT     20H

        END START
```

And add the instructions that will let us accept input:

```
        .MODEL SMALL
        .CODE

        ORG 100H
START:  JMP CAP
        ;Data Area
CAP:    MOV     AH,1     ;Request keyboard input  ←
        INT     21H      ;From INT 21H            ←


EXIT:   INT     20H
        END START
```

After the INT 21H instruction is executed, the ASCII code of the typed character is in AL. The program's job is to capitalize the letter and print it out.

There is an easy way to capitalize letters—ASCII codes for the small letters, (e.g., a) have higher values than the ASCII codes for the small letters (e.g., A). The ASCII codes for A to Z run from 65 to 90; for a to z from 97 to 122:

ASCII Letters

| *Capitals* | *Code* | *Smalls* | *Code* |
|---|---|---|---|
| A | 65 | a | 97 |
| B | 66 | b | 98 |
| C | 67 | c | 99 |
| : | | : | |
| : | | : | |
| Z | 90 | z | 122 |

To capitalize a letter we just have to subtract a number from its ASCII code to move the code from its place in the a...z part of the table to its corresponding place in the A...Z part:

Capitalizing

| *Capitals* | *Code* | | *Smalls* | *Code* |
|---|---|---|---|---|
| A | 65 | — subtract 32 → | a | 97 |
| B | 66 | — subtract 32 → | b | 98 |
| C | 67 | — subtract 32 → | c | 99 |
| : | | | : | |
| : | | | : | |
| Z | 90 | — subtract 32 → | z | 122 |

The number we have to subtract is just equal to ASCII(a)–ASCII(A), which is 97 – 65 = 32, the distance between the two parts of the table. Here's how we capitalize the ASCII value in AL, introducing the new instruction, SUB, for subtract:

```
        .MODEL SMALL
        .CODE
        ORG 100H
START:  JMP CAP
        ;Data Area
CAP:    MOV     AH,1     ;Request keyboard input
        INT     21H      ;From INT 21H
→       SUB     AL,"a"-"A"      ;Capitalize the typed key


EXIT:   INT     20H

        END START
```

## The SUB and ADD Instructions

In Pascal, you can use the – and + operators to perform subtraction and addition; in assembly language, it is the SUB and ADD instructions.

The SUB instruction is used this way:

```
SUB      AL,5
```

here 5 is subtracted from the contents of AL; AL is changed. Similarly, you could execute this instruction:

```
SUB      AX,DX
```

and subtract the contents of DX from AX. AX is changed, DX is not.

If you had a variable named NUMBER_1, you could subtract it or from it like this:

```
SUB      MEMORY_1,DX
SUB      DX,MEMORY_1
```

As usual, however, you cannot subtract a memory location immediately from another memory location (SUB MEMORY_1,MEMORY_2). However, you can subtract an *immediate* number (that is, a constant) from a memory location, like this:

```
SUB      MEMORY_1,3
```

In the same way, there is an ADD instruction. All you have to do is to think of the registers as normal (word-long) integers:

```
ADD      AL,5
ADD      AX,DX
ADD      MEMORY_1,DX
ADD      DX,MEMORY_1
ADD      MEMORY_1,3
```

We will use ADD and SUB frequently, and we'll examine them in more detail in our chapter on fast math, Chapter 7.

The assembler has a preprocessor, and it lets you use expressions like a – A. For instance, we can use a line like this:

```
SUB      AL,"a"-"A"
```

which makes what we are doing much clearer than if we simply said:

```
SUB      AL,32
```

Similarly, expressions like a + A are allowed. Since the assembler understands expressions that include operators like +, – ,/, and *, it's often a good idea to use them to make your code clearer. For example, if you want to read data from a file in 1K sections, and each section was prefaced by a header of 256 bytes, a line like this:

```
MOV      DX, 256 + 1024
```

can make it a lot clearer that you are going to be interested in using a header and one data section than a line like:

```
MOV      DX, 1280
```

In our program, all that is left is to type the newly capitalized letter on the screen. We can do that with INT 21H service 2, as we've already seen.

## Printing Out Capital Letters

INT 21H Service 2, which prints a character on the screen, expects the ASCII code of the character that it is to print in DL. So far in CAP.ASM, the ASCII code is still in the AL register because service 1 returned it there. We have to move the code from AL to DL and then print the character:

```
        .MODEL SMALL
        .CODE
        ORG 100H
START:  JMP CAP
        ;Data Area
CAP:    MOV     AH,1     ;Request keyboard input
        INT     21H      ;From INT 21H
        SUB     AL,"a"-"A"      ;Capitalize the typed key
        MOV     DL,AL    ;Set up for service 2.
        MOV     AH,2     ;Request character output ←
        INT     21H      ;Type out character.     ←
EXIT:   INT     20H

        END START
```

CAP.ASM is complete. We read in a typed key with INT 21H service 1, capitalize it ourselves, and then print it out with INT 21H service 2. Type it in, assemble and produce CAP.COM—give it a try.

When you run it, you see this:

```
A>cap
```

The program waits for a key to be typed. As soon as you type a letter, say s, it echoes the letter and prints out a capital S. Then it simply exits:

```
A>cap
sS
A>
```

If we wanted to rewrite CAP so that the s wasn't echoed on the screen, we could have used service 8, for example, instead of service 1:

```
        .MODEL SMALL
        .CODE
        ORG 100H
START:  JMP CAP
        ;Data Area
        CAP:    MOV     AH,8     ;Request keyboard input ←
        INT     21H     ;From INT 21H
```

```
        CMP     AL,"a"  ;Compare the incoming ASCII code to "a".
        JB      EXIT    ;If the letter is not lower case, exit.
        CMP     AL,"z"  ;Compare the incoming ASCII code to "z".
        JA      EXIT    ;If the letter is not lower case, exit.
        SUB     AL,"a"-"A"      ;Capitalize the typed key
        MOV     DL,AL   ;Set up for service 2.
        MOV     AH,2    ;Request character output
        INT     21H     ;Type out character.
EXIT:   INT     20H

        END START
```

This new CAP.COM will wait for your typed-in key, capitalize it, and print only the result on the screen.

Although it is gratifying to get the result we expected, there are a number of problems with this progam. Perhaps the most serious one is: What happens if you type in some character other than a lowercase letter? Odd characters will be printed, since we are ready to handle small letters only.

This problem may be fixed if we check the incoming ASCII code to make sure that it actually represents a lowercase letter—we have to check to make sure that the ASCII code is between the values for a and z. This type of checking brings us to the topic of conditional jumps, which are extremely important in assembly language since they are almost the only branch instructions available.

# Conditional Jumps

We want to check that the incoming ASCII code is between a and z. If it isn't, we exit. We have to divide the process into two steps: The first step is to check whether AL is greater than or equal to a; the second step is to check if AL is less than or equal to z. If both tests pass, we capitalize the letter, type it, and exit.

## The CMP Instruction

Checking a value against some known comparison value is done with the assembly language instruction compare, CMP. To branch on the results of the comparison, we then use a *conditional jump* immediately after the CMP instruction.

In Pascal, you might have an expression like this:

```
if number < 5 then number := 3;
```

Here you check the value in number and then take appropriate action all in one step.

Unlike Pascal, comparisons are a two-step process in assembly language. For example, here is the same thing in assembly language (JB means jump if below):

```
CMP     NUMBER, 5
JB      BELOW5
```

```
        MOV     NUMBER, 3
BELOW5:
```

Take a look at the code to check whether AL is above or equal to "a":

```
        .MODEL SMALL
        .CODE

        ORG 100H
START:  JMP CAP
        ;Data Area
CAP:    MOV     AH,1    ;Request keyboard input
        INT     21H     ;From INT 21H
→       CMP     AL,"a"  ;Compare the incoming ASCII code to "a".
→       JB      EXIT    ;If the letter is not lower case, exit.

        SUB     AL,"a"-"A"      ;Capitalize the typed key
        MOV     DL,AL   ;Set up for service 2.
        MOV     AH,2    ;Request character output
        INT     21H     ;Type out character.
EXIT:   INT     20H

        END START
```

We compared AL to the ASCII value for "a", and then immediately followed this with a JB—Jump if Below—instruction:

```
CMP     AL,"a"  ;Compare the incoming ASCII code to "a".
JB      EXIT    ;If the letter is not lower case, exit.
```

If the comparison showed that the value in AL (the first item in the CMP instruction) was below a in value, we will jump to the label EXIT at the end of the program and leave without capitalizing the ASCII code.

The process works like this: first, the microprocessor's *flags* are set by the CMP instruction, then the JB instruction checks these internal flags and acts accordingly:

```
CMP     AL,"a"  ← Sets Flags
JB      EXIT    ← Reads Flags
```

As you saw briefly in Chapter 1, a number of flags are inside the 80x86. Many instructions, particularly the conditional jump instructions, rely on those flags to tell them what to do. One way of setting those flags is with a CMP instruction. You can compare a register to memory, or a register to a register, or even a memory location to a constant:

```
CMP     AL,5
CMP     AX,DX
CMP     MEMORY_1,DX
CMP     DX,MEMORY_1
CMP     MEMORY_1,3
```

Now we have to compare the value in AL once again, to check if it is above z. This is done with an instruction whose name you could probably guess: JA, or Jump if Above:

```
         .MODEL SMALL
         .CODE
         ORG 100H
START:   JMP CAP
         ;Data Area
CAP:     MOV      AH,1     ;Request keyboard input
         INT      21H      ;From INT 21H
         CMP      AL,"a"   ;Compare the incoming ASCII code to "a".
         JB       EXIT     ;If the letter is not lower case, exit.
→        CMP      AL,"z"   ;Compare the incoming ASCII code to "z".
→        JA       EXIT     ;If the letter is not lower case, exit.
         SUB      AL,"a"-"A"     ;Capitalize the typed key
         MOV      DL,AL    ;Set up for service 2.
         MOV      AH,2     ;Request character output
         INT      21H      ;Type out character.
EXIT:    INT      20H

         END START
```

That completes the program CAP.ASM, our first real assembly language program. It both accepts input and generates output; and it even checks for errors. If we give it a letter outside what we've defined as an acceptable range, it exits without trying to capitalize it.

## More Conditional Jumps

We have seen the two instructions, JA and JB. These follow a CMP—compare—instruction, and, depending on the result, a jump may be made. There are many conditional jumps. In fact, there are even variations of JA and JB. Besides these two, there are JAE (Jump if Above or Equal), JBE (Jump if Below or Equal), JNA (Jump if Not Above), JNB (Jump if Not Below), JNAE (Jump if Not Above or Equal), and JNBE (Jump if Not Below or Equal). All of these are used after a CMP instruction.

Probably the two most common conditional jumps are JE, Jump if Equal, and JNE, Jump if Not Equal, and we will be using these soon. Here are a number of conditional jumps and their meanings:

| *Conditional Jump* | *Means* |
|---|---|
| JA/JG | Jump if Above/Greater |
| JB/JL | Jump if Below/Less |
| JAE/JGE | Jump if Above/Greater or Equal |
| JBE/JLE | Jump if Below/Less or Equal |
| JNA/JNG | Jump if Not Above/Not Greater |

| *Conditional Jump* | *Means* |
|---|---|
| JNB/JNL | Jump if Not Below/Not less |
| JNAE/JNGE | Jump if Not Above/Greater or Equal |
| JNBE/JNLE | Jump if Not Below/Less or Equal |
| JE | Jump if Equal |
| JNE | Jump if Not Equal |
| JZ | Jump if result was Zero |
| JNZ | Jump if result was Not Zero |
| JCXZ | Jump if CX = 0 (Used at end of loops) |

You can see that there is a rich selection of jump instructions. Without such a selection of conditional jumps, assembly language would be very difficult to use. As it is, there are conditional jumps that meet most needs. If you are new to assembly language, it might take you a while to become practiced in their use.

You can see that for a number of jumps there are two variations: Jump if Above (JA) or Jump if Greater (JG), for example. The difference has to do with signed and unsigned numbers, and the way the computer treats them. So far, we have been dealing with only unsigned numbers but, of course, that's only half the story.

All the jumps with G or L in them deal with signed numbers. In Pascal, you make numbers signed by declaring them so. In assembly language, 16-bit numbers are just 16-bit numbers; the way you treat them as signed is by using the signed conditional jumps, not the unsigned ones (the ones with A or B in them are unsigned). However, that is a topic for Chapter 7. We will stick to unsigned math until then.

# DEHEXER.ASM

We can put our new expertise to work at once. Let's develop a program that will change four digit hex numbers to decimal. Working with hex is not an easy task unless you get used to it (or have a hexadecimal programmer's calculator). This routine can help you to display program output or values while debugging. We start with the .COM file shell:

```
        .MODEL SMALL
        .CODE
        ORG 100H
ENTRY:  JMP DEHEXER

        ;Data will go here.

        DEHEXER:
```

```
        ;Program will go here.

        INT     20H

        END     ENTRY
```

First, we have to read the hex number in from the keyboard. This is where we find the assembly language analog of readln(). DOS provides a buffer input service to read strings until a carriage return is pressed. We can use it if we set up a buffer in memory with the DB directive, like this (you can give it any name, not just BUFFER):

```
BUFFER DB #, 0, 0, 0, 0, 0, 0, 0, 0, 0, 0, 0
```

To fill the buffer, we will use DOS INT 21H, service 0AH—get string. We set the number (# above) in the beginning of the buffer ourselves. INT 21H service 0AH needs that number—the buffer length—so it won't overfill the buffer. Service 0AH always sets the last byte of the buffer to ASCII 13 (a carriage return) as an end-of-string marker, so we set # to one more than the number of characters we expect as input.

The second byte in the buffer will be filled by service 0AH with the number of bytes actually typed. If we're careful, we can set up our buffer with some foresight by giving names to the important bytes in it:

```
          .MODEL SMALL
          .CODE
          ORG 100H
ENTRY:    JMP DEHEXER
          PROMPT DB "Type in a 4 digit hex number:$"
    →     BUFFER DB 5
    →     NUM_TYPED         DB 0
    →     ASCII_NUM         DB 3 DUP (0)
    →     END_NUM           DB 0
    →     CRLF   DB 0
DEHEXER:MOV     AH,9
          MOV     DX,OFFSET PROMPT
          INT     21H
          MOV     AH,0AH
          MOV     DX,OFFSET BUFFER
          INT     21H

          INT     20H
          END     ENTRY
```

Note how easy it was to structure our data this way and give a label to each byte in the string. Notice we also added a prompt to be typed out, named PROMPT. Service 9, the string-printing service, is the writeln() of DOS. To print out our prompt, we have to pass service 9 the address of the string to print. It expects an offset address in DX and expects the string to be terminated with $:

```
         .MODEL SMALL
         .CODE
         ORG 100H
ENTRY:   JMP DEHEXER
         PROMPT DB "Type in a 4 digit hex number:$"
         BUFFER DB 5
         NUM_TYPED        DB 0
         ASCII_NUM        DB 3 DUP (0)
         END_NUM          DB 0
         CRLF    DB 0
DEHEXER:MOV      AH,9
   →     MOV      DX,OFFSET PROMPT
   →     INT      21H
```

After printing the prompt:

```
Type in a 4 digit hex number:
```

we use service 0AH to read the four-digit hex number from the keyboard. This is the number we will convert to decimal and print out. We have to pass the offset (in DX) of the beginning of the buffer for service 0AH to use, so we move the offset of BUFFER into that register:

```
         .MODEL SMALL
         .CODE
         ORG 100H
ENTRY:   JMP DEHEXER
         PROMPT DB "Type in a 4 digit hex number:$"
         BUFFER DB 5
         NUM_TYPED        DB 0
         ASCII_NUM        DB 3 DUP (0)
         END_NUM          DB 0
         CRLF    DB 0
DEHEXER:MOV      AH,9
         MOV      DX,OFFSET PROMPT
         INT      21H
         MOV      AH,0AH
   →     MOV      DX,OFFSET BUFFER
   →     INT      21H

         INT      20H
         END      ENTRY
```

Next we issue an INT 21H instruction and accept the hex number. The <cr> at the end of the returned string will go into the byte marked CRLF, and we can ignore it.

You might notice the use of the directive DUP:

```
ASCII_NUM        DB 3 DUP (0)
```

This directive saves us time. This expression is equal to ASCII_NUM DB 0, 0, 0; not such a big saving for 3 bytes, but what if you needed to reserve space for 32,000 bytes?

You can also allocate space on the heap (although assembly language doesn't call it a heap—it's simply available memory) in assembly language by using the assembly-language equivalents of malloc() and realloc(), which are the DOS INT 21H services referred to as GETBLOCK and SETBLOCK. They operate a little like New(). We'll have more to say about memory soon. Also, see the section in the Appendix on DOS and BIOS interrupts.

## Pointers in Assembly Language

After the buffer has been filled with input from the keyboard, the ASCII string extends from the pointers ASCII_NUM to END_NUM in memory. We have to convert that string into a number.

If this was the number:

```
1234H
```

we'd just have to point to the last number, 4, convert it from ASCII to binary, then point to the next number, 3, convert it to binary, multiply by 16, and add it to the 4 we already have, and so on. In this way we loop over all characters.

That is the method we will use. We have labeled the last ASCII digit in memory as END_NUM:

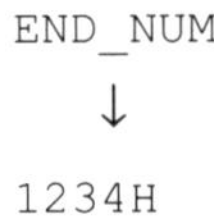


And we are familiar with data labels—to get the ASCII character from that location, we can just say MOV AL, END_NUM. But how do we point to the previous digits?

We can use a register as a pointer. You are probably familiar with the use of pointers in Pascal. In assembly language, the BX register was designed explictly to be used as a pointer (except for the 80386, the only other registers that can function as pointers are the SI and DI registers, which we'll cover soon). Let's examine how that's done.

We'll need a loop to read all four digits, so we start off by loading BX with the address of END_NUM:

```
        .MODEL SMALL
        .CODE
        ORG 100H
ENTRY:  JMP DEHEXER
        PROMPT DB "Type in a 4 digit hex number:$"
        BUFFER DB 5
```

```
        NUM_TYPED           DB 0
        ASCII_NUM           DB 3 DUP (0)
        END_NUM             DB 0
        CRLF                DB 0
DEHEXER:MOV     AH,9
        MOV     DX,OFFSET PROMPT
        INT     21H
        MOV     AH,0AH
        MOV     DX,OFFSET BUFFER
        INT     21H

        MOV     CX, 0
        MOV     AX,0
  →     MOV     BX, OFFSET END_NUM
LOOP1:
        :
        :
        :
        JB      LOOP1


        INT     20H

        END     ENTRY
```

Now we'll load the ASCII character into the DL register. We can do that like this:

```
        .MODEL SMALL
        .CODE

        ORG 100H
ENTRY:  JMP DEHEXER
        PROMPT              DB "Type in a 4 digit hex number:$"
        BUFFER              DB 5
        NUM_TYPED           DB 0
        ASCII_NUM           DB 3 DUP (0)
        END_NUM             DB 0
        CRLF                DB 0
DEHEXER:MOV     AH,9
        MOV     DX,OFFSET PROMPT
        INT     21H
        MOV     AH,0AH
        MOV     DX,OFFSET BUFFER
        INT     21H

        MOV     BX, OFFSET END_NUM
LOOP1:  MOV     DL, BYTE PTR [BX]       ←
        DEC     BX                      ←
        :
        :
```

```
        JB      LOOP1

        INT     20H

        END     ENTRY
```

Putting BX inside square brackets—[BX]—means that the microprocessor will use the address stored in BX to reference memory. You may recall that in Chapter 1, memory references in the disassembled sort_ab were just numbers put into brackets:

```
C7063E000300  →  MOV    WORD PTR [003E],0003
C70640000500  →  MOV    WORD PTR [0040],0005
A13E00        →  MOV    AX,[003E]
3B064000      →  CMP    AX,[0040]
7E12          →  JLE    0135
A13E00        →  MOV    AX,[003E]
A34200        →  MOV    [0042],AX
A14000        →  MOV    AX,[0040]
A33E00        →  MOV    [003E],AX
A14200        →  MOV    AX,[0042]
A34000        →  MOV    [0040],AX
```

Each number in brackets above, like [003E], stands for a memory reference. In the same way, you can use BX like this: [BX].

The expression BYTE PTR:

```
        MOV     BX, OFFSET END_NUM
LOOP1:  MOV     DL, BYTE PTR [BX]       ←
        DEC     BX
        :
        :
```

means byte pointer, and it is frequently used with [BX]. Here we are indicating to the assembler that the value we want to put into DL is a byte.

The type cast is not actually needed here since the DL register is one byte long, which means that [BX] must be taken as a one-byte expression. On the other hand, this expression:

```
MOV [BX], 0
```

is not clear; we might want to overwrite the byte pointed to by the value in BX, or we might want to overwrite the word starting at that location. Here we would have to use a type cast directive such as BYTE PTR or WORD PTR, to indicate what we want.

After moving the byte into DL, we decrement the pointer BX with DEC, which works just like Dec() in Pascal. (INC is also available to increment operands).

Decrementing BX points us to the previous ASCII character in preparation for the next time through the loop.

Now the ASCII character is in DL, and we must convert it into binary. If the character is between 0 and 9, we can subtract the ASCII value for 0 from it to convert it into the corresponding number. In other words, if you subtract 0 from 5, you get 5.

If the number is between A and F, we have to subtract A from it, then add 10. In other words, 0BH is really the number 11: If you subtract the ASCII code for A from B, you get 1—you still have to add 10 to get 11.

We do that in the program in the following way:

```
         .MODEL SMALL
         .CODE
         ORG 100H
ENTRY:   JMP DEHEXER
         PROMPT DB "Type in a 4 digit hex number:$"
         BUFFER DB 5
         NUM_TYPED        DB 0
         ASCII_NUM        DB 3 DUP (0)
         END_NUM          DB 0
         CRLF    DB 0
DEHEXER:MOV      AH,9
         MOV      DX,OFFSET PROMPT
         INT      21H
         MOV      AH,0AH
         MOV      DX,OFFSET BUFFER
         INT      21H

         MOV      BX, OFFSET END_NUM
LOOP1:   MOV      DX,0
         MOV      DL, BYTE PTR [BX]
         DEC      BX
         CMP      DL,"9"                        ←
         JBE      UNDER_A                       ←
         SUB      DL, "A" - "0" - 10            ←
UNDER_A:SUB       DL, "0"                       ←
         :
         JB       LOOP1

         INT      20H

         END      ENTRY
```

It's a little clumsy-looking, but DL now holds the numerical value of current hex digit.

To convert the entire four-digit number to decimal, we have to multiply each digit by the appropriate power of 16 and add it to the running total. In other words, if the hex number was 0ABCDH, and the running total was stored in AX, then the conversion would go like this:

```
MOV AX,0
ADD AX, D x 16^0
ADD AX, C x 16^1
ADD AX, B x 16^2
ADD AX, A x 16^3
```

In the first step, we make sure that AX holds 0. Then we systematically add each digit from the number 0ABCDH, multiplying it by the correct power of 16. There is an easy way to multiply by 16: We can *shift* the value in DL left—shifting left by four places is the same as multiplying by 16. You can shift right and left in assembly language just as you can with the Shl and Shr operators in Pascal.

## SHL and SHR

SHL and SHR *shift* operands left or right by a specified number of binary spaces. SHL shifts left and SHR shifts right. For example, taking this binary number:

```
00000001B
```

and shifting it left by one place would yield:

```
00000010B
```

This is just the same as multiplying by 2. Conversely, shifting right by one place, would convert:

```
00000010B
```

back to:

```
00000001B
```

Shifting to the right has the same effect as dividing by 2. This is the easy way to multiply in our computer—as long as you can do it in multiples of 2. You can shift 8-bit registers, 16-bit registers, and memory locations too. To shift AL left by one bit, for example, would go like this:

```
SHL     AL,1
```

You'd think that shifting it left by two bits would be SHL AL,2. Unfortunately not, at least in the 8088 and 8086. In these two processors, you can shift only left or right by 1 or by a value held in CL; these are the only two valid ways of shifting AL left:

```
SHL     AL,1
```

or

```
SHL     AL,CL
```

where CL has previously been filled with some value (the same format holds for SHR). On the 80186-80386 processors, there is no problem; you don't have to use CL.

```
SHL      AL,5
```

is OK (here we'll stick to what the 8088 can handle, as usual, for compatibility with those readers who don't have a later processor).

> The 80386 also supports the use of double words—32 bits—and can shift them with one instruction, SHLD or SHRD.

The plan is to shift the current hex digit, now in DL, left by the correct power. When we shift DL left by more than two hex places, however, the result will be bigger than a byte can hold. Instead, we must use the whole DX register to hold the value, not just DL. After it is shifted, we have to add this current hex digit to the running total in AX. In other words, we have to add DX to AX each time we loop through. It looks like this:

```
          .MODEL SMALL
          .CODE
          ORG 100H
ENTRY:    JMP DEHEXER
          PROMPT              DB "Type in a 4 digit hex number:$"
          BUFFER              DB 5
          NUM_TYPED           DB 0
          ASCII_NUM           DB 3 DUP (0)
          END_NUM             DB 0
          CRLF                DB 0
DEHEXER:MOV        AH,9
          MOV        DX,OFFSET PROMPT
          INT        21H
          MOV        AH,0AH
          MOV        DX,OFFSET BUFFER
          INT        21H

→         MOV        CX, 0
→         MOV        AX,0
          MOV        BX, OFFSET END_NUM
LOOP1:    MOV        DX,0   ←
          MOV        DL, BYTE PTR [BX]
          DEC        BX
          CMP        DL,"9"
          JBE        UNDER_A
          SUB        DL, "A" - "0" - 10
UNDER_A:SUB        DL, "0"
→         SHL        DX, CL
→         ADD        AX, DX
→         ADD        CX,4
→         CMP        CX,16
          JB         LOOP1
```

```
        INT     20H

        END     ENTRY
```

Note that we had to load DX with 0 at the top of the loop to make sure DH was clear (so we wouldn't be adding leftover data into AX after we shifted DX). Now, every time through the loop, we load the ASCII value into DL, make it into a binary number, shift it to the left, and add it to the running total in AX.

After four loops, the ASCII string has been converted into binary—but we still have to convert it back to (decimal) ASCII.

The way to do that is to successively peel off the decimal digits by dividing the number in AX by 10. Each time we divide by 10, the remainder is a decimal digit.

## The DIV and MUL Instructions

There is a divide instruction in assembly language called DIV. It is just like Div—the integer divide instruction—in Pascal (not like normal division). There is no 80x86 assembly language instruction corresponding to normal floating point division. However, it's a different story with the 80x87, as we'll see in Chapter 8.

If you load the number to divide into AX and divide by a byte-long register like this:

```
DIV BL
```

then the 80x86 divides AX by BL—AX is assumed to hold the number to divide when you divide by a byte. The quotient is returned in AL and the remainder in AH:

```
DIV BL → AX Div BL → Quotient in AL and remainder in AH
```

For example, if AX contained 16 and BL 3, DIV BL would leave 5 in AL and 1 in AH.

On the other hand, if you give this instruction: DIV BX, the microprocessor assumes that you are dividing the double-word number (32 bits long, that is, a longint) in DX:AX by the specifed general-purpose register, here BX.

```
DIV BX → DX:AX Div BX → Quotient in AX and remainder in DX
```

The terminology DX:AX is an unfortunate way of specifying double words, since addresses are also specifed with a colon—however, when segment registers are used, you can be sure it's an address.

The multiply instruction, MUL, works similarly. MUL BL will multiply AL by BL and leave the result in AX:

```
MUL BL → AL * BL → Result in AX
```

MUL BX will multiply BX by AX and leave the result in DX:AX.

```
MUL BX → DX:AX * BL → Result in DX:AX
```

> We will explore MUL and DIV in the fast math chapter. MUL and DIV treat their operands as unsigned, by the way; the signed versions are IMUL and IDIV.

If we use the DIV BX instruction, the number in DX:AX will be divided by BX. AX already holds the binary number we want to systematically divide by 10, so we should load DX with 0 and BX with 10.

After the DIV BX instruction, AX will hold the quotient (ready to be divided by 10 again in the next pass to peel off the next decimal digit) and DX holds the remainder. The remainder is what we want—it's the current decimal digit. Note that we are peeling the digits off in backward order. For example, if we had the number 4321 (decimal) in AX, the first time we divided by 10 we would get a remainder of 1, the next time a remainder of 2, and so on.

## PUSH and POP

To store these decimal digits, we push them on the *stack*, using the instruction PUSH DX. The stack is simply made up of words in memory. As you may recall, it has its own segment address. When a program starts, the SS register is loaded with that address, and a special register, SP, holds the address of the *top* of the stack (that is, the top of the stack's address is SS:SP). The reason it's called the top of the stack is that it is at the top of the memory area put aside for the stack:

When you execute the instruction PUSH DX, the contents of DX—let's say that's 4—is placed at SS:SP and SP is *decremented*:

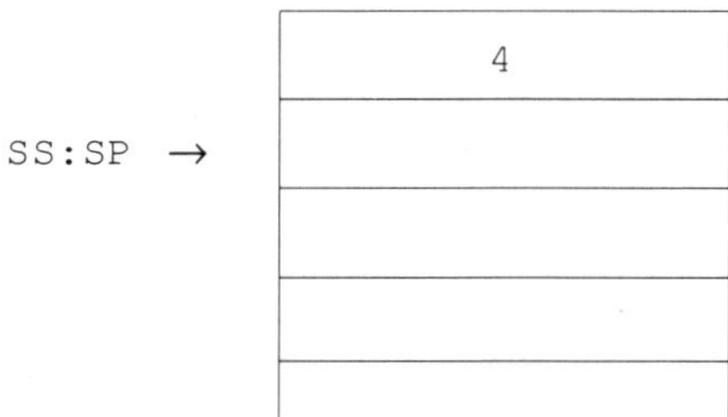

Next, we might push the numbers 3, 2, and 1 onto the stack:

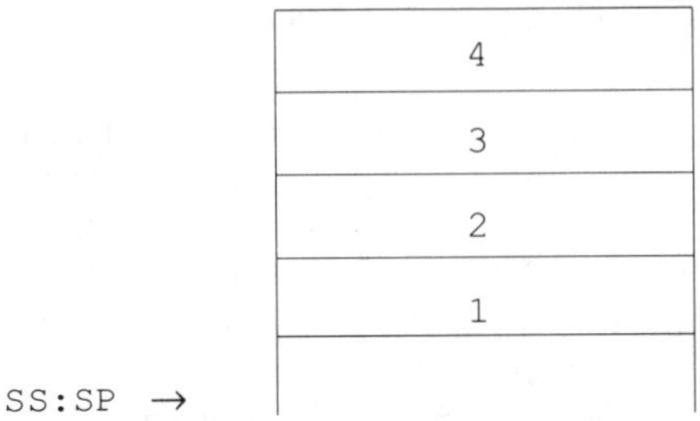

```
              +-----------+
              |     4     |
              +-----------+
              |     3     |
              +-----------+
              |     2     |
              +-----------+
              |     1     |
              +-----------+
SS:SP  →      |           |
```

We say the stack grows downward in memory.

The opposite instruction is POP. POP operand pops a value into the operand. For example, POP DX at this point would place 1 in DX, and SP would be incremented. If you executed four pops, you would pick off the numbers in the reverse order that we've placed them on the stack: 1, 2, 3, and then 4.

In DEHEXER, we keep track of how many numbers we've pushed in the CX register so we can POP them later (a four-digit hex number may give from 1 to 5 decimal digits). PUSHing and POPing these digits will do more than just store them, however: It will reverse their order as well. Here's the way it looks:

```
          .MODEL SMALL
          .CODE

          ORG 100H
ENTRY:    JMP DEHEXER
          PROMPT             DB "Type in a 4 digit hex number:$"
          BUFFER             DB 5
          NUM_TYPED          DB 0
          ASCII_NUM          DB 3 DUP (0)
          END_NUM            DB 0
          CRLF               DB 0
DEHEXER:MOV       AH,9
          MOV       DX,OFFSET PROMPT
          INT       21H
          MOV       AH,0AH
          MOV       DX,OFFSET BUFFER
          INT       21H
          MOV       CX, 0
          MOV       AX,0
          MOV       BX, OFFSET END_NUM
LOOP1:    MOV       DX,0
          MOV       DL, BYTE PTR [BX]
          DEC       BX
          CMP       DL,"9"
          JBE       UNDER_A
          SUB       DL, "A" - "0" - 10
UNDER_A:SUB       DL, "0"
          SHL       DX, CL
```

```
        ADD     AX, DX
        ADD     CX,4
        CMP     CX,16
        JB      LOOP1
        MOV     CX,0    ←
        MOV     BX, 10  ←
LOOP2:  MOV     DX,0    ←
        DIV     BX      ←
        PUSH    DX      ←
        INC     CX      ←
        CMP     AX,0    ←
        JA      LOOP2   ←


        INT     20H

        END     ENTRY
```

At this point, we're almost done. The decimal digits are on the stack, and the number of digits is in CX. Let's print out a message saying "That number in decimal is: " with service 9 of INT 21H:

```
CODE_SEG        SEGMENT
        ASSUME  CS:CODE_SEG, DS:CODE_SEG, ES:CODE_SEG, SS:CODE_SEG

        ORG 100H
ENTRY:  JMP DEHEXER
        PROMPT          DB "Type in a 4 digit hex number:$"
        BUFFER          DB 5
        NUM_TYPED       DB 0
        ASCII_NUM       DB 3 DUP (0)
        END_NUM         DB 0
        CRLF            DB 0
→       ANS_STRING      DB 13, 10, "That number in decimal is: $"
DEHEXER:MOV     AH,9
        MOV     DX,OFFSET PROMPT
        INT     21H
        MOV     AH,0AH
        MOV     DX,OFFSET BUFFER
        INT     21H

        MOV     CX, 0
        MOV     AX,0
        MOV     BX, OFFSET END_NUM
LOOP1:  MOV     DX,0
        MOV     DL, BYTE PTR [BX]
        DEC     BX
        CMP     DL,"9"
        JBE     UNDER_A
        SUB     DL, "A" - "0" - 10
UNDER_A:SUB     DL, "0"
        SHL     DX, CL
```

```
        ADD     AX, DX
        ADD     CX,4
        CMP     CX,16
        JB      LOOP1
        MOV     CX,0
        MOV     BX, 10
LOOP2:  MOV     DX,0
        DIV     BX
        PUSH    DX
        INC     CX
        CMP     AX,0
        JA      LOOP2

  →     MOV     AH,9
  →     MOV     DX,OFFSET ANS_STRING
  →     INT     21H

        INT     20H
CODE_SEG        ENDS

        END     ENTRY
```

And then just print out the digits using service 2 of INT 21H and POP DX (we pop the digits back into DX since service 2 expects the ASCII character to print to be in DL):

```
CODE_SEG        SEGMENT
        ASSUME  CS:CODE_SEG, DS:CODE_SEG, ES:CODE_SEG, SS:CODE_SEG

        ORG 100H
ENTRY:  JMP DEHEXER
        PROMPT          DB "Type in a 4 digit hex number:$"
        BUFFER          DB 5
        NUM_TYPED       DB 0
        ASCII_NUM       DB 3 DUP (0)
        END_NUM         DB 0
        CRLF            DB 0
        ANS_STRING      DB 13, 10, "That number in decimal is: $"
DEHEXER:MOV     AH,9
        MOV     DX,OFFSET PROMPT
        INT     21H
        MOV     AH,0AH
        MOV     DX,OFFSET BUFFER
        INT     21H

        MOV     CX, 0
        MOV     AX,0
        MOV     BX, OFFSET END_NUM
LOOP1:  MOV     DX,0
        MOV     DL, BYTE PTR [BX]
        DEC     BX
        CMP     DL,"9"
```

```
        JBE     UNDER_A
        SUB     DL, "A" - "0" - 10
UNDER_A:SUB     DL, "0"
        SHL     DX, CL
        ADD     AX, DX
        ADD     CX,4
        CMP     CX,16
        JB      LOOP1

        MOV     CX,0
        MOV     BX, 10
LOOP2:  MOV     DX,0
        DIV     BX
        PUSH    DX
        INC     CX
        CMP     AX,0
        JA      LOOP2

        MOV     AH,9
        MOV     DX,OFFSET ANS_STRING
        INT     21H

        MOV     AH,2        ←
LOOP3:  POP     DX          ←
        ADD     DX,"0"      ←
        INT     21H         ←
        LOOP    LOOP3       ←

        INT     20H
CODE_SEG        ENDS

        END     ENTRY
```

Note that we had to add ASCII 0 to each digit to turn it into a character that can be printed.

This introduces us to the LOOP instruction, which we use to loop over the pushed digits, pop them, and print them out.

## The LOOP Instruction

To use LOOP, just fill CX with the number of times you want to loop, define a label, and loop like this:

```
        MOV     CX,5
LOOP_1:
        :
        :
        LOOP    LOOP_1
```

Here, the body of LOOP_1 will be executed 5 times. It works much like a for loop in Pascal.

In DEHEXER (and with a little foresight), the previous loop left the number of digits in CX already, so the loop index CX is all set. All we have to do is to use LOOP—we will loop once for each digit, decrementing the number of digits in the loop index CX each time. We add ASCII 0 to the digit to make it into an ASCII character and print it out.

The program works—give it a try. It accepts four-digit hex numbers and prints out the correct decimal version. Go through this program several times—it contains many basic assembly language skills.

On the other hand, there is still one difference between it and most .ASM files—most .ASM files have at least one procedure defined inside them.

# Procedures

We can make DEHEXER into a single procedure like this:

```
         .MODEL SMALL
         .CODE

         ORG 100H
ENTRY:   JMP DEHEXER
         PROMPT          DB "Type in a 4 digit hex number:$"
         BUFFER          DB 5
         NUM_TYPED       DB 0
         ASCII_NUM       DB 3 DUP (0)
         END_NUM         DB 0
         CRLF            DB 0
         ANS_STRING      DB 13, 10, "That number in decimal is: $"
DEHEXER  PROC                               ←
         MOV     AH,9
         MOV     DX,OFFSET PROMPT
         INT     21H
         MOV     AH,0AH
         MOV     DX,OFFSET BUFFER
         INT     21H

         MOV     CX, 0
         MOV     AX,0
         MOV     BX, OFFSET END_NUM
LOOP1:   MOV     DX,0
         MOV     DL, BYTE PTR [BX]
         DEC     BX
         CMP     DL,"9"
         JBE     UNDER_A
         SUB     DL, "A" - "0" - 10
UNDER_A: SUB     DL, "0"
         SHL     DX, CL
         ADD     AX, DX
```

```
        ADD     CX,4
        CMP     CX,16
        JB      LOOP1

        MOV     CX,0
        MOV     BX, 10
LOOP2:  MOV     DX,0
        DIV     BX
        PUSH    DX
        INC     CX
        CMP     AX,0
        JA      LOOP2

        MOV     AH,9
        MOV     DX,OFFSET ANS_STRING
        INT     21H

        MOV     AH,2
LOOP3:  POP     DX
        ADD     DX,"0"
        INT     21H
        LOOP    LOOP3

        INT     20H
DEHEXER ENDP                    ←

        END     ENTRY
```

We have added the PROC and ENDP directives, which define procedures. Usually, code is enclosed inside procedures. (However, if you only have one procedure in your program, you don't have to use the PROC and ENDP directives to define it.)

When you have more than one procedure, however, you must use these directives. The PROC directive lets the assembler know that you want to define a procedure, and the ENDP directive indicates that the procedure definition is finished.

There is more to the PROC directive than we're using here. Ever since MASM 5.1 or TASM 1.0, PROC has become a lot more like procedures in high level languages. You can now specify, for example, the arguments that a procedure is called with, and what values it returns. This capability is used only when you link to high level languages, however; you cannot pass parameters to procedures in assembly language (except by loading the registers), and you cannot return values (so there are no assembly language functions).

> When we link assembly language and Pascal, we will see how to mimic both Pascal procedures and functions using PROC.

Unless you are in the main procedure, you have to end the procedure with a return, or RET instruction. Let's break up DEHEXER to see how this is done:

```
        .MODEL SMALL
        .CODE

        ORG 100H
ENTRY:  JMP DEHEXER
        PROMPT          DB "Type in a 4 digit hex number:$"
        BUFFER          DB 5
        NUM_TYPED       DB 0
        ASCII_NUM       DB 3 DUP (0)
        END_NUM         DB 0
        CRLF            DB 0
        ANS_STRING      DB 13, 10, "That number in decimal is: $"
DEHEXER PROC
        MOV     AH,9
        MOV     DX,OFFSET PROMPT
        INT     21H
        MOV     AH,0AH
        MOV     DX,OFFSET BUFFER
        INT     21H

        MOV     CX, 0
        MOV     AX,0
        MOV     BX, OFFSET END_NUM
LOOP1:  MOV     DX,0
        MOV     DL, BYTE PTR [BX]
        DEC     BX
        CMP     DL,"9"
        JBE     UNDER_A
        SUB     DL, "A" - "0" - 10
UNDER_A:SUB     DL, "0"
        SHL     DX, CL
        ADD     AX, DX
        ADD     CX,4
        CMP     CX,16
        JB      LOOP1

        CALL    PRINT_NUM       ←

        INT     20H
DEHEXER ENDP

PRINT_NUM       PROC            ←
        MOV     CX,0
        MOV     BX, 10
LOOP2:  MOV     DX,0
        DIV     BX
        PUSH    DX
        INC     CX
        CMP     AX,0
        JA      LOOP2

        MOV     AH,9
        MOV     DX,OFFSET ANS_STRING
```

```
        INT     21H

        MOV     AH,2
LOOP3:  POP     DX
        ADD     DX,"0"
        INT     21H
        LOOP    LOOP3
        RET                         ←
        PRINT_NUM           ENDP    ←

        END     ENTRY
```

Here we have broken DEHEXER up into two procedures, DEHEXER itself and PRINT_NUM, like this:

```
CODE_SEG        SEGMENT
        ASSUME  CS:CODE_SEG, DS:CODE_SEG, ES:CODE_SEG, SS:CODE_SEG

        ORG 100H
ENTRY:  JMP DEHEXER
        ;Data
DEHEXER PROC
        :
        :
        CALL    PRINT_NUM       ←
        INT     20H
DEHEXER ENDP


PRINT_NUM       PROC            ←
        :
        :
        RET
PRINT_NUM       ENDP

CODE_SEG        ENDS
        END     ENTRY
```

It works as you'd expect it to—when you call PRINT_NUM, control is transferred to the first line there. Execution continues until the return instruction, RET, is reached, and control returns to the line just after the CALL PRINT_NUM instruction in the main procedure.

Procedures in assembly language don't specifically return any values, as functions can in Pascal. Instead, when you want to return information from an assembly language procedure, you must place it in the registers, or, in some cases, in the flags. For example, a procedure may set a special flag called the *carry flag* to indicate an error, and you can check for that condition by following the call to the procedure immediately with a JC, Jump if Carry Flag Set, instruction.

Let's make one more refinement to DEHEXER.ASM. In Pascal, you can make use of command-line parameters with ParamCount (the number of command-line parameters) and ParamStr(i) (an array of strings holding the command-line parameters). The same is true in assembly language.

## Command-Line Arguments

If you've ever wondered what happens to the characters you type after a program's name, like the string FILE.TXT here:

```
A>EDIT FILE.TXT
```

then here's the answer: They go into the program segment prefix, the header installed for the program, ready to be read. Every program, from huge editors to the small programs we've been writing can read what was typed on the command line. All the command line characters are placed in the header that DOS sets up for the program in memory—this is the header we referred to when we first discussed .COM files.

Since the way the characters are stored there are very much like the way we've set up our buffer BUFFER in DEHEXER, we can convert DEHEXER to use this information very easily. This way, you'll be able to use DEHEXER like this:

```
A>DEHEXER 12AF
```

The characters typed after the program's name on the command line can be found in a .COM file's Program Segment Prefix (PSP), starting at location CS:0080H. This first byte holds the number of characters that were typed—including the space that separated them from the program's name. In other words, for this command:

```
A>PROG abcxdef
```

PROG would find the string in the PSP at CS:0080:

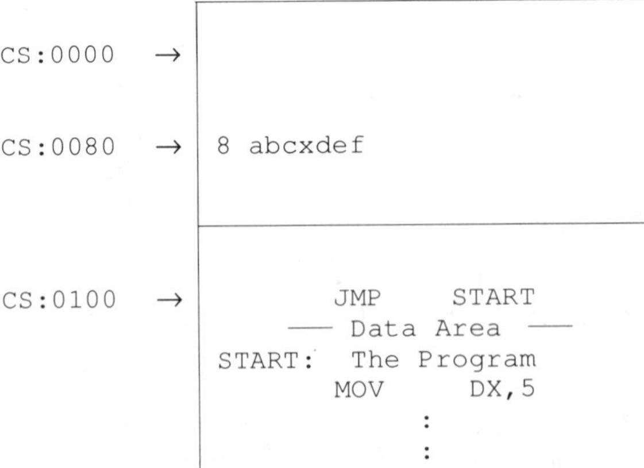

The area at CS:0080H would look like this:

```
CS:80H 81H 82H 83H 84H 85H 86H 87H 88H 89H
    8   " "  "a"  "b"  "c"  "x"  "d"  "e"  "f"  0DH
```

where a means the ASCII code for a and so on. The first byte contains the number of bytes typed—8 including the leading space—and at the end is the byte 0DH, which is the ASCII code for a carriage return (note that this string is set up much like a Pascal one). This buffer always ends with the 0DH carriage return byte, and this final byte is not included in the byte count.

Since this information is very similar to what we have in DEHEXER, we can easily change DEHEXER to use this buffer instead of the one we have set aside. Using this default buffer will allow us to accept input without using INT 21H service 0AH.

Here's the new program:

```
CODE_SEG        SEGMENT
        ASSUME  CS:CODE_SEG, DS:CODE_SEG, ES:CODE_SEG, SS:CODE_SEG

        ORG 100H
ENTRY:  JMP DEHEXER
        ANS_STRING      DB 13, 10, "That number in decimal is: $"
DEHEXER PROC

        MOV     CX,0
        MOV     AX,0
        MOV     BX, 85H        ←
LOOP1:  MOV     DX,0
        MOV     DL, BYTE PTR [BX]
        DEC     BX
        CMP     DL,"9"
        JBE     UNDER_A
        SUB     DL, "A" - "0" - 10
UNDER_A:SUB     DL, "0"
        SHL     DX, CL
        ADD     AX, DX
        ADD     CX,4
        CMP     CX,16
        JB      LOOP1

        CALL    PRINT_NUM

        INT     20H
DEHEXER ENDP

PRINT_NUM       PROC
        MOV     CX,0
        MOV     BX, 10
LOOP2:  MOV     DX,0
        DIV     BX
        PUSH    DX
        INC     CX
```

```
        CMP     AX,0
        JA      LOOP2

        MOV     AH,9
        MOV     DX,OFFSET ANS_STRING
        INT     21H

        MOV     AH,2
LOOP3:  POP     DX
        ADD     DX,"0"
        INT     21H
        LOOP    LOOP3
        RET
PRINT_NUM       ENDP

CODE_SEG        ENDS

        END     ENTRY
```

Nothing's changed except that we've removed BUFFER, the prompt and the code to type it out. Instead, we know that we will find the number of characters typed at CS:0080. At CS:0081, there is a space, and following that, the number to convert, which must therefore end at CS:0085. In order to read that number, we load BX with 85H, not the offset of END_NUM.

```
DEHEXER PROC

MOV     CX,0
MOV     AX,0
MOV     BX, 85H         ←
:
:
```

The buffer in the Program Segment Prefix is the same as the one we set aside earlier (BUFFER); so from then on, the process is just the same as with the original version of DEHEXER.

We've been dealing with character strings in a limited way—decrementing a pointer through a four digit hex number. However, there are many more sophisticated methods of working with strings in assembly language, and because of their speed and power, they are very important.

# Introduction to the String Instructions

What a programmer wants to regard as a string of bytes in memory is just unconnected bytes to the microprocessor. Originally, working with such strings was a weak point in assembly language with the Intel chips until the string instructions were added. These instructions are as follows (don't memorize them):

| *Instruction* | *Action* | *Explanation* |
|---|---|---|
| LODSB | Loads | Load byte from DS:SI into AL |
| SCASB | Scans | Scan byte string at ES:DI for byte in AL |
| CMPSB | Compares | Compare byte string at ES:DI to one at DS:SI |
| MOVSB | Moves | Move byte string byte by byte from DS:SI to ES:DI |
| STOSB | Stores | Store byte in AL to string at ES:DI |

Starting with the 80286, two more string instructions were added, INSB and OUTSB, input string from a port, and output string to a port. A port is how I/O devices are connected to the PS/2 or PC: port 60H is where data comes in from the keyboard, for example.

These instructions will be crucial later, so we're introducing them early. With them, you can rapidly scan strings to find a certain element, compare strings, move strings in memory, or store string elements from the registers to memory.

Each of the string instructions listed above has two forms, one to be used if your string is made up of bytes, one to use if your string is made up of words. For example, SCASB can be used as either SCASB or SCASW. Simply by changing the final letter—B for byte or W for word—you can let the string instructions know what type of string to operate on. Here are the word versions of the string instructions:

| *Instruction* | *Action* | *Explanation* |
|---|---|---|
| LODSW | Loads | Load word from DS:SI into AX |
| SCASW | Scans | Scan word string at ES:DI for word in AX |
| CMPSW | Compares | Compare word string at ES:DI to one at DS:SI |
| MOVSW | Moves | Move word string word by word from DS:SI to ES:DI |
| STOSW | Stores | Store word in AX to string at ES:DI |

In the 80386, the string instructions can be used with *double words*; for example, the instruction SCASW can become SCASD there.

The idea of word strings is new to us. In them, each element is one word long, not just one byte long. We will be able to store words in memory in a way similar to that used to store bytes, except that instead of DB, we will use the directive DW. The use of DW is close to DB, but with word-length items. Here are two examples:

```
ALL_FULL  DW 0FFFFH
NUMBERS   DW 1234H, 5678H, 9ABCDH
```

When the assembler sees the definition of ALL_FULL, for instance, it will set aside one word (two bytes) for it. We can work with ALL_FULL this way:

```
MOV     AX,ALL_FULL
MOV     ALL_FULL,DX
```

But we cannot do the following:

```
MOV     AL,ALL_FULL
```

ALL_FULL was defined with DW, Define Word, and AL is only an eight-bit register, so there is a type mismatch. The data types must match inside an instruction: The assembler will not place a value that was defined as byte-length (or that comes in a byte-length register) into one that was defined as word-length (or a word-length register). If we try to do so, the assembler will give us an error.

## Byte and Word Strings in Memory

Storing a byte is easy with DB; here we can do it in DEBUG:

```
-A100
0EF1:0100 DB        5
0EF1:0101
```

DEBUG provides a way of examining memory that is very useful; the DEBUG D command. With it, we can see the 5 in memory at location CS:0100:

```
-D100         ↓

0EF1:0100  05 EC 04 02 0F 8B E5 5D-CB 00 00 00 00 00 00 00   .......].......
0EF1:0110  00 00 2E F6 06 00 00 01-74 0E BA DA 03 EC A8 08   ........t.......
0EF1:0120  74 FB BA D8 03 B0 21 EE-C3 2E F6 06 00 00 01 74   t.....!........t
0EF1:0130  06 BA D8 03 B0 29 EE C3-8C D8 8E C0 8B 3E 4C F6   .....).......>L.
0EF1:0140  8B 0E 96 F6 B0 0A FC C3-E8 ED FF 8B 1E 48 F6 2B   .............H.+
0EF1:0150  1E 58 F6 74 0D FD 4F 4F-F2 AE 83 EB 50 75 F9 47   .X.t..OO....Pu.G
0EF1:0160  47 FC C3 E8 E2 FF 89 3E-4C F6 CB E8 CA FF 2B CF   G......>L.....+.
0EF1:0170  F2 AE E3 03 EB 16 90 B8-00 00 CB E8 BA FF 3B 3E   ..............;>
```

We've just put that 5 there ourselves. However, things are not so straightforward with DW. Here we can use DW 0102H, for example:

```
-A100
0EF1:0100 DW        0102
0EF1:0102
```

And also dump it:

```
-D100         ↓

0EF1:0100  05 EC 04 02 0F 8B E5 5D-CB 00 00 00 00 00 00 00   .......].......
0EF1:0110  00 00 2E F6 06 00 00 01-74 0E BA DA 03 EC A8 08   ........t.......
0EF1:0120  74 FB BA D8 03 B0 21 EE-C3 2E F6 06 00 00 01 74   t.....!........t
0EF1:0130  06 BA D8 03 B0 29 EE C3-8C D8 8E C0 8B 3E 4C F6   .....).......>L.
0EF1:0140  8B 0E 96 F6 B0 0A FC C3-E8 ED FF 8B 1E 48 F6 2B   .............H.+
0EF1:0150  1E 58 F6 74 0D FD 4F 4F-F2 AE 83 EB 50 75 F9 47   .X.t..OO....Pu.G
0EF1:0160  47 FC C3 E8 E2 FF 89 3E-4C F6 CB E8 CA FF 2B CF   G......>L.....+.
0EF1:0170  F2 AE E3 03 EB 16 90 B8-00 00 CB E8 BA FF 3B 3E   ..............;>
```

You might have expected to see 01 02 in memory, not 02 01. However, 0102H is stored as 02 01 because the 80x86 *reverses* the order of the bytes in a word that it stores in memory. The high byte (01) is stored at a higher memory location. This won't affect the way you store or read words, however. If you defined:

```
WORD_VARIABLE    DW       0
```

And then used that word like this:

```
MOV      WORD_VARIABLE,0102H       ← Storing
MOV      AX,WORD_VARIABLE          ← Reading
```

then AX would be left with 0102H, as you'd expect. How the bytes of a word are stored is important only if you examine the individual bytes of a stored word in memory. We'll run into it again when we look at the internal representation of floating point numbers in Pascal.

Now that we understand a little more about strings in memory, we can use the string instructions with them. Those instructions assume the use of two new registers, DI and SI.

## The DI and SI registers

SI and DI are two registers specially put aside for string operations. String manipulation is so important that both these registers were designed to be used with them exclusively. DI stands for destination index, and SI stands for source index.

String instructions *assume* that the address of the source string is in the SI register, and that of the target string is already loaded into the DI.

> To be exact, the string instructions assume that DS:SI is set up as a pointer to the beginning of the source string, and that ES:DI is set up as a pointer to the beginning of the target string.

Every time you execute the instruction MOVSB, one byte is taken from the location DS:SI and copied to ES:DI. DS:SI is the *source* pointer, and ES:DI is the *destination* pointer. Also, like all string instructions, MOVSB automatically increments the string registers it uses. In this case, that is both SI and DI:

```
ES:DI    ← MOVSB —     DS:SI
 ↓                      ↓

  1, 2, 3...             8, 9, 0...


   ES:DI                  DS:SI
    ↓                      ↓

  8, 2, 3...             8, 9, 0...
```

You should know that SI and DI can automatically be set to *decrement* instead of increment, by setting the *direction flag*. Just use the instruction STD, Set Direction Flag, to do this. To clear the flag, use CLD, Clear Direction Flag. We will not use the direction flag ourselves—when programs are loaded, string instructions are set to increment as the default.

Just using MOVSB by itself, however, only moves one byte. If you had this line in your program:

```
        MOV     AH,2
LOOP3:  POP     DX
        ADD     DX,"0"
        INT     21H
        MOVSB   ←
        LOOP    LOOP3
        RET
```

then every time the line was executed, the microprocessor would read the byte at DS:SI, make a copy of it, place the copy at ES:DI, and then increment both DI and SI. However, MOVSB alone, like any string instruction alone, only works on one byte or word every time it is executed. To do more, you have to use *REP*.

## The REP Prefix

The REP Prefix can augment any string instruction so that it is performed a number of times. This is very useful if you want to copy a whole string of data, for example, or search a string for a matching byte.

REP stands for repeat: It will repeat a string operation a number of times. This number is set by the value in the CX register. For example,

```
        MOV     CX,5
REP     MOVSB
```

will copy five bytes, in order, from DS:SI to ES:DI. If the bytes at those locations looked like this to begin with:

```
DS:SI                      ES:DI
↓                          ↓
0, 1, 2, 3, 4, 5, 6...     9, 9, 9, 9, 9, 9...
```

they will look this way after REP MOVSB (where CX was 5 to start):

```
               DS:SI                      ES:DI
               ↓                          ↓
0, 1, 2, 3, 4, 5, 6...     0, 1, 2, 3, 4, 9...
```

There are three forms of REP: REP, REPE, and REPNE. REP repeats the string instruction CX times, REPE means Repeat While Equal (up to CX times), REPNE means Repeat While Not Equal (also up to CX times).

For example, a popular string instruction is REPNE SCASB. This instruction means Repeat While Not Equal, Scan for Byte. It scans a string at ES:DI up to CX bytes for a match to the byte in AL. It keeps scanning while the bytes do not equal the byte in AL; if a match is found, the instruction terminates.

To use REPNE SCASB to find a byte, we load ES:DI with the address of the string to be scanned, put the byte we want to find in AL (often the first byte of a substring we are searching for), and set CX to the number of bytes in the string. Then we just give the instruction REPNE SCASB:

```
ZEBRA_STRING       DB "There is a zebra over there."
                   :
        MOV        DI, OFFSET ZEBRA_STRING
        MOV        CX,28    ;The number of bytes in the string.
        MOV        AL,"z"   ;The byte we want to find.
REPNE   SCASB      ←
```

When the instruction finishes, one of two things happened: Either a match was found to the byte in AL, or we ran out of bytes to compare (CX became 0). In order to check if we found a match or reached the end, REPNE SCASB is often followed by the JCXZ instruction—which stands for Jump if CX is zero:

| JCXZ is designed for just such cases—there is no JBXZ instruction, for example).

```
ZEBRA_STRING       DB "There is a zebra over there."
                   :
        MOV        DI, OFFSET ZEBRA_STRING
        MOV        CX,28    ;The number of bytes in the string.
        MOV        AL,"z"   ;The byte we want to find.
        REPNE      SCASB
 →      JCXZ       REACHED_END
 →      FOUND_MATCH:        ;We found z.
```

If we do not jump to the label REACHED_END in this example, we've found a match to the byte we were looking for, z. In this case, ES:DI will be pointing at the byte just *after* the match.

We've seen how SCASB and MOVSB work. The STOSB instruction, Store Byte, just makes duplicates of the byte in AL and stores it at location ES:DI, and then increments DI. STOSW does the same thing with the word in AX, and DI gets incremented by 2 to point to the next word in memory. You can use both forms with the REP prefixes.

The CMPSB string instruction is more interesting. With it, you can compare two strings to see where they start matching (using REPNE CMPSB) or where they start differing (using REPE CMPSB). Here's an example — we use REPE CMPSB (Repeat While Equal, Compare String Byte) to compare two strings, DATA_1 and DATA_2:

```
CODE_SEG        SEGMENT
        ASSUME  CS:CODE_SEG, DS:CODE_SEG, SS:CODE_SEG, ES:CODE_SEG
ORG     100H
ENTRY:  JMP     START
DATA_1  DB      "A rose by any other name would smell as sweet."
DATA_2  DB      "A nose by any other name would smell as sweetly."
MSG     DB      "The strings started differing at character $"
START:  MOV     DI,OFFSET DATA_1
        MOV     SI,OFFSET DATA_2
        MOV     CX,47   ;The length of DATA_1.
REPE    CMPSB
        JCXZ    EXIT    ;If we ran out of bytes to compare, strings matched.
        MOV     DX,OFFSET MSG   ;Mismatch must have been found - print MSG.
        MOV     AH,9
        INT     21H
        SUB     DI,OFFSET DATA_1        ;Like subtracting pointers.
        ADD     DI,"0"
        MOV     DX,DI   ;Get ASCII place number in DL for INT 21H service 2.
        MOV     AH,2
        INT     21H     ;Print place number out.
EXIT:   INT     20H

CODE_SEG        ENDS
        END     ENTRY
```

REPE CMPSB keeps comparing bytes until two bytes are unequal. Depending on how the instruction stopped (did we run out of bytes to compare?), we know where the mismatch starts, and can print that location out. The result of this program is:

```
The strings started differing at character 3
```

The 80x86's string instructions are fast. If you're a programmer, they represent a great asset of the machine—when you want to use them, just drop into assembly language and you can pick up some speed. And we'll see how to do that in Chapter 6.

# 3

# How About Files?

So far, we've covered the basics of input and output for assembly language programs and developed the assembly language instruction set needed to accomplish those tasks. We've made great progress—in developing our example programs so far, we've seen many instructions and directives:

| *80x86 Instructions* | *Directives* |
|---|---|
| MOV, JMP, PUSH, POP, DEC, INC, INT, ADD, SUB, CALL, RET, LOOP, CMP, JA, JB, JE, JCXZ, SCASB, MOVSB, CMPSB, MOVSB, REP. | PROC, ENDP, END, DB, DW, DD, OFFSET, ORG, EQU, +, –. |

We understand addressing, have been introduced to indirect addressing, and know how to use INT 21H services 1, 2, 6, 7, 8, 9 and 0AH, as well as INT 20H. All our new expertise will be put to good use right here, in the current chapter.

Here, we're going to work with some real data in the PS/2 or PC—as we dig into file handling.

The real goal of computing is to produce something useful that can be seen outside the program. Output on the screen is one such method; but without files, computers would be hopelessly lost. Files represent the long-term storage of the PS/2 or PC, and they're still there when you turn your machine off. They can be printed out. They can be arranged to hold data and letters to the editor; they can be programs. And DOS meets the challenge with its rich set of file-handling services, again in INT 21H.

> The services of INT 21H represent most of the resources that the assembly language programmer uses in DOS. Besides INT 20H (end program), and the interrupts that make files memory-resident, the only other really useful DOS interrupts are the disk-reading and writing ones, INT 25H and INT 26H. Meanwhile, the number of services that INT 21H provides just keeps growing. In DOS 4.0, we are up to service 6CH.

## File Control Blocks

Before DOS 2.0, DOS used to work with files through what were called *File Control Blocks*, or FCBs. FCBs held information about files: their names, the drive they were on, and, although it was in the "reserved" system part, their sizes. However, FCBs restricted filenames to 11 characters, (eight characters of filename plus three of extension, like BASEBALL.BAT) and this proved to be their fatal flaw.

Beginning with DOS 2.0, IBM introduced directories, and suddenly filenames had to include pathnames as well. There is just no way to fit C:\PROGRAMS\ASSEMBLER\MASM.EXE into 11 characters. So *file handles* were introduced.

# File Handles

A file handle is a 16-bit word that stands, to DOS, for a file. When you want to use a file, you give DOS a file name, and DOS returns a file handle in a register (usually AX). Whenever you want to do something with that file—rename it, open it, read from it—the INT 21H service will need that 16-bit file handle in some register (usually BX).

A typical sequence for copying a file is a lot like it is in Pascal—we will open, read, write, and close files—but now we will use DOS services instead. It runs like this: Set up the file name as a string in memory, and make the last byte a 0 (not as ASCII 0, but a byte whose value is 0). As mentioned, this is referred to as an ASCIIZ string (ASCII zero) and tells the INT 21H service that the filename is ended:

```
FILE_36 DB "C:\Novel\Chapter.89",0
```

Now we open the file and get a file handle for it (INT 21H service 3DH). Create a new file (service 3CH). Read from the first file (service 3FH), write to the new file (service 40H), and then close them both (service 3EH).

Service 3FH is much like Read(), and Service 40H is much like Write(). As in Pascal, you aren't limited to using these services with files on disk; you can also treat devices as logical files. In particular, we use *predefined* handles to refer to various physical devices. Here are the predefined handles:

| *Handle* | *Device* |
|---|---|
| 0 | Standard Input (STDIN), usually keyboard |
| 1 | Standard Output (STDOUT), usually screen |
| 2 | Standard Error device (STDERR) |
| 3 | Standard Auxiliary device (STDAUX) |
| 4 | Standard Printer (STDPRN) |

For example, if we chose service 40H and passed 04H as the file handle, output would go to the printer.

# The DOS File Handle Services

There are so many INT 21H file handle services that it's easy to get lost. To avoid that, we will list all the usual file handle services DOS offers here instead of stringing them over the whole chapter. Table 3.1 collects the services we will use into one convenient table, which you can refer to later easily. Looking over it now shows the file services available in DOS.

Table 3.1 File Handle Services

| *File Handle Service* | *Number* | *You Set* | *It Returns* |
|---|---|---|---|
| Create Subdirectory | 39H | DS:DX to ASCIIZ string | If CY=1, AX has error |
| Delete Subdirectory | 3AH | DS:DX to ASCIIZ string | If CY=1, AX has error |
| Change Directory | 3BH | DS:DX to ASCIIZ string | If CY=1, AX has error |
| Create File | 3CH | DS:DX to ASCIIZ string<br>CX=attribute | If CY=1, AX has error<br>If CY=0 |
| Open File | 3DH | DS:DX to ASCIIZ<br>AL=mode | If CY=1, AX has error<br>If CY=0, AX=File Handle |
| Close File | 3EH | BX=File Handle | If CY=1, AX has error |
| Read from File | 3FH | BX=Handle<br>CX=#Bytes wanted<br>DS:DX=Buffer | If CY=1, AX has error<br>If CY=0, AX=#Bytes Read |
| Write to File | 40H | BX=Handle<br>CX=#Bytes<br>DS:DX=Buffer | If CY=1, AX has error |
| Delete a File | 41H | DS:DX to ASCIIZ string | If CY=1, AX has error |
| Move Read/Write Pointer | 42H | CX:DX=#Bytes to move<br>BX=File Handle<br>AL="method" | If CY=1, AX has error<br>If CY=0 DX:AX = new location in file. |

*Table 3.1, continued*

| | | | |
|---|---|---|---|
| Find 1st Matching File (use with wildcards) | 4EH | DS:DX to ASCIIZ<br>CX=Attribute | If CY=1, AX has error<br>If CY=0 then DTA has<br>21 bytes reserved<br>1 byte: file's attrib.<br>1 word: file's time<br>1 word: file's date<br>1 Dword: file's size<br>13 bytes: ASCIIZ name |
| Find Next Matching File | 4FH | DTA as set by service 4EH | Same as for 4EH |
| Rename File | 56H | DS:DX to ASCIIZ<br>ES:DI to new name (also ASCIIZ) | If CY=1, AX has error |

As you can see, there are plenty of services, including ones that create temporary files, get or set file's times or dates, and so on. (For more details, see the Appendix.) Let's begin to unpack some of this information right now, as we develop a small example program, RUBOUT, whose only purpose is to delete a specified file.

## The Program RUBOUT

About the simplest program we could write that works with files is one that deletes them, using service 41H. This service doesn't even require a file handle to delete the file: All that is needed is an ASCII character string, followed by a 0 byte—an ASCIIZ string—holding the file's pathname and filename.

We have already written programs that can read typed input into a buffer, and we'll use that knowledge in RUBOUT to read the file's name that we are to delete. Here's the program shell:

```
        .MODEL SMALL
        .CODE

        ORG 100H
START:  JMP RUBOUT
        THE_BUFFER        DB 50              ←
        BYTES_TYPED       DB 0
        CHARACTERS        DB 50 DUP(0)       ←
RUBOUT  PROC NEAR                            ←
        MOV      AH,0AH
        MOV      DX,OFFSET THE_BUFFER
        INT      21H
         :
         :
EXIT:   INT      20H
RUBOUT  ENDP                                 ←

        END START
```

Here we have made the buffer 50 characters long to accept both path and filenames and made the code into a procedure named RUBOUT. What the program does so far is to fill THE_BUFFER with the ASCII string we type to RUBOUT, which will be the name of the file we want deleted.

> There are easier ways of deleting files than writing RUBOUT, but it is worth noting that DOS itself—in the DEL command—uses these same services to delete files too.

When the ASCII string is typed in, the last character put into the buffer will be 0DH, which is the ASCII code for a carriage return. On the other hand, we want our ASCII string to end with 0, to make it ASCIIZ. To do this, we must replace the 0DH with 00H. This is not so hard.

We do not know in advance the location of the byte we have to make zero: It will be at the end of the ASCII string. This is where indirect addressing comes in handy. We will simply put the offset of the begining of the string (the offset of the label CHARACTERS) into the BX register, add the number of bytes actually typed to BX, and then make the 0DH into 00H with an instruction MOV BYTE PTR [BX],0. (Remember that service 0AH does not count the final 0DH in the total count of characters that were typed.) Notice that since [BX] can refer to either a byte or a word, we had to specify the size with BYTE PTR.

BX is a word-long register. To add BYTES_TYPED (a byte, defined with DB) to it, we will have to be careful. Here is how we do it: We first fill BH with zero, followed by MOV BL,BYTES_TYPED. Now the value of BYTES_TYPED is in BX. Then we can ADD BX, OFFSET CHARACTERS:

```
RUBOUT   PROC NEAR
         MOV      AH,0AH
         MOV      DX,OFFSET THE_BUFFER
         INT      21H
         MOV      BH,0  ←
         MOV      BL,BYTES_TYPED ←
         ADD      BX,OFFSET CHARACTERS     ←
         :
```

BX is all set with the address of the 0DH byte that we want to make into 0. Here's the line that we add next:

```
         .MODEL SMALL
         .CODE
         ORG 100H
START:   JMP RUBOUT
         THE_BUFFER       DB 50
         BYTES_TYPED      DB 0
         CHARACTERS       DB 50 DUP(0)
RUBOUT   PROC NEAR
         MOV      AH,0AH
         MOV      DX,OFFSET THE_BUFFER
```

```
         INT      21H
         MOV      BH,0
         MOV      BL,BYTES_TYPED
         ADD      BX,OFFSET CHARACTERS
         MOV      BYTE PTR[BX],0              ←
         :
         :
EXIT:    INT      20H
RUBOUT   ENDP

         END START
```

To delete a file, we check the entry in our DOS file services table earlier:

| *File Handle Service* | *Number* | *You Set* | *It Returns* |
|---|---|---|---|
| Delete a File | 41H | DS:DX to ASCIIZ string | If CY=1, AX has error |

All we have to do is to direct DS:DX to CHARACTERS, where the ASCIIZ string will start, and execute INT 21H, service 41H to delete the file whose name is at CHARACTERS:

```
         .MODEL SMALL
         .CODE
         ORG 100H
START:   JMP RUBOUT
         THE_BUFFER       DB 50
         BYTES_TYPED      DB 0
         CHARACTERS       DB 50 DUP(0)
RUBOUT   PROC NEAR
         MOV      AH,0AH
         MOV      DX,OFFSET THE_BUFFER
         INT      21H
         MOV      BH,0
         MOV      BL,BYTES_TYPED
         ADD      BX,OFFSET CHARACTERS
         MOV      BYTE PTR[BX],0
         MOV      DX,OFFSET CHARACTERS      ←
         MOV      AH,41H                    ←
         INT      21H                       ←
EXIT:    INT      20H
RUBOUT   ENDP

         END START
```

RUBOUT.ASM is ready to be assembled and run. We will find that it works as written, but that while running, it is very mysterious. When we type RUBOUT at the DOS prompt, the program just silently waits for us to type a filename for it to delete. This is less than user friendly.

We can easily add a prompt to RUBOUT, so that when run, it will prompt: "File to delete?". This is done with service 9 of INT 21H, the string printing service. We simply define a string to print (called PROMPT here), and type it out in the beginning:

```
        .MODEL SMALL
        .CODE
        ORG 100H
START:  JMP RUBOUT
        THE_BUFFER      DB 50
        BYTES_TYPED     DB 0
        CHARACTERS      DB 50 DUP(0)
        PROMPT          DB "File to delete? $"      ←
RUBOUT  PROC NEAR
        MOV     DX,OFFSET PROMPT        ←
        MOV     AH,9                    ←
        INT     21H                     ←
        MOV     AH,0AH
        MOV     DX,OFFSET THE_BUFFER
        INT     21H
        MOV     BH,0
        MOV     BL,BYTES_TYPED
        ADD     BX,OFFSET CHARACTERS
        MOV     BYTE PTR[BX],0
        MOV     DX,OFFSET CHARACTERS
        MOV     AH,41H
        INT     21H
EXIT:   INT     20H
RUBOUT  ENDP

        END START
```

This simple addition makes RUBOUT much clearer to use.

Use $ to terminate strings printed out by service 9. Many system programs use service 9 to print out their messages. If you debug COMMAND.COM—type

```
DEBUG COMMAND.COM<cr>
```

and repeatedly type D<cr>, DEBUG's command to dump memory—you will see all the errors COMMAND.COM can give you, followed by $s ("Terminate Batch Job (Y/N) $" etc.). String structure is quite different from Pascal, where the details are handled automatically.

# Error Checking

When we are dealing with files, we encounter something that we haven't seen before: the possibility of an error in carrying out an instruction. What if the name of the file was misspelled? What if it can't be found on the specified disk or in the specified subdirectory? RUBOUT should let the user know.

Error checking is a major part of programming when using files. For that reason, we will build (rudimentary) error checking into our example RUBOUT. If you check the table at the beginning of this chapter, you will see the line "If CY=1, AX has error" in the entry for service 41H (delete file):

| *File Handle Service* | *Number* | *You Set* | *It Returns* |
|---|---|---|---|
| Delete a File | 41H | DS:DX to ASCIIZ string | If CY=1, AX has error |

The CY stands for one of the internal flags that we've met briefly—the carry flag—and setting the carry flag is DOS' normal way of indicating that there has been an error of some kind.

The carry flag is normally set when a math operation produced a carry while combining two numbers—and we'll use it in our fast math chapter. When DOS sets the carry flag, however, a DOS error code is usually returned in the AX register.

## Error Codes

There are 91 different error codes in DOS 4.0, too many to cover here. However, here are the more common ones (they are returned in AX):

| *Error Code* | *Means* |
|---|---|
| 1 | Invalid function number |
| 2 | File not found |
| 3 | Path was not found |
| 4 | Too many files open at once |
| 5 | Access denied for this operation |
| 6 | File Handle used is invalid |
| 7 | Memory Control Blocks destroyed |
| 8 | Insufficient memory |
| 15 | Invalid drive was specified |
| 16 | Cannot delete current directory |
| 19 | Cannot write on a write-protected diskette |
| 21 | Drive not ready |
| 23 | Disk data error |
| 25 | Disk seek error |
| 27 | Sector not found |
| 28 | Printer needs paper |
| 29 | Write fault |
| 30 | Read fault |
| 61 | Print queue is full |

All these and more information may be found in a volume called the *DOS Technical Reference* manual. This book contains all the INT 21H services and can be quite useful. To deal with errors, we could use service 59H, get extended error; this service returns information on the error that has occurred, where it is, and even suggests what you should do. Information about this advanced service can be found in the DOS Technical Reference manual.

We aren't going to get very complex in RUBOUT. We are just going to assume that if there was no error, the file was deleted, and if there was an error, that it wasn't. Therefore, we will want to check the carry flag with the JC and JNC conditional jumps.

## JC and JNC

If the carry flag is 1, it is set. If it is set, the instruction JC OVER_THERE will cause the program to jump to the label OVER_THERE. Conversely, JNC will cause a jump if the carry flag *isn't* set. We will do the following: immediately after service 41H was requested, we will put a JNC instruction that will cause the message

```
File deleted
```

to print. If the JNC isn't taken, we will print out a message

```
File NOT deleted
```

and jump to the exit. Here's how it looks:

```
        .MODEL SMALL
        .CODE
        ORG 100H
START:  JMP RUBOUT
        THE_BUFFER       DB 50
        BYTES_TYPED      DB 0
        CHARACTERS       DB 50 DUP(0)
        PROMPT DB "File to delete? $"
        OK_MESSAGE       DB "File deleted $"        ←
        NOT_OK_MESSAGE   DB "File NOT deleted $"    ←
RUBOUT  PROC NEAR
        MOV     DX,OFFSET PROMPT
        MOV     AH,9
        INT     21H
        MOV     AH,0AH
        MOV     DX,OFFSET THE_BUFFER
        INT     21H
        MOV     BH,0
        MOV     BL,BYTES_TYPED
        ADD     BX,OFFSET CHARACTERS
        MOV     BYTE PTR[BX],0
```

```
          MOV     DX,OFFSET CHARACTERS
          MOV     AH,41H
          INT     21H
          JNC     ALL_OK                          ←
          MOV     DX,OFFSET NOT_OK_MESSAGE        ←
          JMP     PRINT                           ←
ALL_OK:   MOV     DX,OFFSET OK_MESSAGE            ←
PRINT:    MOV     AH,9                            ←
          INT     21H                             ←
EXIT:     INT     20H
RUBOUT    ENDP

END START
```

Notice our use of JNC right after the return from INT 21H. We have to check the carry flag immediately, before it is changed by another instruction.

That's it for RUBOUT, which has taught us about deleting files, ASCIIZ, the PTR directive, and error handling. To do anything more than delete files, you need to work with file handles, and our next example does that often enough.

# The Program BACK.ASM

Using file handles to work with files has made a difficult task into a (if not pleasant, at least) mercifully short business. This is the clean approach of assembly language—there are no layers buffering you from the data. If you want 12 bytes here in memory, just put them there. If you want to read in 279 bytes from a file and not worry about records or readln() or anything, assembly language is for you.

BACK.ASM is a program that will demonstrate the fluid way that assembly language can work with data. All we'll do in BACK.ASM is make a backup copy of a file you specify, changing the file's extension to ".BAK". For example, if you type:

```
BACK<cr>NOVEL.ONE<cr>
```

then BACK will copy NOVEL.ONE into a new file named NOVEL.BAK.

BACK is just a demonstration program. Since we are going to have to fit all data and code into the same segment, we will restrict BACK.COM to work with only files of less than, say 60K. It is not difficult to modify BACK.ASM so that it will read files larger than 60K in installments, and write them out the same way, letting the program handle files of any size. We'll point out where this can be done.

In addition (to thoroughly destroy any utility the program may have had), we are going to limit BACK to accepting filenames with eight letter names and three letter extensions—no pathnames. This is to avoid having to do fancy string manipulations when we copy the name over and substitute .BAK for the extension. Again, this can be changed with a little work, but these details of string handling would detract from the main points of file handling.

## The .COM File Stack

Here is a point that will be important when you deal with large amounts of data, as file copying programs can. The stack—which DOS uses to store addresses to return to when CALLs are made or that we use with PUSH and POP—shares the same segment as our program. In fact, you may have wondered where it was. It is at the top of the segment.

The final two registers in the 80x86 deal with the stack, and we won't really cover them until we deal with connecting assembly language to Pascal. However, we can discuss them a little here; their names are SP and BP.

The current location in the stack is always pointed to by SS:SP, and BP is an auxilary stack pointer. When the program begins, SP is set to the end of the segment (as you can see in DEBUG R commands we used earlier). It is vital that the program not write over the stack; if it does, it will crash. This means that you shouldn't allow anything to come closer to the end of the segment than about 256 words, or you stand a chance of overwriting the stack:

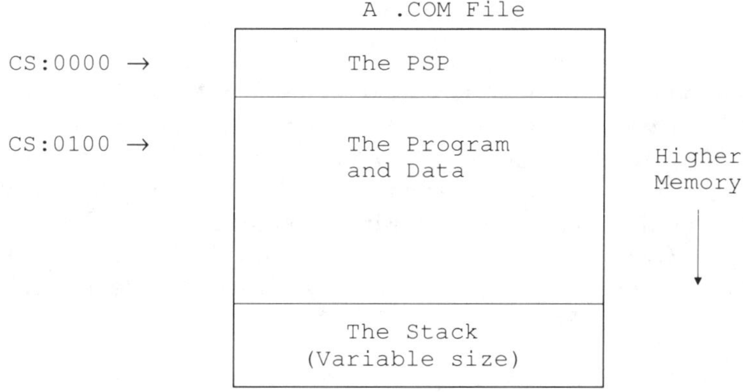


We will examine the stack later, but one thing you should know is that it has a variable size—the more it is used, the bigger it gets. As mentioned earlier, the stack grows downward—every time you push a word, SP is *decremented.*

In .COM files, the stack starts off as just the single word at the top of the segment and grows downward word by word as you push values.

> If a .COM file is made memory-resident, on the other hand, the stack that it uses from then on is DOS' own internal one, and there is no need to worry.

## BACK.ASM in Outline

We'll start out by taking what we need from RUBOUT. Here the program BACK will ask for a file to back up, accept a name, and make an ASCIIZ string out of it:

```
        .MODEL SMALL
        .CODE
        ORG 100H
START:  JMP BACK
        THE_BUFFER      DB 13
        BYTES_TYPED     DB 0
        FILE_ONE        DB 12 DUP(0)
        MAKE_ME_ZERO    DB 0
        FILE_TWO        DB 8 DUP(0), ".BAK",0
        PROMPT DB "Filename to back up: $"
BACK    PROC NEAR
        MOV     DX,OFFSET PROMPT
        MOV     AH,9
        INT     21H
        MOV     AH,0AH
        MOV     DX,OFFSET THE_BUFFER
        INT     21H
         :
         :
EXIT:   INT     20H
BACK    ENDP

        END START
```

Note that we've changed the label CHARACTERS to FILE_ONE, since that will be where the first file's name will appear. Also, we've added FILE_TWO, with the extension .BAK already. We've set THE_BUFFER to accept 13 characters—eight bytes of filename, the ., the three byte extension, and one last byte for the trailing 0DH that is always returned as the last byte in the buffer by service 0AH. Keep in mind that BACK, as written, will work *only* with 12-character filenames—so we can always count on the 13th byte being 0DH. To make it easy to write over this byte, we give it a label, MAKE_ME_ZERO:

```
→       THE_BUFFER      DB 13
        BYTES_TYPED     DB 0
→       FILE_ONE        DB 12 DUP(0)
→       MAKE_ME_ZERO    DB 0
→       FILE_TWO        DB 8 DUP(0), ".BAK",0
        PROMPT          DB "Filename to back up: $"
```

Note that if we didn't restrict the file's name to exactly 12 characters, we could use indirect addressing to find the end of buffer character—0DH—and set it to zero, as we did in RUBOUT. Even if service 0AH did not tell us how many characters were typed, we could find the 0DH by steadily incrementing the value of BX along the buffer and checking the value of BYTE PTR [BX].

We set MAKE_ME_ZERO to 0, making the read-in filename an ASCIIZ string, this way:

```
        ORG 100H
START:  JMP BACK
        THE_BUFFER      DB 13
        BYTES_TYPED     DB 0
        FILE_ONE        DB 12 DUP(0)
        MAKE_ME_ZERO    DB 0
        FILE_TWO        DB 8 DUP(0), ".BAK",0
        PROMPT DB "Filename to back up: $"
BACK    PROC NEAR
        MOV     DX,OFFSET PROMPT
        MOV     AH,9
        INT     21H
        MOV     AH,0AH
        MOV     DX,OFFSET THE_BUFFER
        INT     21H
        MOV     MAKE_ME_ZERO,0  ←
        :
```

If the file's name was BASEBALL.BAT, then THE_BUFFER would have looked like this before we made MAKE_ME_ZERO zero:

```
                                                         MAKE_ME_ZERO ──┐
                                                                        ↓
THE_BUFFER 13 12 "B" "A" "S" "E" "B" "A" "L" "L" "." "B" "A" "T" 0DH
```

and this afterwards:

```
                                                                        ↓
THE_BUFFER 13 12 "B" "A" "S" "E" "B" "A" "L" "L" "." "B" "A" "T" 0
```

## The Second Filename

Now we need to duplicate the filename with the extension .BAK. Since we've insisted on eight letter names and three letter extensions and have already placed .BAK in FILE_TWO, all we have to do is move eight letters from FILE_ONE to FILE_TWO using MOVSB. MOVSB means move string byte, and it is one of the string instructions that we've already had a brief introduction to. In Pascal, we have the luxury of copying strings without a second thought, but in assembly language, we have to take care of the details ourselves.

The MOVSB and MOVSW instructions give the names source index to SI and destination index to DI. MOVSB assumes that bytes come from DS:SI and that they go to ES:DI, all the while incrementing SI and DI. To use MOVSB, we can set DS:SI to FILE_ONE and ES:DI to FILE_TWO:

```
        ORG 100H
START:  JMP BACK
        THE_BUFFER      DB 13
        BYTES_TYPED     DB 0
        FILE_ONE        DB 12 DUP(0)
```

```
              MAKE_ME_ZERO     DB 0
              FILE_TWO         DB 8 DUP(0), ".BAK",0
              PROMPT DB "Filename to back up: $"
BACK          PROC NEAR
              MOV     DX,OFFSET PROMPT
              MOV     AH,9
              INT     21H
              MOV     AH,0AH
              MOV     DX,OFFSET THE_BUFFER
              INT     21H
              MOV     MAKE_ME_ZERO,0
              MOV     SI,OFFSET FILE_ONE        ←
              MOV     DI,OFFSET FILE_TWO        ←
               :
               :
EXIT:         INT     20H
BACK          ENDP
```

And then just move the eight bytes of the name by using the REP prefix for MOVSB. To use REP, we have to fill CX with 8, and this is how we do it:

```
              ORG 100H
START:        JMP BACK
              THE_BUFFER       DB 13
              BYTES_TYPED      DB 0
              FILE_ONE         DB 12 DUP(0)
              MAKE_ME_ZERO     DB 0
              FILE_TWO         DB 8 DUP(0), ".BAK",0
              PROMPT DB "Filename to back up: $"
BACK          PROC NEAR
              MOV     DX,OFFSET PROMPT
              MOV     AH,9
              INT     21H
              MOV     AH,0AH
              MOV     DX,OFFSET THE_BUFFER
              INT     21H
              MOV     MAKE_ME_ZERO,0
              MOV     CX,8  ←
              MOV     SI,OFFSET FILE_ONE
              MOV     DI,OFFSET FILE_TWO
REP           MOVSB          ←
               :
               :
EXIT:         INT     20H
BACK          ENDP
```

The ASCIIZ name of the original file is in FILE_ONE. And now the ASCIIZ name of the new, backup file is in FILE_TWO. We will want to copy from file one to file two. To start, let's open file one.

There are three ways to open a file—for reading only (like Pascal's Reset()), for writing only (like Pascal's Rewrite() and Append()), and for reading and writing.

Each of these can be selected with the *access mode* passed in AL to the open file service, service 3DH. Here's what that information looked like in the table at the beginning of this chapter:

| *File Handle Service* | *Number* | *You Set* | *It Returns* |
|---|---|---|---|
| Open File | 3DH | DS:DX to ASCIIZ string<br>AL=mode | If CY=1, AX has error<br>If CY=0, AX=File Handle |

The access mode, seen in Table 3.2, is passed in AL. It is 0 for reading only, 1 for writing only, and 2 for both.

Table 3.2 File Access Modes

| *Access Mode for Opening Files* | *Means* |
|---|---|
| 0 | Open file for read only |
| 1 | Open file for write only |
| 2 | Open file for both read and write |

We will set AL to 0. Here's how we open file one:

```
        ORG 100H
START:  JMP BACK
        THE_BUFFER      DB 13
        BYTES_TYPED     DB 0
        FILE_ONE        DB 12 DUP(0)
        MAKE_ME_ZERO    DB 0
        FILE_TWO        DB 8 DUP(0), ".BAK",0
        HANDLE_1        DW 0 ←
        HANDLE_2        DW 0
        PROMPT DB "Filename to back up: $"
BACK    PROC NEAR
        MOV     DX,OFFSET PROMPT
        MOV     AH,9
        INT     21H
        MOV     AH,0AH
        MOV     DX,OFFSET THE_BUFFER
        INT     21H
        MOV     MAKE_ME_ZERO,0
        MOV     CX,8
        MOV     SI,OFFSET FILE_ONE
        MOV     DI,OFFSET FILE_TWO
REP     MOVSB
        MOV     DX,OFFSET FILE_ONE      ←       ;Open first file
        MOV     AX,3D00H                ←
        INT     21H                     ←
        MOV     HANDLE_1,AX             ←
```

```
                :
                :
EXIT:       INT      20H
BACK        ENDP
```

Notice that we have combined the process of loading AH with 3DH and AL with 0 into one instruction, MOV AX,3D00H. The *file handle* for file one is returned by service 3DH in AX. We will store the handle (the way we will reference file one from now on) in HANDLE_1.

> The top three bits of AL, bits 7,6,5, can also be set in service 3DH, in DOS versions after 2.10, to indicate a network sharing mode. These modes set bits 7,6,5 this way for various *modes*: 000 = compatible with all, 001 = deny read/write, 010 = deny write, 011 = deny read, 100 = deny none. Sharing modes are very important under OS/2.

After opening the first file, we'll have to create the new, backup version of the file. To do this, we'll use INT 21H service 3CH. Here is Service 3CH from the table of file handling services at the beginning of the chapter:

| *File Handle Service* | *Number* | *You Set* | *It Returns* |
|---|---|---|---|
| Create File | 3CH | DS:DX to ASCIIZ string<br>CX=attribute | If CY=1, AX has error<br>If CY=0, AX=File Handle |

When you create a file you can set its attribute. Here are a list of possible attributes you can set:

| *File Attribute* | *Means* |
|---|---|
| 0 | Plain old file |
| 1 | Read-Only |
| 2 | Hidden file (hidden from directory searches) |
| 4 | A system file (like IBMDOS.COM) |
| 8 | Used for the volume label of a disk |
| 10H | This file name is the name of a subdirectory |

To select the attribute, you must load it into CX for service 3CH. We will select an attribute of 0. Service 3CH then returns a file handle for file two in AX, and we will store that in HANDLE_2:

```
        .MODEL SMALL
        .CODE
        ORG 100H
START:  JMP BACK
        THE_BUFFER      DB 13
        BYTES_TYPED     DB 0
        FILE_ONE        DB 12 DUP(0)
        MAKE_ME_ZERO    DB 0
        FILE_TWO        DB 8 DUP(0),  ".BAK",0
```

```
        HANDLE_1        DW 0
        HANDLE_2        DW 0 ←
        PROMPT          DB "Filename to back up: $"
BACK    PROC NEAR
        MOV     DX,OFFSET PROMPT
        MOV     AH,9
        INT     21H
        MOV     AH,0AH
        MOV     DX,OFFSET THE_BUFFER
        INT     21H
        MOV     MAKE_ME_ZERO,0
        MOV     CX,8
        MOV     SI,OFFSET FILE_ONE
        MOV     DI,OFFSET FILE_TWO
REP     MOVSB
        MOV     DX,OFFSET FILE_ONE              ;Open first file
        MOV     AX,3D00H
        INT     21H
        MOV     HANDLE_1,AX
        MOV     DX,OFFSET FILE_TWO  ←
        MOV     AH,3CH              ←           ;Create backup file.
        MOV     CX,0                ←
        INT     21H  ←
        MOV     HANDLE_2,AX         ←
         :
         :
EXIT:   INT     20H
BACK    ENDP

        END START
```

Now file one is ready to be read from, and file two ready to be written to:

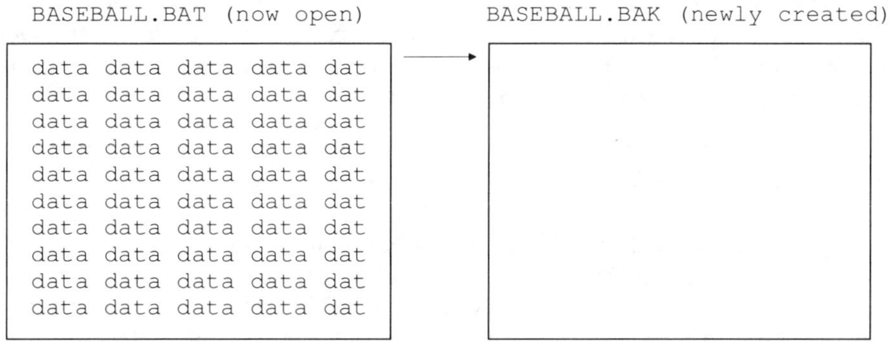


We will have to read the data from the first file into a data area in memory before writing it out to the second file. We can prepare a data area simply by adding a label, say DATA, at the end of the program, but still inside the code segment. This point, immediately after the program, is where data will be read in:

```
        ORG 100H
START:  JMP BACK
        :
BACK    PROC NEAR
        :
        MOV     DX,OFFSET FILE_ONE                  ;Open first file
        MOV     AX,3D00H
        INT     21H
        MOV     HANDLE_1,AX
        MOV     DX,OFFSET FILE_TWO
        MOV     AH,3CH                              ;Create backup file.
        MOV     CX,0
        INT     21H
        MOV     HANDLE_2,AX
         :
         :
EXIT:   INT     20H
BACK    ENDP
DATA:                               ←

        END START
```

Using a label outside our procedure might be surprising, but it is fine. All it means is that all our data will go immediately after the program in memory. Notice that it wasn't necessary to reserve space in DATA with DB. This is because, after our program code, we have the whole rest of the segment (excluding the stack at the high end) to work with. On the other hand, unless we deliberately set aside space in the normal .COM file data area with DB or DW, no space would be reserved. By using the DATA label at the end of our program, we avoid having to set up a 60K data buffer with DB, which would make our program BACK.COM larger than 60K on disk.

In Pascal, we do not have this luxury unless we allocate memory, which is effectively what we are doing here. Theoretically, we should use the DOS GETBLOCK and SETBLOCK services as described in the appendix, but because DOS gives us the whole segment, we might as well use it.

## Reading From Files

Now we have to read the data in from file one into the data area at the end of the program. There are three logical types of files in Pascal—text, typed, and untyped. In text files, you expect to find <cr><lf>s (that is, #13,#10) at the end of a line. Typed files contain only data of one particualr type, and you must declare that type in advance. Untyped files are unstructured and considered only as unrelated bytes.

All files in assembly language are treated as untyped.

Let's see how that works when reading from files. Service 3FH (the Read() of assembly language) reads from an open file. We don't know the file's length, so we don't know how many bytes to read in. However, all we have to do is to ask for the maximum possible, 60K, and service 3FH will read in as many as it can. It returns the actual number of bytes read in AX, and that is all we need—we will tell the writing service, service 40H (like Write()), to write that many to the second file. This is common practice when working with files in assembly language—it does not generate an error.

> This is where we could modify BACK.ASM to work with files greater than 60K. If service 3FH reports that a full 60K bytes were read in, as requested, then you should write those bytes, and go back to check if there were more, using service 3FH again.

This is how to use Service 3FH, from our file handle services table:

| *File Handle Service* | *Number* | *You Set* | *It Returns* |
|---|---|---|---|
| Read from File | 3FH | BX=Handle<br>CX=#Byte wanted<br>DS:DX=Buffer | If CY=1, AX has error<br>If CY=0, AX=#Bytes Read |

Service 3FH needs this input—point DS:DX to the buffer used for data (our label DATA), load BX with the file handle (HANDLE_1), and CX with the number of bytes to read (60K). Here we read the data in from file one:

```
        ORG 100H
START:  JMP BACK
        THE_BUFFER      DB 13
        BYTES_TYPED     DB 0
        FILE_ONE        DB 12 DUP(0)
        MAKE_ME_ZERO    DB 0
        FILE_TWO        DB 8 DUP(0), ".BAK",0
        HANDLE_1        DW 0
        HANDLE_2        DW 0
        PROMPT DB "Filename to back up: $"
BACK    PROC NEAR
        MOV     DX,OFFSET PROMPT
        MOV     AH,9
        INT     21H
        MOV     AH,0AH
        MOV     DX,OFFSET THE_BUFFER
        INT     21H
        MOV     MAKE_ME_ZERO,0
        MOV     CX,8
        MOV     SI,OFFSET FILE_ONE
        MOV     DI,OFFSET FILE_TWO
REP     MOVSB
        MOV     DX,OFFSET FILE_ONE               ;Open first file
        MOV     AX,3D00H
        INT     21H
        MOV     HANDLE_1,AX
        MOV     DX,OFFSET FILE_TWO
        MOV     AH,3CH                           ;Create backup file.
```

```
        MOV     CX,0
        INT     21H
        MOV     HANDLE_2,AX
        MOV     AH,3FH              ←
        MOV     CX,60*1024          ←
        MOV     DX,OFFSET DATA      ←
        MOV     BX,HANDLE_1         ←
        INT     21H                 ←
          :
          :
EXIT:   INT     20H
BACK    ENDP
DATA:
```

You may have noticed the use of a new assembler operator here, *, which is a math operator like + or – (keep in mind that operators are like directives—they are instructions to the assembler and generate no code). This operator makes the assembler multiply for us; in particular, it multiplies 60 times 1024 and places the result in the assembled program. This is handy, because, reading the code, it's clear that we want 60K here, and it wouldn't be so clear if we had typed in 61440 instead.

## Writing the Data to File Two

Next we write the data out to file two, the backup file, with Service 40H. Because all data from files is considered untyped, we don't have to worry about the number of lines to write, or the number of data items; only the number of bytes, and we already have that available. Here's how to use it from our file handle service table:

| *File Handle Service* | *Number* | *You Set* | *It Returns* |
|---|---|---|---|
| Write to File | 40H | BX=Handle<br>CX=#Bytes<br>DS:DX=Buffer | If CY=1, AX has error<br>If CY=0, AX=#Bytes actually written |

To use this service, you must point DS:DX at the data (our label DATA), fill CX with the number of bytes to write (returned from the read operation in AX), and BX with the file handle (HANDLE_2). The only trick here is loading CX for service 40H with the number of bytes actually read, returned in AX by service 3FH. All we'll have to do is transfer the value in AX to CX and then write the bytes in DATA out:

```
        ORG 100H
START:  JMP BACK
        THE_BUFFER      DB 13
        BYTES_TYPED     DB 0
        FILE_ONE        DB 12 DUP(0)
        MAKE_ME_ZERO    DB 0
        FILE_TWO        DB 8 DUP(0), ".BAK",0
        HANDLE_1        DW 0
        HANDLE_2        DW 0
```

```
        PROMPT DB "Filename to back up: $"
        BACK    PROC NEAR
        MOV     DX,OFFSET PROMPT
        MOV     AH,9
        INT     21H
        MOV     AH,0AH
        MOV     DX,OFFSET THE_BUFFER
        INT     21H
        MOV     MAKE_ME_ZERO,0
        MOV     CX,8
        MOV     SI,OFFSET FILE_ONE
        MOV     DI,OFFSET FILE_TWO
REP     MOVSB
        MOV     DX,OFFSET FILE_ONE              ;Open first file
        MOV     AX,3D00H
        INT     21H
        MOV     HANDLE_1,AX
        MOV     DX,OFFSET FILE_TWO
        MOV     AH,3CH                          ;Create backup file.
        MOV     CX,0
        INT     21H
        MOV     HANDLE_2,AX
        MOV     AH,3FH
        MOV     CX,60*1024
        MOV     DX,OFFSET DATA
        MOV     BX,HANDLE_1
        INT     21H
→       MOV     CX,AX   ;Set number of bytes to write to number actually read.
→       MOV     AH,40H
→       MOV     BX,HANDLE_2
→       INT     21H
          :
          :
EXIT:   INT     20H
BACK    ENDP
DATA:
```

After this step, we've copied file one to file two on the disk:

```
  BASEBALL.BAT (now open)          BASEBALL.BAK (newly created)

  data data data data dat   ──→    data data data data dat
  data data data data dat          data data data data dat
  data data data data dat          data data data data dat
  data data data data dat          data data data data dat
  data data data data dat          data data data data dat
  data data data data dat          data data data data dat
  data data data data dat          data data data data dat
  data data data data dat          data data data data dat
  data data data data dat          data data data data dat
  data data data data dat          data data data data dat
  data data data data dat          data data data data dat
```

Now that it's done, all that remains is to close the two files. That is done with service 3EH (just like Close()). From our table:

| *File Handle Service* | *Number* | *You Set* | *It Returns* |
|---|---|---|---|
| Close File | 3EH | BX=File Handle | If CY=1, AX has error |

All this service needs is the file's handle in BX (we'll give it both HANDLE_1 and HANDLE_2). Here it is:

```
        .MODEL SMALL
        .CODE
        ORG 100H
START:  JMP BACK
        THE_BUFFER      DB 13
        BYTES_TYPED     DB 0
        FILE_ONE        DB 12 DUP(0)
        MAKE_ME_ZERO    DB 0
        FILE_TWO        DB 8 DUP(0), ".BAK",0
        HANDLE_1        DW 0
        HANDLE_2        DW 0
        PROMPT          DB "Filename to back up: $"
BACK    PROC NEAR
        MOV     DX,OFFSET PROMPT
        MOV     AH,9
        INT     21H
        MOV     AH,0AH
        MOV     DX,OFFSET THE_BUFFER
        INT     21H
        MOV     MAKE_ME_ZERO,0
        MOV     CX,8
        MOV     SI,OFFSET FILE_ONE
        MOV     DI,OFFSET FILE_TWO
REP     MOVSB
        MOV     DX,OFFSET FILE_ONE               ;Open first file
        MOV     AX,3D00H
        INT     21H
        MOV     HANDLE_1,AX
        MOV     DX,OFFSET FILE_TWO
        MOV     AH,3CH                          ;Create backup file.
        MOV     CX,0
        INT     21H
        MOV     HANDLE_2,AX
        MOV     AH,3FH
        MOV     CX,60*1024
        MOV     DX,OFFSET DATA
        MOV     BX,HANDLE_1
        INT     21H
        MOV     CX,AX   ;Set number of bytes to write to number actually read.
        MOV     AH,40H
        MOV     BX,HANDLE_2
        INT     21H
```

```
        MOV     AH,3EH          ←
        MOV     BX,HANDLE_1     ←
        INT     21H             ←
        MOV     BX,HANDLE_2     ←
        INT     21H             ←
EXIT:   INT     20H
BACK    ENDP
DATA:

        END START
```

And that's it! Assemble it and give it a try, but make sure to give it the name of a file with an eight letter name and a three letter extension, like BASEBALL.BAT. BACK.COM will produce and fill BASEBALL.BAK (up to 60K, of course). Our program can copy files; it's not so difficult in assembly language, and it works at high speed too.

# Inside Files

In this chapter, we have seen how to delete files, simply by storing their names in memory, pointing to them, and using service 41H of INT 21H. There's not much work that goes on in just deleting files, however.

Next we saw how to work with the entire file—all the data at once—by copying the file whole and producing a backup copy. This was also pretty easy to do. All we had to do was to open the file we wanted to back up, create a new file, copy from file one into file two, and then close them both. We also saw that all files are treated as untyped.

On the other hand, we did very little with the data actually in the file itself. BACK.COM can swallow whole files at once and write them back elsewhere on the disk, but it knows nothing about what's in them. This is where all the protocol one finds in Pascal was designed to come in—by formatting your file. You can think of a typed file as formatted into records—if we want to use records in assembly language, we are responsible for maintaining them.

## Records

A record works like this: Suppose you wanted to store all your friends' telephone numbers—a pretty simple example. Each *record* might then be simply, say, 16 bytes that you set aside for the person's name, and another 16 bytes that you set aside for their telephone number. For example this might be a record, the way we've set it up:

```
←— 16-Bytes —→
................     ← The person's name will go here.
................     ← The telephone number will go here.
```

> In the old days, using FCBs, we did have definite record sizes and block lengths and so on. Using file handles, where we simply select the number of bytes to be read in, is much easier.

You could define such a record with DB in memory, like this:

```
NAME     DB 16 DUP(0)
NUMBER   DB 16 DUP(0)
```

This means that each record is 32 bytes long and begins at label NAME. If you had a name of a good friend to store, say, Albert Einstein, and a number, say, 299-7980, you could put those bytes—or rather, their ASCII equivalents, into NAME and NUMBER, leaving the leftover bytes at the end untouched.

Both NAME and NUMBER are fields; the record as a whole has two fields, NAME and NUMBER. You could set up NAME and NUMBER in advance, like this:

```
NAME     DB "Albert Einstein", 0
NUMBER   DB "299-7980", 8 DUP(0)
```

The formal way of setting up records in assembly language is setting up what is referred to as a data structure, with the advanced directive STRUC. Take a look at this Pascal record that has two fields:

```
PHONE_RECORD = record
        NAME : string;
        NUMBER : string;
        end;
```

You refer to elements like this: RecordName.FieldName. You can do the same in assembly language, like this:

```
PHONE_RECORD     STRUC
        NAME     DB "$$$$$$$$$$$$$$$$"
        NUMBER   DB "$$$$$$$$$$$$$$$$"
PHONE_RECORD     ENDS
```

This creates a structure type named PHONE_RECORD; no physical data structure exists yet. To allocate space for data (i.e., to set aside a labeled data area as DB does), use PHONE_RECORD in place of DB, like this:

```
PHONE_DATA       PHONE_RECORD <"Albert Einstein", "299-7980">
```

In this case, we have created a data structure named PHONE_DATA of type PHONE_RECORD. We have overridden the default NAME and NUMBER fields to hold Albert Einstein's name and phone number. In memory, it looks like this:

```
PHONE_DATA:
        NAME     DB "Albert Einstein$"
        NUMBER   DB "299-7980$$$$$$$$"
```

Simple fields—ones that contain one data item or a string—can be overridden this way. Complex fields—ones with elements separated by commas or defined with DUP—cannot. Now we can refer to the string 'Albert Einstein' by PHONE_DATA.NAME.

> If an overriding string is shorter than the initial string, the space to the right is padded with blanks; if the overriding string is longer, it is trunctated.

You can see that STRUC acts very much like data records in Pascal. STRUC is an advanced directive, however, and is usually used only when data handling is complex. In our case, we only have one record with two fields, so we'll leave it like this:

```
NAME     DB 16 DUP(0)
NUMBER   DB 16 DUP(0)
```

Note that in each case, we carefully added zeroes at the end of the field to make sure that the field length in memory stayed the same. This way, every record will be the same length in the file when we write it out, and it is critical that they should be so. A fundamental property about records that you want to retrieve from anywhere in a file is that they have the same length to make finding them easier. Each of our records are 32 bytes long, and here is how Albert Einstein's would look:

```
Albert Einstein.    ← The person's name will go here.
299-7980........    ← The telephone number will go here.
```

Making sure records have the same length makes it easy to choose a record at random from anywhere in a file, and this is called random access—the only type of file formatting we'll deal with here. The other method allows you to have variable length records, but constrains you to put end-of-record markers into the file to show the boundaries between records. For example, this end-of-record marker is a carriage return line feed pair in Pascal text files. Since you have to read from the beginning of the file to know the number of the present record this way, it is called sequential access.

To write this record out to a file, open or create the file, point at NAME, and tell service 40H to write 32 bytes. That's how a record is written in assembly language—as long as you know the record length, you'll always know where you are or where a given record number is in a file, because the INT 21H services let you specify the number of bytes you want and you can just choose the record length.

You can then make another record with another name and number, say Enrico Fermi, whose number might be 271-8281. This is the way the record would look:

```
←— 16-Bytes —→
Enrico Fermi....
271-8281........
```

where the dots indicate a zero byte. You can add this information to your data file, which we can call NUMBERS.DAT. To add Enrico Fermi, just write out the 32 bytes of this record. Since we've already written out Albert Einstein, Enrico Fermi will be placed right after him:

```
       The data file
   ┌────────────────────┐
   │ Albert Einstein.   │  ← First record
   │  299-7980........  │
   │ Enrico Fermi....   │  ← Second record
   │  271-8281........  │
   │         :          │  ← Third record, etc.
   │         :          │
   └────────────────────┘
```

You can continue in this manner until NUMBERS.DAT is as full as you want it. NUMBERS.DAT will always be a multiple of 32 bytes in length. After NUMBERS.DAT is fully stocked, however, there might come a day when you realize that you've forgotten Enrico Fermi's telephone number, and want to look it up. How would you do that?

## Retrieving Data From Files

There's not much point in writing excellent data files unless you can use them. And using them isn't so hard as you might think. Here we want to read in a record—the second record of NUMBERS.DAT, that is, Enrico Fermi's name and telephone number.

You might expect that we can simply open NUMBERS.DAT and request to read in 64 bytes, which encompasses both the first two records; and, of course, we can. But this method demands that we read in two records, and it is clear this method might use up a lot of memory if we wanted record 32,001.

Another method might be to read in the first record, 32 bytes, and then to read in the second record in the same location in memory, so that it will overwrite the first record. Then we'd have record 2 at no additional memory expense. Of course, if we wanted record 32,001, we'd have to wait a long time to reach it. Fortunately, there is a better way.

## The Read/Write Pointer

This better way is quite simple. You can simply set the location in the file that you want to start reading bytes from, and that location is called the read/write pointer. In other words, this is how NUMBERS.DAT looks now:

```
NUMBERS.DAT

Albert Einstein.  ───┐
299-7980........  ───┘  Record 1
Enrico Fermi....  ───┐
271-8281........  ───┘  Record 2
Wolfgang Pauli..  ───┐
314-1592........  ───┘  Record 3
        :
        :
←── 16-Bytes ──→
```

And to read the second record, we could simply position the read/write pointer 32 bytes into the file, that is, at the beginning of record 2:

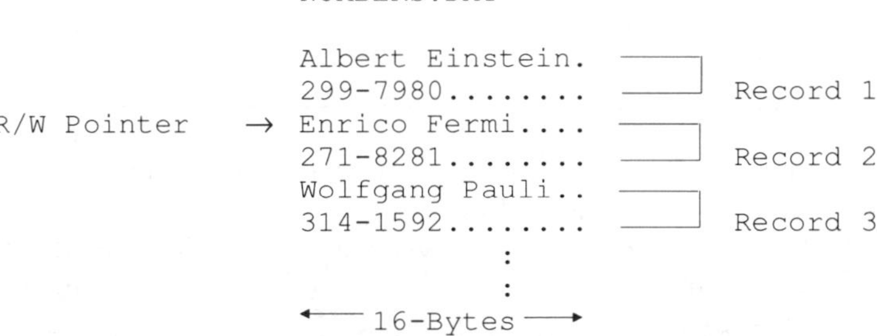


And then read in that record—ask for 32 bytes to be read in. It's simple.

The place you read from a file or write to it is where the read/write pointer is. By setting this pointer yourself, you can position yourself in any file.

To position the read/write pointer, use service 42H, Move read/write Pointer. Here's the entry for Service 42H in our file handle services table:

| *File Handle Service* | *Number* | *You Set* | *It Returns* |
|---|---|---|---|
| Move Read/Write Pointer | 42H | CX:DX=#Bytes to move<br>BX=File Handle<br>AL="method" | If CY=1, AX has error<br>If CY=0 DX:AX = new location in file. |

To use this service, just set CX:DX to the number of bytes that you want to move. The reason two words are specified for this distance is that you may want to move more than 64K bytes, and 64K–1 is the largest number that a word can hold. If the number is larger than that, you'll need more than 16 bits to indicate it.

For example, 68K in hex is 11000H; if you wanted to move the read/write pointer that many bytes, you'd set the low word—in DX—to 1000H, and the high word—in CX—to 0001H. Together, CX and DX as CX:DX would make 0001:1000 = 00011000H.

Besides setting up the number of bytes to move, BX must hold the file's handle so service 42H knows which file you mean to use.

> As its name implies, you can either read or write at the read/write pointer's location—it sets where the next read or write operation will take place in the file.

In addition, you have to tell service 42H *how* to move the read/write pointer. This is called the *method* and can range from 0 to 2. The method is passed to service 42H in AL; the possible methods are shown in Table 3.3.

Table 3.3 Methods for INT 21H Service 42H

| *Method (in AL)* | *Means* |
|---|---|
| 0 | Set R/W pointer to CX:DX bytes from the beginning of the file. |
| 1 | Mov R/W pointer CX:DX bytes from where we are now. |
| 2 | Set R/W pointer to CX:DX bytes from end of file. |

Note: New location of R/W pointer returned in DX:AX.
If CY = 1, error code will be in AX.

The standard method is to move the read/write pointer the specified number of bytes from the beginning of the file. This is method 0.

The next method, method 1, moves the read/write pointer CX:DX from the read/write pointer's current position. For example, if the read/write pointer was at byte 32,000 in a file, and you specified method 1, and a distance of one byte, you would end up positioned at 32,001.

The last method, method 2, moves the Read/Write pointer to the end of the file, plus the value stored in CX:DX (that is, past the end of the file)—this method is almost always used only for determining the length of the file.

You start at the beginning of the file, use method 2 to place the read/write pointer at the end of the file, and set CX:DX to 0000:0000. In other words, we are asking that the read/write pointer be placed at the end of the file. When service 42H returns, it always sets the new location of the pointer in DX:AX (DX is the high word, AX the low word), and, in this case, DX:AX will simply hold the length of the file, from beginning to end, in bytes.

## Using the Read/Write Pointer

This means that we can get any record we want. If we know each record is 32 bytes long, and we want the second record, we can use service 42H, method 0, to position the pointer 32 bytes from the beginning of the file, after the first record, and then read in the second record. If we wanted record 32,001, we would position the pointer at byte 32,000*32 and read the record there.

Let's put this knowledge to work and see how it works in practice, with a new example program. We can even use the file we have been talking about,

NUMBERS.DAT. The program, which will look up phone numbers for us, will be called PHONE.COM.

# PHONE.ASM

It would be a long, strenuous exercise to write the program that creates NUMBERS.DAT for us, and then a second program, PHONE.ASM to read it in. So we'll cheat a little. We will create NUMBERS.DAT using DEBUG, and not an assembly language program, since the point here is data retrieval—we've already written to files. PHONE.ASM will get us started working with the Read/Write pointer.

## Making the Data File NUMBERS.DAT

First let's make NUMBERS.DAT. We want to make it just as a program would write it—with thirty-two bytes, that is, ASCII characters, for each record. Instead of padding the record fields with 0's to fill them out, however, let's use the character $. This will be a shortcut for us in PHONE.ASM, since then we can use just the string printing service, INT 21H service 9, to print both name and phone number—service 9 stops printing when it reaches a $, the end of the NAME or NUMBER field.

Start DEBUG:

```
A>DEBUG
```

We can use the DEBUG *Fill* command, F, to fill memory with $ characters. Let's give NUMBERS.DAT three records, each 32 bytes long, for a total of 3 times 32 equals 96 bytes. In other words, our file, NUMBERS.DAT, will be 96 bytes long. DEBUG starts us off at location CS:0100, so we want to fill the 96 bytes (60H) from CS:0100 to CS:015F with $s. This is the way to do it:

```
A>DEBUG
-F 100 15F "$"
```

Let's check to make sure, with the Dump command. D will dump memory locations for you, letting you know what's there:

```
A>DEBUG
-F 100 15F "$"
-D100  ←
0EF1:0100  24 24 24 24 24 24 24 24-24 24 24 24 24 24 24 24   $$$$$$$$$$$$$$$$
0EF1:0110  24 24 24 24 24 24 24 24-24 24 24 24 24 24 24 24   $$$$$$$$$$$$$$$$
0EF1:0120  24 24 24 24 24 24 24 24-24 24 24 24 24 24 24 24   $$$$$$$$$$$$$$$$
0EF1:0130  24 24 24 24 24 24 24 24-24 24 24 24 24 24 24 24   $$$$$$$$$$$$$$$$
0EF1:0140  24 24 24 24 24 24 24 24-24 24 24 24 24 24 24 24   $$$$$$$$$$$$$$$$
0EF1:0150  24 24 24 24 24 24 24 24-24 24 24 24 24 24 24 24   $$$$$$$$$$$$$$$$
0EF1:0160  24 FC C3 E8 E2 FF 89 3E-4C F6 CB E8 CA FF 2B CF   .......>L.....+.
0EF1:0170  F2 AE E3 03 EB 16 90 B8-00 00 CB E8 BA FF 3B 3E   ..............;>
```

It looks like we're all set. Now we have to enter our names and numbers. There will be two lines of $s (each line is 16 characters in the DEBUG dump—just the size of our fields) for each record, and since there are six lines of $s, we will be able to put in three records.

Unfortunately, DEBUG makes a particularly bad editor. We have to enter our data with the deposit byte, DB directive, just as if we were writing a program. Each field will be easy to locate since it is just 16—that is, 10H—bytes apart. We have to assemble (the A command) at the beginning of each field and use DB to put the string in. Here's how it looks for the NUMBERS.DAT we've developed, as we (tediously) fill each of the six fields:

> You might try this with your word processor, but the reason DEBUG was selected for this exercise is that word processors usually insert unwanted carriage returns.

```
-A100 ←
0EF1:0100 DB "Albert Einstein"
0EF1:010F
-A110 ←
0EF1:0110 DB "299-7980"
0EF1:0118
-A120 ←
0EF1:0120 DB "Enrico Fermi"
0EF1:012C
-A130 ←
0EF1:0130 DB "271-8281"
0EF1:0138
-A140 ←
0EF1:0140 DB "Wolfgang Pauli"
0EF1:014E
-A150 ←
0EF1:0150 DB "314-1592"
0EF1:0158
```

Now that memory should be set up correctly, let's dump it again and check:

```
-D100  ←
0EF1:0100  41 6C 62 65 72 74 20 45-69 6E 73 74 65 69 6E 24   Albert Einstein$
0EF1:0110  32 39 39 2D 37 39 38 30-24 24 24 24 24 24 24 24   299-7980$$$$$$$$
0EF1:0120  45 6E 72 69 63 6F 20 46-65 72 6D 69 24 24 24 24   Enrico Fermi$$$$
0EF1:0130  32 37 31 2D 38 32 38 31-24 24 24 24 24 24 24 24   271-8281$$$$$$$$
0EF1:0140  57 6F 6C 66 67 61 6E 67-20 50 61 75 6C 69 24 24   Wolfgang Pauli$$
0EF1:0150  33 31 34 2D 31 35 39 32-24 24 24 24 24 24 24 24   314-1592$$$$$$$$
0EF1:0160  24 FC C3 E8 E2 FF 89 3E-4C F6 CB E8 CA FF 2B CF   .......>L.....+.
0EF1:0170  F2 AE E3 03 EB 16 90 B8-00 00 CB E8 BA FF 3B 3E   ..............;>
```

Everything is there, ready to be written out. This is exactly the way NUMBERS.DAT would look if it had been written out by a program. We can write NUMBERS.DAT with DEBUG's W command, first filling CX with the number of bytes to fill—60H—

and then naming the file with the N command, as we've seen when we used DEBUG as an assembler:

```
-NNUMBERS.DAT
-RCX
CX 0000
:60
-W
Writing 0060 bytes
-Q
```

Our data file, NUMBERS.DAT, is all set. Now that we've got the data file, we've got to read it in.

# Writing PHONE.ASM

We're ready for the program itself. PHONE will not be so hard to write, because we already know what file we'll be reading in, NUMBERS.DAT. Let's make an ASCIIZ string containing NUMBERS.DAT and open the file here in the beginning of PHONE.ASM, storing the file handle in FILEHANDLE:

```
        .MODEL SMALL
        .CODE
        ORG 100H
START:  JMP PHONE
        FILENAME        DB "NUMBERS.DAT",0          ←
        FILEHANDLE      DW 0                        ←
PHONE   PROC NEAR
        MOV     DX,OFFSET FILENAME      ←
        MOV     AL,0    ;Read Only      ←
        MOV     AH,3DH                  ←
        INT     21H                     ←
        MOV     FILEHANDLE,AX           ←
          :
          :
EXIT:   INT     20H
PHONE   ENDP

        END START
```

Note that we set the access mode, in AL, to 0 (read only) so that we can only read NUMBERS.DAT. If your program wants to write data as well as read it, use access mode 2 (read and write). We open the file and store the handle, returned in AX, for future use.

In preparation for reading in records, let's set up the two fields that we will need and might as well call PERSON_NAME and NUMBER, as we did before:

```
.MODEL SMALL
.CODE
```

```
        ORG 100H
START:  JMP PHONE
        FILENAME        DB "NUMBERS.DAT",0
        FILEHANDLE      DW 0
        PERSON_NAME     DB 16 DUP(0)                ←
        NUMBER          DB 16 DUP(0)                ←
PHONE   PROC NEAR
        MOV     DX,OFFSET FILENAME
        MOV     AL,0     ;Read Only
        MOV     AH,3DH
        INT     21H
        MOV     FILEHANDLE,AX
          :
          :
EXIT:   INT     20H
PHONE   ENDP

        END START
```

Next we'll have to find out what to do from the user: Which record—1, 2, or 3—should we read in? Or should we quit? Let's type out a prompt that lists the available options:

```
        .MODEL SMALL
        .CODE
        ORG 100H
START:  JMP PHONE
        FILENAME        DB "NUMBERS.DAT",0
        FILEHANDLE      DW 0
        PERSON_NAME     DB 16 DUP(0)
        NUMBER          DB 16 DUP(0)
        PROMPT          DB "Get phone number (1-3) or Quit (Q): $" ←
PHONE   PROC NEAR
        MOV     DX,OFFSET FILENAME
        MOV     AL,0     ;Read Only
        MOV     AH,3DH
        INT     21H
        MOV     FILEHANDLE,AX
ASK:    MOV     DX,OFFSET PROMPT          ←
        MOV     AH,9                      ←
        INT     21H                       ←
        MOV     AH,1                      ←
        INT     21H                       ←
          :
          :
EXIT:   INT     20H
PHONE   ENDP

        END START
```

Here we also use service 1 to get a one-letter response. If that response is Q, as indicated in the prompt, we should quit. Before we do, however, we must close the files.

Service 1 delivers the typed key's ASCII code in AL. To check whether this is Q, we use CMP. If our response turned out indeed to be Q, then we have to close the file (service 3EH) and exit, like this:

```
        .MODEL SMALL
        .CODE
        ORG 100H
START:  JMP PHONE
        FILENAME        DB "NUMBERS.DAT",0
        FILEHANDLE      DW 0
        PERSON_NAME     DB 16 DUP(0)
        NUMBER          DB 16 DUP(0)
        PROMPT          DB "Get phone number (1-3) or Quit (Q): $"
PHONE   PROC NEAR
        MOV     DX,OFFSET FILENAME
        MOV     AL,0     ;Read Only
        MOV     AH,3DH
        INT     21H
        MOV     FILEHANDLE,AX
ASK:    MOV     DX,OFFSET PROMPT
        MOV     AH,9
        INT     21H
        MOV     AH,1
        INT     21H
        CMP     AL,"Q"          ←
        JE      QUIT            ←
         :
         :
QUIT:   MOV     BX,FILEHANDLE   ←       ;Close the files.
        MOV     AH,3EH          ←
        INT     21H             ←
EXIT:   INT     20H
PHONE   ENDP

        END START
```

If the response wasn't Q, then we'll assume it was a number, 1 to 3. To convert the ASCII code now in AL to a record number, we have only to subtract ASCII 0 from AL. This converts the ASCII digit to a hex one.

After getting the record number, we have to set the read/write pointer. To read in the first record, we want the read/write pointer at offset 0; for the second record, at offset 32, and for the third, at 64. In other words, the location of the pointer will be (record number – 1) times 32 bytes from the beginning of the file. Here's how we get the record number and calculate the number of bytes to move the pointer:

```
        .MODEL SMALL
        .CODE
```

```
        ORG 100H
START:  JMP PHONE
        FILENAME        DB "NUMBERS.DAT",0
        FILEHANDLE      DW 0
        PERSON_NAME     DB 16 DUP(0)
        NUMBER          DB 16 DUP(0)
        PROMPT          DB "Get phone number (1-3) or Quit (Q): $"
PHONE   PROC NEAR
        MOV     DX,OFFSET FILENAME
        MOV     AL,0    ;Read Only
        MOV     AH,3DH
        INT     21H
        MOV     FILEHANDLE,AX
ASK:    MOV     DX,OFFSET PROMPT
        MOV     AH,9
        INT     21H
        MOV     AH,1
        INT     21H
        CMP     AL,"Q"
        JE      QUIT
        SUB     AL,"0"  ←
        MOV     CL,5    ←
        DEC     AL      ←
        SHL     AL,CL   ←
          :
          :
QUIT:   MOV     BX,FILEHANDLE  ;Close the files.
        MOV     AH,3EH
        INT     21H
EXIT:   INT     20H
PHONE   ENDP

        END START
```

Here we were lucky enough to be able to use the SHL command, which is an easy way to multiply by factors of two in the PS/2 and PC. When CL equals 5, the SHL AL,CL instruction will have the effect of multiplying AL by 32, just the length of a record.

We've taken the number in AL from ASCII character to record number by subtracting ASCII 0, then adjusted it and multiplied it so that it now holds the offset into the file at which we want to start reading. Now we can set the Read/Write pointer.

## Setting the Read/Write Pointer

To set the Read/Write pointer in PHONE, we must move the number of bytes to move (in AL) into CX:DX. We will only be using the lowest byte of this combination—DL (since our maximum distance to move will be 64 bytes). To set up CX:DX, we set CX and DH to 0, and then transfer our value from AL (the byte position of the Read/Write pointer) to DL.

After the byte offset is ready, we will load the file handle (from FILEHANDLE) into BX. Service 42H also needs a method—the position from which to set the pointer—and we will use method 0. This method will set the pointer CX:DX bytes from the beginning of the file. Here is how we set the pointer to the desired record:

```
        .MODEL SMALL
        .CODE
        ORG 100H
START:  JMP PHONE
        FILENAME        DB "NUMBERS.DAT",0
        FILEHANDLE      DW 0
        PERSON_NAME     DB 16 DUP(0)
        NUMBER          DB 16 DUP(0)
        PROMPT          DB "Get phone number (1-3) or Quit (Q): $"
PHONE   PROC NEAR
        MOV     DX,OFFSET FILENAME
        MOV     AL,0     ;Read Only
        MOV     AH,3DH
        INT     21H
        MOV     FILEHANDLE,AX
ASK:    MOV     DX,OFFSET PROMPT
        MOV     AH,9
        INT     21H
        MOV     AH,1
        INT     21H
        CMP     AL,"Q"
        JE      QUIT
        SUB     AL,"0"
        MOV     CL,5
        DEC     AL
        SHL     AL,CL
→       MOV     CX,0
→       MOV     DH,0
→       MOV     DL,AL
→       MOV     AH,42H
→       MOV     AL,0     ;Set the method.
→       MOV     BX,FILEHANDLE
→       INT     21H
          :
          :
QUIT:   MOV     BX,FILEHANDLE         ;Close the files.
        MOV     AH,3EH
        INT     21H
EXIT:   INT     20H
PHONE   ENDP

        END START
```

Now we just read in the data—the 32-byte record—into our prepared record area, which starts at the label PERSON_NAME:

```
        .MODEL SMALL
        .CODE
        ORG 100H
START:  JMP PHONE
        FILENAME        DB "NUMBERS.DAT",0
        FILEHANDLE      DW 0
        PERSON_NAME     DB 16 DUP(0)
        NUMBER          DB 16 DUP(0)
        PROMPT          DB "Get phone number (1-3) or Quit (Q): $"
PHONE   PROC NEAR
        MOV     DX,OFFSET FILENAME
        MOV     AL,0    ;Read Only
        MOV     AH,3DH
        INT     21H
        MOV     FILEHANDLE,AX
ASK:    MOV     DX,OFFSET PROMPT
        MOV     AH,9
        INT     21H
        MOV     AH,1
        INT     21H
        CMP     AL,"Q"
        JE      QUIT
        SUB     AL,"0"
        MOV     CL,5
        DEC     AL
        SHL     AL,CL
        MOV     CX,0
        MOV     DH,0
        MOV     DL,AL
        MOV     AH,42H
        MOV     AL,0    ;Set the method.
        MOV     BX,FILEHANDLE
        INT     21H
→       MOV     DX,OFFSET PERSON_NAME
→       MOV     BX,FILEHANDLE
→       MOV     CX,32
→       MOV     AH,3FH
→       INT     21H
         :
         :
QUIT:   MOV     BX,FILEHANDLE          ;Close the files.
        MOV     AH,3EH
        INT     21H
EXIT:   INT     20H
PHONE   ENDP

        END START
```

Now the record is in memory. The person's name is in the field we have labeled PERSON_NAME, and the phone number is in the field we have named NUMBER. In Enrico Fermi's case, the second record, this is how things look:

```
PERSON_NAME      "Enrico Fermi$$$$"
  NUMBER "271-8281$$$$$$$$"
```

We can print out both the name and number using service 9, the string printing service of INT 21H, simply by pointing DS:DX at the correct field to print. After we print out the correct field, let's jump back up to the top of the program again to see if there's another record we should print out (jumping back to the place where we print out the prompt, the label ASK). Here is the final program:

```
         .MODEL SMALL
         .CODE
         ORG 100H
START:   JMP PHONE
         FILENAME          DB "NUMBERS.DAT",0
         FILEHANDLE        DW 0
         PERSON_NAME       DB 16 DUP(0)
         NUMBER            DB 16 DUP(0)
         PROMPT            DB "Get phone number (1-3) or Quit (Q): $"
PHONE    PROC NEAR
         MOV      DX,OFFSET FILENAME
         MOV      AL,0     ;Read Only
         MOV      AH,3DH
         INT      21H
         MOV      FILEHANDLE,AX
ASK:     MOV      DX,OFFSET PROMPT
         MOV      AH,9
         INT      21H
         MOV      AH,1
         INT      21H
         CMP      AL,"Q"
         JE       QUIT
         SUB      AL,"0"
         MOV      CL,5
         DEC      AL
         SHL      AL,CL
         MOV      CX,0
         MOV      DH,0
         MOV      DL,AL
         MOV      AH,42H
         MOV      AL,0     ;Set the method.
         MOV      BX,FILEHANDLE
         INT      21H
         MOV      DX,OFFSET PERSON_NAME
         MOV      BX,FILEHANDLE
         MOV      CX,32
         MOV      AH,3FH
         INT      21H
```

```
→       MOV     AH,9
→       MOV     DX,OFFSET PERSON_NAME
→       INT     21H
→       MOV     DX,OFFSET NUMBER
→       INT     21H
→       JMP     ASK
QUIT:   MOV     BX,FILEHANDLE   ;Close the files.
        MOV     AH,3EH
        INT     21H
EXIT:   INT     20H
PHONE   ENDP

        END START
```

PHONE.COM as it stands is not very user friendly. There is no error checking, a serious oversight when working with files, and the prompt is pretty terse. Even worse, it prints entries one after the other, without even putting in carriage returns. This is easily fixed by printing a carriage return linefeed pair (ASCII 13 and 10, respectively), when necessary, with INT 21H service 9:

```
CR_LF   DB 13,10,"$"
```

Even so, PHONE gets the point across. You can store data efficiently and in easily accessible form in the PS/2 and PC, just by using files. As you see, retrieving any record that you have stored away is not so difficult using the read/write pointer. We've gained a good deal of mastery here in working with files.

# 4

# Screen Handling and Fast Graphics

In Pascal, we're used to a rich assortment of screen functions—we can draw ellipses or polygons or other shapes. However, most graphics functions are pretty slow. In assembly language, the situtation is reversed; there is little support for graphics (except under the OS/2 Presentation Manager—see Chapter 10), but what there is operates with great speed—including writing directly to the screen buffer, as we'll see in this chapter.

Screen displays on the PC machines have gotten steadily better over time—a popular improvement. The original Color Graphics Adapter (CGA) could display only four colors at a time—with a poor resolution of 320 by 200 (320 vertical colums, 200 horizontal rows) and it flickered badly. The individual pixels on the screen were so large that they were better called squares than dots.

The other option, the Monochrome Display Adapter (MDA) didn't flicker, had good resolution, but it also didn't do graphics: All it used were alphanumeric characters. With the introduction of other competing machines (i.e., Apple's Macintosh), graphics obviously was an up and coming issue in hardware, and IBM eventually followed the lead.

In 1984, IBM introduced what has since become very popular: the Enhanced Graphics Adapter (EGA). The EGA can select 16 colors to display at once from a selection of 64, doesn't flicker, and has pretty good resolution: 640 by 350 (almost as good as the monochrome display, which has 720 by 350). In addition, the EGA could display anything that the CGA or MDA could—it even used the same character set as the monochrome screen. The improvement can be readily seen in the difference in memory size allocated to the CGA—16K—versus the EGA—(up to) 256K.

Then, in April 1987, along with the introduction of the PS/2, VGA was born. The Video Graphics Adapter, built with an IBM chip, can do everything the EGA can do (in turn, the EGA can do everything that the CGA and MDA could do) and more. In particular, there was an expansion in the numbers of colors that could be displayed—in low resolution mode, the VGA can display 256 colors at once, chosen from a selection of 256K possibilities. This immense number is slightly qualified by the poor resolution in this mode: only 320 by 200. Other VGA graphics modes allow higher resolution display (such as 640 by 480), but with a correspondingly fewer number of available colors.

Graphics and color on the PC and PS/2 had clearly become an important issue.

# An Outline

This chapter on screen handling and graphics will largely be an exploration of BIOS INT 10H (remember, BIOS was assigned the low interrupt numbers), because, for most purposes, it *is* screen handling and graphics at the assembly language level. Even the services of INT 21H that print on the screen (only alphanumerics) call BIOS to do it. BIOS is the software in ROM (augmented now by what is read in from disk), and is the lowest-level of support in your PC—even below DOS.

Our primary goal in this chapter is to explore what assembly language can do well on the screen. Even so, we'll examine the most pertinent of the other services of INT 10H as well—there are 20 total—but not all of them (we'll skip light pen support, for example).

This is our first introduction to BIOS, but the INT instruction works just as it did before: Load a service number into AH, load any other required registers, and execute the INT instruction.

One thing you should know before we even begin unraveling the huge INT 10H is that you can't count on it to preserve the AX, SI, and DI registers when it returns from the call. When we use it, we'll have to protect those ourselves. DOS would return those registers without problem, but this is the lowest level of our machine—BIOS.

> The term pixel is a condensation of "picture element," and refers to each dot on the screen. A pixel can be made to display many different colors, depending on the monitor.

# The BIOS Screen-Handling Services

We'll begin by scrutinizing the screen-handling services. We'll look at the ways that BIOS can put characters on the screen; it can do many things that DOS cannot. For example, this is where we learn about colored characters, the video or screen buffer, character attributes, and how to move the cursor around or scroll the screen. When we've finished with the screen-handling services, we'll turn to graphics.

We'll begin with the first screen-handling services available. What could be more fundamental to screen handling than moving the cursor around? And that's what these services, services 2 and 3, do.

```
Services 2 and 3 - Set or Get Cursor Position
---- Service 2, Set Cursor - Set these things:
AH =2
DH,DL = Row, Column of new position (0,0 is upper left of screen)
BH = Page Number (usually 0)

---- Service 3, Get Cursor - Set these things:
AH =3
BH = Page Number (usually 0)

Returns:
DH, DL = Row, Column of current cursor position.
```

There are two services here—service 2 and service 3. Service 2 sets the cursor position (like GotoXY in Pascal), and service 3 gets the current cursor position (like WhereX and WhereY) for you.

We'll use service 2 in our program CHECKER.COM very soon. This service gives you the chance to position the cursor where you want it on the screen. The cursor position is always given as coordinates like: (row, column). To set this position, just put the row and column numbers in DH, DL respectively. The upper left of the screen is (0,0), and values increase from there:

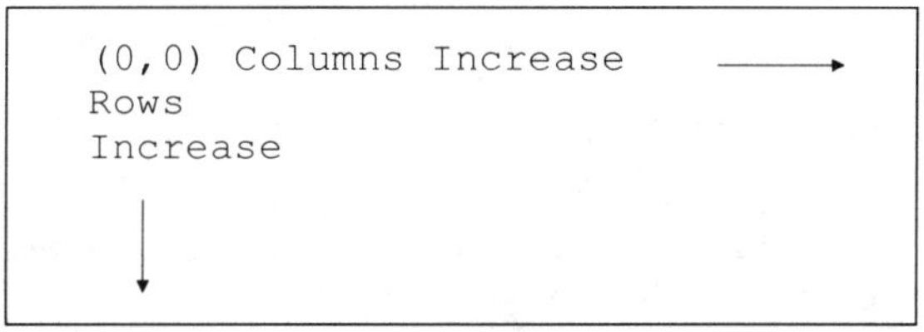

```
(0,0) Columns Increase    ——→
Rows
Increase

  |
  ↓
```

Service 3 allows you to get the current cursor position. This is useful if you are writing, say, a popup program (see Chapter 5), and want to use an INT 10H service to write a notepad on the screen. With service 3, you can get the original cursor position (before you popped up) so that you can restore it later, after writing your notepad.

## Page Numbers

You also have to load the *page number* into BH to use these services. The page number takes a little more explaining: the video memory can be divided up, in some video modes, into *pages*. Although we will not deal with pages here, we can at least examine the concept.

Some video modes require more memory than others. If there is some unused memory in some particular video mode, IBM lets you use it as extra *pages* of screen display.

When it is doing pixel-by-pixel graphics, the CGA requires 16K instead of the 4K it uses for its alphanumeric mode (as we'll see shortly). This memory is always available on the CGA card, and since it is enough to make up four full screens of text, IBM allows us to use pages when in alphanumeric mode. This is how pages were born. Normally, all pages are copies of each other, and page 0 is displayed. With BIOS, though, it is possible to skip around and selectively write to particular pages. The default page is 0, and that's the one we will always use here (the use of pages is not common).

To use the cursor services, set the page number in BH to 0. If we want to set the cursor position, we can pass new coordinates to service 2 in (DH,DL). If we want to get the current position, service 3 will return it in the same way. We'll have the chance to set the cursor for ourselves later.

There is more to screen handling than just using the cursor—besides working with the cursor, we can scroll the screen up or down (in OS/2, you can even scroll it *sideways*). This is done with services 6 and 7.

## Services 6 and 7—Scroll Active Page Up or Down

Set these things:

AH = 6 → Scroll Up
= 7 → Scroll Down
AL = Number of lines to scroll (blank lines will be inserted). AL = 0 means blank the whole active window.
(CH,CL) = Row, Column of upper left corner of scroll window.
(DH,DL) = Row, Column of lower right corner of scroll window.
BH = Attribute to be used on blank line.

This is how scrolling is done in the PS/2 and PC: You can even scroll some small section of the screen independently, and it makes a startling effect. Here you set the scroll area's boundaries with (CH,CL)—row, column of upper left corner of scroll window, and (DH,DL)—row, column of lower right corner of scroll window. To scroll this window up, use INT 10H service 6; to scroll down, use service 7.

We could go from this:

```
It was a dark
and stormy
night. Heath-
cliffe jumped
```

to this, by scrolling up:

```
and stormy
night. Heath-
cliffe jumped
```

Blank lines are inserted into the window, and they are ready for you to type into:

```
and stormy
night. Heath-
cliffe jumped

```

You can select the color of the new line yourself—this is our first introduction to color. To select the color in alphanumeric modes, you choose what is called the *attribute.*

## Attributes

The screen attribute is a one-byte long value that determines how a character will appear on the screen. For example, you can select green characters on a blue background or yellow characters on a red background. When you set the attribute of the new line, every position in it is given the same attribute byte (even though there is no character there yet). This will determine what the characters that you print there will look like. That is, if you print new characters there, they will use the attribute already set for that line (it is also possible to set attributes character by character when printing, if we want to do it that way).

The attribute byte looks like this:

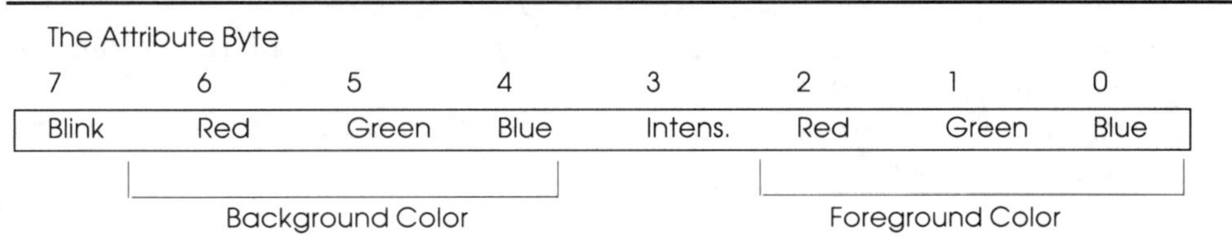


One attribute byte is reserved for each position on the screen. By setting the attribute byte for a character, you can select the mix of red, green, and blue for both the foreground color (the color of the character) and the background color (the color of the screen around the character). Also, you can set bit 3 for high intensity display, and bit 7 to make the character blink.

For example, a red foreground on a green background would have an attribute byte of 00100100B, or 24H:

You can mix the colors too by adding the respective bit values together. Here are the bit values to add in forming your attribute byte:

| *Bit Value* | *Color Generated* | |
|---|---|---|
| 1 | Blue | Foreground |
| 2 | Green | Foreground |
| 4 | Red | Foreground |
| 8 | High Intensity | |
| 16 | Blue | Background |
| 32 | Green | Background |
| 64 | Red | Background |
| 128 | Blinking | |

For example, to get a normal setting of white on black, you would turn all the foreground colors (the letter itself) on this way: 1 + 2 + 4 = 7. All the background colors are off, so they are set to 0. This value of 7 is the normal, startup screen attribute value. If you wanted to make that high intensity, you would add 8 to give 15 = 0FH. If you wanted blinking reverse video in white, set all the background colors on, and add 128 to make it blink: 16 + 32 + 64 + 128 = 240 = 0F0H.

On monochrome displays we can't use the individual colors, but we can use the normal attribute (7), high intensity (0FH), blinking normal (87H), blinking reverse video (F0H), and underlined, which graphics monitors don't have. To turn on underlining, use a blue foreground (making an attribute of 1). We can also use intense underlining (attribute of 9).

We will use the attribute byte character by character when we print out colored characters with service 9.

## The Screen Buffer and Attribute Bytes

A character's ASCII and attribute bytes are stored in the screen buffer. This buffer, therefore, carries two bytes per character in alphanumeric modes. The bytes go like this: character, attribute, character, attribute, and so on. The first character in the buffer goes on the top left of the screen.

There are 25 lines (numbered 0–24) times 80 columns (numbered 0–79) = 2000 positions on the screen, so the screen buffer requires 4000 bytes of memory (about 4K) to display a single alphanumeric page. In monochrome (MDA) monitors, this memory starts at B000:0000, and in graphics monitors at B800:0000. For the EGA and VGA modes, this memory starts at A000:0000.

> Unless you specifically set the video mode, the EGA and VGA both run in CGA modes, so their screen buffers start at B800:0000. In EGA- or VGA-only modes, the screen buffer starts at A000:0000.

In graphics mode, things work similarly, but with pixels, not bits. For example, in the CGA 320 by 200 mode, there are 320 by 200 = 64000 pixels. In that mode, the CGA allows four colors, so each pixel needs two bits in memory; this means that the total CGA memory requirement will be 64000 pixels times 2 bits/pixel / 8 bits/byte = 16000 bytes. This is rounded up to 16K.

Say that we wanted to write directly to a monochrome adapter's (MDA) memory. We could use the DEBUG *edit* command like this:

```
A>DEBUG
-EB000:0000
B000:0000  20.     ←
```

DEBUG will let us edit the byte at B000:0000, the first byte in the monochrome video buffer, with the E command. We use the command EB000:0000 to edit that byte; use EB800:0000 for a CGA, EGA, or VGA. DEBUG tells us that this byte is currently a 20H = 32 = the ASCII space character. We can type our own value, which will appear directly after the . Let's use ASCII 41H ( = 65 = ASCII "A"):

```
A>DEBUG
-EB000:0000
B000:0000  20.41   ← Type 41
```

Now type a space; the A appears on the screen in the upper lefthand corner. We have edited the first byte in the screen buffer:

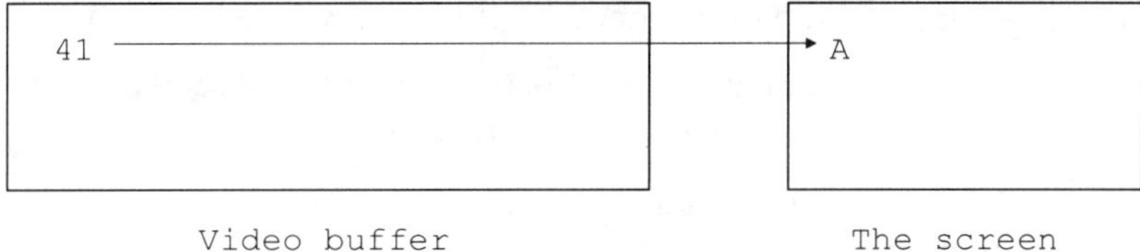


Video buffer            The screen

DEBUG now indicates the next byte to edit (at B000:0001):

```
A>DEBUG
-EB000:0000
B000:0000  20.41   07.
-Q
```

This next byte to edit has a value of 07—it is the attribute byte of the first screen position. Let's change it from normal video (attribute 7) to blinking reverse video (attribute F0H), followed by a space bar, then a <cr> to quit editing:

```
A>DEBUG
-EB000:0000
B000:0000  20.41   07.F0   20.   ← type a <cr>
-Q
```

This enters a flashing A on the screen, writing directly to the monochrome video buffer.

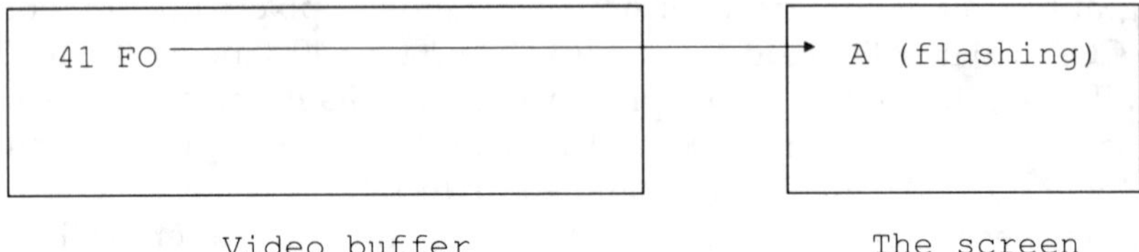


Video buffer    The screen

For each screen location, both an ASCII code and an attribute byte are stored. Writing directly to the buffer to change these values is the way professional word processors often work.

We can write characters with attributes that we select too, as we'll do now.

## Service 9—Write Attribute/Character at Cursor Position

Set these things:

AH = 9
AL = ASCII code of character to write.
BH = Page Number (usually 0)
BL = Character's attribute
CX = Number of times to write character (restricted to 1 line on screen)

This is the way to type out colored characters on the screen—you can even type out multiple copies of the same character if you set CX to a value greater than one.

> When you are typing multiple copies of the same character, however, this service will not type more than one line—it doesn't add carriage returns.

However, the cursor is not automatically moved to the next space after this call is done—it remains pointing at the just-typed character! If you want to use this service to type both characters and attributes, you will have to take care of the cursor yourself, which we'll do immediately in an example.

> To type out with cursor advancement, use Service 0EH, "teletype write." However, Service 0EH will not type attributes.

# An Example: CHECKER.ASM

Let's dig into an example named CHECKER.ASM. This will bring home the screen handling services we've been seeing. CHECKER prints out all the 255 ASCII characters that the PC or PS/2 is capable of, and each one will have an attribute matching its ASCII code (0–255). This way we'll get a look at everything that the PC or PS/2 can type, and in color.

Start with the normal .COM file shell:

```
        .MODEL  SMALL
        .CODE
        ORG     100H
ENTRY:
                :
                :
        INT     20H
        END     ENTRY
```

We will use LOOP to loop over all characters and attributes. This means that we must set the loop index, CX, to 255. Also, INT 10H service 9, which prints out characters and attributes, requires the ASCII code in AL and the attribute in BL, as we just saw. Let's initialize them both to 0:

```
        .MODEL  SMALL
        .CODE
        ORG     100H
ENTRY:  MOV     CX,255  ←       ;Loop over all 255 combinations
        MOV     AL,0    ←       ;Start with character 0
        MOV     BL,0    ←       ;And attribute 0
        :
        :
        INT     20H
        END     ENTRY
```

Since this is a BIOS character printing service, we'll have to set the cursor ourselves. That is done with INT 10H service 2, which expects the new cursor row to be in DH, and its column to be in DL. Let's start off at, say row 4 and column 0—(4,0). We need to set DH and DL, and then we can enter our character printing loop:

```
        .MODEL  SMALL
        .CODE
        ORG     100H
ENTRY:  MOV     CX,255          ;Loop over all 255 combinations
        MOV     AL,0            :Start with character 0
        MOV     BL,0            ;And attribute 0
        MOV     DL,0    ←       ;Start at column 0
        MOV     DH,4    ←       ;And row 4
COLOR_LOOP:             ←
```

```
    ......PUSH     AX          ←
    :      MOV     AH,2        ←          ;Set cursor
    :      INT     10H         ←
    :      POP     AX          ←
    :      :
    :.....LOOP     COLOR_LOOP  ←          ;Keep going
           INT     20H
CODE_SEG           ENDS
           END     ENTRY
```

We also want to set the cursor position inside our loop, since each time through the loop we will have to change it. Note that, since we can't count on AX being returned from INT 10H safely, we have enclosed our call to INT 10H with PUSH AX and POP AX:

```
           .MODEL SMALL
           .CODE
           ORG     100H
ENTRY:     MOV     CX,255                 ;Loop over all 255 combinations
           MOV     AL,0                   ;Start with character 0
           MOV     BL,0                   ;And attribute 0
           MOV     DL,0                   ;Start at column 0
           MOV     DH,4                   ;And row 4
COLOR_LOOP:
    ......PUSH     AX          ←
    :      MOV     AH,2                   ;Set cursor
    :      INT     10H
    :      POP     AX          ←
    :      :
    :.....LOOP     COLOR_LOOP  ←          ;Keep going
           INT     20H
           END     ENTRY
```

Now we're ready to print out the character, having set our position on the screen. We can use service 9, which requires this information:

AH = 9
AL = ASCII code of character to write.
BH = Page Number (usually 0)
BL = Character's attribute
CX = Number of times to write character (restricted to 1 line on screen)

We've already loaded AL (ASCII code) and BL (attribute), so we just execute INT 10H, service 9. As you can see, service 9 requests a character count in CX, which will be 1 for us. Since we are also using CX as a loop index, we will push it (as well as AX) before executing the INT 10H instruction and restore it afterward; with a limited number of registers available, making them serve double duty is a common occurence:

```
        .MODEL SMALL
        .CODE
        ORG     100H
ENTRY:  MOV     CX,255          ;Loop over all 255 combinations
        MOV     AL,0            ;Start with character 0
        MOV     BL,0            ;And attribute 0
        MOV     DL,0            ;Start at column 0
        MOV     DH,4            ;And row 4
COLOR_LOOP:
  ......PUSH    AX
  :     MOV     AH,2            ;Set cursor
  :     INT     10H
  :     POP     AX
  :     MOV     AH,9            ;Now type character/attribute
  :     PUSH    AX      ←
  :     PUSH    CX      ←
  :     MOV     CX,1    ←
  :     INT     10H     ←
  :     POP     CX      ←
  :     POP     AX      ←
  :     :
  :.....LOOP    COLOR_LOOP      ;Keep going
        INT     20H
        END     ENTRY
```

We've printed out our first character and attribute. Now we have to increment both the ASCII code (in AL) and the attribute (in BL) to prepare us for printing again:

```
        .MODEL SMALL
        .CODE
        ORG     100H
ENTRY:  MOV     CX,255          ;Loop over all 255 combinations
        MOV     AL,0            ;Start with character 0
        MOV     BL,0            ;And attribute 0
        MOV     DL,0            ;Start at column 0
        MOV     DH,4            ;And row 4
COLOR_LOOP:
  ......PUSH    AX
  :     MOV     AH,2            ;Set cursor
  :     INT     10H
  :     POP     AX
  :     MOV     AH,9            ;Now type character/attribute
  :     PUSH    AX
  :     PUSH    CX
  :     MOV     CX,1
  :     INT     10H
  :     POP     CX
  :     POP     AX
  :     INC     AL      ←       ;Select next character
  :     INC     BL      ←       ;And next attribute
  :     :
  :.....LOOP    COLOR_LOOP      ;Keep going
        INT     20H
        END     ENTRY
```

Also, of course, we have to prepare DH and DL with the new row and column number to set the cursor to. We just increment the column number. If we are at the end of the screen (compare DL to 79), then we reset the column number to zero (MOV DL,0), and increment the row, moving us down to the next line (INC DH):

```
          .MODEL SMALL
          .CODE
          ORG       100H
ENTRY:    MOV       CX,255               ;Loop over all 255 combinations
          MOV       AL,0                 ;Start with character 0
          MOV       BL,0                 ;And attribute 0
          MOV       DL,0                 ;Start at column 0
          MOV       DH,4                 ;And row 4
COLOR_LOOP:
          PUSH      AX
          MOV       AH,2                 ;Set cursor
          INT       10H
          POP       AX
          MOV       AH,9                 ;Now type character/attribute
          PUSH      AX
          PUSH      CX
          MOV       CX,1
          INT       10H
          POP       CX
          POP       AX
          INC       AL                   ;Select next character
          INC       BL                   ;And next attribute
          INC       DL          ←        ;Find new cursor column
          CMP       DL,79       ←        ;Might have to go to next row
          JB        OK_CURSOR   ←
          MOV       DL,0        ←
          INC       DH          ←        ;Go to next row
OK_CURSOR:                      ←
          LOOP      COLOR_LOOP           ;Keep going
          INT       20H
          END       ENTRY
```

That completes the loop, and, with it, CHECKER. ASM. When you run it, you'll notice that halfway through the display, the blinking bit (bit 7 in the attribute byte) gets set, so the second half of the display blinks.

What if we wanted to print on the screen, but didn't want to have to set the attribute as well? For example, when we scroll a line with the scrolling services, we can set the attribute of the whole line. We might want to preserve those attributes when we print in that new line.

In that case, we could use INT 10H, Service 0AH. Service 0AH is useful when you're printing on the screen and don't want to disturb the colors already there (which is often). Since it's so useful, let's take a look at this service.

## Service 0AH—Write Character Alone at Current Cursor Position

Set these things:

```
AH = 0AH
AL = ASCII code of character to write.
BH = Page Number (usually 0)
CX = Number of times to write character (restricted to 1 line on screen)
```

This is the same as service 9, except that it does not change the attribute as it writes. In other words, if the character it overwrites was red on blue, the new character will be red on blue too. Also, just as service 9, this service leaves the cursor pointing at the just-typed character.

There is one remaining character-handling service before we head into graphics, and this is Service 0EH, the "teletype write" service. This is the BIOS printing service that *does* handle the cursor correctly.

## Service 0EH—Teletype Write

Set these things:

```
AH = 0EH
AL = Character to write
```

This service types characters more the way we might expect. Services 9 and 0AH type characters but do not advance the cursor past the last character typed. They also put symbols on the screen for screen control characters like the linefeed or carriage return characters.

Service 0EH both advances the cursor and treats carriage returns and linefeeds as commands, not characters to print. However, this service will not print out atttributes. You'll either have to handle the cursor yourself when you print out, or forgo attributes and use this service, 0EH.

That's all the BIOS options: printing with attributes, printing without attributes, and printing with cursor advancement. That's also the end of our screen-handling (alphanumeric) work in INT 10H. Let's turn from screen handling to handling graphics instead.

# Graphics

Despite the rich number of colors now available to us, the actual BIOS programming support for drawing graphics is terrible. The graphics support in BIOS allows you to write only one dot (that is, pixel). This support is minimal, compared certainly to a machine like the Macintosh, which has built in Toolbox routines (like QuickDraw), or the system routines available to us under the OS/2 Presentation Manager that can draw circles, lines, boxes, fill shapes, and so on.

In Chapter 10, we'll use the Presentation Manager services available to do exactly that: draw circles, lines, boxes, and fill shapes.

Later on in this chapter we'll develop a program that will draw boxes on the screen, a small improvement at least. There are a number of fast line-drawing algorithms in assembly language (as described in *Advanced Assembly Language for the IBM PC*, by Steven Holzner, Brady Books, 1987), and even though they don't use fancy methods, they can still take up many pages. Later on in this chapter, we'll see how to access individual pixels directly in the screen buffer, and see that it's not such an easy task.

Before we start to draw boxes, we'll have to learn how to select what mode (that is, resolution and color options) the screen is running in, and how to specify what color the dot on the screen will be. We can select graphics modes or alphanumeric modes. All that is done in INT 10H, Service 0.

## INT 10H Service 0—Set Video Mode

Set these things:

```
AH = 0
AL = New Video Mode
```

This is a big one. Here we will see all the modes possible on all the PS/2 and PC machines—how many colors they support and how many lines they use on the screen. Whenever you want to do graphics, you'll first have to set the mode to the desired resolution. After that has been done, it stays that way until it is set some other way. Setting the mode is usually done quite early in graphics programs. To set the video mode for your particular screen (CGA, MDA, EGA, or VGA), put 0 in AH and the new mode in AL. Table 4.1 shows all the possible screen modes.

Table 4.1 Screen Modes

| *Mode (in AL)* | Display Lines | *Number of Colors* | *Adapters* | *Maximum Pages* |
|---|---|---|---|---|
| 0 | 40x25 | B&W text | CGA, EGA, VGA | 8 |
| 1 | 40x25 | Color text | CGA, EGA, VGA | 8 |
| 2 | 80x25 | B&W text | CGA, EGA, VGA | 4 (CGA) 8 (EGA, VGA) |
| 3 | 80x25 | Color text | CGA, EGA, VGA | 4 (CGA) 8 (EGA, VGA) |
| 4 | 320x200 | 4 | CGA, EGA, VGA | 1 |
| 5 | 320x200 | B&W | CGA, EGA, VGA | 1 |
| 6 | 640x200 | 2 (on or off) | CGA, EGA, VGA | 1 |
| 7 | 80x25 | Monochrome | MDA, EGA, VGA | 1 (MDA) 8 (EGA, VGA) |
| 8 | 160x200 | 16 | PCjr | 1 |
| 9 | 320x200 | 16 | PCjr | 1 |
| A | 640x200 | 1 | PCjr | 1 |
| B | Reserved for future use. | | | |

*Table 4.1 continued*

| | | | | |
|---|---|---|---|---|
| C | Reserved for future use. | | | |
| D | 320x200 | 16 | EGA, VGA | 8 |
| E | 640x200 | 16 | EGA, VGA | 4 |
| F | 640x350 | monochrome | EGA, VGA | 2 |
| 10H | 640x350 | 16 | EGA, VGA | 2 |
| 11H | 640x480 | 2 | VGA | 1 |
| 12H | 640x480 | 16 | VGA | 1 |
| 13H | 320x200 | 256 | VGA | 1 |

Some of these modes are alphanumeric—that is, they are text modes that don't support graphics (modes 0–3, and 7). You can still use text as usual in graphics modes, but there is no cursor. You can see how the modes are partitioned by adapter—modes 0–6 are used on the CGA (and EGA and VGA, since they're compatible). Mode 7 is the monochrome display adapter. MDA (and EGA and VGA again since they can mimic the MDA) modes 8–0AH are the PCjr; modes 0DH-10H are the EGA and VGA (here the VGA is emulating the EGA for compatibility); and modes 11H–13H are just for the VGA (mode 13H is the 256-color one):

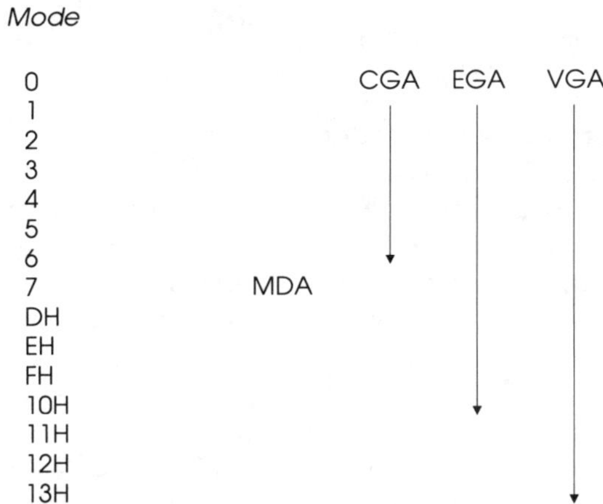


## Black and White vs. Color

The CGA can work with monitors that have all colors (color monitors) or black and white ones (B&W—often black and green on monitors without color). Its text modes are set up accordingly: Modes 0 and 1 are the same, except that mode 0 is B&W, and mode 1 displays in color, modes 2 and 3 are B&W and color respectively.

Next come the CGA graphics modes: mode 4 is color, mode 5 is B&W, as indicated in the table. In addition, in mode 6, pixels can only be on or off—even though 2 colors are listed, one is black, the other white.

To set the screen the way you want it, just select from the listed modes, and use INT 10H, Service 0. That's it. Now that we've set up the screen, let's see if we can't select some colors to use.

## Service 0BH—Set CGA Color Palette (Colors in CGA 320x200 mode ONLY)

Set these things:

AH = 0BH
BH = Palette Color ID (0 or 1, see below.)
BL = Color(s) to set with that Palette Color ID (see below.)

BH = 0
    BL = Background Color (0–31) From now on, this will be color value 0 to be used in Write and Read Dot. What colors 0–15 actually mean (blue, red, etc) is discussed below.
    * In alphanumeric modes, this background color will determine the screen border color (0–31; 16–31 means high intensity.)
BH = 1
    BL = Palette to be used
        BL = 0 Selects Green/Red/Yellow Palette. Color value 1 in Write and Read Dot will be Green, color value 2 will be red, 3 will be yellow.
        BL = 1 Selects this palette and color values: Cyan (color value will be 1) /Magenta (2)/White (3).

This is another big service. Here you set the four colors the CGA (and the EGA and VGA when operating in the CGA modes) can draw in its 320 by 200 resolution mode. The additional colors that the EGA or VGA can use are set by Service 10H—this service is only for the CGA compatibility screen modes.

There are actually three modes of resolution in the CGA low, medium, and high. The number of pixels up and down (in the Y direction) is always the same—200. The number in the across direction (the X direction) varies from 160 (low resolution), through 320 (medium resolution) to 640 (high resolution).

You can display the maximum number of colors available, 16, only in low resolution mode. However, there is no support in the PC or PS/2's software, BIOS or DOS, for low resolution. The graphics video controller can be put in low resolution mode, though; so if you want to take the time, you can provide support yourself. As it is, we will concentrate here only on medium- and high-resolution graphics.

## Palettes

In medium resolution graphics on the CGA (320 by 200) you can display four colors at any pixel, and in high resolution (640 by 200) only two—black and white (on and off). Here are the CGA's graphics modes:

| | Mode (in AL) | Display Lines | Number of Colors | Adapters | Maximum Pages |
|---|---|---|---|---|---|
| | 0 | 40x25 | B&W text | CGA, EGA, VGA | 8 |
| | 1 | 40x25 | Color text | CGA, EGA, VGA | 8 |
| | 2 | 80x25 | B&W text | CGA, EGA, VGA | 4 (CGA) 8 (EGA, VGA) |
| | 3 | 80x25 | Color text | CGA, EGA, VGA | 4 (CGA) 8 (EGA, VGA) |
| → | 4 | 320x200 | 4 | CGA, EGA, VGA | 1 |
| → | 5 | 320x200 | B&W | CGA, EGA, VGA | 1 |
| → | 6 | 640x200 | 2 (on or off) | CGA, EGA, VGA | 1 |

Even the four colors of medium resolution are an illusion, because you are free to pick only one of the four; the other three (colors 1,2, and 3) can only be chosen by picking one of two *palettes.*

There are two CGA palettes: green, red, yellow; or cyan, magenta, white. When you turn a pixel on the screen on with the write dot service, you specify which color value—0, 1, 2, or 3—to make it. The palette colors make up color values 1, 2, and 3 in order (the background color will make up color value 0).

Let's see this more clearly. To select which palette to use, use this service, Service 0BH. For this service:

Set these things:

AH = 0BH
BH = Palette Color ID (0 or 1, see below.)
BL = Color(s) to set with that Palette Color ID (see below.)

BH = 0
    BL = Background Color (0-31) From now on, this will be color value 0 to be used in Write and Read Dot. What colors 0-15 actually mean (blue, red, etc) is discussed below.
    * In alphanumeric modes, this background color will determine the screen border color (0-31; 16-31 means high intensity.)
BH = 1
    BL = Palette to be used
        BL = 0 Selects Green/Red/Yellow Palette. Color value 1 in Write and Read Dot will be Green, color value 2 will be red, 3 will be yellow.
        BL = 1 Selects this palette and color values: Cyan (color value will be 1) /Magenta (2)/White (3).

Set BH to 1, to indicate that you want to select a three-color palette. Then set BL to either 0 or 1, depending on which palette you want. (Palette 0 is green, red, yellow; palette 1 is cyan, magenta, white.)

After you've selected the palette, you've selected colors 1–3 of the colors that will be used by the CGA. Whenever you write a dot on the screen, you can pass a color value that is 0–3 (when in 320 by 200 CGA resolution mode). For example, if you select palette 1, you can write cyan, magenta, or white dots on the screen. The write dot service that we will cover requires a color value for the dot. If you pass it color value 1 with this CGA palette, you will draw a cyan dot.

## The CGA Background Color

Color values 1–3 come from the palette, and color value 0 is the background color, which you can choose out of 16 choices:

```
CGA Possible Color Values:  0,        1,        2,        3
                            |         |__________________|
                            |
                            |          Set by choice of palette
                            |
                            |_________ Background color:
                                          chosen from 16 choices
```

To choose the color that will become color value 0, let's look at our table for this service again:

Set these things:

AH = 0BH
BH = Palette Color ID (0 or 1, see below.)
BL = Color(s) to set with that Palette Color ID (see below.)

BH = 0
- BL = Background Color (0-31) From now on, this will be color value 0 to be used in Write and Read Dot. What colors 0-15 actually mean (blue, red, etc) is discussed below.
  * In alphanumeric modes, this background color will determine the screen border color (0-31; 16-31 means high intensity.)

BH = 1
- BL = Palette to be used
  - BL = 0 Selects Green/Red/Yellow Palette. Color value 1 in Write and Read Dot will be Green, color value 2 will be red, 3 will be yellow.
  - BL = 1 Selects this palette and color values: Cyan (color value will be 1) /Magenta (2)/White (3).

First, set BH to 0, to inform this service that you want to select the CGA background color. Then put the background color number that you want in BL and execute Service 0BH.

There are 32 possible colors to choose from—16 colors and 16 more high-intensity versions of the same colors. The colors available to fill BL with (add 16 to make the color high intensity) are shown in Table 4.2.

Table 4.2 Colors Available (CGA)

| *Color Number* | *Color* |
|---|---|
| 0 | Black (off) |
| 1 | Blue |
| 2 | Green |
| 3 | Cyan (Green+Blue) |
| 4 | Red |

*Table 4.2, continued*

| | |
|---|---|
| 5 | Magenta (Red+Blue) |
| 6 | Brown |
| 7 | White |
| 8 | Black |
| 9 | Light Blue |
| 10 | Light Green |
| 11 | Light Cyan |
| 12 | Light Red |
| 13 | Light Magenta |
| 14 | Yellow |
| 15 | Light White |

| These are also the default first 16 color numbers for the EGA and VGA.

In setting the background color, note that the *whole* background will no longer be black but will become the color you've selected.

This is how you select the color values 0–3 that you will pass to the write dot service later to draw on the screen: select one of two palettes to select color values 1–3 and select the background color to select color value 0. When you want to specify a color to be used, this color value (0–3 in the CGA) is what you will pass.

## High Resolution CGA Mode

In high resolution CGA mode, 640 by 200 pixels (mode 6), you cannot choose 4 colors, but only two: on or off, 0 or 1. With the amount of memory available to it, the CGA can only save one bit per pixel in this higher resolution mode (i.e., 320 by 200 vs. 640 by 200). Since there are 200 lines down (on graphics monitors characters are 8 scan lines high, and 8 times 25 lines equals 200) and 640 lines across, there are 640 times 200 equals 128,000 bits needed. This makes 16,000 bytes, rounded up in the CGA's video buffer to 16K.

In medium resolution, 320 by 200, we can specify one of four colors for each pixel; so we need two bits to hold the possible values for each pixel. Since there are only half as many pixels (320 across vs. 640 across), we still use the same size video buffer, 16K. Now we've set the screen mode and selected our colors—it's time to draw on the screen.

## Service 0CH—Write Dot

Set these things:

```
AH = 0CH
DX = Row Number (0–199, 0–349, 0–479)
CX = Column Number (0–319 or 0–639)
AX = Color Value
BH = Page number (0 based) for multi-paged graphics modes.
```

Here it is! DOS graphics on the PS/2 and PC, right here. To set a pixel anywhere on any screen (if you've set the mode, service 0, correctly), use write dot. Set DX = Row Number (0-199, 0-349, 0-479), and CX = Column Number (0-319 or 0-639). (0,0) is at the top left of the screen.

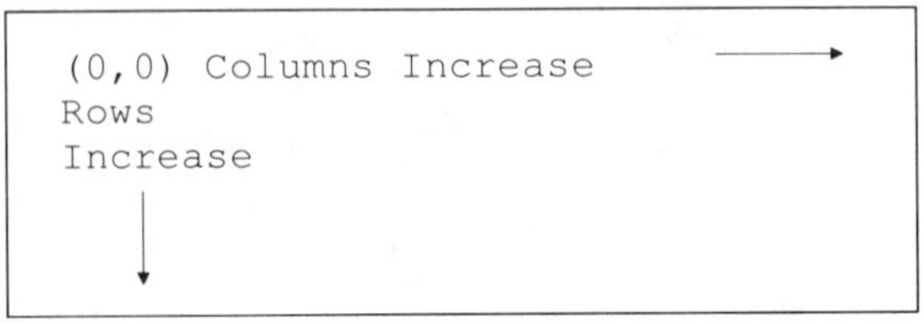

```
(0,0) Columns Increase          ──────►
Rows
Increase
   │
   ▼
```

The big issue in the write dot service is in the innocuous line AX = Color Value, because the color value has three different interpretations under the three different graphics standards: CGA, EGA, and VGA.

The color value can range from 0–3 on CGA (but only 0–1 in high CGA resolution, 640 by 200), 0–15 on EGA, and 0–255 on VGA (but only in VGA mode 13H—otherwise it's 0–15). In CGA modes, these color values are set with service 0BH; in EGA and VGA modes with Service 10H. Once the color values are set, you can draw anywhere on the screen with this service—that's what it's designed for.

Let's put write dot to use at once. Here is where we can draw boxes on the screen—our first graphics work.

## Putting Graphics to Use

We will take all the graphics knowledge we've acquired and put it to use here. Any graphics tools we design will help augment the PS/2 and PC BIOS services. Unfortunately, these kinds of tools usually aren't easy to write—not because of graphics complexities, but the difficulty of doing integer math when you really need floating point math.

Even drawing a line becomes a real struggle when you have to try to preserve accuracy in the slope as you go from pixel to pixel. You might be able to imagine how difficult it is to write a program that can draw circles or ellipses (where squares and square roots can be involved).

> That kind of work is easier if you have a math coprocessor—see Chapter 8.

We don't need to draw ellipses to get started though—we can introduce ourselves to assembly language graphics by drawing rectangular boxes. Provided with the coordinates of the box's upper lefthand corner and the coordinates of the lower righthand corner, we can use write dot to get the job done effectively. Let's give this a try.

Our program will be called BOX.ASM. Even though the two corner coordinates are already written into the data area, you can change the program easily to ask for user input or pass the coordinates in registers when calling BOX from a larger program (make the procedure BOX part of your .ASM file, in the code segment, and call it).

# BOX.ASM

Our aim in BOX is to draw rectangles on the screen. First we take a standard .COM file shell:

```
         .MODEL  SMALL
         .CODE
         ORG      100H
START:   JMP      BOX
         :
BOX      PROC
         :
         INT      20H
BOX      ENDP

         END      START
```

And add at least the things we know we'll need; space for the corner coordinates of the box, and the color value that will be used. For this demonstration program, let's choose CGA video mode 6 (640 by 200 high resolution CGA graphics—two color), just to make sure that this program can be used by almost everyone. In this mode, any non-zero color value turns the pixel on—so we'll set the color value to 15 (0FH). To make your rectangle colored, just set the color value you want and then choose a mode that your machine can support to display it in (instead of 6).

We should also set some values for the corner coordinates: the CGA screen coordinates range from 0–199 and 0–319, so let's set these values for our first box:

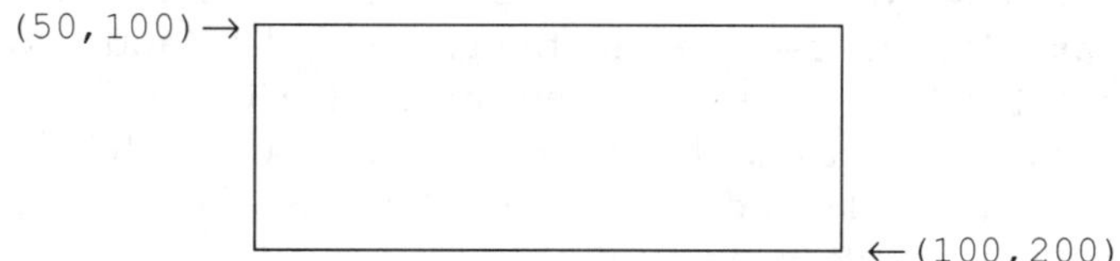


Here's what our new data area looks like:

```
         .MODEL  SMALL
         .CODE
         ORG      100H
START:   JMP      BOX
         TOPROW   DW       50        ←
         TOPCOL   DW       100       ←
         BOTROW   DW       100       ←
         BOTCOL   DW       200       ←
         COLOR    DB       15        ←
BOX      PROC
```

```
        :
        INT     20H
BOX     ENDP

        END     START
```

First, we set the video mode, using (naturally) INT 10H:

```
        .MODEL SMALL
        .CODE
        ORG     100H
START:  JMP     BOX
        TOPROW  DW      50
        TOPCOL  DW      100
        BOTROW  DW      100
        BOTCOL  DW      200
        COLOR   DB      15
BOX     PROC
→       MOV     AH,0
→       MOV     AL,6
→       INT     10H
        :
        INT     20H
BOX     ENDP

        END     START
```

This is where you can set the mode to whatever you want on your own machine if desired. If you're curious to see what a particular color looks like on your monitor, you can use that color as COLOR in BOX (and use a screen mode other than 6, which displays only white or black).

Here is how we will proceed: We will draw the box from the top to bottom, using LOOP. First, we will draw the top of the box, then the sides, and finally the bottom. This will take three loops. To make things easier, let's add a little procedure to actually write the dot on the screen. Here, in WRITEDOT, we will set everything up for the Write Dot service and then write the dot. To use WRITEDOT, we will need some way of passing the dot's coordinates. Let's use the SI and DI registers, since they are not doing anything just now:

```
        .MODEL SMALL
        .CODE
        ORG     100H
START:  JMP     BOX
        TOPROW  DW      50
        TOPCOL  DW      100
        BOTROW  DW      100
        BOTCOL  DW      200
        COLOR   DB      15
BOX     PROC
        MOV     AH,0
        MOV     AL,6
```

```
          INT     10H
          :
          INT     20H
BOX       ENDP

WRITEDOT          PROC
          PUSH    AX
          PUSH    CX
          PUSH    DX
          MOV     DX,SI
          MOV     CX,DI
          MOV     AL,COLOR
          MOV     AH,0CH
          INT     10H
          POP     DX
          POP     CX
          POP     AX
          RET
WRITEDOT          ENDP

          END     START
```

Note in particular the use of PUSHes and POPs in WRITEDOT to save the registers that WRITEDOT uses. If BOX called WRITEDOT and WRITEDOT changed all the registers that BOX was counting on, it would be a serious problem. Notice also the use of RET at the end of WRITEDOT, which returns us to BOX after the call is completed. To use WRITEDOT, we'll load the row number into SI and the column number into DI.

Now let's add the first loop, the one that draws the top of the box. Here we will want to write dots starting with (TOPROW,TOPCOL) at the left and ending with (TOPROW,BOTCOL) on the right. In other words, here is our box with all four corners:

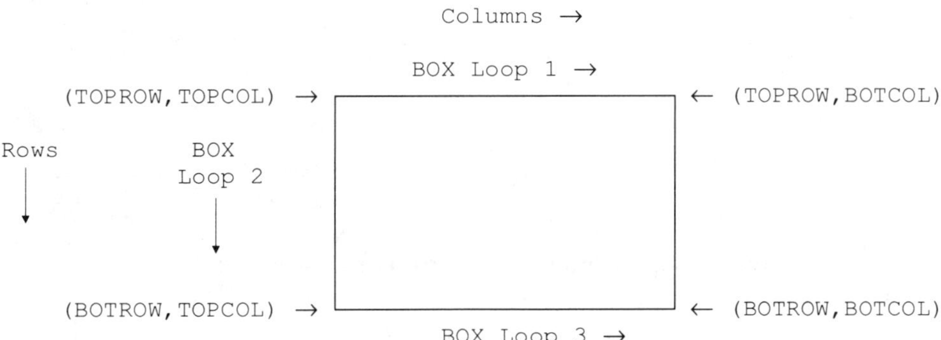


In this first loop, we'll have to increment the column number from TOPCOL to BOTCOL, in other words, we want to loop BOTCOL–TOPCOL times, drawing a dot each time. To do this, we'll put BOTCOL–TOPCOL in CX, which LOOP uses to determine the number of times to loop. Here it is:

```
        .MODEL SMALL
        .CODE
        ORG     100H
START:  JMP     BOX
        TOPROW  DW      50
        TOPCOL  DW      100
        BOTROW  DW      100
        BOTCOL  DW      200
        COLOR   DB      15
BOX     PROC
        MOV     AH,0
        MOV     AL,6
        INT     10H
        MOV     CX,BOTCOL   ←   ;Draw the top of the box
        SUB     CX,TOPCOL   ←   ;Find number of columns to loop over
        MOV     SI,TOPROW   ←   ;SI holds row number of current pixel
        MOV     DI,TOPCOL   ←   ;DI holds column number of current pixel
TOPLOOP:CALL    WRITEDOT    ←   ;Loop over the columns
        INC     DI          ←
        LOOP    TOPLOOP     ←
        :
        INT     20H
BOX     ENDP

WRITEDOT        PROC
        PUSH    AX
        PUSH    CX
        PUSH    DX
        MOV     DX,SI
        MOV     CX,DI
        MOV     AL,COLOR
        MOV     AH,0CH
        INT     10H
        POP     DX
        POP     CX
        POP     AX
        RET
WRITEDOT        ENDP

        END     START
```

Next we have to loop through Loop 2, drawing the sides:

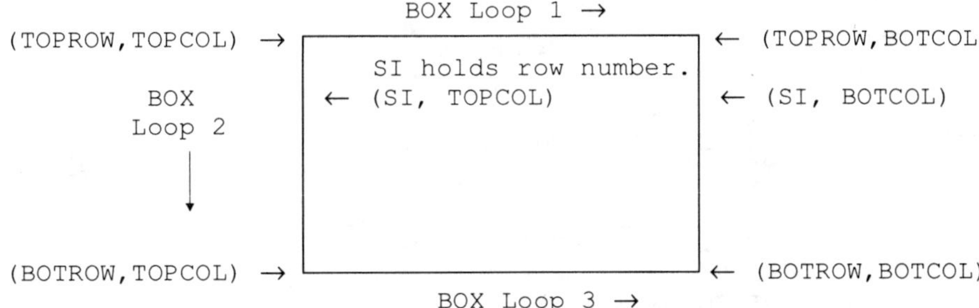


Here we move downward in rows, starting at row TOPROW and ending at row BOTROW. In other words, we want to loop BOTROW–TOPROW times (remember, (0,0) is at top left on the screen, so BOTROW is larger than TOPROW). Now we will put BOTROW–TOPROW into CX. In each row we want to write a dot on the left side and on the right side. As we loop through loop 2, the row number which is stored in SI will be steadily incremented. By looking at the diagram, we see that we have to draw the dot for the left side at (SI,TOPCOL), and the dot for the right side at (SI,BOTCOL). Here's what that is in code:

```
        .MODEL SMALL
        .CODE
        ORG     100H
START:  JMP     BOX
        TOPROW  DW      50
        TOPCOL  DW      100
        BOTROW  DW      100
        BOTCOL  DW      200
        COLOR   DB      15
BOX     PROC
        MOV     AH,0
        MOV     AL,6
        INT     10H
        MOV     CX,BOTCOL       ;Draw the top of the box
        SUB     CX,TOPCOL       ;Find number of columns to loop over
        MOV     SI,TOPROW       ;SI holds row number of current pixel
        MOV     DI,TOPCOL       ;DI holds column number of current pixel
TOPLOOP:CALL    WRITEDOT        ;Loop over the columns
        INC     DI
        LOOP    TOPLOOP
        MOV     CX,BOTROW
        SUB     CX,TOPROW
        MOV     SI,TOPROW
SIDELOOP:               ←
        MOV     DI,TOPCOL   ←
        CALL    WRITEDOT    ←
        MOV     DI,BOTCOL   ←
        CALL    WRITEDOT    ←
        INC     SI          ←
        LOOP    SIDELOOP    ←
```

```
        :
        INT     20H
BOX     ENDP

WRITEDOT        PROC
        PUSH    AX
        PUSH    CX
        PUSH    DX
        MOV     DX,SI
        MOV     CX,DI
        MOV     AL,COLOR
        MOV     AH,0CH
        INT     10H
        POP     DX
        POP     CX
        POP     AX
        RET
WRITEDOT        ENDP

        END     START
```

The last step is to draw the bottom of the box, loop 3. This is similar to drawing the top, except that instead of going from (TOPROW,TOPCOL) to (TOPROW,BOTCOL), we'll be going from (BOTROW,TOPCOL) to (BOTROW,BOTCOL). This means that we want to draw BOTCOL–TOPCOL pixels, each in a different column (so we'll increment DI, which holds the column number).

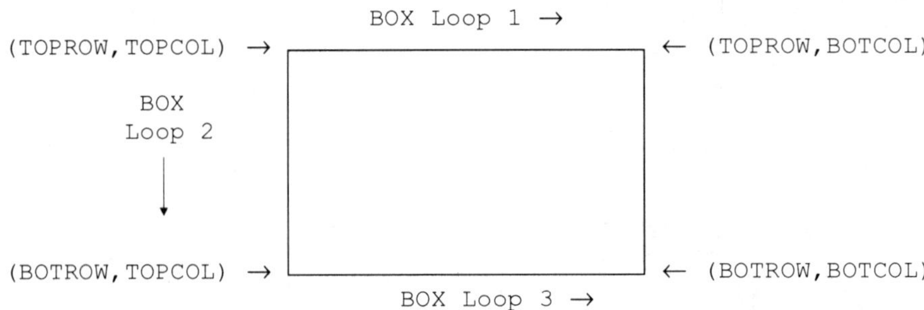


Here that is:

```
        .MODEL SMALL
        .CODE
        ORG     100H
START:  JMP     BOX
        TOPROW  DW      50
        TOPCOL  DW      100
        BOTROW  DW      100
        BOTCOL  DW      200
        COLOR   DB      15
BOX     PROC
        MOV     AH,0
```

```
        MOV     AL,6
        INT     10H
        MOV     CX,BOTCOL       ;Draw the top of the box
        SUB     CX,TOPCOL       ;Find number of columns to loop over
        MOV     SI,TOPROW       ;SI holds row number of current pixel
        MOV     DI,TOPCOL       ;DI holds column number of current pixel
TOPLOOP:CALL    WRITEDOT        ;Loop over the columns
        INC     DI
        LOOP    TOPLOOP
        MOV     CX,BOTROW
        SUB     CX,TOPROW
        MOV     SI,TOPROW
SIDELOOP:
        MOV     DI,TOPCOL
        CALL    WRITEDOT
        MOV     DI,BOTCOL
        CALL    WRITEDOT
        INC     SI
        LOOP    SIDELOOP
        MOV     CX,BOTCOL     ←
        SUB     CX,TOPCOL     ←
        MOV     SI,BOTROW     ←
        MOV     DI,TOPCOL     ←
BOTLOOP:CALL    WRITEDOT      ←
        INC     DI            ←
        LOOP    BOTLOOP       ←
        INT     20H
BOX     ENDP

WRITEDOT        PROC
        PUSH    AX
        PUSH    CX
        PUSH    DX
        MOV     DX,SI
        MOV     CX,DI
        MOV     AL,COLOR
        MOV     AH,0CH
        INT     10H
        POP     DX
        POP     CX
        POP     AX
        RET
WRITEDOT        ENDP

        END     START
```

BOX.COM is complete—give it a try. It may be rudimentary, but at least it does a little graphics on the screen. From this example, we can see that graphics can take some work. It can be more difficult if you want to draw slanted lines.

The 45-degree case is easy—all you do is increment the row and column number each time:

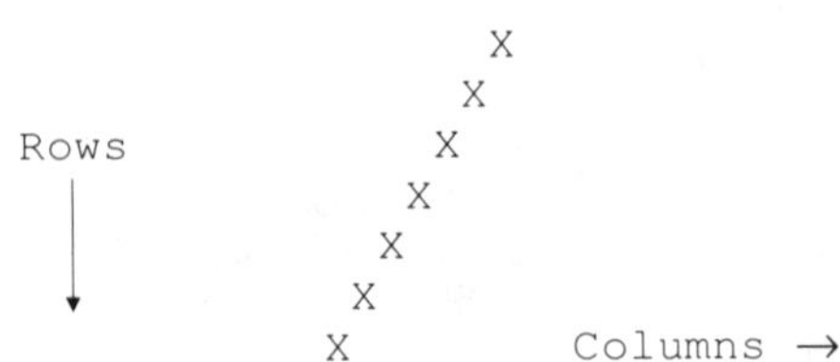


However, if you wanted to draw a line at some different angle—not quite straight up and down, but like this:

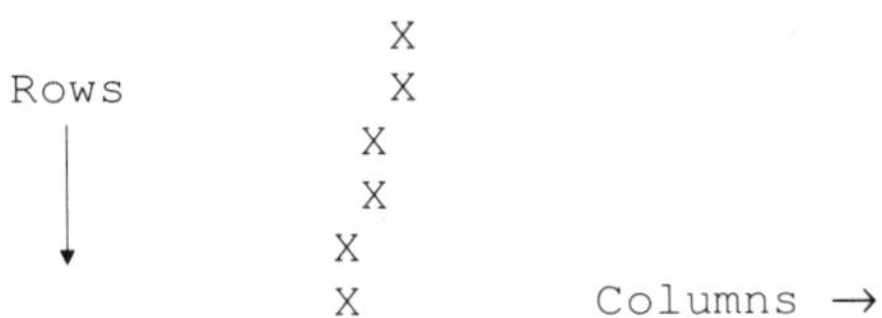


Here you can see that a simple loop would not work. Even though each pixel has a different row number, some pixels have the same column number as others—you could not just loop over column numbers. As you go to different angles, this problem has to be faced.

# Beyond CGA

There are other adapters beyond the CGA—way beyond. We will want to be able to handle the EGA and VGA as well. The write dot service will work as before, but we can handle more colors now. To do that, we have to learn how to set the 16 colors the EGA can handle—and the up to 256 colors of the VGA. To select these colors, the new BIOSes use service 10H of INT 10H, just as the CGA used service 0BH to set its palette. You can modify BOX fairly easily to work in any of these colors after you select them.

The EGA uses a palette just like the CGA does, but now it's bigger. In the EGA palette, registers go from 0 to 15, not 0 to 3, and you can select each color independently from 64 choices. Let's start off our investigation of higher resolution monitors by understanding how the EGA works.

## The EGA

For each pixel, the EGA has two levels of intensity for each of the three primary colors: red, green, and blue. There are both low intensity (we will refer to those levels as r, g, b) and medium intensity (R, G, B). When they are both on at some pixel location, the result is high intensity (like r + R)—when they are both off, the result is nothing. Thus there are four levels of *combined* intensity for each of the three colors. In the case of pure red, the levels would be: off = 0, low = r, medium = R, and high

= r + R. Using both low and medium intensity at the same time, we can fill six bits—rgbRGB—to create a color. With these six bits, we can specify values from 0 to 63—and this is where the 64 choices of the EGA come from. You can set the 16 palette colors (color values 0–15) from among these 64 possibilities in any 16-color mode.

When the PS/2 or PC is turned on, default EGA color values are set in the EGA palette, and they may be good enough for most purposes. The color values (given to the write dot service), colors, and rgbRGB settings for the default colors are given in Table 4.3.

Table 4.3 Default Palette Colors (0–15) on EGA

| *Color Value* | *Color* | *rgbRGB* |
|---|---|---|
| 0 | Black | 000000 |
| 1 | Blue | 000001 |
| 2 | Green | 000010 |
| 3 | Cyan | 000011 |
| 4 | Red | 000100 |
| 5 | Magenta | 000101 |
| 6 | Brown | 010100 |
| 7 | White | 000111 |
| 8 | Dark Gray | 111000 |
| 9 | Light Blue | 111001 |
| 10 | Light Green | 111010 |
| 11 | Light Cyan | 111011 |
| 12 | Light Red | 111100 |
| 13 | Light Magenta | 111101 |
| 14 | Yellow | 111110 |
| 15 | Intense White | 111111 |

This means that if you select a color value of 3 and pass that on to the write dot service in a 16-color EGA or VGA mode, a cyan dot will appear (unless you change the defaults).

## Designer Colors in the EGA

You can make up your own colors for the EGA by selecting which of the six bits you want set in each palette register. Palette registers go from 0 to 15—one for each color value. To specify a color to use for a particular color value, you can fill the palette registers with the appropriate rgbRGB number (0–63).

Say you load a value of 000011B = 3 (cyan) into palette register 5. From then on, when you ask for color value 5 in 16 color modes, rgbRGB will be set to 000011B, or 3, and you'll get cyan. Let's jump in and see how to set one of the EGA palette registers ourselves.

## The Service 10H Functions

All the EGA and VGA services use INT 10H, Service 10H to set colors. The way you distinguish between EGA and VGA services is by the setting in AL. In this first service, where we will set an EGA palette register, AL is 0. This is also referred to as INT 10H, Service 10H, *function 0*.

## Service 10H Function 0—Set Individual EGA Palette Register (Set 1 of 16 colors for 16-color mode)

Set these things:

```
AH = 10H
AL = 0
BL = EGA Palette register to set (0-15)
BH = rgbRGB value to set it to (0-63)
```

Here's where you set any of the 16 color values in the EGA palette. You can assign a particular rgbRGB setting to any of the EGA palette registers:

```
                                    10H   →   AH
                                      0   →   AL
          Color value to change (0-15)   →   BL
rgbRGB value to change it to (0-63)      →   BH
```

To do that, select an rgbRGB setting in six bits and put it into BH. Select a palette register (which is the same as the color value, the number that write dot will see) from 0 to 15 and put it into BL. Then use this function and, congratulations, you've just installed a color for use by your program.

For example, color value 5 is magenta under the default settings. Let's change that to cyan, rgbRGB = 000011B = 3. In other words, we want to change palette register 5 to use an rgbRGB setting of 3:

```
                  10H   →   AH
                    0   →   AL
 Palette register 5    →   BL
New rgbRGB setting 3   →   BH
```

In code it looks like this:

```
→       MOV     AH,10H      ;Use INT 10H service 10H
→       MOV     AL,0        ;Function 0
→       MOV     BL,5        ;Change palette register 5
→       MOV     BH,3        ;To rgbRGB = 3, cyan
→       INT     10H
```

It's simple. From now on, when you pass color value 5 to write dot, you'll get cyan instead of magenta. That's it for the EGA palette.

> Note that every time the mode is reset, the palette colors return to the default setting.

The EGA palette can set the colors used in 16-color modes whether you're using an EGA or VGA. By setting this palette, you can select from 64 choices. If you're really using a VGA, however, you might want to select these 16 colors from among its 256K choices instead. Or you might want to use its 256-color mode (mode 13H). Let's take some time to examine these possibilities.

## The VGA

The VGA is different from other displays in that it is an *analog* display. Internally, this means that the VGA has what is called a digital to analog converter, or DAC, to help in selecting color.

The DAC has 256 registers, and they can act like the palette registers we've just seen. This is quite an enhancement over the 16 palette registers—here color values can go from 0–255. In each of the 256 DAC registers there is an 18-bit number, so DAC registers can hold numbers ranging up to 256K. In other words, if you use the DAC registers to set colors, you have a choice of up to 256K colors to work with.

## From CGA to EGA to VGA

In CGA modes, you select the background color and choose from one of two palettes for a total of four colors. Color values range from 0–3.

In EGA modes, you can select up to 16 colors using the EGA palette. These numbers, 0–15, become the color values you can pass to write dot. Each color can be selected individually as a six-bit rgbRGB setting; to set color value 2 we'd load palette register 2:

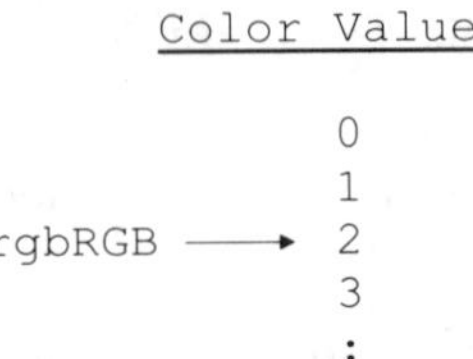


In any VGA 16-color mode, you can also set the colors using the EGA palette registers, just as with the EGA. When you set a palette register, you are setting that color value (0–15) from a six-bit selection (rgbRGB), giving you 64 possibilities.

On the other hand, in 16-color modes, the VGA is really using the first 16 DAC registers (since it's a VGA, it always uses the DAC registers). These first 16 DAC registers correspond to the 16 available color values. If you set a color in an EGA palette register while using a VGA, your rgbRGB setting will be translated into an 18-bit setting for the corresponding DAC register. Setting color value 2 looks like this:

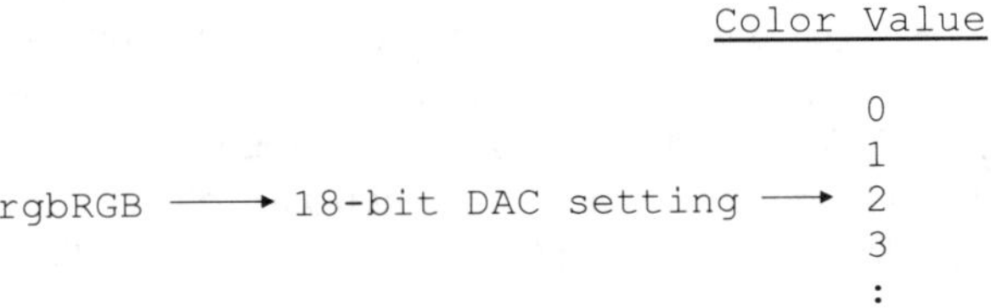


This means that you can set the 16 colors of a VGA *either* by changing the EGA palette, where you can select from among 64 rgbRGB possibilities, or by changing a DAC register directly, where you can use 18-bit numbers—giving you a choice of 256K colors.

```
                              Color Value

                                   0
                                   1
        18-bit DAC setting  →      2
                                   3
                                   :
```

> The default for the VGA is using the first 16 DAC registers as the first 16 color values—we could select which set of DAC registers to use by selecting *color pages*, which we will not do here.

For example, if we wanted to change color value 5 from its default of magenta in the VGA, we could do it by setting palette register 5 to another of the 64 possible colors (we've used cyan before). Your rgbRGB setting would then be translated into an 18-bit number for DAC register 5.

Or you could set this DAC register directly, by putting a new 18-bit number in DAC register 5. With 18 bits to work with, you can specify 256K colors this way. To be able to change a DAC value like that, we've got to be able to decode the 18-bit DAC numbers, which we'll do next.

## Using the DAC Registers

The way 18 bits are used in a DAC register is as follows: the first six bits give the intensity of the red in this color; the next six bits the intensity of the green, and the last six bits the intensity of the blue. This means that you can always design new DAC colors for yourself.

```
DAC Register. 18 bits:  rrrrrrggggggbbbbbb
                        ↑     ↑     ↑
                        |     |     └──────── Blue intensity (6 bits)
                        |     └────────────── Green intensity (6 bits)
                        └──────────────────── Red intensity (6 bits)
```

Let's see how to set one of these DAC registers ourselves. We will use Service 10H, with AL = 10H. (That makes this INT 10H, Service 10H, function 10H.)

## Service 10H Function 10H—Set DAC Register (Set 1 of 255 VGA Colors)

Set these things:

AH = 10H
AL = 10H
BX = register to set (0 - 255)
CH = Green Intensity
CL = Blue Intensity
DH = Red Intensity

Here's where we select 1 of the 16 or 256 colors (depending on the screen mode) that the VGA can display from 256K possible choices. Decide on the relative intensities of the green, blue, and red you want in your color, convert them into six-bit arguments, and place them in their respective registers:

CH ← Green Intensity
CL ← Blue Intensity
DH ← Red Intensity

Then execute this service, and you've set a color for use by the VGA. The default settings of the first 16 DAC registers give the same colors as the default colors of the EGA (although they use 18 bits and the EGA palette uses six, the DAC values are set to closely match the EGA colors).

But we can change that. Let's work through our earlier example and say that we wanted to change DAC register 5 from its default setting (magenta) to an intense green (green value = 00111110B). Here's how we would do that:

```
MOV     AH,10H          ;Select Service 10H
MOV     AL,10H          ;Select subservice 10H
MOV     BX,5            ;Select DAC register to change
MOV     CH,00111110B    ;Select new green value
MOV     CL,0            ;Set new red and blue values to 0
MOV     DH,0
INT     10H
```

Now, DAC register 5 holds a value corresponding to green. When we pass a color value of 5 to the write dot service in a VGA mode, green will appear. Besides 16-color modes, the VGA can handle 256-color modes. Let's look at what makes them different.

## VGA 16-Color Modes

As we've seen, in 16-color modes on the VGA, you can select colors in two ways. The first way is simply by loading one of the possible EGA colors—rgbRGB (0–63)—into the a register of the EGA palette. What this really does is to set the corresponding DAC register to that color. In other words, your rgbRGB setting gets translated into an 18-bit DAC register value, and it's stored in the corresponding DAC register.

The second way is by changing one of the first 16 DAC register contents directly:

```
                                  Color Value

                                       0
                                       1
        rrrrrrggggggbbbbbb  ------>    2
                                       3
                                       :
```

In 16-color modes in the VGA, the first 16 DAC register numbers and the color values are all the same things.

It's worth noting that if you set colors the first way, you can choose from only 64 choices, while if you change one of the DAC registers (which are what really hold the color settings anyway), you can select from 256K choices.

## VGA-Only 256-Color Mode

In 256-color VGA mode, you can make up colors by selecting red, green, and blue values (six bits each) and putting your values into any of the DAC registers. As usual, the DAC register number is the color value (now 0–255) you will pass to write dot. Only the first 64 DAC registers are initialized with default values. In fact, you may even want to stick to the first 16 default color values, which are the same as the EGA ones.

# Writing Graphics Images Directly in Memory

Most professional programs do not use the BIOS Write Dot routine, since it is quite slow, but instead write directly to memory (which is a number of times as fast). However, the procedure in writing to memory is different for all the IBM monitors, and that fact is encouragement to use the BIOS routines only (the monitor may be different, but Write Dot will take care of that).

Probably the easiest of the EGA or VGA modes to directly work with in memory is, almost paradoxically, the 256 VGA color mode (320 by 200). This is because an entire byte is set aside for each pixel to hold 256 colors that can be displayed. The video buffer starts at A000:0000; to set the color of the pixels, you can work byte by byte. You can find more about this and other aspects of the EGA and VGA in Sutty and Blair's book: *Programmer's Guide to the EGA/VGA* (Brady Books).

Let's get an idea of what directly writing to the screen in graphics modes is like. In the CGA, for example, there is a 16K buffer. In high resolution CGA mode (640 by 200), dots can either be on or off—that's it. Each dot is stored as one bit in a certain area of memory named the video or screen buffer. We will go into that buffer and work with individual pixels.

## The CGA Screen Buffer in Graphics Mode

In high resolution mode, 640 by 200 pixels, you can choose only on or off, 0 or 1. The PC needs to save only one bit per pixel in this case. Since there are 200 lines down (on graphics monitors characters are 8 scan lines high, and 8 by 25 lines equals 200) and 640 lines across, there are 640 by 200 equals 128,000 bits needed. This makes 16,000 bytes, rounded up in the PC's graphics video buffer to 16K.

It seems natural that if you wanted to turn the pixel on at location (0,0), the top left corner of the screen, you would set the first bit in the video buffer to 1. That is actually how it works. To turn the next pixel in the top row (row 0) on, you would set the next bit to 1, and so forth to the end of the first line on the screen, the first 640 pixels (numbers 0–639).

It also seems natural that if you wanted to turn on the first pixel of the second row (row 1), you would set bit 640 in the video buffer to 1, since the first line goes from 0 to 639. Unfortunately, that is not how it works.

## CGA Buffer Memory Blocks

IBM decided to separate the graphics video buffer into two blocks of 8K each. The first block, starting at location B800:0000, holds the even scan lines on the screen; the second block, starting at B800:2000, holds the odd scan lines. This is done because the video controller scans over all the even lines on the screen first, and then does all the odd ones. To facilitate its operation, IBM gives it the bits in the order needed. This is an added complication for any program; now it has to split up its image between two blocks in memory:

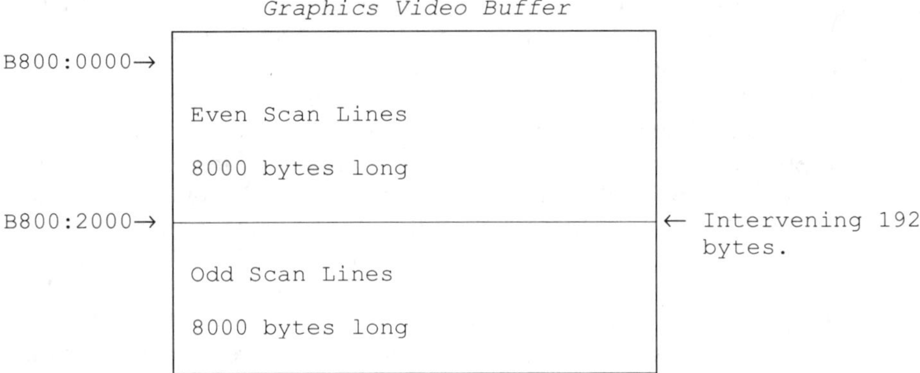


The scheme in medium resolution is similar, but in that case, there can be four colors, not just two. Four colors demand two bits, so every two bits in the screen buffer can be grouped together into one pixel. Since there are only one-half as many pixels on a line, but twice as many bits per pixel, there are the same number of memory bits corresponding to each screen line, 640.

## The Program PUT_PIXEL

Here's a small program, PUT_PIXEL, that will turn high resolution pixels on:

```
PUT_PIXEL        PROC
      ;SUPPLY DX=ROW,CX=COLUMN. ASSUMES ES=B800H and screen in High
      ; Resolution mode (Use BIOS INT 10H Service 0).
      XOR      BX,BX
      SHR      DX,1
      JNC      CALC
```

```
        ADD     BX,8*1024
CALC:   MOV     AX,DX              ;GET 80*DX
        SHL     DX,1
        SHL     DX,1
        ADD     DX,AX
        MOV     AX,CX
        MOV     CL,4
        SHL     DX,CL              ;DX NOW MULTIPLIED BY 80 (16*5)
        ADD     BX,DX              ;ADD TO INDEX
        MOV     DX,AX
        AND     DX,7               ;GET X3 INTO DX
        MOV     CL,3
        SHR     AX,CL              ;CX/8
        ADD     BX,AX              ;FIND BYTE ALONG ROW
        NEG     DL
        ADD     DL,7
        MOV     CL,DL              ;GET BIT TO TURN ON
        MOV     AL,1
        SHL     AL,CL
        OR      ES:[BX],AL
        RET
PUT_PIXEL       ENDP
```

PUT_PIXEL is about three times as fast as the equivalent BIOS service call. Notice that the calling program must have left B800H in ES; because it takes time to load ES, we do not want to do it every time through PUT_PIXEL.

The first job of PUT_PIXEL is to determine whether the pixel is to be put in an even or odd row. The pixel's coordinates are given to PUT_PIXEL in DX ( = row, 0–199) and CX ( = column, 0–639). We have to check if DX is odd or even. The first 8K of the screen buffer holds lines 0,2,4,6,8, and so on; the second 8K holds lines 1,3,5,7,9 and so forth as shown in Table 4.4.

Table 4.4 CGA Even and Odd Scan Lines

| *Screen Row #* | *1st or 2nd 8K* | *Line inside 8K Block* |
|---|---|---|
| 0 | 1 | 0 |
| 1 | 2 | 0 |
| 2 | 1 | 1 |
| 3 | 2 | 1 |
| 4 | 1 | 2 |

For each even line across the screen, there is a row of 640 bits in the first 8K block, and for each odd line, a row of 640 bits in the second 8K block. To find which line of 640 bits a particular pixel is in, just divide the row number by two and disregard the remainder (see Table 4.4). This is the same as shifting once to the right with the SHR instruction, which moves all bits right one place and places the bit shifted out into the carry bit. Since we have to check the low bit of DX (the block number) anyway, we can shift that bit into the carry bit and use JNC:

```
PUT_PIXEL          PROC
        ;SUPPLY DX=ROW,CX=COLUMN. ASSUMES ES=B800H
        XOR     BX,BX
    →   SHR     DX,1
    →   JNC     CALC
    →   ADD     BX,8*1024
CALC:   MOV     AX,DX            ;GET 80*DX       ←
                :
                :
```

DS:[BX] will be used to point to the byte in the screen buffer we have to change. If the pixel is in an odd row, we just add 8K to BX so it points to the second 8K block.

These commands both check which block the pixel is in and set DX to that pixel's row of 640 bits. To find what offset from the beginning of the 8K block that makes in bytes, we have to multiply the number in DX by 640 bits/8 bits per byte = 80 bytes per row on the screen. Multiplying DX by 80 will give us the byte offset of the pixel's line from the beginning of its block.

The 80x86 has a multiply command, of course, but it is very slow. We should try to avoid using it when speed is of the essence, as it is in graphics. To multiply by 80, we could just multiply by 5 and then by 16, or—even better—we could multiply DX by 4, add DX to it again to make five times, and then multiply by 16. Multiplying by powers of two, of course, is done by shifting to the left. To include the 8088, let's use the CL register for shifting (the 8088 cannot take immediate values above 1) like this:

```
MOV     CL,3
SHL     DX,CL
```

Here's our multiplication by 80:

```
PUT_PIXEL          PROC
        ;SUPPLY DX=ROW,CX=COLUMN. ASSUMES ES=B800H and screen in High
        ; Resolution mode (Use BIOS INT 10H Service 0).
        XOR     BX,BX
        SHR     DX,1
        JNC     CALC
        ADD     BX,8*1024
CALC:   MOV     AX,DX  ←       ;GET 80*DX
        SHL     DX,1   ←
        SHL     DX,1   ←
        ADD     DX,AX  ←
        MOV     AX,CX  ←
        MOV     CL,4   ←
        SHL     DX,CL  ←       ;DX NOW MULTIPLIED BY 80 (16*5)
        ADD     BX,DX            ;ADD TO INDEX
                :
                :
```

DX now holds the byte offset, inside the 8K block, of the line in which our pixel lies. Here's what we've done so far:

```
DX=Row Number on Screen.
Low Bit(DX) → 8K Block Number
SHR DX,1=Row Number in its 8K Block.
(SHR DX,1)x80=Offset of correct line in 8K Block.
```

```
        B800:0000→ ...........80 Bytes...........
                   ...........80 Bytes...........
                   ...........80 Bytes...........
B800:(SHR DX,1)x80→

        B800:2000→ 

                   8000 bytes long
```

To point to the correct line that holds the pixel we want to change with [BX], we add (SHR DX,1) times 80 to BX. Once we're in the right row, we still have to find which byte to work on and that depends on the column required, 0–639. Since each of these 640 places is a bit, to find the correct byte we have to divide CX by 8 and add that to BX. This process is like this:

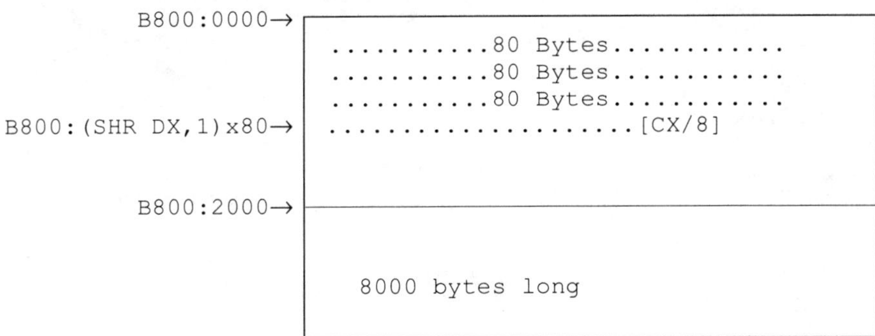


Here it is in code:

```
PUT_PIXEL         PROC
        ;SUPPLY DX=ROW,CX=COLUMN. ASSUMES ES=B800H and screen in High
        ; Resolution mode (Use BIOS INT 10H Service 0).
        XOR     BX,BX
        SHR     DX,1
        JNC     CALC
        ADD     BX,8*1024
```

```
CALC:   MOV     AX,DX           ;GET 80*DX
        SHL     DX,1
        SHL     DX,1
        ADD     DX,AX
        MOV     AX,CX
        MOV     CL,4
        SHL     DX,CL           ;DX NOW MULTIPLIED BY 80 (16*5)
        ADD     BX,DX           ;ADD TO INDEX
    →   MOV     DX,AX
        AND     DX,7            ;GET X3 INTO DX
    →   MOV     CL,3
    →   SHR     AX,CL           ;CX/8
    →   ADD     BX,AX           ;FIND BYTE ALONG ROW
                :
                :
```

At the same time, we have to calculate which bit in that byte to set to 1. If CX (which can range from 0 to 639) was 0, we would want to turn on the leftmost bit of the 0th byte of that line, bit 7. In general, the bit we want to turn on is 7 – (CX Mod 8), where CX Mod 8 is the remainder of dividing CX by 8.

However, CX Mod 8 is just AND CX,7, so we end up with these instructions:

```
PUT_PIXEL       PROC
        ;SUPPLY DX=ROW,CX=COLUMN. ASSUMES ES=B800H and screen in High
        ; Resolution mode (Use BIOS INT 10H Service 0).
        XOR     BX,BX
        SHR     DX,1
        JNC     CALC
        ADD     BX,8*1024
CALC:   MOV     AX,DX           ;GET 80*DX
        SHL     DX,1
        SHL     DX,1
        ADD     DX,AX
        MOV     AX,CX
        MOV     CL,4
        SHL     DX,CL           ;DX NOW MULTIPLIED BY 80 (16*5)
        ADD     BX,DX           ;ADD TO INDEX
        MOV     DX,AX
    →   AND     DX,7            ;GET X3 INTO DX
        MOV     CL,3
        SHR     AX,CL           ;CX/8
        ADD     BX,AX           ;FIND BYTE ALONG ROW
    →   NEG     DL
    →   ADD     DL,7
    →   MOV     CL,DL           ;GET BIT TO TURN ON
        MOV     AL,1
        SHL     AL,CL
        OR      ES:[BX],AL
        RET
PUT_PIXEL       ENDP
```

At the end, we put a 1 into AL and shift it DL (=7 – AND(CL,7)) times, then OR the result with whatever byte is in the screen buffer at location [BX]. And that, finally, turns on the pixel. It's pretty clear that working with graphics directly in the PC isn't an especially easy job.

On that note, we end our BIOS graphics work. Graphics on the PC and PS/2 have improved many-fold over the years. It may not be particularly easy to use, but the results can be worth it.

# 5

# Pop-Up Programs

Assembly language is popular because it can run behind the scenes, so to speak, and support pop-up, memory-resident programs. They have become so prevalent that they can hardly be left out of a book on assembly language programming, and it is not difficult to write them.

> Although it is possible to write pop-up programs in Pascal, we will not do that here, sticking instead to the much more space-efficient assembly language code.

Popular examples of memory-resident programs include calculators that can "pop up" onto the screen even when you're running another program, screen clocks that are always there, notepads, utilities that can dial phone numbers, report on the printer, catch disk errors, let you run DOS commands, and so forth.

Memory-resident programs do just that: They stay in memory, even when you start to run other programs. Usually, the program loader in COMMAND.COM loads programs in memory right after the space used by DOS, runs your program, and then exits, marking that space as free once again. With a memory-resident program, that final step doesn't occur. Instead, the space that is marked as DOS' is increased, until the code you've written is protected from being written over by the next program to be run. In this way, it becomes part of DOS. Only .COM files, with their compact format, can be made memory-resident unless you take special precautions.

> What memory-resident programs can appear to do—let two programs run at once, for example, when you pop up a calculator—OS/2 does for real. With a pop-up, you have to select it explicitly to run it. Under OS/2, the machine can automatically give time to many different programs.

## Writing Memory-Resident Code

Even though it may sound difficult, making programs memory-resident is really simple. The real problem to be solved is this: Even if you add a section of code to DOS, it won't do anything by itself until called. Just making it memory-resident doesn't mean it will run—it will lie dormant until you can enter it again. For example, we could add the commands:

```
MOV     AX,5
  MOV     DX,32001
  INC     DI
```

to the end of DOS rather easily with either of the two DOS interrupts (INT 27H or INT 31H) designed to make code memory-resident. This would work simply by setting a few registers and ending the program with one of those interrupts, and not INT 20H as we have usually done. Now that those instructions are there, however, they are just bytes in memory—there is no reason they will run until CS:IP is set to them. In the same way, the code in DOS and BIOS doesn't all run at once everywhere—it waits until called.

> In the language of OS/2, we say DOS has only one *thread*. OS/2 can have multiple threads—meaning many programs can be active at once.

There is really only one way to run memory-resident code like this—with software or hardware interrupts. Software interrupts we know about—they are just the INT instruction. Hardware interrupts aren't generated by a program, but instead they occur when something happens in the PS/2 or PC's peripherals. For example, if you touch a key on the keyboard, an interrupt, interrupt 9, is generated. The disk can generate other hardware interrupts if some operation takes place there, as can an internal clock inside the PS/2 and PC (the clock interrupt is in fact made 18.2 times a second, unless you turn it off).

A hardware interrupt causes the PS/2 or PC to stop temporarily—interrupt—the program it is running and attend instead to the hardware interrupt. Hardware interrupts can be "turned off" (except for some low level ones) by programs with the CLI instruction, Clear Interrupt flag. This internal flag is there simply to do this: indicate whether hardware interrupts will be recognized or ignored by the microprocessor. If your program executes a CLI instruction, no typed keys will be recognized or recorded, for example. You can reset this flag with STI, Set Interrupt flag, which allows hardware interrupts to be recognized again.

Typically, memory-resident programs are popped onto the screen with a *hot key*—a key that, when pressed, will pop the calculator or whatever onto your screen. This is because they make use of the keyboard interrupt. Hardware interrupts are much like software interrupts in that every time they occur, a program can be run, in this case, our memory-resident one. For memory-resident code in pop-up programs, we use hardware and not software interrupts. This is because the software interrupts would have to be executed by the program then running, while you could interrupt that program with a hot-key hardware interrupt at any time. And that is what we are aiming for.

However, hardware and software interrupts share the way the microprocessor finds the address of the program to run when they occur. If your program executes an INT 10H instruction, for example, the microprocessor searches for the program that is to be run to handle it in the same way that it does if you pressed a key on the keyboard and generated an INT 9.

Since it is our intention to get our program to run when a hardware interrupt is generated, we'll have to understand what this process is.

# Interrupts

As mentioned near the beginning of the book, Intel added interrupts to its microprocessors so that the microprocessor's instruction set could be expanded. They wanted to let the builders of computers add their own code so that operations like opening a file would seem to be just another simple instruction (using, in this case, INT 21H). In our microprocessor, we can have up to 256 of these interrupts.

What actually occurs when an interrupt (hardware or software) is executed is this: The microprocessor loads the address of the program for that interrupt from a specially designed table in low memory, called the *interrupt vector table.* This important table is such a large part of what the microprocessor does that it is given the very first position in memory, starting at 0000:0000.

## The Interrupt Vector Table

The idea behind this important-sounding name, the interrupt vector table, is actually easy to understand. For each interrupt, two words are stored: the segment address and the offset address of the program that is to be run when that interrupt occurs.

The first two words in memory correspond to interrupt 0, the next two correspond to interrupt 1, and so on:

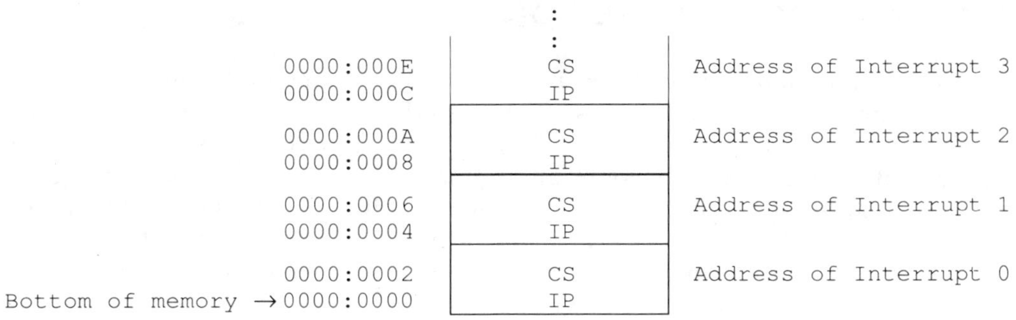

```
                                 :
                                 :
                   0000:000E     CS      Address of Interrupt 3
                   0000:000C     IP
                   0000:000A     CS      Address of Interrupt 2
                   0000:0008     IP
                   0000:0006     CS      Address of Interrupt 1
                   0000:0004     IP
                   0000:0002     CS      Address of Interrupt 0
Bottom of memory →0000:0000     IP
```

Remember, as you look at the addresses corresponding to the interrupts, that the addresses are in bytes, and both the segment address and the offset address take up one word. Therefore, the addresses of these words go: 0000:0000, 0000:0002, 0000:0004, and so forth.

To find the address of the interrupt handling routine, the microprocessor turns to the interrupt vector table. It multiplies the interrupt number by 4 (actually, it shifts it left twice) and produces the address at which the interrupt's vector (that is, the full address of the interrupt's routine) is stored. Each interrupt vector takes up 4 bytes.

Then the microprocessor pushes three words onto the stack to preserve them for later use: the current value of all the flags (these are stored as bits in one 16-bit word), the current value of IP, and the current value of CS. Then, it heads off to handle the interrupt. After the interrupt is done, the microprocessor can pop these values from the stack, restoring them, and continue with the program that was in progress when the interrupt occurred (even down to the flags). This is done for either software or hardware interrupts.

At the end of the interrupt routine, you might expect a RET instruction. However, since three words were pushed onto the stack—the full return address and the settings of the flags, there is a special 80x86 instruction to handle returns from interrupts, IRET.

## IRET

If you write a procedure for an interrupt, it must end with IRET, not RET. IRET pops all three words off the stack, restores them, and the interrupted program can continue.

For example, in a notepad program, let's say we press a key. An INT 9 is generated, and code will have been added that checks every INT 9 to see if the hot key has been pressed. If not, a normal INT 9, ending with IRET, is executed (the microprocessor finds the address from 4 x 9 = 36 = 24H, or 0000:0024). If the hot key has been pressed, the notepad becomes active. It may have its own program, also ending with IRET, that will handle typed-in keys from then on.

## Intercepting Interrupt Vectors

A clever program will set itself up in memory by changing the interrupt vector stored for a particular interrupt so that when that interrupt occurs, the microprocessor will come to the program, not to the interrupt routine. This is how memory-resident programs are run. For example, our notepad program would change the address stored at 0000:0024, the INT 9 vector, to point to itself instead. It might store the original address of INT 9 to let it handle what the notepad doesn't want.

Here's the way the interrupt vector might start out in the interrupt vector table:

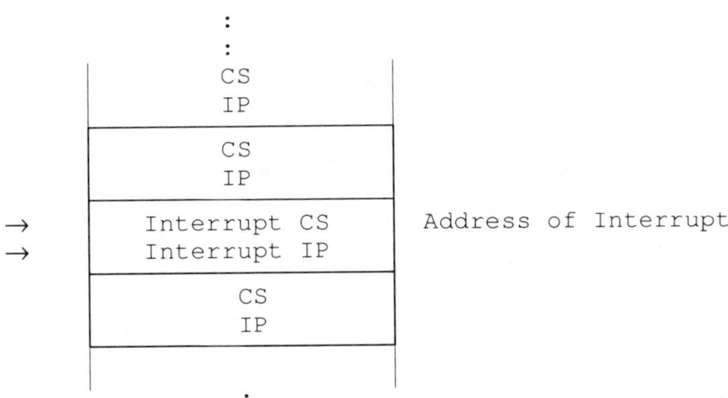


And our program might be at some high point in memory, at a specific value of CS:IP:

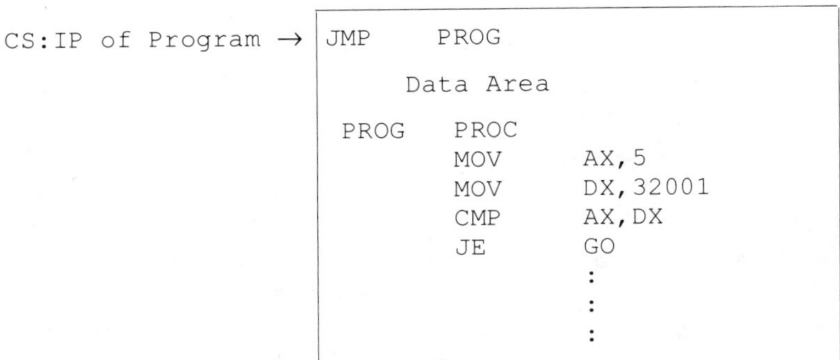


What we want to do is to supplant the routine that services the interrupt with our own program, PROG. In other words, we want the two words in the interrupt vector table called Interrupt CS and Interrupt IP to be changed to the corresponding values of our program's beginning location, Program CS and Program IP:

```
              :
              :
              CS
              IP
       ----------------
              CS
              IP
       ----------------
→        Program CS        Address of Interrupt
→        Program IP
       ----------------
              CS
              IP
       ----------------

              :
              :
```

Usually, a program that intercepts an interrupt doesn't handle all the functions of that interrupt but occasionally passes on those things it doesn't want to do to the old interrupt routine. For this reason, Interrupt CS and Interrupt IP are stored in the data area of the program:

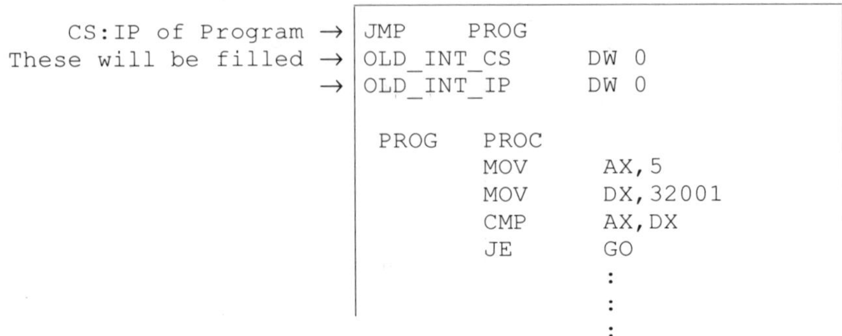


That's all there is to it; when that interrupt occurs, control will come to us, not to the old interrupt routine. Our program PROG was loaded by COMMAND.COM into the beginning of available memory—when we make it memory-resident, PROG will stay where it is (that is, Program CS and Program IP will not change), and the address at which programs get loaded will be moved to the end of PROG.

At this point we have to investigate how to fill the interrupt vector of a selected interrupt with the addresses CS and IP of our own program. The interrupt vectors are at the very bottom of memory; how do we reach them?

After memory-resident programs are installed, how do you un-install them when memory becomes too full? There are a number of programs that you can run before installing memory-resident programs, and they (also memory-resident) will un-install added-on programs for you by resetting the top of available memory and resetting interrupt vectors. Or you could design your program to un-install itself.

## The Get and Set Interrupt Vector Services of INT 21H

DOS INT 21H comes to our aid here. There is a service to get an interrupt's current vector, service 35H. And there is also one to set the interrupt's vector to a new address, service 25H.

Since we will usually want to use the old interrupt routine for some things (for example, we will let the keyboard routine read the keyboard port and interpret the key that was typed for us), we want to retain its address before setting the vector to point to us. We can do that by storing the original interrupt vector in the data area of our own program. There we will set up two memory words in our program's data area, beginning at our label OLD_INTERRUPT like this:

```
        .CODE
        ORG      100H            ;ORG = 100H to make this into a .COM file
FIRST:  JMP      LOAD_PROG       ;First time through jump to initialize routine
        :
→       OLD_INTERRUPT   DW 2 DUP(0)
        :
PROG    PROC                     ;The keyboard interrupt will now come here.
```

Now we can copy the old interrupt vector into these two words at OLD_INTERRUPT in our program's data area. To get this old vector, we use INT 21H, service 35H, Get Vector:

```
INT 21H Service 35H Get Vector

Input: AH= 35H
       AL = Interrupt Number
Output:ES:BX = Interrupt's Vector
```

## Getting the Old Vector

To get the old interrupt vector, we'll put service 35H to work. Let's say that we want to intercept the keyboard interrupt, interrupt 9. In that case, we could set a constant named INTERRUPT_NUMBER to 9:

```
INTERRUPT_NUMBER          EQU      9
```

The EQU directive lets you define constants, just as you can declare them with the keyword const in Pascal. In this case, the assembler will substitute 9 whenever it sees INTERRUPT_NUMBER throughout our code. You can see the INTERRUPT_NUMBER is a lot more informative than simply 9.

Using INTERRUPT_NUMBER, we get the old interrupt vector like this:

```
        INTERRUPT_NUMBER      EQU 9
        :
        :
→       MOV      AH,35H             ;Get old vector into ES:BX
→       MOV      AL,INTERRUPT_NUMBER     ;See EQU at beginning
→       INT      21H
        :
```

It's simple. If we want to change the interrupt we're intercepting, all we have to do is to change the value of INTERRUPT_NUMBER at the top of the program. Service 35H returns the interrupt's vector in ES:BX, and we want to store this address in the space we have set aside in the data area—the two words named OLD_INTERRUPT:

```
        .CODE
        ORG       100H              ;ORG = 100H to make this into a .COM file
FIRST:  JMP       LOAD_PROG         ;First time through jump to initialize routine
        :
→      OLD_INTERRUPT   DW 2 DUP(0)
        :
PROG    PROC                        ;The keyboard interrupt will now come here.
```

## Doublewords in Memory

Later, we are going to treat these two words as a single, double-word quantity. You may recall that the 80x86 has a funny way of storing objects larger than bytes in memory—it stores doublewords with the low word first. For example, 01020304H would be stored like this: 04 03 02 01 (remember that the 80x86 also exchanges the bytes in a word). This means that the offset address of the old interrupt's vector (in BX) goes into the first word of our storage place:

```
        INTERRUPT_NUMBER     EQU 9
        :
        :
        MOV      AH,35H            ;Get old vector into ES:BX
        MOV      AL,INTERRUPT_NUMBER      ;See EQU at beginning
        INT      21H
→       MOV      OLD_INTERRUPT,BX         ;Store old interrupt vector
        :
```

And the segment address (in ES) goes into the second word. That can be done with a line like this:

```
        INTERRUPT_NUMBER     EQU 9
        :
        :
        MOV      AH,35H            ;Get old vector into ES:BX
        MOV      AL,INTERRUPT_NUMBER      ;See EQU at beginning
        INT      21H
        MOV      OLD_INTERRUPT,BX         ;Store old interrupt vector
→       MOV      OLD_INTERUPT[2],ES
        :
```

## Indexed Addressing and Arrays

This is a new way of using indirect addressing, called *indexed addressing*. OLD_INTERRUPT[2] refers to the location two bytes (that is, one word) after the label OLD_INTERRUPT.

This method can prove quite useful—we can also index an array using BX, like this: ARRAY[BX]. Just set BX to the location of the byte in ARRAY, and we're set.

For example, we might have an array set up like this:

```
ARRAY    DB 50 DUP(0)
```

We could use it like this:

```
            ARRAY    DB 50 DUP(0)
                     :
                     :
→           MOV      AX,ARRAY[2]
```

Here we have defined an area of 50 bytes called ARRAY (there is nothing special about the name; we could have called it ARRAY_15, or anything). To move the first byte of ARRAY into AX, we would say MOV AX,ARRAY[0], to move the second byte into AX we would say MOV AX,ARRAY[1], and so on.

| Note: MOV AX,ARRAY and MOV AX,ARRAY[0] are identical to the assembler.

Two dimensional arrays are possible as well, like this:

```
MOV         DX,ARRAY[BX][SI]
```

(This really indicates the item at ARRAY[BX+SI]. See the assembler manual for more details.)

In our case, we want to point to the word after OLD_INTERRUPT, so we simply use OLD_INTERRUPT[2]; we use 2 since addressing always is measured in bytes, and a word is 2 bytes:

```
     INTERRUPT_NUMBER      EQU 9
     :
     :
     MOV      AH,35H            ;Get old vector into ES:BX
     MOV      AL,INTERRUPT_NUMBER      ;See EQU at beginning
     INT      21H
     MOV      OLD_INTERRUPT,BX         ;Store old interrupt vector
→    MOV      OLD_INTERUPT[2],ES
     :
```

## Resetting the Interrupt Vector

It's time to move ourselves into the interrupt vector table. We want to be able to change the vector to point to us, not to the old interrupt routine. That is, we want to load our program's IP and Program CS into the interrupt's vector.

To do this, we can use INT 21H, service 25H, Set Vector:

```
INT 21H Service 25H Set Vector

Input: AH= 25H
       AL = Interrupt Number
       DS:DX = New Interrupt Handler Address
Output: (None)
```

What we've done so far is to store the old interrupt vector:

```
  INTERRUPT_NUMBER      EQU 9
  :
  :
  MOV     AH,35H              ;Get old vector into ES:BX
  MOV     AL,INTERRUPT_NUMBER      ;See EQU at beginning
  INT     21H
→ MOV     OLD_INTERRUPT,BX         ;Store old interrupt vector
→ MOV     OLD_INTERUPT[2],ES
  :
```

And now we can add some lines to reset the interrupt vector to us. We have to give service 25H the new address—the address of our program—in DS:DX. Since we haven't changed DS in our .COM file, we can leave that alone, but we do have to get the offset of our program let's call it PROG—into DX. We can do that with a new instruction, LEA:

```
  INTERRUPT_NUMBER      EQU 9
  :
  :
  MOV     AH,35H              ;Get old vector into ES:BX
  MOV     AL,INTERRUPT_NUMBER      ;See EQU at beginning
  INT     21H
  MOV     OLD_INTERRUPT,BX         ;Store old interrupt vector
  MOV     OLD_INTERUPT[2],ES

→ MOV     AH,25H              ;Set new interrupt vector
→ LEA     DX,PROG
→ INT     21H
  :
```

## The LEA Instruction

LEA means Load Effective Address. An instruction like LEA DX,PROG is just like MOV DX,OFFSET PROG, except that LEA will load only offset addresses into registers—if you had a memory location named APPLES, you couldn't say LEA APPLES,PROG. We'll see LEA later in the chapter on linking.

At this point, we have changed the interrupt's interrupt vector so that it points to our program. Every time that interrupt is executed, we will get control. We have reset the interrupt vector in the interrupt vector table:

```
         :                              :
|        CS        |        |        CS        |
|        IP        |        |        IP        |
|------------------|        |------------------|
|        CS        |        |        CS        |
|        IP        |        |        IP        |
|------------------|        |------------------|
|   Interrupt CS   |   →    |    Program CS    |
|   Interrupt IP   |   →    |    Program IP    |
|------------------|        |------------------|
|        CS        |        |        CS        |
|        IP        |        |        IP        |
|------------------|        |------------------|
|                  |        |                  |
         :                              :
```

# Making Code Memory-Resident

Our code can now reset the interrupt so that it will come to us instead of the old interrupt handling routine. But how do we make sure that our program will stay in memory? There are two ways to do this: DOS INT 27H and INT 21H service 31H. To use INT 27H, simply set DS:DX to the last address you want to keep in memory, and execute INT 27H; that's it.

INT 21H service 31H can give a *return code*, which can be examined by the ERRORLEVEL batch command, or with another INT 21H service (4DH). Since we're not going to use return codes in this book, we will be using INT 27H. Nonetheless, to use INT 21H service 31H, set the number of *paragraphs* that you want to keep in memory into DX. A paragraph is 16 bytes. Move the number you want to use as the return code into AL, set AH to 31H and execute INT 21H.

Here's how we will use INT 27H. As do most programs that install themselves in memory, we will set up a small initialization part of the program at the very end of the code. This part is only to install the program in memory, and it will be jettisoned when the program is installed. For this reason, it is occasionally called the *transient* part of the program. Our program is called PROG; let's call the transient part LOAD_PROG. LOAD_PROG will come after PROG in the .ASM file.

When we first run the .COM file that will attach itself in memory, we start at ORG 100H. At this location, we have been used to seeing the instruction JMP PROG. In this case, that will change to JMP LOAD_PROG. What LOAD_PROG will do, the first time that the .COM file is run, is to reset the appropriate interrupt vectors so that they point to PROG. We do not want to run PROG when we run the .COM file (so we didn't say JMP PROG at ORG 100H)—we want PROG to run only when the interrupts it is intercepting are executed.

Instead, this first time, LOAD_PROG is run. After resetting the correct interrupt vectors to PROG, LOAD_PROG will point DS:DX at the very beginning of itself, LOAD_PROG, and execute an INT 27H. This means that INT 27H will retain in memory all our program up to the point where LOAD_PROG starts. The next program that is loaded will therefore preserve PROG but write over LOAD_PROG. Here's how it looks (PROG will become memory-resident, LOAD_PROG will be jettisoned after the INT 27H):

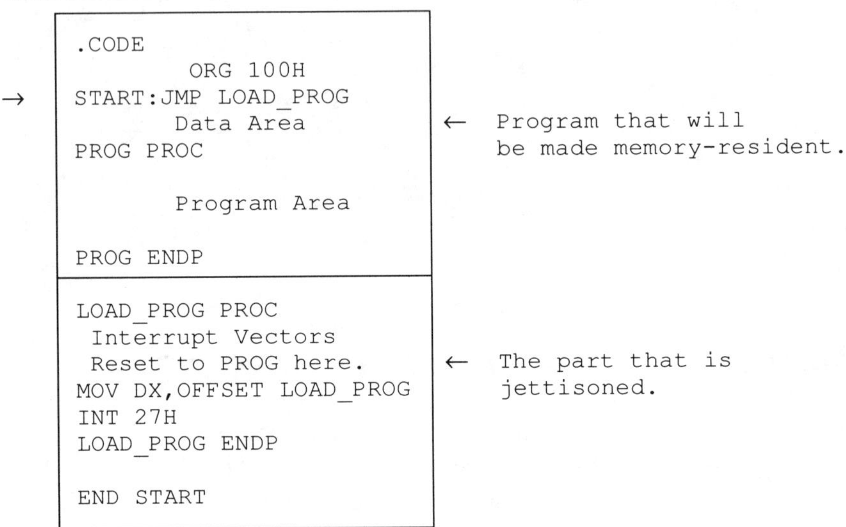


We have already written the transient part that resets the interrupt vector. All we have to add is the part that secures PROG in memory. That looks like this:

```
        :
        :
        :
PROG    ENDP

LOAD_PROG       PROC            ;This procedure intializes everything

        MOV     AH,35H          ;Get old vector into ES:BX
        MOV     AL,INTERRUPT_NUMBER     ;See EQU at beginning
        INT     21H
        MOV     OLD_KEY_INT,BX        ;Store old interrupt vector
        MOV     OLD_KEY_INT[2],ES

        MOV     AH,25H          ;Set new interrupt vector
        LEA     DX,PROG
        INT     21H

EXIT2:  MOV     DX,OFFSET LOAD_PROG     ←
        INT     27H                     ←
LOAD_PROG        ENDP
```

Now PROG is safely installed in memory. This is the entire LOAD_PROG procedure—the whole transient part of our program. Soon we will bring all this together into a .COM file shell that can be made memory-resident, but first we have to make sure that PROG can handle interrupts.

## Writing a Program That Can Handle Interrupts

We've finished designing the transient part of our program. Now we come to more familiar territory: the program itself, which simply handles whatever we want it to when the interrupt is executed. Let's look at that part in detail.

In outline, the program, which we'll call PROG for this example, will fit in like this:

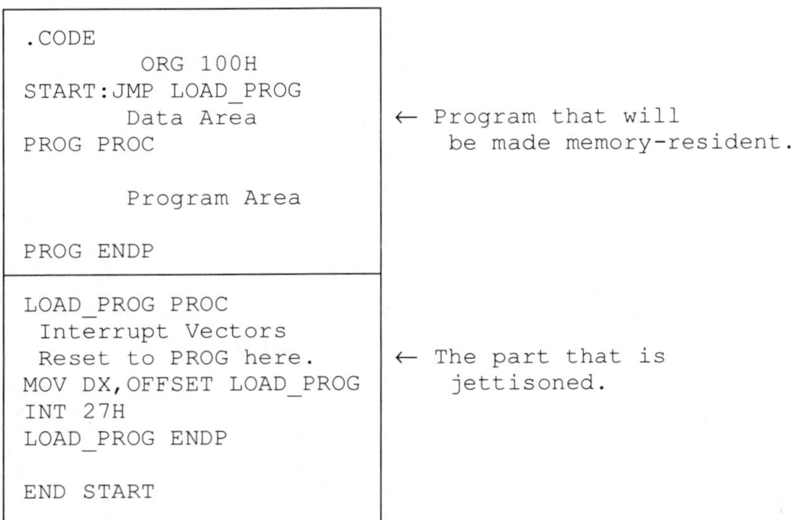


And after the transient part has installed the program, all we'll be left with is this:

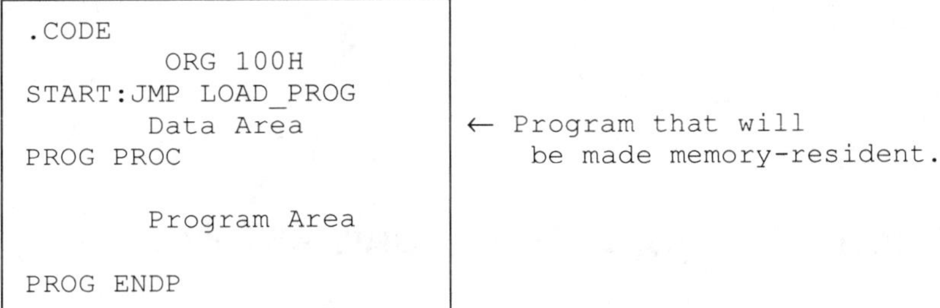


This program has the normal data area and code areas that we're used to. In essence, it will be like any other program we've written, with one or two changes.

Those changes are these: We will usually include a call to the original interrupt routine to let it handle some things (like reading keys from the keyboard port—and then we'll read the key from memory). Also, we'll be extra careful in the beginning and end of the program, saving and then restoring all registers.

The reason we save and then restore all registers is a commonsense one: Imagine that you had just pressed a hot key for your pop-up calculator program. When you're done, you press it again, and the program you had been running takes up where it left off. You can see how things would be if all the registers had been changed—it's like changing all the variables in mid-program, which will most likely cause the program to crash. To avoid this, we'll push all registers and pop them before exiting. Here is PROG in outline:

```
        .MODEL SMALL
        .CODE
        ORG     100H            ;ORG = 100H to make this into a .COM file
FIRST:  JMP     LOAD_PROG       ;First time through jump to initialize routine
        :
        Data Area
        :
PROG    PROC                    ;The keyboard interrupt will now come here.
        PUSH    AX              ;Save the used registers for good form
        PUSH    BX
        PUSH    CX
        PUSH    DX
        PUSH    DI
        PUSH    SI
        PUSH    DS
        PUSH    ES

        ;Prog goes here.

EXIT:→  POP     ES      ;Having done Pushes, here are the Pops
        POP     DS
        POP     SI
        POP     DI
        POP     DX
        POP     CX
        POP     BX
        POP     AX
→       IRET                    ;An interrupt needs an IRET
PROG    ENDP
```

## Segment Register Details and ASSUME

Also, we have ended our program PROG with IRET, the proper end for an interrupt routine. At the end of every executed INT instruction, there is an IRET or something equivalent. IRET is a normal FAR return (that is, both CS and IP are retrieved from the stack) with the flags added on. We can push all the microprocessor's flags with the instruction PUSHF and pop them again, restoring all flags, with POPF. It is important to realize that we can no longer rely on DS and ES being set to our code segment: If we interrupt another program, then the segment registers will naturally be set to the ones it was using at the time we take over control. This means that we will often fill those registers from the CS value, giving us the environment we are used to—using only one segment.

Here we find another 80x86 peculiarity. The segment registers can be loaded only from the general-purpose registers. In other words, we cannot say MOV DS,NEW_SEG, where NEW_SEG is some memory operand; nor can we say MOV DS,CS. However, we can use instructions like these:

```
MOV AX,CS then MOV DS,AX.
```

The one exception is that you can load segment registers directly from memory if that memory is the stack; it is a common programmer's trick to load a segment register this way: PUSH NEW_SEG then POP DS. This saves a few bytes over the double MOVs above.

Whenever you reload a segment register like this, you must inform the assembler of the new contents so that they may be coded into the executable file. The assembler has no way of knowing what the segment registers will hold unless you tell it: You have to use an *ASSUME* directive.

For example, if you want to load DS from CS, you can do it this way:

```
MOV     AX,CS
MOV     DS,AX
```

But the assembler must know at all times which segment will be loaded into which segment register so that it can generate offsets correctly. In this case, you should add a line like this:

```
ASSUME  DS:@CODE ←
MOV     AX,CS
MOV     DS,AX
```

The @CODE keyword is translated into the same segment name as the .CODE directive. If you use another segment directive, such as .DATA, you can use @DATA. These two keywords are called *predefined equates*. @CODE and @DATA are the only two we'll need in this book; for other predefined equates, see the assembler manual. Using ASSUME like this is a fact of life every time you reload a segment register if you want the assembler to generate offsets. In fact, the simplified segment directives like .CODE have ASSUME built right into them. We are going to switch segments only in this chapter, but it's important that you know that ASSUME is necessary when you do. As we'll see later in this chapter, it's possible to name your own segment, such as the ROM_BIOS_DATA segment we'll set up below. To load DS to that segment, we first have to include the line ASSUME DS:ROM_BIOS_DATA. Because the @CODE keyword is translated to the name of the current code segment, we can also use it with ASSUME as we did above: ASSUME DS:@CODE.

## Calling the Old Interrupt

Usually, we will want the old interrupt to do things for us. As mentioned, the keyboard interrupt reads keys that were struck directly from the keyboard, port 60H on the I/O bus. This information would be practically meaningless to us—the keyboard interrupt does a lot of processing to convert that key into an ASCII code (it has to look up the bytes it receives in an internal table, for example)—work that we don't want to duplicate.

However, when the key is interpreted, it is placed in memory in the *keyboard buffer*, a section of memory that we will discuss later in this chapter. It is a simple matter to read the keyboard buffer to see what was typed and whether the key was our hot key. For this reason, we'll want to call the keyboard interrupt to read the struck key and interpret it for us. Before we return to the program that was interrupted by the keystroke, we will be able to examine the key that was struck in the keyboard buffer.

That's why we often want to call the old interrupt routine—we can let it do its work and, before we return to the interrupted program, examine what happened.

Even if we don't want to use the old interrupt routine for anything, it is often a good thing to call it anyway, in case another memory-resident program has already been installed which intercepts this interrupt—unless we called the old interrupt, this earlier memory-resident program would never be run.

Let's see how the call will work. We've already stored the old interrupt routine's address in the data area of PROG (LOAD_PROG did that). Now all we have to do is call it.

## Indirect Calls and the DD and LABEL Pseudo-Ops

There is a simple way of calling such addresses. Up until now, we've had to name our procedures and call them by name, like this:

```
          ORG       100H
          FIRST:    JMP PROG_A
                    :
              Data Area
                    :
          PROG_A    PROC
                    :
→                   CALL      PROG_B
                    :
          PROG_A    ENDP

          PROG_B    PROC
```

```
              :
              RET
        PROG_B ENDP
```

On the other hand, we could have said this:

```
        ORG       100H
        FIRST:    JMP PROG_A
→       PROG_B_ADDR       DW 0
        PROG_A    PROC
                  :
→                 MOV       PROG_B_ADDR,OFFSET PROG_B
→                 CALL      PROG_B_ADDR
                  :
        PROG_A    ENDP

        PROG_B    PROC
                  :
                  RET
        PROG_B ENDP
```

We've simply stored the offset address of the label PROG_B in a memory word, PROG_B_ADDR. Then, the microprocessor allows us to execute an instruction like this: CALL PROG_B_ADDR, which is the same thing as CALL PROG_B. This is helpful to us here, since we do not know in advance where the old interrupt routine will be in memory, and therefore cannot give it a name like PROG_B.

In our case, however, we cannot assume that only the offset address is needed—the old interrupt routine is almost certainly not in our current segment. Instead, we will have to use both words of the address—offset and segment addresses. We have already stored these in locations we named OLD_INTERRUPT and OLD_INTERRUPT[2]; but we cannot call either one of them, since they are just a word long—the assembler knows how many words to use in determining the called address from the declaration DW. Doublewords, which we've seen briefly before, can be declared with the DD directive. If we can just store the old interrupt's address in OLD_INTERRUPT_ADDR, declared like this:

```
OLD_INTERRUPT_ADDR       DD       ?        ;Location of old interrupt
```

then we'll be fine, and can CALL OLD_INTERRUPT_ADDR to execute the old interrupt routine.

> Besides DB, DW, and DD, there is DQ—Define Quadword—and DT—Define Ten Bytes. On the 80386, there is an additional directive: DF, for Define Fword, a 6-byte entity made up of a 16-bit segment address and a 32-bit offset address. We'll stick to DB, DW, and DD.

On the other hand, now we'll have problems loading the old address into OLD_INTERRUPT_ADDR, because the assembler finds itself trying to load single words into something that was defined with DD, not DW, and it will refuse to do it. This is much like a type mismatch in Pascal.

Remember, this is how we filled THE_INTERRUPT in LOAD_PROG, storage for the old interrupt's address (and what we now want to call OLD_INTERRUPT_ADDR, defined with DD):

```
LOAD_PROG       PROC            ;This procedure intializes everything

        MOV     AH,35H          ;Get old vector into ES:BX
        MOV     AL,INTERRUPT_NUMBER     ;See EQU at beginning
        INT     21H

→       MOV     THE_INTERRUPT,BX        ;Store old interrupt vector
→       MOV     THE_INTERRUPT[2],ES

        MOV     AH,25H          ;Set new interrupt vector
        LEA     DX,PROG
        INT     21H

EXIT2:  MOV     DX,OFFSET LOAD_PROG     ;Set up everything but LOAD_PROG to
        INT     27H                     ;stay and attach itself to DOS
LOAD_PROG        ENDP
```

In other words, we now want to refer to the same memory location two different ways—as if it were a word and a doubleword. This can be solved using the directive LABEL, which is built into the macro assembler for exactly this type of case.

## The LABEL Directive

We will define OLD_INTERRUPT_ADDR with DD this way in the data area of our program:

```
        .CODE
        ORG     100H            ;ORG = 100H to make this into a .COM file
FIRST:  JMP     LOAD_PROG       ;First time through jump to initialize routine
→       OLD_INTERRUPT_ADDR      DD      ?       ;Location of old interrupt

PROG    PROC                    ;The interrupt will now come here.
        PUSH    AX              ;Save the used registers for good form
        PUSH    BX
        PUSH    CX
        PUSH    DX
        PUSH    DI
        PUSH    SI
        PUSH    DS
        PUSH    ES
        PUSHF                   ;First, call old interrupt
        CALL    OLD_INTERRUPT_ADDR

        ;Prog goes here.
```

```
EXIT:   POP     ES      ;Having done Pushes, here are the Pops
        POP     DS
        POP     SI
        POP     DI
        POP     DX
        POP     CX
        POP     BX
        POP     AX
        IRET                    ;An interrupt needs an IRET
PROG    ENDP
```

so that we can CALL OLD_INTERRUPT_ADDR. And then we will LABEL the first word as OLD_INTERRUPT like this:

```
        .CODE
        ORG     100H            ;ORG = 100H to make this into a .COM file
FIRST:  JMP     LOAD_PROG       ;First time through jump to initialize routine
→       OLD_INTERRUPT   LABEL   WORD
→       OLD_INTERRUPT_ADDR      DD      ?       ;Location of old interrupt

PROG    PROC                    ;The interrupt will now come here.
        PUSH    AX              ;Save the used registers for good form
        PUSH    BX
        PUSH    CX
        PUSH    DX
        PUSH    DI
        PUSH    SI
        PUSH    DS
        PUSH    ES
        PUSHF                   ;First, call old interrupt
        CALL    OLD_INTERRUPT_ADDR

        ;Prog goes here.

EXIT:   POP     ES      ;Having done Pushes, here are the Pops
        POP     DS
        POP     SI
        POP     DI
        POP     DX
        POP     CX
        POP     BX
        POP     AX
        IRET                    ;An interrupt needs an IRET
PROG    ENDP
```

LABEL gives the current location a name, just like DD or DW does, except that it doesn't reserve any space for it in memory. LABEL is most useful when you have to refer to a particular memory location in two ways, as if, for example, it was defined with DW *and* DD. LOAD_PROG is satisfied, since it will be able to load individual words into OLD_INTERRUPT, and PROG itself is satisfied, because it will be able to CALL OLD_INTERRUPT_ADDR as a doubleword.

> We can label data with these keywords: BYTE, WORD, DWORD, QWORD, TBYTE, FWORD, or a structure name.

## Using PUSHF

Waiting at the end of the old interrupt routine that we are about to call, however, is not a normal return, but an IRET, and IRET pops the flags off the stack (this is the final word it pops before returning to the calling program). To take care of this, we will not simply call OLD_INTERRUPT_ADDR this way:

```
CALL     OLD_INTERRUPT_ADDR
```

but instead will add the flags to the stack first with PUSHF:

```
PUSHF                         ;First, call old interrupt
  CALL     OLD_INTERRUPT_ADDR
```

And now we are all set to call the old interrupt without trouble.

# Use This Shell

Here is the way our entire memory-resident .COM file shell looks:

```
        .MODEL SMALL
INTERRUPT_NUMBER        EQU      9   ← Put the INT number here

        .CODE
        ORG      100H               ;ORG = 100H to make this into a .COM file
FIRST:  JMP      LOAD_PROG          ;First time through jump to initialize routine
        OLD_INTERRUPT    LABEL      WORD
        OLD_INTERRUPT_ADDR          DD       ?       ;Location of old interrupt

PROG    PROC                        ;The interrupt will now come here.
        PUSH     AX                 ;Save the used registers for good form
        PUSH     BX
        PUSH     CX
        PUSH     DX
        PUSH     DI
        PUSH     SI
        PUSH     DS
        PUSH     ES
        PUSHF                       ;First, call old interrupt
        CALL     OLD_INTERRUPT_ADDR

        ;Prog goes here.
```

```
EXIT:   POP     ES          ;Having done Pushes, here are the Pops
        POP     DS
        POP     SI
        POP     DI
        POP     DX
        POP     CX
        POP     BX
        POP     AX
        IRET                        ;An interrupt needs an IRET
PROG    ENDP

LOAD_PROG       PROC                ;This procedure intializes everything

        MOV     AH,35H              ;Get old vector into ES:BX
        MOV     AL,INTERRUPT_NUMBER         ;See EQU at beginning
        INT     21H

        MOV     OLD_INTERRUPT,BX            ;Store old interrupt vector
        MOV     OLD_INTERRUPT[2],ES
        MOV     AH,25H              ;Set new interrupt vector
        LEA     DX,PROG
        INT     21H

EXIT2:  MOV     DX,OFFSET LOAD_PROG         ;Set up everything but LOAD_PROG to
        INT     27H                         ;stay and attach itself to DOS
LOAD_PROG       ENDP

        END     FIRST   ;END "FIRST" so 80x86 will go to FIRST first.
```

Now that it's built, we can simply use this shell, instead of building it from scratch each time. As it stands, this shell is a little barren; we will add some code to it specifically so that it can intercept the keyboard interrupt (the most widely intercepted interrupt) and report the character that was typed in DX a little later. Before we do that, we will develop an example, using the shell as it stands.

## Some Things You Can't Do

It would be great if we could do anything from a memory-resident program; however, you cannot. We cannot, for example, use any DOS interrupts (including DOS INT 21H)! We can, however, use the BIOS interrupts without problem. The reason is that the DOS interrupts are comparatively fragile—if our main program is executing something in INT 21H, and then we take over with a memory-resident program and try to run the same code, we'll destroy the memory variables that were already set for the first program. When we finish, and go back to the first program, everything will be in a shambles. BIOS doesn't have this failing. The BIOS interrupts make up the interrupts up to 1FH; we are going to use INT 10H, the BIOS video interrupt, to print on the screen while memory-resident, not INT 21H.

> In computer language, DOS is not *re-entrant* (OS/2 is re-entrant). The DOS interrupts actually *can* be used, if you add a tremendous amount of programming, but we're not going to do that here.

## Some Things You Can Do

One thing we can do is to write an example program right now. After having developed all the technology of memory-resident programs, let's put it into practice.

For example: There is no cursor on the screen in graphics modes, but we can make a program that will add one. Actually, it will be very simple to accomplish. There is a certain hardware interrupt that is very useful to memory-resident programs, and that is the timer interrupt, INT 8. This interrupt is made 18.2 times a second all the time—the PC or PS/2 is stopping work 18.2 times a second to check on the timer (unless we turn off hardware interrupts).

We'll intercept that interrupt and use it, 18.2 times a second, to print out an underscore, _ , as a cursor at the current cursor position with INT 10H service 0AH (recall that although INT services 9 and 0AH write out characters, they do not advance the cursor). Our program PROG will be very easy. All we really have to do is make sure we set INTERRUPT_NUMBER to 8 and then print out _. Here's the program:

```
INTERRUPT_NUMBER        EQU     8        ←
        .MODEL SMALL
        .CODE
        ORG     100H                    ;ORG = 100H to make this into a .COM file
FIRST:  JMP     LOAD_PROG               ;First time through jump to initialize routine
        OLD_INTERRUPT   LABEL   WORD
        OLD_INTERRUPT_ADDR      DD      ?       ;Location of old interrupt

PROG    PROC                            ;The interrupt will now come here.
        PUSH    AX                      ;Save the used registers for good form
        PUSH    BX
        PUSH    CX
        PUSH    DX
        PUSH    DI
        PUSH    SI
        PUSH    DS
        PUSH    ES
        PUSHF                           ;First, call old interrupt
        CALL    OLD_INTERRUPT_ADDR
→       MOV     AH,0AH
→       MOV     CX,1
→       MOV     BH,0
→       MOV     AL,"_"
→       INT     10H
        POP     ES      ;Having done Pushes, here are the Pops
        POP     DS
        POP     SI
```

```
        POP     DI
        POP     DX
        POP     CX
        POP     BX
        POP     AX
        IRET                    ;An interrupt needs an IRET
PROG    ENDP

LOAD_PROG       PROC            ;This procedure initializes everything

        MOV     AH,35H          ;Get old vector into ES:BX
        MOV     AL,INTERRUPT_NUMBER     ;See EQU at beginning
        INT     21H
        MOV     OLD_INTERRUPT,BX        ;Store old interrupt vector
        MOV     OLD_INTERRUPT[2],ES

        MOV     AH,25H          ;Set new interrupt vector
        LEA     DX,PROG
        INT     21H

EXIT:   MOV     DX,OFFSET LOAD_PROG     ;Set up everything but LOAD_PROG to
        INT     27H                     ;stay and attach itself to DOS
LOAD_PROG        ENDP

        END     FIRST   ;END "FIRST" so 80x86 will go to FIRST first.
```

The body of PROG just types out this cursor, _. We select graphics page 0 (the usual page) with MOV BH,0; set the count of characters to write to 1 with MOV CX,1; select service 0AH with MOV AH,0AH, and type a _ by placing that character in AL:

```
MOV     AH,0AH
MOV     CX,1
MOV     BH,0
MOV     AL,"_"
INT     10H
```

This is our first memory-resident program. To use it, just type it in, assemble, link, and run it through EXE2BIN. Then put yourself in a graphics mode on the screen, as we discussed in the previous chapter (note there is no cursor), and run CURSOR.COM.

A cursor will appear; just the unblinking, somewhat sullen-looking underscore. But it will stay there wherever the cursor is. Unfortunately, sometimes the cursor is moved around on the screen discontinuously—that is, no character is typed to overwrite the _ before the cursor moves on. Most of the time this isn't the case, but sometimes you will see little underscores in odd places on the page.

You can easily make the cursor blink by counting the number of times the timer interrupt has been called, and typing either a _ or a blank space. You can also fix the problem of left-behind cursors (when the cursor is moved discontinuously), if you really want to, but you will have to intercept INT 10H also and check when the move cursor service, service 2, is called.

# Intercepting the Keyboard Interrupt

This is the big one, the interrupt that most pop-up type programs really use, the keyboard interrupt. As mentioned before, whenever a key is struck, an INT 9 is generated. The PS/2 or PC stops work to go off to the keyboard interrupt routine (whose vector is at 4 x 9 = 36 =24H; 0000:0024); this routine reads in the key codes and places the key's ASCII code into the keyboard buffer, along with its scan code.

## The Keyboard Buffer and Scan Codes

For each of the 83 keys on the basic PC keyboard or the 101 keys on the PS/2 keyboard, there is a code called a scan code, which the microprocessor in the keyboard sends to the PC when a key is typed. All the scan codes are listed in many PC and PS/2 manuals, as well as Pascal manuals. For example, the A key has an ASCII code of 41H and a scan code of 1EH. The S key, next to it, has an ASCII code of 53H and a scan code of 1FH.

Both the typed character's scan code and its ASCII code are stored in the keyboard buffer (two bytes total).

The keyboard buffer itself is a set of 16 words in memory in the BIOS data area. These bytes are set up to be what is called a circular buffer. Since the reading and writing operations to and from this buffer are independent, circular buffering allows you to put in and take out keys easily. At any given time, one of these 16 words, called the *head*, is the position that the next character will be read from.

Another, the *tail*, is the position that the next character can be written to. When keys are typed in, the tail advances. When you read one, the head advances. When either comes to the end of their 16 word range, they wrap around to the beginning again. A good model for this circular buffer is a ring of sixteen words, with the head forever chasing the tail. Two more bytes in the BIOS data area hold the current addresses of the head and the tail.

When everything is read, the head catches up with the tail; the two are at the same address, and the buffer is empty. Conversely, if the tail wraps around and comes up from behind the head, the buffer is full.

## The BIOS Data Area

The keyboard buffer is in the BIOS data area in memory segment 40H. There is an immense amount of information in the BIOS Data Area, as shown in Table 5.1.

Table 5.1 The BIOS Data Area

| Address(es) | | | Contents |
|---|---|---|---|
| 40:0000 | - | 40:0006 | Addresses of RS 232 adapters 1–4 |
| 40:0008 | - | 40:000E | Addresses of printer adapters 1–4 |
| 40:0010 | | | Equipment Flag (returned by Int 11H) |
| 40:0012 | | | Manufacturer's test mark |
| 40:0013 | | | Motherboard memory (in Kbytes) |
| 40:0015 | | | I/O channel memory |
| 40:0017 | | | The Keyboard Flags (see below) |
| 40:0019 | | | Numbers input with Alt key |
| 40:001A | | | Location of Keyboard Buffer Head |
| 40:001C | | | Location of Keyboard Buffer Tail |
| 40:001E | - | 40:003D | Keyboard Buffer |
| 40:003E | | | Status of Diskette Seek |
| 40:003F | | | Status of Diskette Motor |
| 40:0040 | | | Timeout of Diskette Motor |
| 40:0041 | | | Status of Diskette |
| 40:0042 | - | 40:0048 | Status Bytes of Diskette Controller (the NEC) |
| 40:0049 | | | Display Mode (see the section on Clock) |
| 40:004A | | | Number of columns (40 or 80) |
| 40:004C | | | Length of Video Regen. Buffer |
| 40:004E | | | Starting Address in Regen. Buffer |
| 40:0050 | - | 40:005E | Positions of cursors on screen pages 1–8 |
| 40:0060 | | | Mode of the Cursor |
| 40:0062 | | | Active Page Number |
| 40:0063 | | | Address of current display adapter |

While we are here, we should examine the two bytes that begin at 40:0017 because they are often useful to assembly language programmers (it is the byte at 40:17 that INT 16H Service 2 returns in AL). This table is a breakdown of 40:17 and 40:18 bit by bit, starting with bit 0.

| Bit | State | Byte at 40:0017 | Byte at 40:0018 |
|---|---|---|---|
| 0 | Right Shift | 1 → Key is pressed | |
| 1 | Left Shift | 1 → Key is pressed | |
| 2 | Cntrl Shift | 1 → Key is pressed | |
| 3 | | 1 →Alt Shift Pressed | 1 →^Num Lock On |
| 4 | Scroll_Lock | 1 → On | 1 → Key is pressed |
| 5 | Num-Lock | 1 → On | 1 → Key is pressed |
| 6 | Caps-Lock | 1 → On | 1 → Key is pressed |
| 7 | Insert | 1 → On | 1 → Key is pressed |

Any program that can get into these bytes can change the keyboard state of the PC, since the scan codes that come in from the keyboard are interpreted with the aid of this byte. We can write, in DEBUG, a small program named TURNCAPS.COM that simply turns on the CapsLock state of the PC by ORing (we'll see more about OR soon) 40H, or 01000000B, with the status byte at 40:17. Using DEBUG we can write TURNCAPS.COM:

```
A> DEBUG
     NTURNCAPS.COM
     A100
     MOV AX,40
     MOV DS,AX
     MOV BX,17
     OR BYTE PTR [BX],40
     INT 20
     <CR>
     RCX
     D
     W
     Q
```

## Examining the Keyboard Buffer

We are interested in the keyboard buffer for our example program. With DEBUG, we should be able to take a direct look at the keyboard buffer at 40:1E. In particular, we can examine it with the dump command. Let's fill the buffer with A's and then examine it. To avoid having to type D0040:001E, which would fill the buffer up, let's do a dump of 128 bytes before 40:1E so we only have to type D <cr> since dump takes up just where it stopped. Here's how it looks:

```
-D0:39E           ← 128 Bytes before the keyboard buffer
0000:039E  00 00                                             ..
0000:03A0  00 00 00 00 00 00 00 00-00 00 00 00 00 00 00 00   ................
0000:03B0  00 00 00 00 00 00 00 00-00 00 00 00 00 00 00 00   ................
0000:03C0  00 00 00 00 E5 FE 00 F0-E5 FE E5 FE 00 F0 FF FF   ....e~.pe~e~.p..
0000:03D0  5D EF FF FF 40 00 3A EF-00 F0 06 00 00 00 01 00   ]o..@.:o.p......
0000:03E0  40 00 6F EC 00 00 43 E6-80 00 02 00 00 00 01 00   @.ol..Cf........
0000:03F0  00 7C 21 E7 00 F0 46 F2-04 00 CF E5 00 F0 97 F2   .|!g.pFr..Oe.p.r
0000:0400  00 00 00 00 00 00 00 00-BC 03 00 00 00 00 00 00   ........<.......
0000:0410  BD 40 00 00 01 C0 00 40-00 00 38 00 38 00         =@...@.@..8.8.

-AAAAAAAAAAAAAAAA          ← Fill the buffer with "A"
     ^ Error               ← Which DEBUG naturally thinks is an error.
-D                         ← And now examine it.
0000:041E  41 1E                                             A.
0000:0420  41 1E 41 1E 41 1E 41 1E-41 1E 41 1E 41 1E 41 1E   A.A.A.A.A.A.A.A.
0000:0430  41 1E 41 1E 41 1E 41 1E-0D 1C 44 20 0D 1C 03 80   A.A.A.A...D ....
0000:0440  3A 00 04 00 00 0D 01 03-02 07 50 00 00 40 00 00   %.........P..@..
```

```
0000:0450   00 18 00 00 00 00 00 00-00 00 00 00 00 00 00 00   ................
0000:0460   07 06 00 B4 03 29 30 E6-0A 00 00 00 98 4D 11 00   ...4.)0f.....M..
0000:0470   00 00 FF FF 00 00 00 00-14 14 14 14 01 01 01 01   ................
0000:0480   1E 00 3E 00 00 00 00 00-00 00 00 00 00 00 00 00   ..>.............
0000:0490   00 00 00 00 00 00 00 00-00 00 00 00 00 00         ..............
-Q
```

If you look at the ASCII part of the display, you'll see our typed A's. Each A is stored as a 41H (its ASCII code) and a 1EH (its scan code). At the end of the last A the carriage return we typed (i.e., AAAAAAAAAAAAAAA<cr>) is stored as 0DH (=ASCII 13) 1CH (its scan code). Finally, you can see our D<cr> command. This last <cr> leaves us at the top of the buffer. The next key typed would be wrapped around and stored at the beginning at 40:1E.

## Reaching the ROM BIOS Data Area

We can set up labels for all the parts of the keyboard buffer by defining a segment with the *AT* directive. For example, here's how we can set up our ROM_BIOS_DATA segment:

```
ROM_BIOS_DATA   SEGMENT AT 40H  ;BIOS statuses held here, also keyboard buffer

        ORG     1AH
        HEAD DW      ?                    ;Unread chars go from Head to Tail
        TAIL DW      ?
        BUFFER       DW      16 DUP (?)          ;The buffer itself
        BUFFER_END   DW ?

ROM_BIOS_DATA   ENDS
```

This is the way you can set up a segment without the .CODE or .DATA directives. We use the *SEGMENT* directive. After the segment definition is complete, we must end it with the *ENDS* directive. In this case, we are specifying that the segment we name ROM_BIOS_DATA starts at segment address 0040H—that is, at 0040:0000. At location 0040:001AH, we give names to various words. Note that we use ? instead of a value here—using ? doesn't make the assembler initialize those locations.

## Reading From the Keyboard Buffer

When an INT 9 is generated, our memory-resident program takes over. Its first action is to call the old keyboard interrupt, which places the scan and ASCII codes of the struck key into the keyboard buffer.

The actual details of reading the struck key from the keyboard buffer aren't important for us to cover here—they will add no new knowledge, and simply take up much time. So let's review them in outline.

To read a key from the keyboard buffer, we'll have to set DS to the ROM_BIOS_DATA segment (after the appropriate ASSUME) and check where the tail is in the keyboard buffer (the location where the next key will be placed). The key just before that in the keyboard buffer is the new one. We'll read it from the buffer and place its scan code in DH and its ASCII code in DL. Your program can then take over and see if it's the hot key expected. If not, you should just exit—that is, jump to the label EXIT.

## Removing Keys From the Keyboard Buffer

If the key is the one you were expecting, your program might want to spring into action and start intercepting all keys as input. This means that your program will have to remove keys from the keyboard buffer as soon as they are typed (and place them into a notepad, for example).

To remove a key from the keyboard buffer, all you need to do is to move the tail of the buffer to overwrite the key. At the point your program takes over (made clear in the keyboard-intercepting .COM file shell to follow), BX will hold the offset address of the current key in the buffer. To remove this key, just use the instruction MOV TAIL,BX.

```
At the point your program takes over:
          [Check scan code (in DH) and ASCII code (in DL)]
              [Is it a key you want to accept as input?]
                    |                        |
                   Yes                       No
                    ↓                        ↓
          [Remove this key                [JMP to EXIT, leaving this
           from the keyboard               key to be used by other
           buffer with MOV TAIL,BX]        programs.]
          [Do work]
          [JMP to EXIT]
```

For example, if your program wanted to remove all typed ^N's (so they never appeared on the screen or got read by any program), it would check for the correct scan code in DH (31H) and the correct ASCII code in DL (0EH). If it found what it was looking for, it would remove the key. If not, it wouldn't interfere. To do this, all you would need are these instructions in the .COM file shell where you take over:

```
CMP     DX,310EH        ;Is this a ^N?
  JNE     EXIT            ;No, just exit
  MOV     TAIL,BX         ;Yes, remove it
  JMP     EXIT            ;And leave
```

We'll develop an example after introducing our key-intercepting .COM file shell to make this clear.

## The Key-Intercepting .COM File Shell

Here is the keyboard-intercepting .COM file shell, complete with instructions on what to do when your program takes over, and how to accept a typed key as input by removing it from the keyboard buffer (note the ASSUME—if you want to change DS back to the value in CS, you must use another ASSUME just before you do):

```
INTERRUPT_NUMBER        EQU     9

        .MODEL SMALL
ROM_BIOS_DATA   SEGMENT AT 40H  ;BIOS statuses held here, also keyboard buffer

        ORG     1AH
        HEAD DW     ?                   ;Unread chars go from Head to Tail
        TAIL DW     ?
        BUFFER      DW      16 DUP (?)          ;The buffer itself
        BUFFER_END  LABEL   WORD

ROM_BIOS_DATA   ENDS

        .CODE
        ORG     100H            ;ORG = 100H to make this into a .COM file
FIRST:  JMP     LOAD_PROG       ;First time through jump to initialize routine

        OLD_KEY_INT     LABEL   WORD
        OLD_KEYBOARD_INT        DD      ?       ;Location of old kbd interrupt

PROG    PROC                    ;The keyboard interrupt will now come here.
        PUSH    AX              ;Save the used registers for good form
        PUSH    BX
        PUSH    CX
        PUSH    DX
        PUSH    DI
        PUSH    SI
        PUSH    DS
        PUSH    ES
        PUSHF                   ;First, call old keyboard interrupt
        CALL    OLD_KEYBOARD_INT

→       ASSUME  DS:ROM_BIOS_DATA        ;Examine the char just put in
→       MOV     BX,ROM_BIOS_DATA
→       MOV     DS,BX

→       MOV     BX,TAIL                 ;Point to current tail
→       CMP     BX,HEAD                 ;If at head, kbd int has deleted char
→       JE      IN                      ;So leave
→       SUB     BX,2                    ;Point to just read in character
→       CMP     BX,OFFSET BUFFER        ;Did we undershoot buffer?
→       JAE     NO_WRAP                 ;Nope
→       MOV     BX,OFFSET BUFFER_END    ;Yes - move to buffer top
→       SUB     BX,2                    ;Point to just read in character
```

```
NO_WRAP:MOV     DX,[BX]  ←              ;Char in DX now

          [NOTE: Your program takes over here (keep in mind that DS is still
                at ROM_BIOS_DATA segment). The just-struck key's scan code is
               in DH and its ASCII code in DL at this point. If you want to
                remove this key from the keyboard buffer (i.e. accept it as
           input), use the instruction MOV TAIL,BX here. Otherwise, you may
              exit by jumping to the label EXIT.]

        ;MOV    TAIL,BX         ; ←Optional removal of key from buffer.
        :
   [Your code here.]
        :
EXIT:   POP     ES      ;Having done Pushes, here are the Pops
        POP     DS
        POP     SI
        POP     DI
        POP     DX
        POP     CX
        POP     BX
        POP     AX
        IRET                    ;An interrupt needs an IRET
PROG    ENDP

LOAD_PROG       PROC            ;This procedure intializes everything

        MOV     AH,35H          ;Get old vector into ES:BX
        MOV     AL,INTERRUPT_NUMBER     ;See EQU at beginning
        INT     21H

        MOV     OLD_KEY_INT,BX          ;Store old interrupt vector
        MOV     OLD_KEY_INT[2],ES

        MOV     AH,25H          ;Set new interrupt vector
        LEA     DX,PROG
        INT     21H

        MOV     DX,OFFSET LOAD_PROG     ;Set up everything but LOAD_PROG to
        INT     27H                     ;stay and attach itself to DOS
LOAD_PROG        ENDP

        END     FIRST   ;END "FIRST" so 80x86 will go to FIRST first.
```

Let's put together an example!

## SWITCH.ASM: A Memory-Resident Hot Key Program

Here we'll put our keyboard interceptor to work and see how everything fits together. We'll write a program named SWITCH.ASM that lets you switch between two screens, the MDA and CGA, if you have both installed. The hot key will be

Alt-S. In other words, when you are using one screen and type Alt-S, you will switch to the other screen, no matter what program is running.

To switch screens, it is not enough to simply switch video modes. If you are using the same screen, switching video modes is fine, but it will not automatically change the monitor you are using if your current monitor doesn't support the mode you select.

You also must change one of the words in the BIOS data area, the equipment word (also called, inaccurately, the equipment flag). In this case, you load this word from 40:0010 (see the table earlier) into a register—for example, CX. The instruction AND CX,11101111B will reset the appropriate bit to switch to the graphics screen. OR CX,00010000B will set you up for monochrome (then, of course, you must return the contents of CX to memory location 40:0010).

## AND and OR

AND and OR are two 80x86 instructions that are very useful for working with individual bits in a word; we've already seen OR, which is just like Pascal's or operator. If we use OR on two bits, the result will always be 1 unless both bits are 0. Conversely, AND is just like the Pascal and operator; using AND on two bits will always yield 0 unless both bits are 1. OR and AND are frequently used to to change individual bits in a word or byte because of these properties—AND can turn bits off, and OR can make sure they are on.

By checking a particular bit in the equipment word, we can tell whether a monochrome screen or a CGA screen is in use and then toggle to the other option. The hot key here is ALT-S (to supposedly stand for "alternate screen"), which means the scan code we are looking for is 1FH and the ASCII code is 0. DX will hold 1F00H if Alt-S has been typed when our program takes over from the keyboard intercepting shell, and we will spring into action.

If Alt-S *has* been typed, we remove it from the keyboard buffer. In that way, the Alt-S won't be left over after we've finished changing screens. To erase the key, we'll use MOV TAIL,BX. Here is the part of the program that both detects whether the hot key was typed, and if it was, erases it from the buffer (and, if it was not, exits):

```
          MOV     BX,TAIL                 ;Point to current tail
          CMP     BX,HEAD                 ;If at head, kbd int has deleted char
          JE      OUT                     ;So leave
          SUB     BX,2                    ;Point to just read in character
          CMP     BX,OFFSET BUFFER        ;Did we undershoot buffer?
          JAE     NO_WRAP                 ;Nope
          MOV     BX,OFFSET BUFFER_END    ;Yes - move to buffer top
          SUB     BX,2                    ;Point to just read in character
NO_WRAP:MOV       DX,[BX]                 ;Char in DX now
→         CMP     DX,1F00H                ;Is the char an ALT-S?
→         JNE     EXIT                    ;No
→         MOV     TAIL,BX                 ;Yes - delete it from buffer
```

Here is the whole program SWITCH, which just toggles between monochrome and CGA:

```
        ;Uses ALT-S to toggle between screens (Graphics ↔ Monochrome)
INTERRUPT_NUMBER        EQU     9
        .MODEL SMALL
ROM_BIOS_DATA   SEGMENT AT 40H  ;BIOS statuses held here, also keyboard buffer

        ORG     1AH
        HEAD DW      ?                  ;Unread chars go from Head to Tail
        TAIL DW      ?
        BUFFER       DW     16 DUP (?)          ;The buffer itself
        BUFFER_END   LABEL  WORD

ROM_BIOS_DATA   ENDS

        .CODE
        ORG     100H            ;ORG = 100H to make this into a .COM file
FIRST:  JMP     LOAD_PROG        ;First time through jump to initialize routine

        OLD_KEY_INT     LABEL   WORD
        OLD_KEYBOARD_INT        DD      ?       ;Location of old kbd interrupt

PROG    PROC                    ;The keyboard interrupt will now come here.
        PUSH    AX              ;Save the used registers for good form
        PUSH    BX
        PUSH    CX
        PUSH    DX
        PUSH    DI
        PUSH    SI
        PUSH    DS
        PUSH    ES
        PUSHF                   ;First, call old keyboard interrupt
        CALL    OLD_KEYBOARD_INT

        ASSUME  DS:ROM_BIOS_DATA        ;Examine the char just put in
        MOV     BX,ROM_BIOS_DATA
        MOV     DS,BX

        MOV     BX,TAIL                 ;Point to current tail
        CMP     BX,HEAD                 ;If at head, kbd int has deleted char
        JE      EXIT                     ;So leave
        SUB     BX,2                    ;Point to just read in character
        CMP     BX,OFFSET BUFFER        ;Did we undershoot buffer?
        JAE     NO_WRAP                 ;Nope
        MOV     BX,OFFSET BUFFER_END    ;Yes—move to buffer top
        SUB     BX,2                    ;Point to just read in character
NO_WRAP:MOV     DX,[BX]                 ;Char in DX now
        CMP     DX,1F00H                ;Is the char an ALT-S?
        JNE     EXIT                    ;No
        MOV     TAIL,BX                 ;Yes — delete it from buffer

        MOV     BX,10H                  ;Get equipment flag
```

```
        MOV     AX,[BX]
        MOV     CX,AX                   ;Put a copy in CX
        AND     AX,00010000B            ;Is CGA in use?
        CMP     AX,0
        JE      TO_MONOCHROME           ;Yes
TO_GRAPHICS: ←                          ;No, switch to CGA
        AND     CX,11101111B            ;Set up equipment byte
        MOV     [BX],CX                 ;And reinstall it
        MOV     AX,0002                 ;Set up a CGA screen mode
        INT     10H
        JMP     EXIT                    ;And leave
TO_MONOCHROME: ←                        ;Turn on monochrome here
        OR      CX,00010000B            ;Set up equipment byte
        MOV     [BX],CX                 ;And reinstall it
        MOV     AX,0007                 ;Set up monochrome video mode
        INT     10H

EXIT:   POP     ES      ;Having done Pushes, here are the Pops
        POP     DS
        POP     SI
        POP     DI
        POP     DX
        POP     CX
        POP     BX
        POP     AX
        IRET                    ;An interrupt needs an IRET
PROG    ENDP

LOAD_PROG       PROC            ;This procedure intializes everything

        MOV     AH,35H          ;Get old vector into ES:BX
        MOV     AL,INTERRUPT_NUMBER     ;See EQU at beginning
        INT     21H
        MOV     OLD_KEY_INT,BX        ;Store old interrupt vector
        MOV     OLD_KEY_INT[2],ES

        MOV     AH,25H          ;Set new interrupt vector
        LEA     DX,PROG
        INT     21H

        MOV     DX,OFFSET LOAD_PROG     ;Set up everything but LOAD_PROG to
        INT     27H                     ;stay and attach itself to DOS
LOAD_PROG       ENDP
                END     FIRST
```

There's not much to this program: We just check to see if the CGA is in use, and, if it is, turn on monochrome instead by setting the equipment byte and changing to the monochrome video mode. If the CGA wasn't in use, we turn it on by setting up the equipment byte and changing to a CGA video mode. Of course, we restore all registers to the way they were before returning to the program then running (including segment registers).

If we had wanted instead to write a pop-up notepad, we would have simply used BIOS INT 10H, service 9 or 0AH, to write out our notepad on the screen. Then, while the pad was active, we would have removed typed keys from the keyboard buffer (MOV BX,TAIL) and put them into the notepad area of memory. When the hot key was typed again, we would have just stopped intercepting typed characters and taken our notepad off the screen.

So ends our discussion of memory-resident programs. Their uses vary from programs that will take snaphots of the screen, that will log screen output, remember what's gone on the screen many screenfuls ago (and let you scroll through it), pop-up utilities of all descriptions, put in disk caches to let disks go faster and all kinds of things. And now, we too know how to write them. It may have originally looked difficult because of the bewildering number of details, but now that we've developed a working .COM file shell, most of the details are solved.

# 6

# Connecting Assembly Language to Pascal

In this chapter start putting Pascal and assembly language together for the first time. There are two main ways of doing it—using in-line code, and linking assembly-language modules into your program. Both have their uses, and we'll explore them in this chapter, beginning with in-line code.

## In-Line Code

Unlike a language such as C, you cannot place actual assembly language instructions in Pascal programs. With most C compilers, you can place instructions like MOV and SHR right in the code (after a special *inline* keyword), and the compiler can handle it (although if you are using Turbo C, you need to have TASM.EXE in the same directory).

In Pascal, though, the situation is different. Let's work through an example. You might recall our earlier program PRINTZ: It printed out the letter Z and exited. These were the instructions it used:

```
MOV     DL, 5AH
MOV     AH, 2
INT     21H
```

This prints out Z (ASCII code 5AH). We can put this into a Pascal program in a number of ways. For example, we can use the standard Intr() procedure to call INT 21H or the MsDos() procedure. To use Intr(), you must load it this way:

```
Intr(InterruptNumber:byte; var Regs: Registers);
```

where Regs is a special record defined in the Dos unit:

```
type
        Registers = record
                case integer of
                   0: (AX, BX, CX, DX, BP, SI,
                       DI, DS, ES, Flags:word);
                   1: (AL, AH, BL, BH, CL, CH,
                       DL, DH: byte);
                end;
```

Here's what the program looks like:

```
program printz;
uses DOS;

var
   Regs: Registers;
   begin
        Regs.AH := 2;
        Regs.Dl := $5A;
→       Intr($21, Regs);
   end.
```

Or, we can take a shortcut by using the MsDos() procedure like this:

```
program printz;
uses DOS;

var
   Regs: Registers;
   begin
        Regs.AH := 2;
        Regs.Dl := $5A;
→       MsDos(Regs);
   end.
```

Here we used MsDos() to do the same thing; MsDos() is reserved for INT 21H calls.

Although Intr() and MsDos() exist, they provide only the most limited utility. If you want to do anything more than, say, print the screen or something similar, you are better off with in-line code (and even in-line code isn't much better).

Pascal supports only in-line *machine code*. In other words, you have to know the actual machine code bytes and place them in the program.

For example, to create PRINTZ using in-line code, we need to know the machine code instructions. Start up DEBUG:

```
E:>DEBUG

–
```

Now type A100 to start assembling our code:

```
-A100
23C2:0100
```

Type these lines, finishing each with a carriage return:

```
-A100
23C2:0100 MOV     AH,2
23C2:0102 MOV     DL,5A
23C2:0104 INT     21H
23C2:0106

_
```

Now we can unassemble with the DEBUG U command to find the machine code we're looking for:

```
-A100
23C2:0100 MOV     AH,2
23C2:0102 MOV     DL,5A
23C2:0104 INT     21H
23C2:0106
-U        ←
23C2:0100 B402          MOV    AH,02      ←
23C2:0102 B25A          MOV    DL,5A      ←
23C2:0104 CD21          INT    21         ←
23C2:0106 E8AEFF        CALL    00B7
23C2:0109 26            ES:
23C2:010A 803D3D        CMP    BYTE PTR [DI],3D
23C2:010D 75F1          JNZ    0100
23C2:010F 47            INC    DI
23C2:0110 E8A4FF        CALL    00B7
23C2:0113 893E9300      MOV    [0093],DI
23C2:0117 803E900002    CMP    BYTE PTR [0090],02
23C2:011C 762D          JBE    014B
23C2:011E 33FF          XOR    DI,DI
-Q
```

By looking on the left of the listing, you can see that the bytes we want (next to the addresses) are $B4 $02 $B2 $5A $CD $21. We're ready to put them into Pascal.

In in-line code, these bytes must be separated by a slash, like this:

```
program printz;
uses DOS;

var
   Regs: Registers;
   begin
```

```
        INLINE
        (
        $B4/$02/
        $B2/$5A/
        $CD/$21
        );
    end.
```

This is our new program PRINTZ, which uses the inline() procedure. Once again, it prints out Z—even though it's a Pascal program, it uses assembly language code to get the work done. You can see that this method is going to be awkward for anything larger than a few bytes. We can do a few more things with in-line code. For example, we can reference Z as Pascal data. Let's make Z into the variable letterz and access it from our in-line code. Here's what letterz looks like in the Pascal code:

```
program printz;
uses DOS;

var
   Regs: Registers;
   letterz : char;         ←
   begin
        letterz := "Z"; ←
        :
```

To access it from the machine code, we need to find the address of the variable letterz. We can't move an immediate value in DL to print (like MOV DL, 5AH) because theoretically we don't know what value the variable letterz will hold. Instead, we have to assemble the instruction to fetch data from memory—MOV DL,[memory location] and then find the memory location. Let's start off with DEBUG. Assemble these lines:

```
-A100
1230:0100 MOV     AH,2
1230:0102 MOV     DL,[0102]
1230:0106 INT     21H
1230:0108
_
```

Now disassemble them. You see these bytes: $B4 $02 $8A $16 $02 $01 $CD $21. The address we used, 0102H, was just a dummy to show where the actual address will go. We have to replace the bytes $02 $01 with the address of the variable letterz.

Since labels are just addresses to the compiler, we can do that like this:

```
program printz;
uses DOS;

var
   Regs: Registers;
   letterz : char;
```

```
    begin
         letterz := 'Z';
         INLINE
         (
         $B4/$02/
→        $8A/$16/letterz/
         $CD/$21
         );
    end.
```

When you compile the program, the compiler substitutes the address of letterz for the variable letterz. In this way, you can access already declared data. Now we can reach Pascal data from within our code. To take advantage of that, however, we have to take a look at the way Pascal stores data internally.

# Pascal Data Formats

Here are the Pascal integer data types and what they are translated to on an assembly language level:

| *Pascal Type* | *Matching Assembly Language Type* |
|---|---|
| byte | Byte |
| integer | Signed Word |
| longint | Signed Double Word |
| shortint | Signed Byte |
| word | Word |

These are simple enough. The signed numbers are held in two's complement notation, which we'll see in Chapter 7. But what is the internal representation of floating-point numbers?

If we dig into a compiled Pascal file, we find that a number like 10.5 has been stored as 41280000H. Where did it come from? The format for floating-point numbers is complex and takes a little getting used to. A number like 32.1 is just $3x10^1$ plus $2x10^0$, and $1x10^{-1}$. On the other hand, the computer is a binary machine, which means it uses base 2, so a number like 10.5 must be stored as $1x2^3$ plus $1x2^1$ plus $1x2^{-1}$, which is 1010.1, where the point is a binary point. It is possible to store any number in binary that can be stored in decimal, it just takes more places. For instance, 0.75 can be broken down into ½ + ¼, or $2^{-1} + 2^{-2}$, so .75 = .11B.

The numbers stored as floating point are all *normalized*, which means they appear with the binary point near the beginning, so 1010.1 would look like this: $1.0101x2^3$. To expand this, just move the binary point three places to the right, giving 1010.1 again. You can see that the first digit in any normalized binary number is always one. Under Pascal floating-point format, the leading 1 is *implicit*. In other words, all that is stored of the *significand* is 0101. The exponent is still three—but to make matters even more complex, all exponents are stored after being added to some offset or *bias*.

For a single, this bias is 7FH, or 127. For doubles, this number is 3FFH, or 1023. In other words, if our number, 1010.1B, is going to be stored as a single, the exponent will be 3 + 127 = 130 = 82H. Finally, the first bit of any floating-point number is the sign bit. Floating-point numbers are *not* stored in two's complement notation. If the sign bit is 1, the number is negative; if it is 0, the number is positive—that's the only distinction between positive and negative numbers. The float format looks like this:

```
Bit #   31 30    23 22                 0
        +--+------+--------------------+
        |  |      |                    |
        +--+------+--------------------+
          S  Exp.   Significand.
```

So 10.5 = 1010.1B will look like this:

```
                 Sign Bit
                    ↓
                   01000001001010000000000000000000
                    |______| |___________________|
[Exponent + Bias =   82H]       [Significand = 0101B]
```

This can be made into Hex by grouping every four binary digits together:

```
01000001001010000000000000000000
|__||__||__||__||__||__||__||__|
 4   1   2   8   0   0   0   0
```

So 10.5 is stored as 41280000H. In fact, due to the 80x86's method of storing low bytes first inside a word and then low words first, 10.5 actually shows up in memory as 00H 00H 28H 41H. These bytes are a far cry from 10.5. If you are going to work with floating-point numbers, first write a function to translate floating-point format into something you can use (or let Pascal do it for you).

The format for doubles is this:

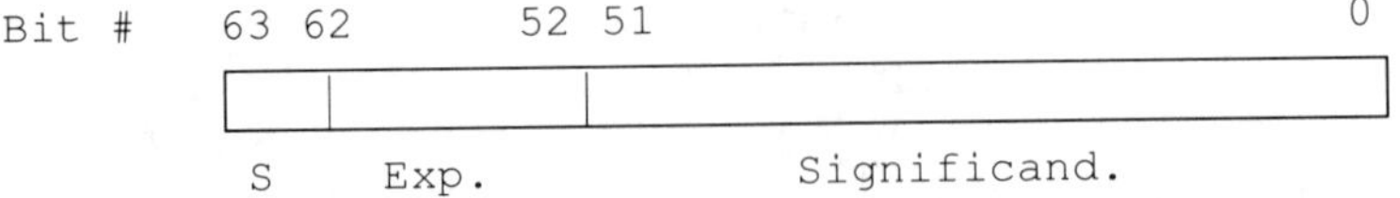


and to use this format, you'll have to write a translating function as well.

It's worth noting that this floating point format is the same format used by the 80x87 coprocessors, so you can interface with them easily. We'll see more about the 80x87 in Chapter 8.

Working directly with variables as we have been doing provides one way of communicating with the Pascal program, but often you don't know the names of the specific variables used in the program. For example, you might be writing some speedy assembly-language code to replace a ponderous standard Pascal library function. In that case, all you'll have are the parameters passed to you. And now we'll pick them right off the stack.

# Passing Parameters

Let's say we wanted a to write a Pascal procedure as in-line code. For example, we can turn PRINTZ into a called procedure:

```
program test;

var
   vble : char;

procedure printz(letterz : char);
          :
          :
begin
     vble := 'Z';
     printz(vble); ←
end.
```

Now we've got to write the procedure printz() in machine code. As we'll see later, Pascal places passed parameters on the stack. We will take advantage of that now by letting the calling procedure pass the letter to us to print (it will be Z). We can pop that value into DX directly, which is where we want it since the ASCII code to print needs to go in DL.

Assemble and then unassemble these lines:

```
-A100
1230:0100 MOV     AH,2
1230:0102 POP     DX
1230:0103 INT     21H
1230:0105
-U
1230:0100 B402           MOV     AH,02
1230:0102 5A             POP     DX
1230:0103 CD21           INT     21
1230:0105 68             DB      68
1230:0106 65             DB      65
1230:0107 207374         AND     [BP+DI+74],DH
1230:010A 61             DB      61
1230:010B 63             DB      63
1230:010C 6B             DB      6B
1230:010D 207769         AND     [BX+69],DH
1230:0110 6C             DB      6C
1230:0111 6C             DB      6C
1230:0112 206C6F         AND     [SI+6F],CH
1230:0115 6F             DB      6F
```

```
1230:0116 6B            DB      6B
1230:0117 206C69        AND     [SI+69],CH
1230:011A 6B            DB      6B
1230:011B 65            DB      65
1230:011C 207768        AND     [BX+68],DH
1230:011F 65            DB      65
-Q
```

When it calls the procedure PRINTZ, Pascal will push the character letterz on the stack (although letterz is only a byte long, a whole word is used because you can't push less than a word). PRINTZ pops a word off the stack, places it into DX, and then prints it. As we can see, the bytes for this process are $B4 $02 $5A $CD $21. Here's what the program looks like:

```
program test;

var
   vble : char;

procedure printz(letterz : char);
     INLINE
     (
     $B4/$02/
     $5A/
     $CD/$21
     );
begin
     vble := 'Z';
     printz(vble);
end.
```

Note that we left out the begin and end of the procedure printz()—the whole thing is just in-line code. Let's take a closer look at how we pass parameters to procedures—and how we return them from functions. In other words, we have to understand Pascal's *calling convention.*

## Calling Conventions

High level languages pass parameters to subroutines and functions on the stack. To interact with high level languages, we are going to have to pick these parameters off the stack. If we had a function named summer() that just sums two numbers—summer(3,2) would return 5, for example—then Pascal would place the parameters 3 and 2 onto the stack before calling the address it has for summer().

However, different languages do this differently. A calling convention indicates the way a high level language passes parameters to routines that it calls. It specifies these things: the order parameters are pushed in, how they are pushed (as addresses or immediate values), and how to reset the stack when we're done. If we are going to successfully interface to Pascal, we have to mimic what it might expect from its own library of routines.

Some languages push parameters in the order you see them and some in reverse order; some languages (like FORTRAN) don't push the values 3 and 2 at all, but rather, push their addresses. Also, at the end of the call, when we are about to return, some languages demand that the stack be reset in the proper way. In BASIC, FORTRAN, and Pascal, that means that after returning to the high level language, the stack should be set the way it was before the parameters were pushed for the call. See the complete list of calling conventions in Table 6.1.

Table 6.1 Calling Conventions

| *Language* | *Parameters Pushed* | *Parameters Passed* | *Return Type* |
|---|---|---|---|
| BASIC | In order | As offset addresses | RET # |
| FORTRAN | In order | As FAR addresses | RET # |
| C | In REVERSE order | As values | RET |
| Pascal | In order | As values | RET # |

Note: Where RET # is used, # = the total size in bytes of all pushed parameters.

Similarly, look at Table 6.2—we will explore the information there later. It indicates how parameter passing works whether parameters are passed by address or by their actual value.

Table 6.2 Parameter Passing by Language

| *Language* | *Near References* | *Far References* | *By Value* |
|---|---|---|---|
| BASIC | Everything | | |
| FORTRAN | | Everything | |
| C | Near Arrays | Far Arrays | Everything else |
| Pascal | VAR, CONST | VARS, CONST | Everything else |

In Pascal, you can change the value only of arguments that you pass to a function or procedure by preceding them with the VAR keyword. If you use VAR, Pascal passes the address of the argument (i.e., its location in memory) so that the called procedure or function can change that memory location directly. It is called passing *by reference.* Values declared with the CONST keyword are also passed this way. String addresses are also placed on the stack, not the string itself. Everything else is passed *by value*, which means that the actual value of the variable is placed onto the stack, like this:

| *To Pass* | *Place on stack* |
|---|---|
| char | 1 word |
| byte | 1 word |
| integer | 1 word |
| shortint | 1 word |
| word | 1 word |
| longint | 2 words (high word pushed first) |
| string | Pass the string address |
| real | 2 words |
| single | 3 words |
| double | 4 words |
| extended | 5 words |
| near pointer | 1 word |
| far pointer | 2 words |

Let's give all this a try with a function of our own; let's write the function summer() mentioned earlier. Our function will simply take two arguments and add them.

## Returning Values Using Functions

Returning values is unexpectedly easy. The convention is to use these registers to return values from functions:

| *Return this* | *In this* |
|---|---|
| char | AL |
| byte | AL |
| integer | AX |
| shortint | AL |
| word | AX |
| longint | DX:AX (high word in DX |
| string | Passed address |
| real | DX:BX:AX |
| near pointer | AX |
| far pointer | DX:AX |

It's very simple: Depending on the return value expected from the function (set with the function prototype), Pascal just reads values from AL, AX, or DX:AX when you return.

To return a byte-long value, just leave the value in AL when you exit the function. If the calling function is expecting a byte-long return value, it will read that byte from AL. Word values (like short integers) are returned in AX. Doubleword values are simply returned in DX:AX (DX = high word, AX = low word).

Let's put this to use when writing summer(). We will accept two ints and return an int value (in AX). We have to pop two values and then add them. Our assembly language would be like this:

```
POP AX
POP DX
ADD AX,DX
```

Here's what it looks like in Pascal:

```
program test;

function summer(a : word; b:word) : word;
    INLINE
    (
    $58/          {pop ax}
    $5A/          {pop dx}
    $01/$D0       {add ax,dx}
    );
begin
     writeln('3 + 2 = ',summer(3,2));
end.
```

This program just leaves the result in AX, and this value therefore becomes the function's return value. Here, Pascal handles the return part of the subroutine itself—when we return to the calling function, we type out a message and the return value of summer(). That is, the program types out 3 + 2 = 5—returning values is that simple.

However, if we add two integers together, the result could be a long integer. We should adjust summer() to allow for such a result. We can return a long integer in DX:AX. Let's put together the code for doing this in DEBUG:

```
E:\>DEBUG
-A100
1230:0100 MOV     DX,0
1230:0103 POP     CX
1230:0104 POP     AX
1230:0105 ADD     AX,CX
1230:0107 ADC     DX,0
1230:010A
-U
1230:0100 BA0000          MOV     DX,0000
1230:0103 59              POP     CX
1230:0104 58              POP     AX
1230:0105 01C8            ADD     AX,CX
1230:0107 83D200          ADC     DX,+00
```

```
1230:010A 803D3D        CMP     BYTE PTR [DI],3D
1230:010D 75F1          JNZ     0100
1230:010F 47            INC     DI
1230:0110 E8A4FF        CALL    00B7
1230:0113 893E9300      MOV     [0093],DI
1230:0117 803E900002    CMP     BYTE PTR [0090],02
1230:011C 762D          JBE     014B
1230:011E 33FF          XOR     DI,DI
```

Here we are anticipating our fast math chapter with the use of ADC (Add with Carry). All ADC DX,0 does is to place the carry bit, if there is one, into DX. This function returns a longint:

```
program test;

function summer(a : word; b:word) : longint;    ←
    INLINE
    (
    $BA/$00/$00/
    $59/
    $58/
    $01/$C8/
    $83/$D2/$00
    );
begin
     writeln('3 + 2 = ',summer(3,2));
end.
```

Now we have considerable expertise in writing in-line code. We can use data that has been declared in Pascal format. We can read parameters passed to us in a function. And we can even return values. This means that we can write whole functions in pure in-line code. However, that is very tedious; there is much more to interfacing assembly language to Pascal than in-line machine code. The second part of this chapter will cover the other, more common technique: writing files in assembly language and linking them in as modules. This is the first step in building your own library of assembly-language Pascal functions to link in.

# Linking in External Files

We have to learn a little about about linking under assembly language before we can link our own streamlined code into Pascal. We will use a simple example—a small program that uses INT 21H service 9 (the writeln() equivalent) to print out the message: Hello, world. Just to make sure we are on solid ground, the first method of printing out "Hello, world." will be familiar to us. We already know how to write a program with one procedure this way:

```
.MODEL SMALL
.CODE
```

```
        ORG      100H
ENTER:  JMP      PRINT
        ALL_OK   DB "Hello, world.$"
PRINT   PROC     NEAR                       ←
        MOV      DX,OFFSET ALL_OK
        MOV      AH,9
        INT      21H
        INT      20H
PRINT   ENDP                                ←
        END      ENTER
```

This works well, and it's a method we're familiar with. If we had more to do, then we might want to call a subprocedure. We've seen how this works as well: Both procedures are in the same file, and one calls the other. We can even put the data into the subprocedure:

```
        .MODEL SMALL
        .CODE
        ORG      100H
ENTER:
PRINT   PROC     NEAR
        CALL     SUB_PRINT
        INT      20H
PRINT   ENDP

SUB_PRINT        PROC NEAR
        JMP      GO
        ALL_OK   DB "Hello, world.$"        ←
GO:     MOV      DX,OFFSET ALL_OK
        MOV      AH,9
        INT      21H
        RET
SUB_PRINT        ENDP
        END      ENTER
```

When we call SUB_PRINT, the first instruction we encounter is JMP GO. That means that we pass over the data and move on to the instructions. Putting purely local data into the procedure that uses it makes sense, and, if you have a lot of procedures, is a good idea.

## Linking

Now we're going to start working with two files and linking them together. Let's break our example up into separate files:

File 1

```
         .MODEL SMALL
         .CODE
         ORG     100H
 ENTER:
PRINT    PROC    NEAR
         CALL    SUB_PRINT
         INT     20H
 PRINT   ENDP
         END     ENTER
```

File 2

```
         .MODEL SMALL
         .CODE
 SUB_PRINT       PROC NEAR
         JMP     GO
         ALL_OK  DB "Hello, world.$"
 GO:     MOV     DX,OFFSET ALL_OK
         MOV     AH,9
         INT     21H
         RET
 SUB_PRINT       ENDP
         END
```

The first thing you might notice is that while the code in both files is enclosed in .CODE definitions, the END ENTER statement and the ORG 100H statements are in the first file only. This is because the whole program can have only one entry point, which we have called ENTER in file 1. In addition, it is clear that since we want the files to end up one after the other in memory like this:

```
        ORG     100H
ENTER:
PRINT   PROC    NEAR
        CALL    SUB_PRINT
        INT     20H
PRINT   ENDP

SUB_PRINT       PROC NEAR
        JMP     GO
        ALL_OK  DB "Hello, world.$"
GO:     MOV     DX,OFFSET ALL_OK
        MOV     AH,9
        INT     21H
        RET
SUB_PRINT       ENDP
```

that we cannot have ORG 100H in the second file.

Now, to link the files, we have to inform the assembler that the procedure SUB_PRINT won't be found in file 1—it will be linked in later. We can do this with an EXTRN directive (just like the corresponding external declaration in Pascal).

To declare a label as EXTRN, you have to tell the assembler what kind of label it is, NEAR or FAR. This way, it can leave the proper length in the code for the address—one word or two—which the linker fills in later. NEAR is for labels that need only one word (offset) addresses because they are in the same segment, and FAR is for two word addresses. An EXTRN statement might look like this, for example:

```
EXTRN    LABEL_1:NEAR, LABEL_2:FAR
```

In addition, we have to do something we wouldn't have to do in Pascal—we have to declare SUB_PRINT as PUBLIC in file 2. The assembler does not save actual labels used in the program as Pascal does. If we want to save a label for the linker's use later, we have to explicitly do so. Here is how our new files look:

File 1

```
EXTRN    SUB_PRINT:NEAR    ←
.MODEL SMALL
.CODE
         ORG      100H
ENTER:
PRINT    PROC     NEAR
         CALL     SUB_PRINT
         INT      20H
PRINT    ENDP
         END      ENTER
```

File 2

```
PUBLIC   SUB_PRINT  ←
.MODEL SMALL
.CODE
SUB_PRINT         PROC NEAR
         JMP      GO
         ALL_OK   DB "Hello, world.$"
GO:      MOV      DX,OFFSET ALL_OK
         MOV      AH,9
         INT      21H
         RET
SUB_PRINT         ENDP
         END
```

They are all set to be linked. We can link them into one .COM file; first we assemble FILE1.ASM and FILE2.ASM, like this (under MASM):

```
C>MASM FILE1;

Microsoft (R) Macro Assembler Version 5.10
Copyright (C) Microsoft Corp 1981, 1988.  All rights reserved.


  50106 + 31315 Bytes symbol space free

      0 Warning Errors
      0 Severe  Errors

C>MASM FILE2;

Microsoft (R) Macro Assembler Version 5.10
Copyright (C) Microsoft Corp 1981, 1988.  All rights reserved.


  50260 + 31161 Bytes symbol space free

      0 Warning Errors
      0 Severe  Errors
```

Then we link them together with the program LINK like this:

```
C>LINK FILE1+FILE2;

Microsoft (R) Overlay Linker  Version 3.64
Copyright (C) Microsoft Corp 1983-1988.  All rights reserved.

LINK : warning L4021: no stack segment
```

This generates an .EXE file named FILE1.EXE. We can take FILE1.EXE, run it through EXE2BIN to create the .COM file, and finally run it:

```
C>EXE2BIN FILE1 FILE1.COM

C>FILE1
Hello, world.
```

We've linked two files together. Using the Turbo assembler, the process is identical, except for one small detail: The label ENTER, which we've used in file 1, is a reserved keyword for 80286 and later microprocessors under MASM, and in TASM at all times. Instead of ENTER, we rename the label ENTER_1:

File 1

```
EXTRN    SUB_PRINT:NEAR
.MODEL SMALL
.CODE
        ORG     100H
ENTER_1:                        ←
PRINT   PROC    NEAR
        CALL    SUB_PRINT
        INT     20H
PRINT   ENDP
        END     ENTER_1         ←
```

File 2

```
PUBLIC  SUB_PRINT
.MODEL SMALL
.CODE
SUB_PRINT       PROC NEAR
        JMP     GO
        ALL_OK  DB "Hello, world.$"
GO:     MOV     DX,OFFSET ALL_OK
        MOV     AH,9
        INT     21H
        RET
SUB_PRINT       ENDP
        END
```

And we're all set. We just use TASM on both files:

```
C>TASM FILE1;
Turbo Assembler  Version 1.0  Copyright (c) 1988 by Borland International

Assembling file:   FILE1.ASM
Error messages:    None
Warning messages:  None
Remaining memory:  381k


C>TASM FILE2;
Turbo Assembler  Version 1.0  Copyright (c) 1988 by Borland International

Assembling file:   FILE2.ASM
Error messages:    None
Warning messages:  None
Remaining memory:  381k  H
```

And then TLINK with the same syntax as we used with LINK:

```
C>TLINK FILE1+FILE2;

Turbo Link  Version 2.0  Copyright (c) 1987, 1988 Borland International
Warning: no stack
```

Finally, we use EXE2BIN as before and run the program:

```
C>EXE2BIN FILE1 FILE1.COM

C>FILE1
Hello, world.
```

Now that we've seen how to link assembly language to assembly language, let's begin to take a look at the process of linking assembly language to Pascal.

# Linking Assembly Language Functions to Pascal

Let's start off with an example right away. Before we do any stack manipulations (picked passed parameters off the stack), we can begin with a simple function that just returns an integer value in AX. One example might be a function named VIDMODE, which uses service 0FH of INT 10H to find the video mode.

Here's the Pascal code that might call VIDMODE:

```
program screener(input, output);
function vidmode(a:integer):integer; extern;
begin
        writeln("The video mode is: ",vidmode(0));
end.
```

We pass a dummy parameter to VIDMODE to satisfy the compiler. This value will just be zero, and we will ignore it. This is what VIDMODE.ASM might look like:

```
        .MODEL   LARGE
        .CODE
                 PUBLIC   VIDMODE          ;For Pascal Interface
        VIDMODE  PROC
                 PUSH     BP
                 MOV      BP,SP

                 PUSH     SI
                 PUSH     DI
                 PUSH     DS

→                MOV      AH,0FH
→                INT      10H
→                MOV      AH,0
```

```
                POP     DS
                POP     DI
                POP     SI

                POP     BP
                RET     2
VIDMODE         ENDP
                END
```

You might note a few things here; we had to declare VIDMODE as PUBLIC, of course. Next, notice that we had to end with RET 2—this special instruction pops an extra word off the stack (i.e., 2 bytes) before returning. This word is the dummy parameter that Pascal pushed onto the stack—we are responsible for taking care of that word before returning.

Finally, note that we used the LARGE memory model. This assembly language function was written for Microsoft Pascal under the LARGE model; in general, we will have to match the memory model used in our assembly language code to that of the Pascal program we want to link to.

## Matching the Memory Model

Defining a memory model is crucial, both to use the simplified segment directives and to link to a high level language. These models set the allowable sizes of the code and data areas. The memory model must match that defined in the high level language program itself, because calls or data references will have to use one or two word addresses depending on the model used.

Until now, we've used only the SMALL memory model, but all the memory model definitions appear in Table 6.3.

Table 6.3 Memory Models

| *Model* | *Means* |
|---|---|
| TINY | .COM file format |
| SMALL | All data fits in one 64K segment, all code fits in one 64K segment. (This means that both data and code can be accessed as near). |
| MEDIUM | All data fits in one 64K segment, but code may be greater than 64K. |
| COMPACT | Data may be greater than 64K (but no single array may be), code must be less than 64K. |
| LARGE | Both data and code may be greater than 64K, but no single array may be. |
| HUGE | Data, Code, and data arrays may be greater than 64K. |

Let's sum up the information in Table 6.3:

| *Model* | *DATA vs. 64K* | *CODE vs. 64K* | *Arrays vs. 64K* | |
|---|---|---|---|---|
| TINY | < | < | < | (One common segment) |
| SMALL | < | < | < | |
| MEDIUM | < | > | < | |
| COMPACT | > | < | < | |
| LARGE | > | > | < | |
| HUGE | > | > | > | |

Using memory models, you can set the size limits of the code and data areas for your program. Use the same model in the Pascal and assembly source codes. What model you will need depends on the compiler that you will be using. Usually, you can specify the memory model that you want the compiler to use. When you do, the size of the addresses used for code and for data references is set.

When you use Turbo Pascal, the whole process is made very easy; you don't have to declare a memory model size at all—just use the TASM directive .MODEL TPASCAL, as we'll do below.

## Reading Passed Parameters From the Stack

The whole process of reading passed parameters has been made easier by the new extended PROC and .MODEL directives as we will see soon. However, it is important that you know in detail what is going on when we take parameters off the stack, so let's work through an example the hard way first.

To take parameters off the stack, our strategy will be the same one that library routines normally use—instead of actually popping parameters off the stack, we will make a copy of the stack pointer, SP, in the BP register. BP is a new register for us; it can be used as a base pointer, which means using indirect addressing like this: MOV AX,SS:[BP], while SP cannot.

In fact, not only can we have instructions like this:

```
MOV     AX,SS:[BP]
```

but we can also have instructions like this:

```
MOV     AX,SS:[BP+8]
```

where we can use the BP pointer as a base and simply pick off words from the stack by adding immediate values to BP. Using BP this way will make it easy to retrieve parameters from the stack without a confusing number of pops and pushes.

> This method of adding immediate numbers will work with *any* form of indirect addressing, [BX] included.

For example, let's return to our Pascal function summer(). If we had this line in the Pascal program:

```
         program add1(input, output);
         function summer(a,b:integer):integer; external;
         var
                 a:integer;
                 b:integer;
         begin
                 a := 3;
                 b := 2;
→                writeln("3 + 2 = ",summer(a,b));
         end.
```

Then Pascal will push the parameters on the stack and then call summer(), like this:

```
PUSH    3
PUSH    2
CALL    SUMMER
```

When we arrive at our procedure summer(), this is what the stack would look like (here we are assuming Pascal integer format for the parameters 3 and 2, which means that they are each stored as one word):

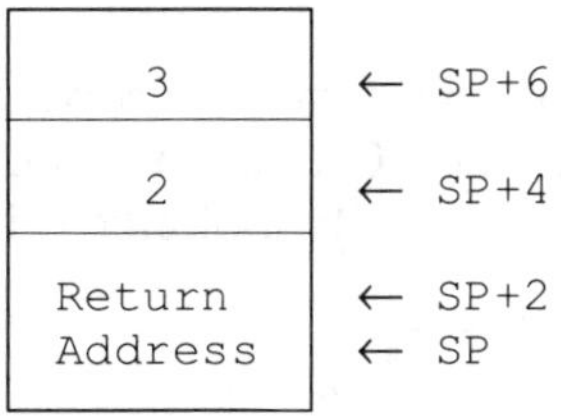

```
+-----------+
|     3     |  ← SP+6
+-----------+
|     2     |  ← SP+4
+-----------+
|  Return   |  ← SP+2
|  Address  |  ← SP
+-----------+
```

Keep in mind that the stack "grows" downwards in memory. That is, SP is decremented *by 2* every time you push something onto the stack. This means that 3 is pushed first:

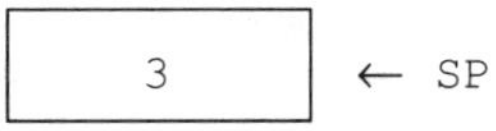

```
+-----------+
|     3     |  ← SP
+-----------+
```

Then 2:

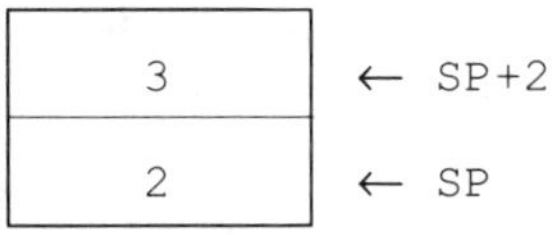

```
+-----------+
|     3     |  ← SP+2
+-----------+
|     2     |  ← SP
+-----------+
```

And then the call is made. Whenever a CALL is executed, the return address is pushed onto the stack: A one word (offset) address is pushed if the call is NEAR, and a two-word (four-byte) address if the call is FAR.

For example, under the LARGE model in Microsoft Pascal, the return address will be FAR. A FAR return address takes up two words, so, when we arrive at SUMMER, this is what we will see:

|  | |
|---|---|
| 3 | ← SP+6 |
| 2 | ← SP+4 |
| Return Address | ← SP+2<br>← SP |

## Using BP

We will first make a backup copy of BP by pushing it onto the stack and then loading it with the current value of SP. That is, the first two lines of SUMMER will look like this:

```
SUMMER  PROC    FAR
PUSH    BP      ←
MOV     BP,SP   ←
 :
```

Doing this is standard. It provides us with a copy of SP in BP, which can now be used to pick parameters off the stack. On the other hand, it also means that the stack that we will have to deal with will really look like this:

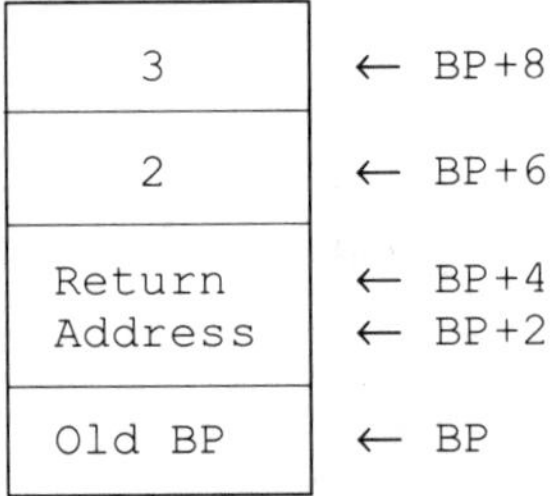


Now if we wanted to, we can just pick the parameters off the stack. In our procedure summer(), we can place the first parameter (3) into AX and the second parameter (2) into BX like this:

```
SUMMER  PROC    FAR
PUSH    BP
MOV     BP,SP
MOV     AX,[BP+8]       ←
MOV     BX,[BP+6]       ←
 :
```

It's easy enough; the only real trouble is keeping track of the number to add to BP.

On the other hand, the high level language usually assumes that some of the registers passed to you with the call will be preserved. At a minimum, you should preserve DI, SI, and DS. Here is what SUMMER looks like with those pushes added:

```
SUMMER  PROC    FAR
        PUSH    BP
        MOV     BP,SP

        PUSH    SI          ←
        PUSH    DI          ←
        PUSH    DS          ←

        MOV     AX,[BP+8]
        MOV     BX,[BP+6]
        :
```

And in the end, before leaving the program, we'll want to restore the saved registers:

```
SUMMER  PROC    FAR
        PUSH    BP
        MOV     BP,SP

        PUSH    SI
        PUSH    DI
        PUSH    DS

        MOV     AX,[BP+8]
        MOV     BX,[BP+6]
        :

        POP     DS          ←
        POP     DI          ←
        POP     SI          ←
```

Note that even though we used the stack here (to save registers with), we did not change the numbers added to BP (e.g., MOV AX,[BP+8] did not change). This is because the value stored in BP has not changed. Although SS:SP is changing, the location pointed to by SS:BP doesn't. If we don't change BP throughout our program, we are free to use the stack as we wish and still use the offsets developed in the examples coming up.

## Returning Data in SUMMER

In our function summer(), we want to return a Pascal integer value, so we will use AX. We have loaded the first parameter (that is, a value of 3) into AX and the second parameter (2) into BX. We can just ADD AX,BX like this:

```
SUMMER  PROC    FAR
        PUSH    BP
        MOV     BP,SP

        PUSH    SI
        PUSH    DI
        PUSH    DS

        MOV     AX,[BP+8]
        MOV     BX,[BP+6]

        ADD     AX,BX     ←

        POP     DS
        POP     DI
        POP     SI
```

In Pascal, we have to make sure that we pop the parameters off the stack at the end of the procedure or function. This means that we will have to end SUMMER with a RET # instruction, where # is the number of bytes that we pushed onto the stack before the call to SUMMER was made.

In other words, when control returns to the calling program, there should be nothing extra on the stack. Here's how the stack looks when we're ready to return in SUMMER (this is after we've restored DS, DI, and SI):

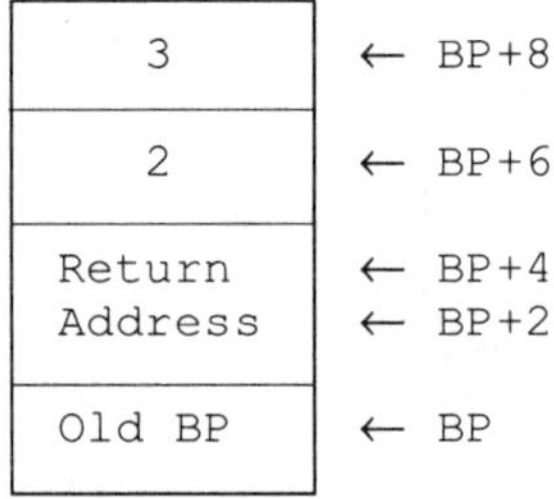


(The first value that would be popped off is at the bottom, Old BP). A normal FAR RET will pop the two words of return address, but we still have four bytes of parameters to release. So, we will do this: first, restore BP with POP BP, then issue a RET 4 instruction.

RET 4 not only returns us to the calling program, but also pops four additional bytes (two words) off the stack. These words go nowhere—they will not be stored in a register. So this is how we end SUMMER:

```
SUMMER  PROC    FAR
        PUSH    BP
        MOV     BP,SP

        PUSH    SI
        PUSH    DI
```

```
        PUSH    DS

        MOV     AX,[BP+8]
        MOV     BX,[BP+6]

        ADD     AX,BX

        POP     DS
        POP     DI
        POP     SI

        POP     BP          ←
        RET     4           ←
SUMMER  ENDP
```

And now SUMMER is ready to be linked into a Pascal program as a function.

# A Better Way

The preceding method was the hard way. Although programmers should be familiar with what goes on with the stack, many of those details can now be made automatic.

Here we are going to use the new MODEL and the newly "extended" (under MASM 5.1 or TASM 1.0) PROC directive. There has been a significant effort to make linking in assembly language even easier. Let's revise SUMMER.ASM. First, we start by specifying that not only is the model SMALL but also that we are using the Pascal calling convention, like this:

```
.MODEL  SMALL, PASCAL ←
        :
        :
```

Other languages you could use here include C, FORTRAN, and BASIC. With Turbo Pascal (only), you can simply say .MODEL TPASCAL in your TASM source file:

```
.MODEL  TPASCAL ←
        :
        :
```

With any other language under TASM, you need to supply the model size and the name (FORTRAN, BASIC, C). Turbo Pascal is the exception.

Let's use Turbo Pascal for this example (the assembly language code will be the same for MASM, except that .MODEL TPASCAL becomes .MODEL SMALL, PASCAL). The next line looks like this:

```
.MODEL   TPASCAL

.CODE
        PUBLIC   SUMMER  ←     ;For Pascal Interface
                 :
                 :
```

Now we declare the procedure by adding more than the usual information after PROC. It looks like this:

```
.MODEL   TPASCAL

.CODE
        PUBLIC   SUMMER          ;For C Interface
SUMMER PROC NEAR USES DI SI, VALUE1:WORD, VALUE2:WORD  ←
        :
        :
```

This will save us a lot of time: We are indicating that PROC is a NEAR procedure that uses the registers DI and SI (note that there are no commas separating them above). MASM or TASM will automatically add the needed pushes and pops to our function to save and restore those registers. Next, we list the arguments passed to SUMMER, in the order they appear in the Pascal call and with the names we will call them in our assembly-language program.

We specify that two parameters are passed, which we refer to as VALUE1 and VALUE2, and that they are both words. Other variable types you could use instead of WORD include BYTE, DWORD, and QWORD (for quad word). The assembler will generate the correct [BP+n] expression whenever we refer to those names from now on, automatically. Here is the rest of our program:

```
.MODEL   TPASCAL

.CODE
SUMMER PROC NEAR USES DI SI, VALUE1:WORD, VALUE2:WORD
        PUBLIC   SUMMER          ;For PASCAL Interface

        MOV      AX,VALUE1
        ADD      AX,VALUE2

        RET
SUMMER ENDP
        END
```

That's it—that's all there is to it. Compare this to our earlier version, and we can see that this new method of using PROC and MODEL saves a lot of time. In particular, note that we can now refer to passed parameters by the names we have given them:

```
.MODEL   TPASCAL

.CODE
SUMMER PROC NEAR USES DI SI, VALUE1:WORD, VALUE2:WORD
        PUBLIC   SUMMER         ;For PASCAL Interface

        MOV      AX,VALUE1 ←
        ADD      AX,VALUE2 ←

        RET
SUMMER ENDP
        END
```

Also, we ended with a simple RET, not a RET #. The assembler (TASM in this case) can put in the correct RET instruction because it now knows what has been passed on the stack.

> Note also that although we specified that we were using SI and DI, that was for demonstration purposes only—we didn't in fact use them in our program, so we didn't have to save them.

This new way of dealing with passed parameters is so much easier that you should use it as often as you can (that is, unless more detailed stack work is required).

Here's what the Turbo Pascal program would look like that calls SUMMER; it is the same as before, except that we had to add the directive {$L summer.obj} so the assembled SUMMER would be linked in:

```
        program add1(input, output);
        function SUMMER(a,b:integer):integer; external;
→       {$L summer.obj}
        var
                a:integer;
                b:integer;
        begin
                a := 3;
                b := 2;
                writeln("3 + 2 = ",SUMMER(a,b));
        end.
```

# How About Data?

That approach is fine if, like summer(), we don't use any data in our assembly language functions. If we do, however, we can use one of two approaches. We can bury the data in the code segment as we did in file 2 above:

File 2

```
PUBLIC  SUB_PRINT
.MODEL SMALL
.CODE
SUB_PRINT        PROC NEAR
        JMP      GO
        ALL_OK   DB "Hello, world.$"   ←
GO:     MOV      DX,OFFSET ALL_OK
        MOV      AH,9
        INT      21H
        RET
SUB_PRINT        ENDP
        END
```

However, that is a little clumsy, and it limits us to the use of the the code segment for our data. On the other hand, Microsoft or Turbo Pascal programs use a data segment, and we can put our data into their data segment with the *.DATA* directive. When linked this way, all the data goes into the same data segment.

The regrettable part is that, unlike other languages like C, you cannot declare initialized data in the .DATA segment when you are linking to a Pascal program. In other words, you might originally think that a program like this might be useful for printing messages:

```
         .MODEL TPASCAL
         PUBLIC  PRINT
→        .DATA
→        ALL_OK  DB "Hello, world.$"

         .CODE
PRINT    PROC    NEAR
         MOV     DX, OFFSET ALL_OK
         MOV     AH,9
         INT     21H
         RET
PRINT    ENDP
         END
```

But you will find that it won't work, because you can't declare initialized variables in code to be linked to Pascal.

However, we *can* make use of Pascal variables from our function if we declare those variables *external*. For example, let's change the Pascal program that uses summer to this:

```
program add1(input, output);
function SUMMER(a,b:integer):integer; external;
{$L summer.obj}
var
        a:integer;
        b:integer;
```

```
        begin
                a := 3;
                b := 2;
→               writeln("3 + 2 = ",SUMMER(4, 5));
        end.
```

In other words, although a and b are still 3 and 2, we are passing the values 4 and 5 instead.

To make sure that we still add a and b in SUMMER and not the passed values, we can change SUMMER to read a and b directly out of memory. That means we have to declare them external, like this:

```
        .MODEL  TPASCAL
→       .DATA
                EXTRN A:WORD, B:WORD
→
        .CODE
        SUMMER PROC NEAR USES DI SI, VALUE1:WORD, VALUE2:WORD
                PUBLIC  SUMMER          ;For PASCAL Interface

                MOV     AX,A
                ADD     AX,B

                RET
        SUMMER ENDP
                END
```

Now we can refer to A and B without trouble, like this:

```
        .MODEL  TPASCAL
        .DATA
                EXTRN A:WORD, B:WORD

        .CODE
        SUMMER PROC NEAR USES DI SI, VALUE1:WORD, VALUE2:WORD
                PUBLIC  SUMMER          ;For PASCAL Interface

→               MOV     AX,A
→               ADD     AX,B

                RET
        SUMMER ENDP
                END
```

You can see that there are now two segments being used—one for data and one for code. Beyond that, nothing special is required; we just assemble, compile, and link as before, and the program runs correctly (3 + 2 = 5). That's the way we can reach Pascal data from inside our external code.

## Using Our Own Data

Also, of course, we can use our own data as long as it hasn't been initialized. For example, we can define a word named OUR_DATA like this:

```
        .MODEL   TPASCAL
        .DATA
                 EXTRN A:WORD, B:WORD
→                OUR_DATA DW ?

        .CODE
        SUMMER PROC NEAR USES DI SI, VALUE1:WORD, VALUE2:WORD
                 PUBLIC   SUMMER           ;For PASCAL Interface

                 MOV      AX,A
                 ADD      AX,B

                 RET
        SUMMER ENDP
                 END
```

Now we're free to use that word, and space will be set aside for it in the data segment of the final .EXE file.

Let's try an example where we use data that we set up in the data segment just like that. Here we set up a function named MAX(), which just returns the maximum of two integers. Here's how the Pascal code looks:

```
program checker1(input, output);
function MAX(a:integer;b:integer):integer; external;
{$L max}
var
        a, b : integer;
begin

a := 12;
b := 27;

writeln("The larger of",a," and ",b," is ",MAX(a,b));
end.
```

And the corresponding assembly language program might look like this (note that we are using the extended PROC and MODEL directives):

```
.DATA
INT1    DW      ?       ←
INT2    DW      ?       ←

.CODE
        PUBLIC  MAX
MAX     PROC NEAR USES BX, PARAM1:WORD, PARAM2:WORD
```

```
        MOV     AX,PARAM1
        MOV     INT1,AX
        MOV     AX,PARAM2
        MOV     INT2,AX

        MOV     AX,INT1
        CMP     AX,INT2
        JA      OVER
        MOV     AX,INT2

OVER:   RET
MAX     ENDP
        END
```

Here we move integers in and out of the data segment. We load INT1 and INT2 by referring to them as PARAM1 and PARAM2, then load them into memory, compare them, and return the larger one in AX. As you can see, using data is pretty easy, except for the restriction on initialized data. All we have to do is to put it into the data segment and use it as we have been in our usual assembly-language programs. That's all there is to linking our assembly-language procedures in as Pascal functions.

These techniques, of course, take practice. And, if speed and size are important, these techniques can be invaluable. With time, you may develop many specialized assembly language routines, able to emulate Pascal functions or procedures, and all ready to be linked in.

# 7

# Fast Math

Computers were made to do at least one thing well—work with numbers. A large part of the 80x86 instruction set is set up exclusively to handle numbers. We will meet some of these instructions in this chapter, like IMUL, IADD, ADC, SHR, NOT, NEG, SBB, ROR, and others. In fact, we will discover that there is a whole new way of looking at numbers in the PS/2 or PC—as signed numbers, where we will use conditional jumps like JG and JL, rather than JA and JB. Our picture of what the computer can do in handling numbers will be made complete in this chapter. Let's begin by covering just how signed numbers can be used in the PS/2 and PC.

## Signed Numbers

The 80x86 instructions work only with integer arithmetic—no floating-point calculations. Math coprocessors, like the 8087, are designed to work with huge floating-point numbers. Of course, you can emulate floating-point work on the 80x86 with Pascal, but it is much slower than on the 80x87.

Up to this point, all the numbers we've been using in assembly language have been unsigned whole numbers. A number could range from 0000H to FFFFH and that was it. Unsigned means, really, positive, and positive numbers are only half the story. Temperatures run negative as well as positive, as do budgets or voltages or any number of categories. To keep track of these, any modern computer has to be able to use signed numbers.

### The Sign Bit

The highest bit—the leftmost bit—in a byte or word is used as the sign bit. What makes a number a signed number is whether you pay attention to this bit. In unsigned bytes or words, this bit was always there, certainly—but it was only the highest bit, and had no other significance. To make a number signed you just have to treat it as signed—which means starting to pay attention to the sign bit. To let us treat this bit specially, there are a whole new set of instructions that we will examine here; for example, conditional jumps like JA change to their signed equivalent JG (jump if greater). What's important to realize is that the byte or word looks the same as before—it is the significance that we give to the highest bit that determines whether we are treating it as signed or not. A 1 in the highest bit will mean that the number, if thought of as signed, is negative.

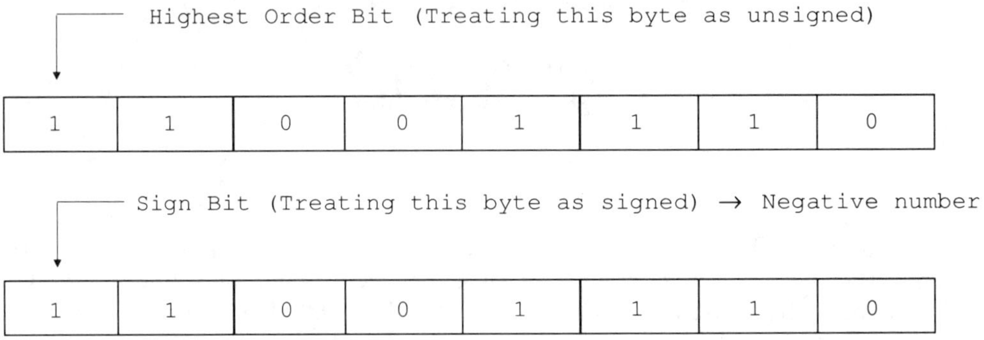

```
┌──── Highest Order Bit (Treating this byte as unsigned)
↓
```

| 1 | 1 | 0 | 0 | 1 | 1 | 1 | 0 |
|---|---|---|---|---|---|---|---|

```
┌──── Sign Bit (Treating this byte as signed) → Negative number
↓
```

| 1 | 1 | 0 | 0 | 1 | 1 | 1 | 0 |
|---|---|---|---|---|---|---|---|

## How Signed Numbers Work

The whole scheme of signed numbers in the 80x86 comes from the simple fact that 1 + (–1) = 0. We realize that if we want to do any calculation with negative numbers in the PS/2 or PC, the number we choose to be –1, when added to 1, has to give 0. Yet this seems impossible. Can you think of an 8-bit number which, when added to 1, will give a result of 0? It seems as if the result must always be 1 or greater.

In fact, if we limit ourselves to the eight bits of the byte, there is an answer. If we add 255 (= 11111111B) and 1:

```
 11111111
      + 1
     ----
100000000
↑
└──── Carry
```

it yields 100000000B; that is, the 8-bit register is left holding 00000000, or 0, and there is a carry, since the 1 is in the $2^8$ place (256), more than the register's capacity to hold. This carry means that the *carry flag* will be set. If we ignore this carry, and look only at the eight bits that fit into the byte, we are left with 00000000B; in other words, FFH + 1 = 0.

This is what happens when we are working with negative numbers: We will ignore the carry flag. The only way it is used is if we explicitly check it (with, for example, JC) and with signed calculations, we ignore the way it is set. Therefore, to us, 11111111B + 1 = 0, when dealing with signed numbers.

## Two's Complement Numbers

It might seem very odd that a number like FFFFH is equal to –1, even if we understand the reasoning. The positive numbers in a byte can range from 00000000B to 01111111B (=127), and there seems to be no problem with that: We can have positive numbers all the way up to the point where the sign bit is set.

But the negative numbers reach from 11111111B = –1 to 10000000B = –128. This seems very odd. On the one hand, we can see that it is true, since 10000000B (–128) + 01111111B (127) = 11111111B (–1), but understanding that the more ones you have in a negative number, the *less* negative it is (–1 is less negative than –128) is difficult.

Let's take a look at a few of these numbers with DEBUG, which provides a way of working in Hex with its Hex, or H, command. We will see that as the numbers get more negative, they seem to decrease in magnitude.

## Using DEBUG's Hex Command

The Hex command is given two numbers, like this: H 0 1. DEBUG both adds and subtracts 0 and 1 and gives you both results. For H 0 1, here is what you would see:

```
C>DEBUG
-H0 1
0001  FFFF
-
```

DEBUG returns both 0 + 1 and 0 – 1:

```
                C>DEBUG
                -H0 1
0+1 = 1  →      0001  FFFF  ←  0-1 = -1 = FFFFH
-
```

We can see that 0 + 1 = 1, and that 0 – 1 = FFFF. Let's take a look at some others:

```
-H0 1              [Subtract 0 - 1]
0001  FFFF         [-1 = FFFF]

-H0 2
0002  FFFE         [-2 = FFFE]

-H0 3
0003  FFFD         [-3 = FFFD]

-H0 4
0004  FFFC         [-4 = FFFC]
```

```
-HO 5
0005   FFFB          [-5 = FFFB]

-HO 80               [-80H = -128 = FF80]
0080   FF80

-HO FFFF             [-(-1) = 1]
FFFF   0001
```

This is the way negative numbers work: It seems that their magnitude is decreasing the more and more negative you get. For example, –1 = FFFFH, but –2 = FFFEH, and –3 = FFFDH. This way of thinking takes a little practice.

> Note that the most negative number you can have for a byte is 80H = –128. Similarly, 8000H is the most negative number you can have in a word, –32768.

## Finding a Two's Complement

As a practical matter, how are these negative numbers found? For instance, if we wanted to know what –109 was, how could we find it? To find –109, we would start with 109 and find what is called its *two's complement*. Two's complement math is the math used in computers—and in Pascal—for dealing with negative numbers. We already know one two's complement: The two's complement of 1 is FFFFH. We can find any number's two's complement easily. We begin by noting that if you take a number like 5, which is 00000101B in binary, then flip all its bits, 11111010B (= FAH), and add the two together, you get all 1s:

```
  00000101  ← 5
+ 11111010  ← 5 with bits flipped [ FAH ]
  --------
  11111111   = FF
```

That is, 5 + FAH = 11111111B. This is close to what we want adding 1 to this sum gives us 0 with a carry. If we ignore the carry, we can see that 5 + FAH + 1 = 0. In other words, adding 5 to (FAH + 1) gives 0 with the (ignored) carry:

```
          5
+ (FAH + 1)
-----------
          0
```

We know that 5 plus –5 equals zero, so –5 must equal (FAH + 1), which is FBH. This is how negative numbers are found. The rule is simple: to find any number's two's complement (and thus to change its sign), just flip the bits and add 1. Thus we see that –1 = Flip(1) + 1 = 11111110B + 1 = 11111111B = FFH (in byte form).

## The NOT and NEG Instructions

To flip the bits in a word or byte, you can use the NOT instruction. For example, if AX was equal to 00000000B, then NOT AX would make AX equal to 11111111B. If BX was equal to 01010101B, then NOT BX would make it 10101010B.

If you NOT a word or byte and then add 1 to the result, you will have that word or byte's two's complement.

There is a special 80x86 instruction that does just this: NEG. NEG is the same as NOT, except that it adds 1 at the end to make a two's complement of the number. If AX held 1, then NEG AX would make it 1111111111111111B or FFFFH.

> Note that NEG flips signs; it doesn't always make signs negative. For example, NEG –1 = 1.

## Ranges

The number of positive numbers you can hold in a word or byte is one less than the number of negative numbers, since 00000000—0—is treated as part of the positive range.

An unsigned byte can hold numbers from 0 to 255. A signed byte can hold numbers from –128 (10000000B = 80H) to 127 (01111111B = 7FH). For words, the unsigned range goes from 0 to 65535. If we treat the word as signed, the range is from –32768 ( = 8000H) to 32767 ( = 7FFFH).

## New Jumps, Not New Numbers

When we decide to use signed numbers, the registers in our machine don't change—they are still the same. The way that we know that we are using signed numbers is by paying special attention to the sign bit and ignoring the carry flag. (In Pascal, by contrast, you let the compiler know that a number is signed by declaring it so.) Besides this, the way we make comparisons will have to change. The way we used to compare two numbers, say FFH (= 11111111B) and 7FH (=01111111B) was with conditional jumps like JA or JB. For example:

```
MOV     AL,11111111B     [FF]
CMP     AL,01111111B     [7F]
JA      AL_BIG
```

If this jump is made, then we'd say that the value in AL, 11111111B, is bigger than the value it's being compared to, 01111111B. That is true if we are using unsigned numbers—FFH is bigger than 7FH. On the other hand, if we want to use signed numbers, we use a new set of conditional jumps that pay attention to the sign. Here, we use JG, or jump if greater:

```
        MOV     AL,11111111B    [ -1  ]
        CMP     AL,01111111B    [ 127 ]
→       JG      AL_BIG
```

The JG instruction sees that 127 is greater than –1. The jump to AX_BIG is NOT made. In this way, we will be able to work with negative as well as positive numbers.

For all the comparison jumps, there is both an unsigned and a signed version. *Above* becomes *greater* and *below* becomes *less*. You can see them in Table 7.1.

Table 7.1 Corresponding Jumps for Unsigned And Signed Numbers

| | *Unsigned* | | *Signed* |
|---|---|---|---|
| JA | Jump if Above | JG | Jump if Greater |
| JNA | Jump if Not Above | JNG | Jump if Not Greater |
| JB | Jump if Below | JL | Jump if Less |
| JNB | Jump if Not Below | JNL | Jump if Not Less |
| JAE | Jump if Above or Equal | JGE | Jump if Greater or Equal |
| JNAE | Jump if Not Above or Equal | JNGE | Jump if Not Greater or Equal |
| JBE | Jump if Below or Equal | JGE | Jump if Greater or Equal |
| JNBE | Jump if Not Below or Equal | JNLE | Jump if Not Less or Equal |

> The N jumps, like JNA and JNB—the N means not. JNA means Jump if Not Above (an unsigned comparison) and JNB means Jump if Not Below (also an unsigned comparison).

Now we've got a pretty good idea how negative numbers work in the PC and PS/2. Here's an example: Let's say we want a program to take the number stored at the memory location NUMBER and put its absolute value at ABS_VAL. We start with a normal .COM file shell:

```
        .MODEL  SMALL
        .CODE
        ORG     100H
ENTRY:  JMP     PROG
        NUMBER  DW -10
        ABS_VAL DW ?
PROG    PROC    NEAR


        INT     20H
PROG    ENDP
        END     ENTRY
```

(As you can see, we can use DW with negative as well as positive numbers. The two's complement is automatically put in.) Our first step is to load NUMBER into

AX. Then we test it: If it is less than zero, we use NEG. Otherwise, we just store it at ABS_VAL:

```
          .MODEL SMALL
          .CODE
          ORG       100H
ENTRY:    JMP       PROG
          NUMBER    DW -10
          ABS_VAL   DW ?
PROG      PROC      NEAR
          MOV       AX,NUMBER          ←
          CMP       AX,0               ←
          JG        LOAD_ABS_VAL       ←
          NEG       AX                 ←
LOAD_ABS_VAL:                          ←
          MOV       ABS_VAL,AX         ←
          INT       20H
PROG      ENDP
          END       ENTRY
```

This little program will leave 10 in ABS_VAL. We can see that in cases like these, we have to use the signed conditional jump JG, and not the unsigned version, JA (remember that JA treats a number like FFFFH as bigger than a number like 0003H).

## The Overflow Flag

There is still a problem with this scheme. Having so cavalierly done away with the carry flag, we've left ourselves without a means of checking on possible overflows. For instance, if we were to add –1 and –128, the result is –129:

```
  11111111
+ 10000000
----------
  101111111
```

Now, –129 is a more negative number than the most negative a number can be and still be in one byte (–128). The byte is left holding 01111111B, which looks like a positive number, not –129 at all. There is a special, new flag, which is set when a number's sign is inadvertently changed—that is, when the result of some math operation gave a result that could not be held in the byte or word's two's complement capacity.

This flag is the *overflow flag*. Before, when we were concerned about the possible size of a result, we could use the carry flag:

```
        ADD       AX,BX
→       JC        TOO_BIG
```

If adding AX and BX gave an unsigned number greater than FFFFH, the carry flag would be set, and, checking it, we could make the appropriate corrections.

When dealing with signed numbers, the overflow flag is used in the same way, with JO (Jump if Overflow) and JNO (Jump if No Overflow):

```
        ADD     AX,BX
→       JO      SIGN_CHANGED
```

If we are worried that the result of a calculation exceeded legal size, we can check with the overflow flag this way.

## Signed Multiplication—IMUL

We've already seen MUL and DIV; the 80x86 also can do multiplication and division that will keep track of the correct sign. These two commands are IMUL and IDIV.

> For accuracy, you might sometimes want to use all bits in a word, even the sign bit. In that case, you should use unsigned numbers, but keep track of the sign yourself, adjusting it correctly at the end of the calculation.

IMUL is the integer multiply instruction. Fundamentally, it is just like MUL, but it works with signed numbers. If you say:

```
IMUL    CL
```

then the microprocessor will multiply AL * CL (including signs) and put the result in (the full 16 bits of) AX. If you say:

```
IMUL    CX
```

then the microprocessor will multiply AX * CX (including signs, of course) and put the result into DX:AX. Let's give this a try by multiplying 5 by –1. We already know that –5 = FBH, so we expect that as an answer. In byte multiplication, you end with a full word answer, so we expect a result of FFFBH.

Changing the byte FBH into the word FFFBH is called *sign extending* it. To sign extend a positive number, pad it on the left with zeros; to sign extend a negative number, pad it on the left with ones. The byte representation of –5 is FBH, the word representation is FFFBH, and the doubleword representation is FFFF:FFFBH.

In DEBUG, we load the registers—let's use BL—assemble an IMUL BL, and then trace through it:

```
A>DEBUG

-RAX                ← Load AL with 5
AX 0000
:5
-RBX                ← Load BL with -1
```

```
BX 0000
:FF
-A100
0EF1:0100 IMUL    BL      ← Get our IMUL instruction ready
0EF1:0102
-R
AX=0005  BX=00FF  CX=0000  DX=0000  SP=FFEE  BP=0000  SI=0000  DI=0000
DS=0EF1  ES=0EF1  SS=0EF1  CS=0EF1  IP=0100   NV UP EI PL NZ NA PO NC
0EF1:0100 F6EB          IMUL    BL
-
```

And we're all ready to trace through IMUL and multiply 5 by –1. Here's the result:

```
-R
AX=0005  BX=00FF  CX=0000  DX=0000  SP=FFEE  BP=0000  SI=0000  DI=0000
DS=0EF1  ES=0EF1  SS=0EF1  CS=0EF1  IP=0100   NV UP EI PL NZ NA PO NC
0EF1:0100 F6EB          IMUL    BL
-T                     ← Trace through IMUL

    ↓

AX=FFFB  BX=00FF  CX=0000  DX=0000  SP=FFEE  BP=0000  SI=0000  DI=0000
DS=0EF1  ES=0EF1  SS=0EF1  CS=0EF1  IP=0102   NV UP EI PL ZR AC PE NC
0EF1:0102 0402          ADD    AL,02
-Q
```

The result, as expected, is FFFBH, the word representation of –5.

Just to see what happens, let's multiply the two bytes FFH (–1) by FFH (–1). We expect an answer of 1 to show up in AX:

```
A>DEBUG

-RAX            ← Load AL with -1
AX 0000
:FF
-RBX            ← Load BL with -1
BX 0000
:FF
-A100
0EF1:0100 IMUL    BL      ← Get ready to IMUL them.
0EF1:0102
-R
AX=00FF  BX=00FF  CX=0000  DX=0000  SP=FFEE  BP=0000  SI=0000  DI=0000
DS=0EF1  ES=0EF1  SS=0EF1  CS=0EF1  IP=0100   NV UP EI PL NZ NA PO NC
0EF1:0100 F6EB          IMUL    BL               ← All set. Let's Trace.
-T
    ↓

AX=0001  BX=00FF  CX=0000  DX=0000  SP=FFEE  BP=0000  SI=0000  DI=0000
DS=0EF1  ES=0EF1  SS=0EF1  CS=0EF1  IP=0102   NV UP EI PL ZR NA PE NC
0EF1:0102 0402          ADD    AL,02
-Q
```

And we find that IMUL handled the sign correctly, –1 * –1 = 1.

## The IDIV Instruction

IDIV is the corresponding signed division instruction. Again, you use it just like DIV, but the signs are kept track of automatically.

If you say:

```
IDIV    CL
```

then AX/CL is calculated and the result goes into AL and the remainder into AH. If you say:

```
IDIV    CX
```

then, as before, DX:AX/CX is calculated; the result goes into AX and the remainder into DX.

| What's wrong with an instruction like IDIV DX?

Using IMUL and IDIV can be important if you want to keep track of signs. Keep in mind that, once you choose, stick with using IMUL and IDIV throughout your program—FFFFH looks like –1 to IMUL and IDIV, but it looks like a big number to MUL and DIV. If you mix these instructions, you'll get mixed results.

# Using the Carry Flag

## ADC—Add with Carry

One word isn't really very long. At best, values up to 65535 can be stored. Can you imagine a calculator that could work only with numbers up to 65535? That's only four places of decimal accuracy. If you wanted to enter a number like 90017, you'd be beyond the calculator's range.

That is just what happens in the 80x86. If you are restricted to one-word numbers, then our accuracy is very poor (unless you have a math coprocessor inside your machine). In an effort to help rectify this, Intel added some instructions that let you chain together a number of addition or subtraction instructions by keeping track of the carry bit. ADC is the instruction for adding when the carry bit is involved—ADC means Add with Carry.

ADC is an add instruction you use after ADD. If you wanted to use doubleword numbers (and couldn't take advantage of the 80386's 32-bit registers) like DX:AX and BX:CX, you can still add them together using ADD followed by ADC. What we want is this:

```
   DX:AX
 + BX:CX
 -------
```

And this can be broken down into adding AX and CX first—this might produce a carry—and then adding the possible carry with DX and BX. In assembly language, this is the way you'd do it:

```
ADD      AX,CX
ADC      BX,CX    ←
```

First we add AX and CX in the usual way. If there was a carry, then the carry flag was set. The ADC BX,CX instruction adds the carry flag (1=set, 0= not set) in with the two registers, BX and CX.

Keep in mind that carries in the binary addition of two numbers can be only zeros or ones—you cannot have a carry of three, for example. Thus, the carry flag is adequate to hold the carry bit.

In this way, the carry from the first addition is correctly treated. Keep in mind that the second addition (ADC BX,CX) could have produced a carry as well, and, to be sure, you should check for it. Here's an example that preserves 48-bit accuracy. If we have a program with six memory word locations—A1–A3 and B1–B3—and we wanted to add them like this:

```
   B3:B2:B1
 + A3:A2:A1
 ----------
```

Then our program might look something like this:

```
        .MODEL SMALL
        .CODE
        ORG     100H
ENTRY:  JMP     PROG
        A3      DW      ?       ← Define A1 - A3
        A2      DW      ?
        A1      DW      ?
        B3      DW      ?       ← Define B1 - B3
        B2      DW      ?
        B1      DW      ?
        CARRY   DW      0       ← Possible carry from whole addition
        PROG    PROC    NEAR
        MOV     AX,A1           ← Put A1, A2, A3 into AX, BX, CX
        MOV     BX,A2
        MOV     CX,A3
        MOV     DX,0            ← Clear DX
        ADD     AX,B1           ← First ADD
```

```
        ADC     BX,B2           ← Then ADC
        ADC     CX,B3
        ADC     CARRY,DX        ← Put carry into CARRY.
        INT     20H
PROG    ENDP

        END     ENTRY
```

What happens here is that first we load the memory words A1–A3 into the registers AX, BX, and CX for easy handling. This is because we cannot ADD A1 to B1 directly—you cannot use two memory locations in the same instruction. We have to add a memory location to a register instead. Then we simply use ADD followed by ADC:

```
ADD     AX,B1           ← First ADD
ADC     BX,B2           ← Then ADC
ADC     CX,B3
```

At the very end, we include this line, having previously set DX to zero:

```
ADC     CARRY,DX        ← Put carry into CARRY.
```

All this does is to keep track of the possible carry from the whole addition A3:A2:A1 + B3:B2:B1. If there is a carry, CARRY will end up being 1. If there is no carry, CARRY will be zero.

The carry from the whole calculation could be treated as an error, if you wanted to. If we wanted to add the number held in DX:AX to the number held in BX:CX and both were unsigned (or could be made so by finding their two's complements), we might use these instructions:

```
ADD     AX,CX           [Add DX:AX + BX:CX]
ADC     DX,BX
JC      ERROR
```

We first add the lower 16 bits of both numbers, held respectively in AX and CX. The result is stored in AX. If this answer is too large to hold in 16 bits, there will be a carry and the carry flag will be set. To include that carry in the subsequent addition of the top 16 bits, we use ADC:

```
   ADD     AX,CX           [Add DX:AX + BX:CX]
→  ADC     DX,BX
   JC      ERROR
```

ADC includes the carry, if there was one, in this addition. The final result is stored in DX:AX. In this calculation we aren't prepared for answers longer than 32 bits (although that can be handled with an additional ADC to as many stages as you desire), so if there was a carry after the second addition, we jump to a location marked Error.

## The SBB Instruction

There is a counterpart for subtraction, SBB. SBB means Subtract with Borrow. After subtracting the two operands, it subtracts the carry flag from the result.

If we subtract a big number from a small one, we have to borrow from higher order places. Intel's designers included the SBB, *subtract with borrow,* instruction expressly for this use:

```
     SUB     AX,CX          [Sub DX:AX - BX:CX]
→    SBB     DX,BX
     JC      ERROR
```

Here we are figuring out what DX:AX – BX:CX is:

```
  DX:AX
- BX:CX
  -----
```

First we subtract CX from AX (with SUB AX,CX). If this left the carry flag set, a borrow from a higher place was required. This is taken into account when we use SBB for the second instruction (with SBB DX,BX). The result will be left in DX:AX.

Again, if there is a net carry, we consider it an error and jump to ERROR, although you could handle it another way if you wished.

## Big Time Multiplying

What if we didn't want to limit ourselves to multiplication results that were only two words long? What if what we were doing required more accuracy? We've just seen how to extend addition and subtraction calculations to arbitrary lengths (by the use of ADD, followed by successive ADCs, or SUB followed by SBBs). Can we do the same for MUL and DIV?

The MUL instruction insists that you start out with the AX register. If you say MUL BX, then the 80x86 multiplies AX by BX and leaves the 32-bit result in DX:AX. If we wanted to multiply AX:DX by BX:CX, we must be prepared for a 64-bit result, using up all our registers.

More common when we deal with multiplication of larger numbers is the use of memory locations. We could, for instance, multiply the number Y1:Y0, held in 16-bit words we've named Y1 and Y0, by the number Z1:Z0, locations Z1 and Z0. We would have to be prepared to store our result in four memory words as the number, say, A:B:C:D.

In other words, this is what we want to do:

```
               Y1  :  Y0
             * Z1  :  Z0
             ___________
                   Z0xY0
              +  Z0xY1
              +  Z1xY0
          +  Z1xY1
          ________________
```

$$2^{32}\ Z1xY1 + 2^{16}\ Z0xY1 + 2^{16}\ Z1xY0 + Z0xY0$$

We supply Y1:Y0 and Z1:Z0—what we want to get out is A:B:C:D, and this number is equal to the final line above:

$$A{:}B{:}C{:}D = 2^{32}\ Z1xY1 + 2^{16}\ Z0xY1 + 2^{16}\ Z1xY0 + Z0xY0$$

Let's write a program to do this, giving us four-word multiplication accuracy. We're not going to go through this program step by step—it would be too tedious. All we are doing is mirroring the normal multiplication process anyway. Here's the program; to use it, load Z1:Z0 and Y1:Y0 in the data area. The result will be left in A:B:C:D;

```
        .CODE
        ORG     100H
ENTRY:  JMP     MULTI
        Y0      DW      0
        Y1      DW      0
        Z0      DW      0
        Z1      DW      0
        A       DW      0
        B       DW      0
        C       DW      0
        D       DW      0
MULTI:  MOV     B,0                 ;Multiplies Y1:Y0 by Z1:Z0 to get A:B:C:D
        MOV     A,0
        MOV     AX,Z0
        MUL     Y0
        MOV     D,AX
        MOV     C,DX
        MOV     AX,Z0
        MUL     Y1
        ADD     C,AX
        ADC     B,DX
        ADC     A,0
        MOV     AX,Z1
        MUL     Y0
        ADD     C,AX
        ADC     B,DX
```

```
ADC     A,0
MOV     AX,Z1
MUL     Y1
ADD     B,AX
ADC     A,DX
INT     20H
END     ENTRY
```

By breaking up the result into partial results, we were able to multiply Y1:Y0 by Z1:Z0 to get A:B:C:D. This result is 64 bits long—not bad as far as accuracy is concerned (although the math coprocessor's registers are 80 bits long).

## Big Time Division

In division our path is less smooth. In all three of the previous cases we were able to divide our calculations into sub-parts and then join the results from those parts. Unfortunately, division cannot be dissected that way. We are reduced to dividing on a bit-by-bit level if we want 32-bit accuracy. Here we will use an actual hardware divide algorithm. This algorithm, usually expressed in cryptic computer design language, is not the fastest available, but it is at least intelligible using the model of long division, and it expresses a wonderful economy in the use of registers that is something of an art in itself.

As we have seen, the 80x86 has an internal DIV command that will divide 32 bits (held in the two registers DX:AX) by a 16-bit number (like this: DIV BX, which divides DX:AX by BX) to return a 16-bit result and a 16-bit remainder. However, we want to maintain our 32-bit accuracy, so here we will develop a bit-by-bit divide algorithm that divides a 64-bit number by a 32-bit number, giving powerful 32-bit results and remainders.

To refresh our memories concerning long division, especially in binary, let's work through a short example. Here we will divide 14 by 6. Our answer will, as all division in the PC does, come out in whole numbers as an answer and a remainder. 14/6 will yield an answer of 2 and a remainder of 2. We start here:

```
A | B     →     6 | 14     →     0110 | 1110
```

To keep the example short we'll use only 4 bits and leave using 64 up to the imagination. Our first move is to compare 0110 against progressively more of the number being divided (B above):

```
0110 | 1 110
         ^
```

Since 0110 is bigger than 1, we place a 0 above it and subtract 0 from it:

```
            0  ←
          ------
0110     | 1110
       - 0
        ---
         1
```

and bring down the next digit of B:

```
            0
          ------
0110     | 1110
       - 0|
        --↓-
         11
```

We're now comparing A, 0110, against the first two digits of B, 11. Since 0110 is also bigger than 11, we put in another 0 up on top, subtract 0 from 11 and bring down another digit, a 1:

```
            00   ←
          ------
0110     | 1110
       - 0  |
        ---  |
         11  |
       - 00  |
        ----↓-
         111
```

Now we are comparing A to the first three digits of B, 111, and 0110 goes smoothly into 111 once, so we put a 1 on top, subtract 0110 from 111 and bring down another digit:

```
            001   ←
          ------
0110     | 1110
       - 0    |
        ---   |
         11   |
       - 00   |
        ----  |
         111  |
       - 110  |
        -----↓-
         0010
```

Now we have to compare 0110 to what is left on the bottom, 0010. Since 0110 is greater than 0010, another 0 goes on top:

```
            0010   Answer
          ┌──────
0110      │ 1110
        - 0
        ──
          11
        - 00
        ───
          111
        - 110
        ────
          0010
        - 0000
        ─────
          0010   Remainder
```

which leaves us with a 4-bit answer, 0010 (2) and a 4-bit remainder, 0010 (also 2). To make an algorithm out of this, we have to decide just what it was that we did at each stage. If the problem looked like this:

```
   ┌────
A  │ B
```

then we compared A to progressively more and more of B, the number being divided. If A was bigger than B, we entered a 0 in the answer, but if A was smaller than B, we entered a 1 and subtracted A. We kept going until we had done this four times, once for every bit in B.

## Computerizing Our Example

Since we compare registers easily in the PC, or in computers in general, we can make a leap and say that to compare A to progressively more of B, we can just compare two registers using CMP. All we have to do is to use CMP AX,BX where AX holds A and BX holds B.

To get more and more of B into BX, we can simply shift B into it one bit at a time. Progressively, then, we can compare A to more and more of B as more and more of B appears in BX. If A is bigger than what we have of B, we put 0 in the answer. If A is smaller, then we subtract B – A and put a 1 into the answer.

In other words, if we start off with AX, BX, and CX loaded like this for 14/6 (treating them as only 4-bit registers):

| AX=6 | BX | CX=14 |
|---|---|---|
| 0110 | 0000 | 1110 |

then we start by shifting the first digit into BX this way:

```
AX=6            BX               CX=14
----           ----              -----
0110           0001      ←        110
```

Since we've got a new BX, we compare AX to it and see immediately that AX > BX. This means that the first bit of the answer is 0.

This algorithm does not waste any space whatsoever. It immediately slips this first bit into the newly vacated rightmost bit of CX. When we are all done, the answer will be fully in CX:

```
AX=6            BX               CX=14
----           ----              -----
0110           0001              110 0     ←
                                     ^
```

With the first bit of the answer secure, we shift CX again to the left:

```
AX=6            BX               CX=14
----           ----              -----
0110           0011      ←       10 0
                                    ^
```

and again compare AX to the new part of B we have in BX. Since again AX > BX, another 0 goes into the answer in CX:

```
AX=6            BX               CX=14
----           ----              -----
0110           0011              10 00     ←
                                    ^
```

Now we have to get a new value in BX, and so shift CX left again:

```
AX=6            BX               CX=14
----           ----              -----
0110           0111      ←       0 00
                                   ^
```

Now when we compare AX to BX, we have enough bits in BX to make AX < BX. Just as in our long division example, this means that we subtract A (in AX) from what we have of B (in BX) and put a 1 into the answer this way:

```
AX=6            BX               CX=14
----           ----              -----
0110           0111              0 001     ←
             - 0110                ^
               ----
               0001
```

This leaves a 1 in BX:

```
AX=6        BX         CX=14
----        ----       -----
0110        0001       0 001
                        ^
```

so we shift the final 0 from CX into BX;

```
AX=6        BX            CX=14
----        ----          -----
0110        0010    ←      001
                          ^
```

Since 0110 > 10, we have to finish by putting a 0 into CX:

```
AX=6        BX            CX=14
----        ----          -----
0110        0010           0010   ←
          Remainder       Answer
```

We've now done our comparison four times so we're done. The leftover bits of B that A didn't divide evenly are the remainder, left in BX, and the final answer that we built bit by bit is in CX. In a direct—although maybe not self-evident—way, this algorithm has provided a clever translation of long division into the language of registers and left shifts.

## How Does it Look in Code?

To get this into code that you can use, let us suppose that we want to divide A:B:C:D by Z1:Z0, 64 bits by 32. The quotient will be left in A:B:C:D. The actual divison code is relatively small, and here it is:

```
        ;64 Bit By 32 Bit Division (memory locations A:B:C:D by Z1:Z0)

        MOV     COUNT,64
        XOR     AX,AX           ;Going to divide A:B:C:D by BX:CX
        XOR     DX,DX           ; End up with quotient in A:B:C:D
        MOV     BX,Z1
        MOV     CX,Z0
SHIF:
     ...CALL    SHLA            ;SHL DX:AX:A:B:C:D by 1 place (96 bits !)
     :  CMP     DX,BX
     :  JB      NOT_YET
     :  JA      HIT
     :  CMP     AX,CX           ;DX = BX, Check AX,CX
     :  JB      NOT_YET
HIT: :  SUB     AX,CX
     :  SBB     DX,BX
     :  ADD     D,1       ;Put in a 1 since divisor went into dividend once
NOT_YET:
```

```
:   DEC       COUNT
:   CMP       COUNT,0
:..JNE       SHIF     ;Keep going all 64 times
```

The variable COUNT will serve as a loop index. We begin by clearing the registers AX and DX and loading BX:CX with Z1:Z0: G

```
MOV       COUNT,64
XOR       AX,AX                 ;Going to divide A:B:C:D by BX:CX
XOR       DX,DX                 ; End up with quotient in A:B:C:D
MOV       BX,Z1
MOV       CX,Z0
```

XOR AX,AX, a method that professional programmers use to clear the AX register, can be found in the BIOS listing. No matter what was in AX before, XOR AX,AX will leave it 0.

AX may be set to zero with MOV AX,0, but you often see the instruction XOR AX,AX instead. This instruction is commonly found in the beginning of .EXE files, so let's review XOR here.

XOR is the Exclusive Or instruction, just like the xor operator in Pascal, and it works by taking two words and matching them up bit by bit. If a zero meets a zero, the result is zero. If a one meets a zero, the result is one. But if a one meets a one, the result is zero:

| XOR | 0 | 1 |
|---|---|---|
| 0 | 0 | 1 |
| 1 | 1 | 0 |

When you XOR a number with itself, all ones are sure to meet ones and all zeroes sure to meet zeros, so the result is zero. XOR AX,AX is sure to make the contents of AX zero.

We will gradually shift more and more of A:B:C:D into DX:AX and compare it to BX:CX. As we shift A:B:C:D into DX:AX, we gradually leave zeroes behind us in D. Every time that DX:AX is greater than BX:CX, however, we will put a 1 in instead.

The whole process begins by shifting a bit from A:B:C:D into DX:AX. In other words, we'd like to execute a command like: SHL DX:AX:A:B:C:D,1. In the absence of such a handy command, though, we have to make one for ourselves. Ours will be called SHLA and can be found here:

```
          ;SHLA, a subroutine to shift 96 bits at once

SHLA      PROC     NEAR
          ;Shifts 96 (!!) bits of DX:AX:A:B:C:D left by 1
          PUSH     BX
          PUSH     CX
          MOV      BX,0
          MOV      CX,0
          SHL      D,1                ;Start with rightmost
```

```
            ADC     BX,0            ;Overflow in BX
            SHL     C,1
            ADC     CX,0            ;New overflow in CX, old in BX
            ADD     C,BX
            MOV     BX,0
            SHL     B,1
            ADC     BX,0    ;BX has new overflow, old in CX
            ADD     B,CX
            MOV     CX,0
            SHL     A,1
            ADC     CX,0    ;CX has new overflow, old in BX
            ADD     A,BX
            MOV     BX,0
            SHL     AX,1
            ADC     BX,0    ;BX has new overflow, old in CX
            ADD     AX,CX
            SHL     DX,1    ;Disregard overflow here
            ADD     DX,BX
            POP     CX
            POP     BX
            RET
    SHLA    ENDP
```

When we shift a 16-bit word to the left one place and end up shifting a 1 out to the left, the carry bit gets set. SHLA follows all those carries up the line with ADC, Add with Carry, into successive words, and that accounts for most of its length.

## Comparing DX:AX and BX:CX

After we've shifted the first part of A:B:C:D into DX:AX, we have to compare it to the number we're dividing by, BX:CX. We could use a CMP DX:AX,BX:CX command here. Instead, we'll have to do the same thing 16 bits at a time, starting with the highest bits.

DX>BX: If DX is greater than BX, then DX:AX is definitely greater than BX:CX and we have a "hit," so we move 1 into A:B:C:D. DX<BX: If DX is less than BX, then DX:AX is less than BX:CX, and we will leave the 0 that was shifted into the end.

DX=BX: If, though, DX = BX, then we must check AX and CX. The entire process goes this way:

```
SHIF:    CALL    SHLA            ;SHL DX:AX:A:B:C:D by 1 place (96 bits !)
   →     CMP     DX,BX
         JB      NOT_YET
         JA      HIT
   →     CMP     AX,CX           ;DX = BX, Check AX,CX
         JB      NOT_YET
HIT:     SUB     AX,CX
         SBB     DX,BX
     :   ADD     D,1      ;Put in a 1 since divisor went into dividend once
NOT_YET: [Shift more of A:B:C:D into DX:AX]
```

Note the use of two conditional jumps, one right after the other. Since conditional jumps don't affect the flags that are set, this will work (check your assembler's documentation to learn which commands affect which flags).

If the part we have of A:B:C:D is bigger than what we're dividing by, we want to subtract it by subtracting DX:AX - BX:CX. This is done at the label HIT:

```
HIT:    SUB     AX,CX
        SBB     DX,BX
    :   ADD     D,1        ;Put in a 1 since divisor went into dividend once
```

And we also put a 1 into the end of A:B:C:D. After we've either let the shifted-in 0 stand or put in a 1, we have to go back and shift more of the number we're dividing into DX:AX and decrement the count.

```
SHIF:
    ...[Shift to the left and compare]
    :        :
    :        :
    :  DEC      COUNT
    :  CMP      COUNT,0
    :..JNE      SHIF     ;Keep going all 64 times
```

When you use this algorithm, load the 64-bit number to divide into A:B:C:D, load the number to divide it by into Z1:Z0, and execute the algorithm. The quotient will be left in A:B:C:D, and the remainder in Z1:Z0.

# Bit Manipulations

It is frequently important in assembly language to work with individual bits in a word or byte. As we have seen, the operating system stores information in the bits of specific bytes in its data areas.

There are a number of assembly language instructions that we can use here. The first are our old friends, SHL and SHR.

> The 80386 has a series of *bit test* instructions—BT, BTC, BTR, and BTS—that can be very useful when needed.

## SHR and SHL

These two, SHR and SHL, shift quantities to the right and left, respectively. You can shift a number of times to the right or left; on the 8088 and 8086, as mentioned, if the number of places to shift is greater than one, place it into CL (then use SHR AX,CL). Otherwise, you can say SHR BX,1 or SHL CX,1. On the 80186–80386, you can use any immediate number, and do not need to use CL.

With SHR and SHL, the bit that is opened up is set to zero. For example, if we shift AL to the right one:

```
AL:       10101010
                 :
     Shift to the right by 1 using SHR
                 :
          01010101
              →
```

In addition, the bit that was shifted out by SHR or SHL—here a zero was shifted off the right-hand side—goes into the carry flag. You can test what this bit was with JC or JNC. In fact, this is a common way of checking bit values (recall we did exactly that in our procedure PUT_PIXEL).

```
Shifting Right    AL: 10101010
                           :
                       SHR AL,1
                           :
                      01010101 → 0 → Carry Flag
                           →

Shifting Left     AL: 10101010
                           :
                       SHL AL,1
                           :
Carry Flag ← 1 ← 01010100
                       ←
```

As we know, SHL may be used for multiplication as well. Every time you shift one place to the left, it is the same as multiplying by two. For example, you could multiply AX by 5 (5 = 2 * 2 + 1) this way:

```
MOV     BX,AX    ← Make a copy of AX
SHL     AX,1     ← Multiply it by 2
SHL     AX,1     ← And 2 again to make 4
ADD     AX,BX    ← Add the copy in BX to make 5
```

Since SHL and ADD combinations are *much* faster than ordinary MUL instructions, use them whenver you can. Graphics routines, where time is crucial, usually try to break up math this way.

In the same way, SHR can be used as a crude version of DIV, since shifting to the right once is equivalent to dividing by 2. The remainder of this division will be put into the carry flag.

## SAR and SAL

Instructions SAR and SAL stand for Arithmetic Shift Right and Arithmetic Shift Left. You can use these on signed numbers.

If you shift a number like 01010101B to the left by 1 with SAL, the sign bit will change (since the new number is 10101010B). On the other hand, SAL will set the overflow flag in this case, and you can check it to see if the sign did change. (For some reason, the overflow flag is set only correctly if you shift to the left once—more than that means that the overflow flag will be undefined.)

The SAR instruction preserves the sign of the operand it is shifting to the right. Let's look at the number 10101010B. This can be regarded as a negative number; SAR would have preserved its sign, whereas SHR wouldn't (remember that SHR always sets the newly-opened bit to 0). SAR will place a 1 in the top bit to preserve the sign bit in this case:

```
AL:     10101010
            :
   Shift to the right by 1 using SHR
            :
        11010101
           →
```

Again, the bit that is pushed off either end will go into the carry flag.

```
Arithmetic Shifting Right   AL: 10101010
                                    :
                                SAR AL,1
                                    :
                                 11010101 → 0 → Carry Flag
                                    →

Arithmetic Shifting Left    AL: 10101010
                                    :
                                 SAL AL,1
                                    :
          Carry Flag ← 1 ← 01010100
                                    ←
```

## The Rotate Instructions: RCL, RCR, ROL, and ROR

Four more instructions work on a bit-by-bit level on either bytes or words. These instructions *rotate* words or bytes.

For example, let's examine ROL, rotate left. When ROL is used, the top-most bit, that is, the leftmost bit, is taken out, and all the other bits are shifted to the left by 1. Then the original leftmost bit goes into the rightmost location. It looks like this if we were to ROL AX,1:

ROL AX,1

```
          AX:      0001000100010001 ← Start like this


          AX:       001000100010001 ← Take leftmost bit.
                   :
                   :......0 →

          AX:   ←001000100010001    ← Shift everything left 1.
                   :
                   :......0


          AX:      001000100010001  ← Move original leftmost
                   :              :        bit into bottom place
                   :              :
                   :......0.......:
                            →

          AX:      0010001000100010 ← Yielding this.
```

We can see that 0001000100010001B rotated once to the left becomes 0010001000100010B. Let's do this exact example in DEBUG. We start off with AX = 0001000100010001B = 1111H (since there are four binary digits per hex digit), and we'll ROL a few times by assembling ROL AX,1 starting at 100H:

```
C>DEBUG
-A100
0EF1:0100 ROL     AX,1            ← Set up our ROLs.
0EF1:0102 ROL     AX,1
0EF1:0104 ROL     AX,1
0EF1:0106 ROL     AX,1
0EF1:0108
-RAX                              ← Set up AX to 1111H.
AX 0000
:1111
-R
AX=1111  BX=0000  CX=0000  DX=0000  SP=FFEE  BP=0000  SI=0000  DI=0000
DS=0EF1  ES=0EF1  SS=0EF1  CS=0EF1  IP=0100   NV UP EI PL NZ NA PO NC
0EF1:0100 D1C0          ROL    AX,1      ← Ready to rotate.
-T
```

We can trace through the first ROL AX,1. As we saw, this changed 0001000100010001B to 0010001000100010B. Here's what happens:

```
-R
AX=1111  BX=0000  CX=0000  DX=0000  SP=FFEE  BP=0000  SI=0000  DI=0000
DS=0EF1  ES=0EF1  SS=0EF1  CS=0EF1  IP=0100   NV UP EI PL NZ NA PO NC
0EF1:0100 D1C0          ROL    AX,1      ← Ready to rotate.
-T             ← Rotate AX to the left once.
```

```
    ↓
AX=2222  BX=0000  CX=0000  DX=0000  SP=FFEE  BP=0000  SI=0000  DI=0000
DS=0EF1  ES=0EF1  SS=0EF1  CS=0EF1  IP=0102   NV UP EI PL NZ NA PO NC
0EF1:0102 D1C0          ROL     AX,1
```

The result is 2222H, as it should be; 0010001000100010B = 2222H. We can rotate again to get 4444H, then 8888H; then a final rotation (the fourth) will move the original ones back into place, one hex digit higher. Here it is:

```
-R  ↓
AX=1111  BX=0000  CX=0000  DX=0000  SP=FFEE  BP=0000  SI=0000  DI=0000
DS=0EF1  ES=0EF1  SS=0EF1  CS=0EF1  IP=0100   NV UP EI PL NZ NA PO NC
0EF1:0100 D1C0          ROL     AX,1     ← Ready to rotate.
-T              ← Rotate AX to the left once.
    ↓
AX=2222  BX=0000  CX=0000  DX=0000  SP=FFEE  BP=0000  SI=0000  DI=0000
DS=0EF1  ES=0EF1  SS=0EF1  CS=0EF1  IP=0102   NV UP EI PL NZ NA PO NC
0EF1:0102 D1C0          ROL     AX,1
-T
    ↓
AX=4444  BX=0000  CX=0000  DX=0000  SP=FFEE  BP=0000  SI=0000  DI=0000
DS=0EF1  ES=0EF1  SS=0EF1  CS=0EF1  IP=0104   NV UP EI PL NZ NA PO NC
0EF1:0104 D1C0          ROL     AX,1
-T
    ↓
AX=8888  BX=0000  CX=0000  DX=0000  SP=FFEE  BP=0000  SI=0000  DI=0000
DS=0EF1  ES=0EF1  SS=0EF1  CS=0EF1  IP=0106   OV UP EI PL NZ NA PO NC
0EF1:0106 D1C0          ROL     AX,1
-T
    ↓
AX=1111  BX=0000  CX=0000  DX=0000  SP=FFEE  BP=0000  SI=0000  DI=0000
DS=0EF1  ES=0EF1  SS=0EF1  CS=0EF1  IP=0108   OV UP EI PL NZ NA PO CY
0EF1:0108 CB            RETF
-Q
```

That's how ROL works. ROR works the same way, except that bits are rotated to the right instead. For example, if we rotated 1111H to the right once, we'd end up with 8888H.

<u>ROR AX,1</u>

```
            AX:    0001000100010001 ← Start like this

            AX:    000100010001000  ← Take rightmost bit.
                                  :
                         ← 1.......:
```

```
AX:      000100010001000→   Shift everything right 1.
                       :
               1.......:

AX:      000100010001000 ← Move original rightmost
        :              :       bit into the top place
        :              :
        :......1.......:
          ←

AX:     1000100010001000 ← Yielding this.
```

## Rotating Through the Carry

RCL and RCR are somewhat different. They include the carry flag in their rotations: The bit that is rotated out becomes the new carry flag, and the carry flag is rotated in to take its place. In other words, these instructions rotate *through* the carry flag. Let's look at RCL. If we had 1111H in AX, and 1 in the carry flag (CY), then here's what would happen when we used RCL AX,1:

RCL AX,1

```
AX:     0001000100010001 ← Start like this

                CY        ← CY = 1

AX:  ← 001000100010001 ← Now RCL

        :              1
        :..0    CY......:
        →          →

AX:     0010001000100011 ← Yielding this

                CY        ← CY = 0
```

In this case, we would have gotten 2223H, since the carry flag was rotated in to make the last digit 3, not 2 (and CY became 0).

If you think of the carry flag as the 9th bit of a byte or the 17th bit of a word, then RCL and RCR rotate these 9-bit bytes or 17-bit words. If you want to examine the carry bit or want to move a bit into the carry bit, this is a good way of doing it.

RCR also rotates through the carry flag but to the right. If we had 0 in the carry flag (CY) and 1111H in AX, this is what RCR AX,1 would look like:

RCR AX,1

```
AX:     0001000100010001 ← Start like this

                CY          ← CY = 0

AX:     000100010001000 →   Now RCR
                          :
        0                 :
        :....CY    1....:
        ←          ←

AX:     0000100010001000 ← Yielding this

                CY          ← CY = 1
```

In this case, RCR AX,1 yields 0888H (and CY = 1). Again, with ROL, ROR, RCL, and RCR, you have to specify the number of times to rotate in CL—if that number is greater than 1—on the 8088 and 8086. With the 80186–80386, you can give immediate values.

# Logical Instructions

There is a last class of math instructions in the PS/2 or PC, and those are the logical instructions: AND, OR, and XOR. We'll include another instruction, TEST, in this group because, as we shall see, it operates much like AND.

We have already seen AND and OR in action, at least briefly. Their chief use in assembly language programs is setting (i.e., setting equal to 1), resetting (setting equal to 0) bits in a byte, or testing the value of a certain bit.

AND does a bit-by-bit comparison of the two operands. When the bits meet, here is how AND calculates the result:

| AND | 0 | 1 |
|---|---|---|
| 0 | 0 | 0 |
| 1 | 0 | 1 |

As you can see, both bit 1 *and* bit 2 have to be 1 before the result will be 1. This is a useful property is making up what are called *masks*.

Suppose that we were interested in bit 1 (that is, the 2's place—the rightmost bit is bit 0) of a byte, which we have in AL.

```
                ↓
AL  =  01010111
```

If we wanted to isolate that bit, and check whether it was set, we could AND AL with a *mask*, which was set to this value in binary: 00000010B. In other words, only bit 1 of this mask is set. When we AND AL,00000010B, then all the other bits in AL will meet zeros, and their results will be zero. If the second bit in AL was set, the result of AND AL,00000010B will be 00000010B, or 2. If the bit was *not* set, the result will be 00000000B, or 0.

Masks are a frequently used tool to isolate individual bits. On the other hand, masks can also be used with OR to set bits. OR works like this on a bit-by-bit level:

| OR | 0 | 1 |
|---|---|---|
| 0 | 0 | 1 |
| 1 | 1 | 1 |

In other words, if either bit 1 *or* bit 2 is one, the result of ORing them will be one. In this case, if we had the same mask, 00000010B, we could OR AL,00000010B. All the bits besides bit 1 will meet zeros. If a zero is ORed with a zero, the result is zero. If a one is ORed with zero, the result is one. That is, all the other bits will have their identities preserved. ORing a byte with 00000000 won't change the byte.

But bit 1's place in the mask is already one. This means that—no matter what bit 1 was before—when it is ORed with one, it will become one. No matter what the bit was before, ORing it with one will set it to one. The bit will be set. When used with OR, masks are tools to set bits in a word or byte. We'll use masks in the next chapter. XOR, or Exclusive OR, is another one we have seen. When XORed, two ones will become zero. Also, two zeroes XORed together become zero. Any two of the same thing XORed together will become zero—that means that anything XORed with itself will become zero.

> Note that XOR is identical to OR except when two ones meet.

The TEST instruction is just like AND, except that it doesn't change either operand being ANDed. Instead, all it does is set up the flags so that an appropriate jump may be made. For example,

```
TEST     AL,00000010B
```

will AND AL with 00000010B—as far as the flags are concerned. It won't actually change the value in AL. If bit 1 (the second bit from the right) was zero, TEST AL,00000010B will give a result of zero. We can check this result with a conditional jump that we have seen before—JZ. The JZ conditional jump is taken if some mathematical operation just resulted in a value of zero. For example, if 0 is in AL, the instructions:

```
TEST     AL,00000010B
JZ       AL_BIT_1_IS_ZERO
```

would cause us to jump to the label AL_BIT_1_IS_ZERO. Using TEST, you can check an individual bit in a word or byte—all you have to do is to set the mask correctly—a one in the bit place(s) you want to test, and a zero in all other places. If the bit was set, the result will not be zero; if the bit was not set, the result will be zero. Following TEST by JZ is not an uncommon sight in assembly language code, and it means that a bit or set of bits is being tested to see if they are set.

That's it for math that we can do with the 80x86. Sometimes, this kind of math can save you a lot of time and code size over instructions generated by the compiler. Next, however, we are going to take a look at the math coprocessors, the 80x87 chips, where math really gets some power.

# 8

# Using The 80x87

## Introduction

Over the years, math coprocessor chips, the 80x87s, have caught on. This chapter introduces us to the assembly language instructions they use.

Starting with MASM release 2.0 (and, of course, also included in TASM 1.0), the macro assembler can assemble about 80 80x87 commands. This is an immense improvement over the old days, when you had to include 80x87 machine language in your program explicitly. The 80x87 is the math coprocessor designed and built to function with the 80x86 already inside the PC. As we know, the 80x86 itself has only some math capability—without further programming, it can multiply up to results not larger than 32 bits, and divide numbers of up to only 32 bits by 16 bits, generating a 16-bit quotient and a 16-bit remainder. This type of division means that, unless we do a lot of work, we cannot count on more than 16 bits of accuracy in the result (four decimal places).

Furthermore, the 80x86 can handle only integer arithmetic. If we want to work with floating-point numbers, we have to write our own algorithms and implement them. In general, this is pretty difficult. Floating-point simulations are usually very slow. And that's just the start—we might want to do more, like calculate sines and cosines, logs and natural logs, square roots and powers as well. It is for such a purpose that the 80x87 was designed. The 80x87 can be counted on to make math calculations go hundreds of times faster. And the 80x87 is more accurate.

The internal accuracy of the 80x87 is considerable. There are eight stack registers (it is a stack-oriented chip), and each one is 80 bits long (ten bytes). For integers, this means an accuracy up to 18 digits, and for floating point numbers an accuracy up to 16 digits. If your PC has an 80x87 in it, you too can enjoy this type of accuracy.

# Getting Started

The assembler does not recognize 80x87 commands immediately; instead, you must include a special directive in your .ASM files like this:

```
→       .8087
        .MODEL SMALL
        .CODE
        ORG      100H
                 :
```

Here we are enabling the assembly of 8087 instructions (other directives include .287 and .387).

The assembler not only assembles 80x87 commands, it also includes a WAIT command to the 80x86 for each one (with the exception of one or two special no-wait commands detailed later). This means that the 80x86 will wait until the 80x87 is done processing before proceeding. Control is coordinated automatically between the two chips this way—we won't have to do anything special besides simply place 80x87 instructions in our programs. When we use DEBUG later on, we will see these WAITs.

# Adding Integers

Let's begin immediately with a simple example—adding two integers; in this case, we add 3 and 1. Here's the code:

```
        .8087
        .MODEL SMALL
        .CODE
        ORG     100H
ENTRY:  JMP     PROG
        OPERAND1 DW     3
        OPERAND2 DW     1
        RESULT  DW      0
PROG:   FILD    OPERAND1
        FIADD   OPERAND2
        FISTP   RESULT
        INT     20H
        END     ENTRY
```

Everything looks the same as usual until we get to the body of the program where the 80x87 instructions are:

```
PROG:   FILD    OPERAND1
        FIADD   OPERAND2
        FISTP   RESULT
```

Every 80x87 instruction begins with an F, as these do (and no 80x86 instructions begin with an F). The first instruction,

```
PROG:   FILD    OPERAND1        ←
        FIADD   OPERAND2
        FISTP   RESULT
```

tells the 80x87 to load the integer number at OPERAND1 in memory onto the top of its stack. FILD is the integer load instruction, as opposed to the floating-point load, FLD. The next instruction,

```
PROG:   FILD    OPERAND1
        FIADD   OPERAND2        ←
        FISTP   RESULT
```

is the instruction for integer addition. Floating point addition, which we'll cover later, uses FADD. Here, OPERAND2 is added to the value in the top of the 80x87's stack. This is the result we want, so we store this number in memory, at the location RESULT:

```
PROG:   FILD    OPERAND1
        FIADD   OPERAND2
        FISTP   RESULT          ←
```

This instruction is an integer store (as opposed to FST, the floating-point store) and pop instruction. The number on the top of the stack is stored in memory and then the stack is popped, leaving it free for further operations.

Popping the stack is an important part of any program; if we don't pop it, the stack fills, and our program stops.

We have stored the result in memory, and we can take a look at it with DEBUG. For this example we will use the shortest integer format available, one word integers, just like the Pascal version. These are defined with DW:

```
OPERAND1 DW     3
OPERAND2 DW     1
RESULT   DW     0
```

This is only one of the six different available formats, and we'll look at some others soon. We can assemble this program since we've included the .8087 directive:

```
        .8087  ←
        .MODEL SMALL
        .CODE
        ORG     100H
ENTRY:  JMP     PROG
        OPERAND1 DW     3
                :
                :
```

Under MASM, for example, all we need to do is to type MASM TEST, link it with LINK TEST, and create TEST.COM with EXE2BIN TEST TEST.COM (and make sure our PC has an 80x87 in it).

The .COM file can be debugged this way:

```
>DEBUG TEST.COM

-R
AX=0000  BX=0000  CX=001A  DX=0000  SP=FFFE  BP=0000  SI=0000  DI=0000
DS=090B  ES=090B  SS=090B  CS=090B  IP=0100   NV UP DI PL NZ NA PO NC
090B:0100 EB07          JMP     0109     ← Here's our first jump.
-T

AX=0000  BX=0000  CX=001A  DX=0000  SP=FFFE  BP=0000  SI=0000  DI=0000
DS=090B  ES=090B  SS=090B  CS=090B  IP=0109   NV UP DI PL NZ NA PO NC
090B:0109 9B            WAIT
```

Let's take a look at the rest of the program by unassembling it:

```
-U
090B:0109 9B            WAIT
090B:010A DF060301      FILD    WORD PTR [0103]
090B:010E 9B            WAIT
090B:010F DE060501      FIADD   WORD PTR [0105]
090B:0113 9B            WAIT
090B:0114 DF1E0701      FISTP   WORD PTR [0107]
090B:0118 CD20          INT     20
090B:011A 36            SS:
090B:011B 9C            PUSHF
090B:011C F6FF          IDIV    BH
090B:011E 76C2          JBE     00E2
090B:0120 9A9A003F0B    CALL    0B3F:009A
090B:0125 FF76C2        PUSH    [BP-3E]
090B:0128 E85ADE        CALL    DF85
```

As you can see, the assembler has added the required wait states for the 80x86 while it waits for the 80x87 to finish processing. From the above addresses, we see that OPERAND1 is at [103], OPERAND2 at [105], and RESULT at [107]. Let's take a look at them by dumping them:

```
-D103
090B:0103  03 00 01 00 00-00 9B DF 06 03 01 9B DE           ......_....^
090B:0110  06 05 01 9B DF 1E 07 01-CD 20 36 9C F6 FF 76 C2  ...._...M 6.v.vB
090B:0120  9A 9A 00 3F 0B FF 76 C2-E8 5A DE E8 CF E5 E9 CB  ...?..vBhZ^hOeiK
090B:0130  00 A1 9A F6 2B 06 98 F6-89 46 C2 A1 4E F6 3B 06  .!.v+..v.FB!Nv;.
090B:0140  98 F6 B9 00 00 72 01 41-3B 06 9A F6 BA 00 00 73  .v9..r.A;..v:..s
090B:0150  01 42 22 CA D1 E9 73 16-BF CA F6 BE C6 FE B9 11  .B"JQis.?Jv>F~9.
090B:0160  00 1E 07 FC F3 A5 9A 79-01 FE 09 E9 89 00 E8 1F  ...|s%.y.~.i..h.
090B:0170  E1 D1 E8 72 03 E9 7F 00-A1 4E F6 3B 06 98 F6 73  aQhr.i..!Nv;..vs
090B:0180  18 89 46                                         ..F
```

The 3 and 1 in OPERAND1 and OPERAND2 are seen immediately. (Recall that the 80x86 stores the low byte at a lower address so they appear as 03 00 01 00 instead of 00 03 00 01.) RESULT holds 0. If we execute the entire program with a Go command, we'll load OPERAND1, add OPERAND2 to it, and then store the result in RESULT. Let's execute the program and dump the results:

```
-G118              ← Execute to the INT 20H instruction.
AX=0000  BX=0000  CX=001A  DX=0000  SP=FFFE  BP=0000  SI=0000  DI=0000
DS=090B  ES=090B  SS=090B  CS=090B  IP=0118   NV UP DI PL NZ NA PO NC
090B:0118 CD20           INT     20

-D103              ← And take a look at RESULT
                          ↓

090B:0103  03 00 01 00 04-00 9B DF 06 03 01 9B DE         ......._....^
090B:0110  06 05 01 9B DF 1E 07 01-CD 20 36 9C F6 FF 76 C2  ...._...M 6.v.vB
090B:0120  9A 9A 00 3F 0B FF 76 C2-E8 5A DE E8 CF E5 E9 CB  ...?..vBhZ^hOeiK
090B:0130  00 A1 9A F6 2B 06 98 F6-89 46 C2 A1 4E F6 3B 06  .!.v+..v.FB!Nv;.
090B:0140  98 F6 B9 00 00 72 01 41-3B 06 9A F6 BA 00 00 73  .v9..r.A;..v:..s
090B:0150  01 42 22 CA D1 E9 73 16-BF CA F6 BE C6 FE B9 11  .B"JQis.?Jv>F~9.
090B:0160  00 1E 07 FC F3 A5 9A 79-01 FE 09 E9 89 00 E8 1F  ...|s%.y.~.i..h.
090B:0170  E1 D1 E8 72 03 E9 7F 00-A1 4E F6 3B 06 98 F6 73  aQhr.i..!Nv;..vs
090B:0180  18 89 46                                        ..F
-Q
```

Now the location RESULT holds 4, as it should. Since the format of word integers is so simple, this is just about the easiest example we could choose. The next easiest example, of course, is subtraction.

## Subtracting Integers

All we have to do here is to replace FIADD with the logical counterpart, FISUB:

```
        .8087
        .MODEL SMALL
        .CODE
        ORG      100H
ENTRY:  JMP      PROG
        OPERAND1 DW      3
        OPERAND2 DW      1
        RESULT   DW      0
PROG:   FILD     OPERAND1
        FISUB    OPERAND2          ←
        FISTP    RESULT
        INT      20H
        END      ENTRY
```

From this we can make a .COM file and use DEBUG as before:

```
-R
AX=0000  BX=0000  CX=001A  DX=0000  SP=FFFE  BP=0000  SI=0000  DI=0000
DS=090B  ES=090B  SS=090B  CS=090B  IP=0100   NV UP DI PL NZ NA PO NC
090B:0100 EB07          JMP     0109
-T

AX=0000  BX=0000  CX=001A  DX=0000  SP=FFFE  BP=0000  SI=000  DI=0000
DS=090B  ES=090B  SS=090B  CS=090B  IP=0109   NV UP DI PL NZ NA PO NC
090B:0109 9B            WAIT
-U
090B:0109 9B            WAIT
090B:010A DF060301      FILD    WORD PTR [0103]
090B:010E 9B            WAIT
090B:010F DE260501      FISUB   WORD PTR [0105]
090B:0113 9B            WAIT
090B:0114 DF1E0701      FISTP   WORD PTR [0107]
090B:0118 CD20          INT     20
090B:011A 6F            DB      6F
090B:011B 8B4606        MOV     AX,[BP+06]
090B:011E 257F00        AND     AX,007F
090B:0121 8B5E0A        MOV     BX,[BP+0A]
090B:0124 89470E        MOV     [BX+0E],AX
090B:0127 81660680FF    AND     WORD PTR [BP+06],FF80
```

Here's how the data area looks before we run the program (note the 0 at [107]):

```
-D103
090B:0103   03 00 01 00 00-00 9B DF 06 03 01 9B DE         ......._....^
090B:0110   26 05 01 9B DF 1E 07 01-CD 20 6F 8B 46 06 25 7F  &..._...M o.F.%.
090B:0120   00 8B 5E 0A 89 47 0E 81-66 06 80 FF 8B 46 06 89  ..^..G..f....F..
090B:0130   47 0A 8B 46 08 89 47 0C-53 C4 46 06 06 50 B8 00  G..F..G.SDF..P8.
090B:0140   00 50 9A EB 03 C1 0C 89-5E 06 8C 46 08 8B 5E 0A  .P.k.A..^..F..^.
090B:0150   8B 47 02 89 46 F6 53 50-9A 06 00 43 09 06 53 8B  .G..FvSP...C..S.
090B:0160   5E F4 FF 77 04 9A 50 03-C1 0C 8B 5E 0A 89 47 06  ^t.w..P.A..^..G.
090B:0170   8B 76 0A 8B 7C 06 8B 4C-04 2B CF 8B 5E F6 8D 39  .v..|..L.+O.^v.9
090B:0180    B0 00 1E                                           0..
```

If we run the program we can find that 3 – 1 is indeed 2:

```
-G118
AX=0000  BX=0000  CX=001A  DX=0000  SP=FFFE  BP=0000  SI=0000  DI=0000
DS=090B  ES=090B  SS=090B  CS=090B  IP=0118   NV UP DI PL NZ NA PO NC
090B:0118 CD20          INT     20

-D103                      ↓
090B:0103   03 00 01 00 02-00 9B DF 06 03 01 9B DE         ......._....^
090B:0110   26 05 01 9B DF 1E 07 01-CD 20 6F 8B 46 06 25 7F  &..._...M o.F.%.
090B:0120   00 8B 5E 0A 89 47 0E 81-66 06 80 FF 8B 46 06 89  ..^..G..f....F..
090B:0130   47 0A 8B 46 08 89 47 0C-53 C4 46 06 06 50 B8 00  G..F..G.SDF..P8.
090B:0140   00 50 9A EB 03 C1 0C 89-5E 06 8C 46 08 8B 5E 0A  .P.k.A..^..F..^.
090B:0150   8B 47 02 89 46 F6 53 50-9A 06 00 43 09 06 53 8B  .G..FvSP...C..S.
090B:0160   5E F4 FF 77 04 9A 50 03-C1 0C 8B 5E 0A 89 47 06  ^t.w..P.A..^..G.
090B:0170   8B 76 0A 8B 7C 06 8B 4C-04 2B CF 8B 5E F6 8D 39  .v..|..L.+O.^v.9
```

```
090B:0180  B0 00 1E                                      0..
-Q
```

The last two easy examples here are multiplication and division.

# Multiplying and Dividing Integers

As might be expected from our previous programs, the two matching instructions for integer multiplication and division, are FIMUL and FIDIV. We can multiply 3 by 2, for example, with this program:

```
        .8087
        .MODEL  SMALL
        .CODE
        ORG       100H
ENTRY:  JMP       PROG
        OPERAND1  DW      3
        OPERAND2  DW      2
        RESULT    DW      0
PROG:   FILD      OPERAND1
        FIMUL     OPERAND2          ←
        FISTP     RESULT
        INT       20H
        END       ENTRY
```

We will find 6 deposited in RESULT. What happens, though, when we try dividing 3 by 2 in integer arithmetic? For example, what if we did this:

```
        .MODEL  SMALL
        .CODE
        .8087
        ORG       100H
ENTRY:  JMP       PROG
        OPERAND1  DW      3
        OPERAND2  DW      2
        RESULT    DW      0
PROG:   FILD      OPERAND1
        FIDIV     OPERAND2          ←
        FISTP     RESULT
        INT       20H
        END       ENTRY
```

We can create a .COM file from the above program, called FIDIV.COM, and DEBUG it:

```
-R
AX=0000  BX=0000  CX=001A  DX=0000  SP=FFFE  BP=0000  SI=0000  DI=0000
DS=090B  ES=090B  SS=090B  CS=090B  IP=0100   NV UP DI PL NZ NA PO NC
090B:0100 EB07          JMP     0109     ← Jump over the data.
-T
```

```
AX=0000  BX=0000  CX=001A  DX=0000  SP=FFFE  BP=0000  SI=0000  DI=0000
DS=090B  ES=090B  SS=090B  CS=090B  IP=0109   NV UP DI PL NZ NA PO NC
090B:0109 9B            WAIT
-U
090B:0109 9B            WAIT
090B:010A DF060301      FILD    WORD PTR [0103]
090B:010E 9B            WAIT
090B:010F DE360501      FIDIV   WORD PTR [0105]            ← Our division.
090B:0113 9B            WAIT
090B:0114 DF1E0701      FISTP   WORD PTR [0107]
090B:0118 CD20          INT     20
090B:011A 6F            DB      6F
090B:011B 8B4606        MOV     AX,[BP+06]
090B:011E 257F00        AND     AX,007F
090B:0121 8B5E0A        MOV     BX,[BP+0A]
090B:0124 89470E        MOV     [BX+0E],AX
090B:0127 81660680FF    AND     WORD PTR [BP+06],FF80
```

Once again, we check to make sure RESULT at [107] is zero before starting:

```
-D103
090B:0103  03 00 02 00 00-00 9B DF 06 03 01 9B DE         ......._....^
090B:0110  36 05 01 9B DF 1E 07 01-CD 20 6F 8B 46 06 25 7F  6..._...M o.F.%.
090B:0120  00 8B 5E 0A 89 47 0E 81-66 06 80 FF 8B 46 06 89  ..^..G..f....F..
090B:0130  47 0A 8B 46 08 89 47 0C-53 C4 46 06 06 50 B8 00  G..F..G.SDF..P8.
090B:0140  00 50 9A EB 03 C1 0C 89-5E 06 8C 46 08 8B 5E 0A  .P.k.A..^..F..^.
090B:0150  8B 47 02 89 46 F6 53 50-9A 06 00 43 09 06 53 8B  .G..FvSP...C..S.
090B:0160  5E F4 FF 77 04 9A 50 03-C1 0C 8B 5E 0A 89 47 06  ^t.w..P.A..^..G.
090B:0170  8B 76 0A 8B 7C 06 8B 4C-04 2B CF 8B 5E F6 8D 39  .v..|..L.+O.^v.9
090B:0180   B0 00 1E                                          0..
```

and then run the program to check RESULT:

```
-G118
AX=0000  BX=0000  CX=001A  DX=0000  SP=FFFE  BP=0000  SI=0000  DI=0000
DS=090B  ES=090B  SS=090B  CS=090B  IP=0118   NV UP DI PL NZ NA PO NC
090B:0118 CD20          INT     20
-D103
090B:0103  03 00 02 00 02-00 9B DF 06 03 01 9B DE         ......._....^
090B:0110  36 05 01 9B DF 1E 07 01-CD 20 6F 8B 46 06 25 7F  6..._...M o.F.%.
090B:0120  00 8B 5E 0A 89 47 0E 81-66 06 80 FF 8B 46 06 89  ..^..G..f....F..
090B:0130  47 0A 8B 46 08 89 47 0C-53 C4 46 06 06 50 B8 00  G..F..G.SDF..P8.
090B:0140  00 50 9A EB 03 C1 0C 89-5E 06 8C 46 08 8B 5E 0A  .P.k.A..^..F..^.
090B:0150  8B 47 02 89 46 F6 53 50-9A 06 00 43 09 06 53 8B  .G..FvSP...C..S.
090B:0160  5E F4 FF 77 04 9A 50 03-C1 0C 8B 5E 0A 89 47 06  ^t.w..P.A..^..G.
090B:0170  8B 76 0A 8B 7C 06 8B 4C-04 2B CF 8B 5E F6 8D 39  .v..|..L.+O.^v.9
090B:0180  B0 00 1E                                         0..
-Q
```

Apparently, 3 divided by 2 is 2. The cause for this is easy to spot, however. In integer arithmetic, numbers are rounded off. When we load 3 with FILD, it is stored in the 80x87 stack in *temporary real* format, a format that uses the full 80 bits the 80x87 is capable of.

| Temporary real format is the same as the extended real format in Pascal.

When we divided by 2, we got a result of 1.5, but FIDIV rounds up any fractional answers by adding .5 to the result and then discarding the fractional part. This process gives us the 2 we finally see. Even if we had used FDIV, which would have given an answer of 1.5, FISTP rounds numbers off in just the same way before storing them—by adding .5 to the number in the stack top and then discarding the fractional part.

This raises the issue of how the 80x87 stores numbers. In itself, this subject takes a little study.

# 80x87 Integer Formats

We already know one format used by the 80x87—word integers, defined with DW:

```
Bit #   15 14   0
        [  |      ]   ← One Word
```

These integers, stored in 16 bits, correspond to the integer type in Pascal. The leftmost bit is used to store the integer's sign; so what is left to hold the number itself are the remaining 15 bits, giving a range of -32,768 to 32,767 (the range is unsymmetric because zero is counted as a positive number). These numbers are stored in just the same way the normal numbers the PC operates on; they are stored in two's complement notation, which we covered in the last chapter.

The next size integer is the so-called *short integer*, which is 32 bits long, and is defined with DD, define doubleword:

```
SHORT_INT  DD  12345678
```

These integers can range from $-2x10^9$ to $2x10^9$. Here's how their bits are stored:

```
Bit #  31 30            0
       [  |               ]   ← Double Word
```

The 80x87 short integer is really the same as Pascal's *long* integer. The sign bit is held in bit 31, the leftmost bit, as usual.

Finally, if you really need *big* integers, there is the *long integer* format (there is nothing comparable in Pascal). This format is 64 bits, and can hold integers from $-9x10^{18}$ to $9x10^{18}$. If you need numbers larger than this, you must go to floating-point notation. As it is, the 80x87 can preserve 18 decimal places of accuracy with long integers. Long integers are defined with DQ, Define Quadword, since four words make up 64 bits:

```
LONG_INT DQ 123456789987654321
```

The bit pattern of Long Integers is as expected, with 63 bits (bits 0–62) of integer and one sign bit (bit 63):

```
Bit #    63 62                                 0
        [  |                                    ]  ← Quadword
```

We are already familiar with two's complement notation, so we know how to set these numbers up. As far as integers go, then, we know how to work with them in Pascal, 80x86, and the 80x87.

We already saw the internal format of the common floating-point types in the last chapter. Pascal's single, double, extended, and comp data types are the same as on the 80x87. But there is one more format that we still have to examine.

## Binary Coded Decimal

One more way of storing numbers in a format recognizable to the 80x87 is in Binary Coded Decimal or BCD. For most people, BCD is particularly easy to work with since it looks just like base 10 numbers. BCD numbers are 10 bytes long (defined with DT, Define Tenbytes) and the largest allowable digit is 9. Again, however, the leftmost bit, bit 79, is used for the sign. Unlike two's complement math, the only difference about numbers like 4 and –4 is the sign bit. If a BCD number is negative, the first byte is 80H; if positive, it is 0:

```
NUMBER  DT 00123456789999999999H
```

The only difference with BCD numbers is that you have to load them with FBLD instead of FILD and store them in memory with FBSTP (store and pop) instead of FISTP. Here is a program that will give a result, in RESULT, of zero:

```
        .MODEL SMALL
        .CODE
        .8087
        ORG     100H
ENTRY:  JMP     PROG
        OPERAND1 DT     00123456789999999999H
        OPERAND2 DT     80123456789999999999H   ;← Note this is -1xOPERAND1.
        RESULT  DW      0
PROG:   FBLD    OPERAND1        ;← Load the two BCD numbers.
        FBLD    OPERAND2
        FADD                    ;Add Stack top plus number below it.
        FISTP   RESULT          ;Store RESULT as an integer.
        INT     20H
        END     ENTRY
```

Here we add the BCD number 00123456789999999999H to the BCD number 80123456789999999999H, which is the same thing, except that the leading bit has been made 1. The result of this addition is 0. Note the use of FBLD in the above program to load the BCD numbers into the coprocessor.

# 80x87 Instructions

There are plenty of coprocessor instructions, but an introductory chapter is not the place to see them all in action. Instead, and for reference, we will list and discuss the most frequently used 80x87 instructions. As noted, these instructions all begin with F. If any instruction begins with F, it is safe to assume it is an 80x87 instruction, because 80x86 instructions don't.

Immediately after the name of the instruction, we see what the instruction does with a line like:

$$2^{ST} - 1 \rightarrow ST$$

This means that the stack (ST) is replaced by the value $2^{ST} - 1$.

## F2XM1 $2^X$ Minus One

Logic: $ST \leftarrow 2^{ST} - 1$

Many 80x87 instructions are hard-to-remember names that are hardly mnemonic. Here, F2XM1 stands for 2 to the X minus 1. This instruction sounds exceptionally useful until you find out that the power to which you raise 2 must be in the interval of 0. to .5. (-1.0 < ST < 1.0 on the 80387). Nevertheless, if you are willing to work with square roots and multiplications, you can fabricate any power of 2 this way.

The abbreviation ST always stands for the stack top, ST(1) for the value on the stack below it, all the way down to ST(7). Don't forget that it is your responsibilty to keep the stack from getting completely filled and, therefore, jammed.

This instruction takes no arguments; it uses only the stack top. Some formulas you might want to keep in mind while using this instruction include:

$$10^{ST} = 2^{ST} \times LOG_2\ 10$$

$$e^{ST} = 2^{ST} \times LOG_2\ e$$

$$Y^{ST} = 2^{ST} \times LOG_2\ Y$$

With these formulas, you can find $10^{ST}$, $e^{ST}$, and $Y^{ST}$ from $2^{ST}$. There are special instructions to load $LOG_2e$ (FLDL2E) and to load $LOG_210$ (FLDL2T). These instructions simply load their respective values into ST.

## FABS Absolute Value

```
Logic:      ST ← ABS(ST)
```

FABS changes the top of the stack to its own absolute value. This instruction provides a fast way of making sure a value is greater than or equal to 0.

## FADD Addition

```
Logic:      ST(1) ← ST(1) + ST, pop stack    (no operands)
            ST ← ST + memory                 (source only)
            ST ← ST + ST(i)                  (destination, source)
```

We have seen this instruction at work already; it simply adds two floating-point numbers. If there are no arguments, the 80x87 adds ST and ST(1) together, loads this new number into ST(1), and then pops the 80x87 stack, leaving the result in ST.

If you use an argument like:

```
FADD     LONG_REAL
```

then LONG_REAL is added to ST, and the answer is left in ST. On the other hand, you can use instructions like:

```
FADD ST,ST(3)
```

in which case ST(3) will be added to ST, and the result will be left in ST. Similarly, the instruction:

```
FADD ST(3),ST
```

will add ST to ST(3), and will leave the result in ST(3)—not ST. The integer version of this instruction is FIADD.

| Note that the stack is popped in the no-operands form only.

## FBLD Load BCD Number

```
Logic:      push stack
            ST ← memory operand
```

FBLD converts a memory operand from BCD (packed decimal) format to temporary real and loads it into ST. The sign of memory operand is preserved.

FBLD, for loading BCD numbers, we have already seen in action. It is simple to use, provided you have stored the BCD number correctly (with DT, Define Tenbytes):

```
FBLD     BCD_NUMBER
```

The counterpart of this instruction is the one that follows, FBSTP.

## FBSTP Store BCD Number

```
Logic:     [memory location] ← ST
           pop stack
```

This accomplishes the reverse of FBLD and also pops the stack. FBSTP stores a number in BCD format. If you wanted to convert from, say, integer to BCD, you could load the integer with FILD and store it with FBSTP. This instruction also keeps the stack trim by popping it.

## FCHS Change Sign

```
Logic:     ST ← -1 * ST
```

FCHS simply changes the sign of the value in ST. It is quicker than multiplying by -1.0.

## FCLEX Clear Exceptions

```
Logic:clear exception flags
```

Like the 80x86, the 80x87 has a set of flags, which will be covered in the following section on errors. The flags are stored in the 80x87's status word. To check them, you have to store the status word in memory. PC users should note that these flags aren't automatically reset. They stay set so that they can propagate through a whole calculation, and we can check any accumulated errors at the end if we wish. FCLEX clears these flags and sets them back to zero. If we intend to use error checking, we should start off any calculation with FCLEX.

## FCOM Comparison

```
Logic:     cmp ST, source
           sets condition codes in the status word:

           C3 C2 C1 C0            Means
           0  0  ?  0      ST > source
           0  0  ?  1      ST < source
           1  0  ?  0      ST = source
           1  1  ?  1      ST not comparable to source
```

FCOM compares a real number to ST and leaves the result encoded in the 80x87 *status word* as shown above. If no source is specified, ST(1) is compared to ST. Otherwise, source is compared to ST.

This is the first of the 80x87's comparison instructions. FCOM is used with real numbers—short or long reals. To use it (the comparison to ST is implicit), just issue a instruction like:

```
FCOM    LONG_REAL_NUMBER
```

The results of this comparison are stored in the 80x87's status word. The condition bits in the status word are of interest here. We can store the status word in memory with the instruction FSTSW (see below) and examine it.

The bits C3–C0 will be returned this way after the comparison:

| C3 | C2 | C1 | C0 | Means |
|---|---|---|---|---|
| 0 | 0 | ? | 0 | ST > source |
| 0 | 0 | ? | 1 | ST < source |
| 1 | 0 | ? | 0 | ST = source |
| 1 | 1 | ? | 1 | ST not comparable to source |

C0 is bit 8 of the status word, and C3 is bit 14. We can use this information immediately in a little test program to check the relative sizes of two memory values, A and B.

## The RECORD and MASK Directives

There is an easy way of working with individual bits in the status word; we will use the new directive *RECORD* to split our status word up into bit-by-bit fields. That way, we can use the *MASK* directive later to generate masks to specify individual bits. We use record to give a name to all the bits in a word this way:

```
M RECORD BY:1,C3:1,TOP:3,C2:1,C1:1,C0:1,IT:1,X:1,P:1,U:1,O:1,Z:1,D:1,I:1
```

Here we define a dummy record, named M, just so we can give names to all the bits in it. The first bit is named BY (which stands for busy), the next bit C3, the following three bits TOP, and so on.

Bit names are short because a RECORD must be completely defined on one line (that is, in 132 characters or less). Note also that the field TOP, which tells you which of the eight 80x87 registers in the stack top currently, is three bits long, because it must be able to hold numbers up to eight.

Now that we've defined the name C3 as part of a word, we can use the MASK directive. When we then use the instruction TEST ST8087,MASK C3, the assembler will substitute the correct hex number for MASK C3. C3 is bit 14, and the assembler will generate a *mask* which has bit 14 set. Here's how the program looks:

```
        .MODEL SMALL
        .CODE
        .8087
        ORG      100H
ENTRY:  JMP      PROG
        A        DQ 10.0
        B        DQ 5.0
        ST8087   DW  0
→       M RECORD BY:1,C3:1,TOP:3,C2:1,C1:1,C0:1,IT:1,X:1,P:1,U:1,O:1,Z:1,D:1,I:1
PROG:   FINIT
        FLD      A
        FCOMP    B
        FSTSW    ST8087
        MOV      DL,'A'
        MOV      AH,2
        INT      21H
        ;C3=0  C0=0 → A>B
        ;C3=0  C0=1 → A<B
        ;C3=1  C0=0 → A=B
→       TEST     ST8087,MASK C3
        JZ       NOTEQ
        MOV      DL,'='
        JMP      SHORT PRINT
NOTEQ:  TEST     ST8087,MASK C0
        JNZ      LESS
        MOV      DL,'>'
        JMP      SHORT PRINT
LESS:   MOV      DL,'<'
PRINT:  MOV      AH,2
        INT      21H
        MOV      DL,'B'
        INT      21H
        FCLEX
        INT      20H
        END      ENTRY
```

We start off with a data area, as usual. Here we make A and B into Pascal single-precision size by using DQ, and store the status word in the word we have labeled ST8087:

```
        .MODEL SMALL
        .CODE
        .8087
        ORG      100H
ENTRY:  JMP      PROG
     →  A        DQ 10.0
     →  B        DQ 5.0
     →  ST8087   DW  0
        M RECORD BY:1,C3:1,TOP:3,C2:1,C1:1,C0:1,IT:1,X:1,P:1,U:1,O:1,Z:1,D:1,I:1
PROG:   FINIT
        :
        :
```

The first instruction used here is the useful FINIT, which initializes the 80x87 and clears the stack. We then load A and compare it to B with FCOMP, the version of FCOM that also pops the stack. Immediately afterward, we store the status word in ST8087. In preparing to type out the answer (either A>B, A<B, or A=B), we first type out A this way:

```
        .MODEL SMALL
        .CODE
        .8087
        ORG     100H
ENTRY:  JMP     PROG
        A       DQ 10.0
        B       DQ 5.0
        ST8087  DW  0
        M RECORD BY:1,C3:1,TOP:3,C2:1,C1:1,C0:1,IT:1,X:1,P:1,U:1,O:1,Z:1,D:1,I:1
PROG:   FINIT
   →    FLD     A                  ;Load A
   →    FCOMP   B                  ;Compare to B
   →    FSTSW   ST8087             ;Store the status word in memory.
   →    MOV     DL,"A"             ;Print out "A"
   →    MOV     AH,2
   →    INT     21H
        :
        :
```

Next we check C3 and C0 after the comparison. If C3=1, then A=B. If C0=1, then A<B. Here's the way the program types out either =, <, or >, followed by B:

```
        .MODEL SMALL
        .CODE
        .8087
        ORG     100H
ENTRY:  JMP     PROG
        A       DQ 10.0
        B       DQ 5.0
        ST8087  DW  0
        M RECORD BY:1,C3:1,TOP:3,C2:1,C1:1,C0:1,IT:1,X:1,P:1,U:1,O:1,Z:1,D:1,I:1
PROG:   FINIT
        FLD     A
        FCOMP   B
        FSTSW   ST8087
        MOV     DL,"A"
        MOV     AH,2
        INT     21H
        ;C3=0  C0=0 → A>B
        ;C3=0  C0=1 → A<B
        ;C3=1  C0=0 → A=B
   →    TEST    ST8087,MASK C3
        JZ      NOTEQ              ;C3 NOT set → jump.
   →    MOV     DL,"="
        JMP     SHORT PRINT
NOTEQ:  TEST    ST8087,MASK C0  ←
```

```
        JNZ     LESS            ;C0 set → jump.
    →   MOV     DL,'>'
        JMP     SHORT PRINT
LESS:   MOV     DL,'<'          ←
PRINT:  MOV     AH,2
        INT     21H
        MOV     DL,'B'
        INT     21H
        FCLEX
        INT     20H
        END     ENTRY
```

We can see not only how to use the status word this way, but also the RECORD and MASK directives.

## FDIV Division

```
Logic:      ST(1) ← ST(1)/ST, pop stack    (no operands)
            ST ← ST/memory location        (source only)
            ST ← ST/ST(i)                  (destination, source)
```

We have seen FDIV before. This is the floating-point divide instruction. If you use it without labels:

```
FDIV
```

it will divide ST(1) by ST, store the result in ST, and pop the stack. If you use a real memory operand:

```
FDIV Long_Real
```

then ST will be divided by the real number and the result is left in ST. Finally, if you use it with both ST and ST(n), then ST will be loaded with ST/ST(n):

```
FDIV ST,ST(n)
```

The integer version of FDIV is FIDIV.

| Note that the stack is popped only in the no-operands form.

## FIADD Integer Add

```
Logic:      ST ← ST + memory operand
```

FIADD adds two integers and leaves the result in the stack top. The source must be a memory word or short integer. The destination implied in the instruction is always ST.

## FICOM Integer Compare

```
Logic:      cmp source, ST
            sets condition codes in the status word:

            C3 C2 C1 C0         Means
            0  0  ?  0      ST > source
            0  0  ?  1      ST < source
            1  0  ?  0      ST = source
            1  1  ?  1      ST not comparable to source
```

FICOM compares two integers and leaves the result encoded in the status word as shown above. The source operand can be either a memory short integer or a memory word integer, and the implied destination is ST.

## FIDIV Integer Divide

```
Logic:      ST ← ST/memory operand
```

FIDIV, an integer division instruction, divides the destination, which is always ST, by the specified memory operand and stores the result in ST. The memory operand can be either a word integer or a short integer.

## FILD Load Integers

```
Logic:      ST ← memory operand
```

FILD is the way you can load integers into ST. Since the only common format for the 80x86 and the 80x87 is the word integer format (16 bits and two's complement signed), this instruction is quite popular. The corresponding instruction to store integers is FIST. If you have done calculations with the 80x87 and now wish to manipulate the results with the 80x86, FIST is often quite useful.

## FIMUL Integer Multiply

```
Logic:      ST ← ST * memory operand
```

FIMUL performs an integer multiplication of the memory operand and ST, and leaves the result in ST. The memory operand can be either a short integer or a word integer.

## FINIT Initialize 80x87

```
Logic: initialize 80x87
```

This especially useful instruction initializes and resets the 80x87. If the stack has become full or if (for any other reason) you want to start from scratch, you can use FINIT. The timing between the 80x87 and the 80x86 is preserved. If, on the other hand, you suspect that the 80x86 and 80x87 are no longer communicating well (i.e., each is waiting for the other to finish), you might use FNINIT, which executes an immediate FINIT, instead of first waiting until the 80x87 signals that it is free.

## FIST Store Integer

```
Logic:     [memory location] ← ST
```

FIST, as mentioned, provides a way of downloading 80x87 results in a manner readable by the 80x86. We can do whatever we want with floating-point numbers and then, finally, load the final answer into memory with FIST, where it can be examined by the 80x86.

## FISTP Store Integer and Pop Stack

```
Logic:     [memory location] ← ST, pop stack
```

FISTP has all the advantages of FIST, and two more. FISTP also pops the stack and keeps it from growing too large. It can also store numbers in the Long_Integer format (64 bits—use DQ), while FIST cannot. As with FIST, you can do all your floating-point calculations first and then store them in integer format so they can be read by the 80x86 CPU.

## FISUB Integer Subtract

```
Logic:     ST ← ST - memory operand
```

FISUB subtracts two integers (ST – memory operand) and leaves the result in the stack top; you use it like this: FISUB MEM_INT. The memory operand must be a word or short integer. The destination implied in the instruction is always ST.

## FLD Load Real

```
Logic:     ST(1) ← ST(1) + ST        (no operands)
           ST ← ST + memory operand  (source only)
           ST ← ST + ST(i)           (destination, source)
```

FLD is the usual way of loading floating-point numbers into ST. With it you can load short or long reals, as well as the temporary real format (80 bits) used internally in the 80x87. The format is simply this:

```
FLD SHORT_REAL
```

as we have already seen. This is the way that the 80x87 operates; we have to load its stack before we can use it. Of course, all numbers that are loaded this way must be stored in the correct floating-point format. To use this format we can do one of four things: We can let Pascal do the dirty work of manipulating the number; we can let the assembler do it by including constants in our .ASM file:

```
LONG_VAL DQ 3.14159
```

we can do the dirty work ourselves; or we can let the 80x87 store the number in an easier (integer) format. Keep track of the number of FLDs you have executed to make sure the stack does not grow uncontrollably.

## FMUL Multiply

```
Logic:    ST(1) ← ST(1) * ST, pop stack  (no operands)
          ST ← ST * memory location      (source only)
          ST ← ST * ST(i)                (destination, source)
```

FMUL is the 80x87's all-purpose real number multiplication instruction. With it you can multiply ST(1) and ST, pop the stack, and move the result from ST(1) into ST:

```
FMUL
```

or you can load a real number into ST with FLD and multiply it by some real number stored in memory:

```
FMUL SHORT_INTEGER
FMUL LONG_INTEGER
```

FMUL can also multiply different stack elements. For example,

```
FMUL ST, ST(7)
```

multiplies ST by ST(7) and leaves the result in ST. The other way around,

```
FMUL ST(7),ST
```

multiplies ST(7) by ST and leaves the results in ST(7).

The integer version of FMUL is FIMUL.

## FNCLEX Clear Exceptions—No Wait

```
Logic: clear exceptions without waiting
```

This is the version of FCLEX that doesn't wait until the 80x87 signals that it is free. Usually, there is no advantage to using FNCLEX instead of FCLEX. If, however, you write what is called an exception handler—analogous to interrupt handlers in the PC—then you have to issue this instruction before returning to the interrupted calculation. We won't deal with exception handlers in this book.

## FNOP No Operation

```
Logic:      ST ← ST
```

FNOP performs no operation and can be used to replace a deleted instruction in an assembly language program while preserving the effective offsets of the remaining instructions. Unfortunately, this instruction is three bytes long, which makes it difficult to replace instructions that are, say, two or five bytes long.

## FNSTSW Store Status—No Wait

```
Logic: store status word without waiting
```

Another instruction that doesn't wait until the 80x87 signals it is free before operating, this instruction is usually used to examine the busy bit (bit 15) of the status word to determine when the 80x87 is no longer busy. Typically, loops are put into 80x86 code that check this bit until it becomes 0, at which time the 80x87 is free.

This instruction is used like this:

```
FNSTSW  WORD_LENGTH_OP
```

## FPATAN Arc Tangent

```
Logic:      T1 ← ARCTAN(ST(1)/ST)
            pop stack
            ST ← T1
```

FPATAN is the instruction for partial arc tangent. This instruction takes no arguments. All we must do is supply it with the ratio Y/X, where X = ST, and Y is ST(1). To load Y, we can use FLD; another FLD for X will push Y into ST(1) and put X into ST. The resulting angle is left in ST and can be stored in memory with FSTP. For the 8087 and 80287, ST must be greater than ST(1), and both must be positive. There is no restriction on ST or ST(1) in the 80387.

## FPREM Partial Remainder

```
Logic:       ST ← repeat (ST - ST(1)) until ST  ST(1)
             If ST > ST(1) then C2 = 1, PREM = ST
             If ST = ST(1) then C2 = 0, REM = 0
             If ST < ST(1) then C2 = 0, REM = ST
```

FPREM calculates ST mod (ST(1)). It leaves the remainder of the division ST/ST(1) in ST. The sign of the remainder is the same as the sign of the original dividend. This instruction also indicates the least-significant three bits of the quotient generated by FPREM in C3 C1 and C0 as follows:

| *C3* | *C2* | *C1* | *C0* | *Meaning* |
|---|---|---|---|---|
| ? | 1 | ? | ? | Incomplete reduction |
| 0 | 0 | 0 | 0 | quotient MOD 8 = 0 |
| 0 | 0 | 0 | 1 | quotient MOD 8 = 4 |
| 0 | 0 | 1 | 0 | quotient MOD 8 = 1 |
| 0 | 0 | 1 | 1 | quotient MOD 8 = 5 |
| 1 | 0 | 0 | 0 | quotient MOD 8 = 2 |
| 1 | 0 | 0 | 1 | quotient MOD 8 = 6 |
| 1 | 0 | 1 | 0 | quotient MOD 8 = 3 |
| 1 | 0 | 1 | 1 | quotient MOD 8 = 7 |

## FPTAN Tangent

```
Logic:       Y/X ← TAN(ST)
             ST ← Y
             push stack
             ST ← X
```

FPTAN is the 80x87's partial tangent instruction. With this instruction, you can also calculate sines and cosines, given the right trigonometric identities. The value of ST must be 0 < ST < Pi/4. Instead of simply delivering a floating-point answer, FPTAN gives us a ratio Y/X (Y in ST(1) and X in ST). This makes it easier to calculate other trigonometric values.

If we want one number, we would divide Y by X with FDIV. The 80387 also lets you calculate sines and cosines directly (with its FCOS and FSINE instructions).

## FSQRT Square Root

```
Logic:sqrt(ST) → ST
```

This instruction just gives us the square root of ST. To not give an undefined answer, ST must be positive. Finding square roots with the 80x87 is actually fast, taking about the same time as division. Needless to say, emulating this instruction with the 80x86 is time-consuming and frustrating.

## FST Store Real

```
Logic:      destination ← ST
```

FST copies the value in ST to the destination. The destination can be a short or long real memory operand, or a coprocessor register, ST(i).

## FSTSW Store Status

```
Logic: status word → memory operand
```

This is a very common instruction used when you are doing error checking. The Status Word, as you'll see in the next section, defines the current state of the 80x87 and includes the error flags. This instruction is preferred over the No-Wait version of the same thing, FNSTSW. FNSTSW is used almost exclusively in tight loops that check when the 80x87 isn't busy by checking the busy bit in the Status Word. We will make more use of the status word later.

## FSUB Subtraction

```
Logic:      ST(1) ← ST(1) - ST, pop stack           (no operands)
            ST ← ST - memory operand                (source only)
            ST ← ST - ST(i)                         (destination,
source)
```

FSUB is the 80x87's real subtraction instruction. It is advisable after any FSUB to check the status word for errors. FSUB can take these forms:

| *Instruction* | *Result* |
|---|---|
| FSUB | (ST(1)–ST → ST(1)), pop stack |
| FSUB SHORT_REAL | (ST–Short_Real → ST) |
| FSUB LONG_REAL | (ST–Long_Real → ST) |
| FSUB ST,ST(3) | (ST–ST(3) → ST) |
| FSUB ST(7),ST | (ST(7)–ST → ST(7)) |

The integer version of this instruction is FISUB.

| Note that the stack is popped in the no-operands form only.

## FTST Test for Zero

```
Logic:      ST ← ST - 0.0
```

FTST compares ST to 0.0. The result of the floating-point comparison is left in the condition codes of the status word:

| C3 | C0 | Means |
|---|---|---|
| 0 | 0 | ST > 0 |
| 0 | 1 | ST < 0 |
| 1 | 0 | ST = +0 or -0 |
| 1 | 1 | ST is not comparable |

## FWAIT Wait

```
Logic:      80x86 wait
```

FWAIT, which causes the 80x86 microprocessor to wait until the current 80x87 instruction is completed, is used to synchronize the 80x86 and 80x87.

FWAIT is the same as the 80x86 WAIT instruction. However, you should use the FWAIT instruction since WAIT may cause an infinite wait under some circumstances.

Note that if an FWAIT instruction is necessary, the assembler will usually put one in.

## FXAM Examine

```
Logic:      sets condition codes according to the value in ST
```

FXAM causes the coprocessor to examine the value currently in ST. The condition codes are set as follows:

| C3 | C2 | C1 | C0 | Means |
|---|---|---|---|---|
| 0 | 0 | 0 | 0 | +Unnormal |
| 0 | 0 | 0 | 1 | +NAN |
| 0 | 0 | 1 | 0 | -Unnormal |
| 0 | 0 | 1 | 1 | -Unnormal |
| 0 | 1 | 0 | 0 | +Normal |
| 0 | 1 | 0 | 1 | +Infinity |
| 0 | 1 | 1 | 0 | -Normal |
| 0 | 1 | 1 | 1 | -Infinity |
| 1 | 0 | 0 | 0 | +0 |
| 1 | 0 | 0 | 1 | Empty |
| 1 | 0 | 1 | 0 | -0 |
| 1 | 0 | 1 | 1 | Empty |
| 1 | 1 | 0 | 0 | +Denormal |

```
C3 C2 C1 C0    Means
1  1  0  1  Empty
1  1  1  0  -Denormal
1  1  1  1  Empty
```

## FXCH Exchange Registers

```
Logic:      T1 ← ST(i)
            ST(i) ← ST
            ST ← T1
```

FXCH exchanges the contents of ST with the contents of the destination register. If no destination is specified, ST is exchanged with ST(1). This instruction is very useful on a stack-based processor like the 80x87.

## FXTRACT Extract Exponent and Significand

```
Logic:      T1 ← exponent(ST)
            T2 ← significand(ST)
            ST ← T1
            push stack
            ST ← T2
```

FXTRACT extracts the exponents and significand of the value in ST. It leaves the exponent in ST(1) and the significand in ST.

## FYL2X Y x Log $X_2$

```
Logic:      T1 ← ST(1) * Log2(ST)
            pop stack
            ST ← T1
```

FYL2X is one of the two instructions in the 80x87 that can calculate $Log_2$ values (the other is FYL2XP1). Nowhere do the 80x87 mnemonics make less apparent sense—what FYL2X means is Y x $Log_2X$. This immediate multiplication is useful, since you can find logs in other bases with the identity:

$$Log_nX = [1/Log_2n] \times Log_2X$$

This is the 80x87's method of raising numbers to powers—you must take the number's log first, multiply by the appropriate power, and then take the antilog by exponentiating (using F2XM1).

# Errors and Error Checking

No math-related computer discussion would be complete without a discussion of errors. Just as we can check the carry flag in the 80x86, so there are provisions in the

80x87 for error checking. Unless you know beforehand just what your input will be, you should check for errors.

The register that holds the 80x87's error flags and status flags is called the Status Word. This word can be stored in memory with FSTSW like this: FSTSW MEM_WORD.

The status word is divided into status bits and exception flags (error flags). The top byte looks like this:

| Bit # | 15 | 14 | 13 | 12 | 11 | 10 | 9 | 8 |
|---|---|---|---|---|---|---|---|---|
| | B | C3 | Top of Stack Register # | | | C2 | C1 | C0 |

The topmost bit, 15, is the busy bit. If this bit is 1, the 80x87 is busy executing some instruction. If this bit is 0, the 80x87 is idle. If you use FSTSW, this bit should always be 0 since this instruction waits until the 80x87 is free before executing. On the other hand, the no-wait form of this instruction, FNSTSW, doesn't wait until the 80x87 is free, and you can check on the 80x87 at any time with it.

The four *condition codes*, C3-C0, are used to hold the results of comparisons, as we saw with FCOM. If we used the instruction FCOM MEM_OP, this is the way the condition codes C3-C0 would be set (C1 is not set for compare instructions):

| *C3* | *C2* | *C1* | *C0* | *Means* |
|---|---|---|---|---|
| 0 | 0 | - | 0 | ST > MEM_OP |
| 0 | 0 | - | 1 | ST < MEM_OP |
| 1 | 0 | - | 0 | ST = MEM_OP |

The 80x87 also has an examine instruction, FXAM, which will set C3–C0 depending on the contents of ST. This instruction is often very useful. The results of FXAM look like this:

| | |
|---|---|
| 0000 | Valid, > 0, Unnormalized |
| 0001 | Invalid, > 0, Zero Exponent |
| 0010 | Valid, < 0, Unnormalized |
| 0011 | Invalid, < 0, Zero Exponent |
| 0100 | Valid, > 0, Normalized |
| 0101 | Positive Infinity |
| 0110 | Valid, < 0, Normalized |
| 0111 | Negative Infinity |
| 1000 | Positive Zero |
| 1001 | Empty |
| 1010 | Negative Zero |
| 1011 | Empty |
| 1100 | Invalid, > 0, Zero Exponent |
| 1101 | Empty |
| 1110 | Invalid, < 0, Zero Exponent |
| 1111 | Empty |

A normalized number is one that fits into the normal format of 80x87 reals—biased exponent and implicit leading one. If, though, a number is very small, it would have leading zeros (not ones) once the smallest exponent for that format has been used. In that case, the number is no longer normalized, but the 80x87 can still operate on it.

The three bits labeled Top of Stack Register # hold the number (0–7) of the register that is the current top of stack (ST). You can watch this number to make sure you know where you are in the stack and that it doesn't overflow.

The bottom eight bits of the status word look like this:

| Bit # | 7 | 6 | 5 | 4 | 3 | 2 | 1 | 0 |
|---|---|---|---|---|---|---|---|---|
| | IR | | P | U | O | Z | D | I |

The IR bit indicates whether an Interrupt Request is pending from the 80x87 to the 80x86.

The six flags—P, U, O, Z, D, and I—indicate exceptions and can be checked after every math operation. Until these flags are cleared with FCLEX or FINIT, however, they stay set once they are set. As mentioned, this means that error flags can propagate through an entire calculation, even an involved one, and can be checked at the end.

If the exception occurred, the corresponding bit is one. Otherwise, the bit is 0. The flags are shown in Table 8.1.

Table 8.1 Exception Flags

| *Flag* | *Means* |
|---|---|
| P | Precision. Some precision has been lost in working with the current operand. |
| U | Underflow. The number's exponent is too small to be represented in the requested format. In other words, the result is non-zero but too small to fit in the format asked for. |
| O | Overflow. The other extreme: the number is too large to fit into the requested format. |
| Z | A divide by zero occurred. |
| D | Denormalization. At least one of the operands used was denormalized, e.g.: it has the smallest possible exponent, but a non-zero significand. |
| I | Invalid operation. Some invalid operations include stack over- and under-flow, dividing zero by zero, taking the negative square root of a number. |

## Using Error Checking

We can put this knowledge to work at once. In this example, we will perform two divisions—one a valid division and one a division by zero. Each time we will check the status word to examine the exception flags. Here's the way the program looks:

```
        .MODEL SMALL
        .CODE
        .8087
        ORG     100H
ENTRY:  JMP     PROG
        OP1     DQ 10.0
        OP2     DQ 5.0
        OP3     DQ 0.0
        NOPROB  DB 'No '
        PROB    DB 'Divide by Zero',13,10,'$'
        ST8087  DW  0
        SW RECORD B:1,C3:1,TOP:3,C2:1,C1:1,C0:1,IT:1,X:1,P:1,U:1,O:1,Z:1,D:1,I:1
PROG:   FINIT
        FLD     OP1
        FDIV    OP2
        MOV     AH,9
        LEA     DX,NOPROB
        FSTSW   ST8087
        TEST    ST8087,MASK Z
        JZ      OK1
        LEA     DX,PROB
OK1:    INT     21H
        FCLEX
        FINIT
        FLD     OP1
        FDIV    OP3
        MOV     AH,9
        LEA     DX,NOPROB
        FSTSW   ST8087
        TEST    ST8087,MASK Z
        JZ      OK2
        LEA     DX,PROB
OK2:    INT     21H
        INT     20H
        END     ENTRY   H
```

To define the bit-by-bit flags in the status word, we use the RECORD directive again. As we saw earlier, the definition of a record has to fit on one line, so we make the abbreviation of each flag rather terse. Here's how the status word is stored in memory:

```
        .CODE
        .8087
        ORG     100H
ENTRY:  JMP     PROG
```

```
    OP1       DQ 10.0
    OP2       DQ 5.0
    OP3       DQ 0.0
    NOPROB    DB 'No '
    PROB      DB 'Divide by Zero',13,10,'$'
 →  ST8087    DW  0
 →  SW RECORD B:1,C3:1,TOP:3,C2:1,C1:1,C0:1,IT:1,X:1,P:1,U:1,O:1,Z:1,D:1,I:1
    :
    :
```

By defining dummy record named SW, we have given names to each bit, and the assembler will recognize these names when we use them again. To check the Zero bit, for instance, we use the 80x86 instruction TEST, along with the directive MASK Z. The assembler knows the place number of the Z bit from our RECORD definition. The MASK directive will make a mask for us; for example, if the Z bit was the third bit place, the mask would be 0000000000000100B, or 0004. Here's how we use MASK Z:

```
PROG:     FINIT
          FLD       OP1
          FDIV      OP2
          MOV       AH,9
          LEA       DX,NOPROB
          FSTSW     ST8087
       →  TEST      ST8087,MASK Z
          JZ        OK1
          LEA       DX,PROB
OK1:      INT       21H
          :
          :
```

We take the operand OP1 and first divide it by OP2. We then reload OP1 and divide by OP3:

```
          .MODEL SMALL
          .CODE
          .8087
          ORG       100H
ENTRY:    JMP       PROG
       →  OP1       DQ 10.0
       →  OP2       DQ 5.0
       →  OP3       DQ 0.0
          NOPROB    DB 'No '
          PROB      DB 'Divide by Zero',13,10,'$'
          ST8087    DW  0
          SW RECORD B:1,C3:1,TOP:3,C2:1,C1:1,C0:1,IT:1,X:1,P:1,U:1,O:1,Z:1,D:1,I:1
          :
          :
```

The first division is just 10.0 divided by 5.0, which won't lead to a division by zero. The second division, 10.0 divided by 0.0, however, will. To do these divisions, we start off with a FINIT to reset the 80x87 and clear all exception flags. We then load OP1 into ST with FLD and divide by OP2:

```
        .MODEL  SMALL
        .CODE
        .8087
        ORG     100H
ENTRY:  JMP     PROG
        OP1     DQ 10.0
        OP2     DQ 5.0
        OP3     DQ 0.0
        NOPROB  DB 'No '
        PROB    DB 'Divide by Zero',13,10,'$'
        ST8087  DW  0
        SW RECORD B:1,C3:1,TOP:3,C2:1,C1:1,C0:1,IT:1,X:1,P:1,U:1,O:1,Z:1,D:1,I:1
PROG:   FINIT           ←
        FLD     OP1     ←
        FDIV    OP2     ←
        :
        :
```

We have to check the status word to make sure there was no divide by zero error. We will print out the results with the string printing function, Service 9 of INT 21H, so we start by optimistically loading DX with the address of the no-error message, NOPROB:

```
        .MODEL  SMALL
        .CODE
        .8087
        ORG     100H
ENTRY:  JMP     PROG
        OP1     DQ 10.0
        OP2     DQ 5.0
        OP3     DQ 0.0
      → NOPROB  DB 'No '
      → PROB    DB 'Divide by Zero',13,10,'$'
        ST8087  DW  0
        SW RECORD B:1,C3:1,TOP:3,C2:1,C1:1,C0:1,IT:1,X:1,P:1,U:1,O:1,Z:1,D:1,I:1
PROG:   FINIT
        FLD     OP1
        FDIV    OP2
      → MOV     AH,9
      → LEA     DX,NOPROB
        FSTSW   ST8087
        TEST    ST8087,MASK Z
        JZ      OK1
        LEA     DX,PROB
OK1:    INT     21H
        :
        :
```

To check if there really was no error, we store the status word in a memory location we have set aside, ST8087, using the instruction FSTSW ST8087. We can check to see if the zero-divide bit was set with TEST ST8087, MASK Z:

```
        .MODEL SMALL
        .CODE
        .8087
        ORG     100H
ENTRY:  JMP     PROG
        OP1     DQ 10.0
        OP2     DQ 5.0
        OP3     DQ 0.0
        NOPROB  DB 'No '
        PROB    DB 'Divide by Zero',13,10,'$'
     →  ST8087  DW  0
     →  SW RECORD B:1,C3:1,TOP:3,C2:1,C1:1,C0:1,IT:1,X:1,P:1,U:1,O:1,Z:1,D:1,I:1
PROG:   FINIT
        FLD     OP1
        FDIV    OP2
        MOV     AH,9
        LEA     DX,NOPROB
     →  FSTSW   ST8087
     →  TEST    ST8087,MASK Z
        JZ      OK1
        LEA     DX,PROB
OK1:    INT     21H
        :
        :
```

If the result of this TEST is zero, the zero-bit flag wasn't set. In that case, we want to print out the default message, NOPROB. Otherwise, of course, there has been an error, so we must load the address of the error message PROB into DX. We print out the results with INT 21H:

```
        .MODEL SMALL
        .CODE
        .8087
        ORG     100H
ENTRY:  JMP     PROG
        OP1     DQ 10.0
        OP2     DQ 5.0
        OP3     DQ 0.0
        NOPROB  DB 'No '
        PROB    DB 'Divide by Zero',13,10,'$'
        ST8087  DW  0
        SW RECORD B:1,C3:1,TOP:3,C2:1,C1:1,C0:1,IT:1,X:1,P:1,U:1,O:1,Z:1,D:1,I:1
PROG:   FINIT
        FLD     OP1
        FDIV    OP2
        MOV     AH,9
        LEA     DX,NOPROB
        FSTSW   ST8087
```

```
      → TEST     ST8087,MASK Z
      → JZ       OK1
      → LEA      DX,PROB
OK1:    INT      21H
        :
        :
```

The code for the second division is the same as for the first. After using FCLEX, then FINIT to be sure, we divide OP1 by OP3 and print out the result in the same way:

```
        .MODEL SMALL
        .CODE
        .8087
        ORG      100H
ENTRY:  JMP      PROG
        OP1      DQ 10.0
        OP2      DQ 5.0
        OP3      DQ 0.0
        NOPROB   DB 'No '
        PROB     DB 'Divide by Zero',13,10,'$'
        ST8087   DW  0
        SW RECORD B:1,C3:1,TOP:3,C2:1,C1:1,C0:1,IT:1,X:1,P:1,U:1,O:1,Z:1,D:1,I:1
PROG:   FINIT
        FLD      OP1
        FDIV     OP2
        MOV      AH,9
        LEA      DX,NOPROB
        FSTSW    ST8087
        TEST     ST8087,MASK Z
        JZ       OK1
        LEA      DX,PROB
OK1:    INT      21H
      → FCLEX
      → FINIT
      → FLD      OP1
      → FDIV     OP3
        MOV      AH,9
        LEA      DX,NOPROB
        FSTSW    ST8087
        TEST     ST8087,MASK Z
        JZ       OK2
        LEA      DX,PROB
OK2:    INT      21H
        INT      20H
        END      ENTRY
```

This second case is the one that does yield an error. In general, error checking on the 80x87 isn't difficult, thanks to the status word.

We've worked our way from doing things correctly to doing them incorrectly; and that finishes our discussion of the 80x87. Now we'll turn to OS/2.

# 9

# An OS/2 Primer

## The PS/2

Computer manufacturers always wonder where to go next with their products. This is a gamble for them—what if their new machines are rejected by the public? IBM isn't immune to it—consider, for example, the PCjr and other fallen stars.

On the other hand, several directions can always be followed with success if you're an established company—more speed and lower cost, for example. Also, the PC had some serious faults—poor graphics capabilities, for one, relatively slow microprocessors and memory restrictions, for two more. So IBM brought out the PS/2.

The PS/2 itself isn't such a marked departure from the PC; for the most part it simply follows the rule: more and faster. More disk space, with faster access; more memory to expand into; faster processors; more keys on the keyboard; faster clocks.

One significant change was PC/2's improved graphics abilities. It was clear—especially because of the success of the Macintosh—that this area had been a disaster before the EGA. Although this doesn't follow the rule of more and faster, improved graphics too was a predictable upgrade.

So when the PS/2 appeared, with its 101-key keyboard, high-capacity hard drives (as well as larger capacity 3.5 inch diskettes), 256-color VGA, and ability to hold megabytes of memory, it was wonderful, but not wholly unexpected.

## Micro Follows Mega

Usually, you can know where microcomputers are going simply by looking at mainframe computers. Mainframes represent an established, successful market. Over the years, they have taken their present forms—every part of them has proven itself in the marketplace. For example, it was clear even in 1981 that hard disks were on the way, along with bigger memories. The development of the PC has followed this course, within the confines of the microprocessor chips that it has to work with.

However, the Intel chips not only have gotten faster, but they have also augmented the instruction set and allowed for an altogether new ability—*multitasking*.

Of course, multitasking itself isn't new, and it was put into the Intel chips mostly because it also follows the development of mainframe machines, which are multitasking machines. It is inconceivable today to think of a modern mainframe computer that cannot support many users at the same time. Intel decided that it could do no less in the development of its chips; its multitasking follows the development of the big, proven machines.

## Single-User Multitasking

On the other hand, what *is* new is the idea of single-user multitasking.

Most IBM microcomputers are single-user machines. Although networks exist, most machines aren't connected. Now, although multitasking originated on mainframe computers to handle multiple users, it's being brought to a single-user machine. Single-user multitasking that can run many programs at the same time? This is new, and, to a large extent, it's a risk on IBM's part. And it's the idea behind OS/2.

Being able to multitask isn't an easy thing to accomplish. In fact, OS/2 brings with it most of the classical parts of a mainframe mulitasking operating system, like the use of (we'll examine these soon) hardware gates, protection rings, semaphores that programs can use to communicate with each other, pipes, queues, and other things. Much of OS/2 is devoted to these new, and, to us, perhaps strange things.

## OS/2 is Not So Different

On the other hand, you shouldn't get the idea that programming in OS/2 is so different from what we have been doing—it's not. The writers of OS/2 went to great pains to include DOS compatibility. Pascal is still Pascal, even under OS/2. There is a *DOS compatibility mode* under OS/2, which you can select easily. For most purposes, this puts you back in DOS. Programs that won't run under OS/2 will run here. And many programs that will run under OS/2 have been specially designed to run under DOS as well.

Assembly language instructions like JMP, CMP, JAE, ADD and so on haven't changed. The chips used do not change when we use OS/2; they still use the same instruction set that they always have. But that's not the only thing. Most of the DOS interrupt services that we have so carefully developed until now in this book are also available in OS/2—under, however, different names.

> If you recall, DOS functions could not be used from a memory-resident program, since DOS is not *reentrant*. OS/2 *is* reentrant. You can use any OS/2 function from any program running. This is a tremendous advantage.

Before, under BIOS and DOS, we called these services using the INT instruction in our programs. Now, BIOS and DOS are no longer there. Instead, we will be calling OS/2. In fact, calling is the appropriate term for the way we will use OS/2. Under DOS and BIOS, we used system services by loading some registers and using INT. Under OS/2, we will push the values we used to load into registers onto the stack and then *call* OS/2.

Here's an example. If we wanted to print the message "No Worries." under DOS, here is how we could do it:

```
MESSAGE             DB        "No Worries.$"
          :
          MOV       DX,OFFSET MESSAGE
          MOV       AH,9
          INT       21H
```

We would just use service 9 of INT 21H, the major DOS interrupt. We load AH with the number of the service we want, load the data's address into DS:DX, and we're off.

Frequently, services like this led to some disorganization with the interrupts. As you may recall, some interrupts became huge like INT 21H, or INT 10H—the BIOS screen interrupt. Another huge interrupt is INT 13H, the disk interrupt. Like most interrupts that have become huge, it did so because more was added to the system. Disks became more and more complex, and INT 13H (originally designed to deal only with diskettes) developed not only an immense number of services, but also, some of the services started developing many subservices. Although this system still works, it doesn't give the impression of a well-thought-out design.

OS/2 is different in this regard. Here you call services by name, not as services under an INT. Here is how we would print out the same message under OS/2:

```
MESSAGE             DB        "No Worries."
MESSAGELENGTH       EQU       $-MESSAGE

          PUSH      DS
          PUSH      OFFSET MESSAGE
          PUSH      MESSAGELENGTH
          PUSH      0                   ;Video handle
          CALL      VioWrtTTY
```

Instead of loading the address into DS:DX, we push DS, then push MESSAGE's offset address. Instead of terminating the string with $, we explicitly tell OS/2 how long the string to print is by pushing MESSAGELENGTH. Then we push 0 to make sure we use the standard video handle (the "video handle" will always be 0 for us), and CALL a routine named VioWrtTTY.

Notice the way we found the length of MESSAGE in this example: with MESSAGELENGTH EQU $-MESSAGE. The $ symbol refers to the offset from the beginning of the current segment (here the code segment). The $ symbol is a very important operator in assembly language.

This is how we reach the system resources—with a CALL, not an INT. VioWrtTTY is the OS/2 service that prints a character string at the current cursor position, the writeln() of low-level OS/2. Notice that since it is a call, and the procedure for VioWrtTTY is not present in our program, we will have to declare VioWrtTTY as EXTRN. Somewhere in the program, we will have to have the line: EXTRN VioWrtTTY:FAR.

This is the case for ALL OS/2 services, which will all have to be declared EXTRN, and these references will be picked up at link time. This doesn't mean that the full code for VioWrtTTY will be linked into your program, as would be normal for linking (that would make all OS/2 programs prohibitively large). Instead, what is linked is a reference to VioWrtTTY, not the whole thing. This is called *dynamic linking*, which we'll see in a moment. When your program is loaded to run, and only then, the rest of VioWrtTTY will be attached.

## Understanding OS/2

Despite the similar setup, to understand OS/2, we'll have to become familiar with a new way of looking at the computer and a new set of concepts (such as the idea of threads, which is central to OS/2). This will take some examination on our part of just what is going on. To start understanding OS/2, we'll examine the chip that fathered it, the 80286.

# The 80286

The 80286 chip has two modes of operating: real and protected modes. The two operating systems for the PS/2 match these modes—DOS (real) and OS/2 (protected).

Real mode is what we have been working in until now. The memory—all 1 M of it, is available to the user (minus the BIOS 384K at the top, leaving 640K for general use). Here we use segments and interrupts, and only one program runs at a time.

Protected mode is, as its name suggests, a mode in which multiple programs can run, protected from each other. There are various levels of hierarchy in the computer. And in protected mode, we no longer use segments, but, rather, segment selectors.

## Segment Selectors

Segment selectors look to our programs just like real segment addresses. That is, they are 16-bit numbers that fit into the segment registers. We will work with them here in the same way we used to work with segment addresses.

What they are really is a different story. In reality, a segment selector points to a table called the segment descriptor table. The segment descriptor pointed to in the table holds the real information about the real segment in memory.

This means that we could have 1343H in the CS register when our program is loaded, and we could think that we are dealing with segment 1343H—that is, 1343:0000 in memory—but we aren't. This selector points to an entry in the segment descriptor table, where the real segment address is stored. And this real address does not use the 20 bits we are used to, but 24. This means that we can now address up to 16 M of memory—quite an improvement.

The reason selectors are useful for multitasking is that OS/2 can move the real segment in memory around wherever it wanted to put it—and the same selector (in a register like CS or DS) would still point to it (although indirectly). If a program finished, segments in memory could be moved around until memory was compacted. Keep in mind that these segments can be of various lengths—they aren't necessarily 64K (which is their maximum length, unless you have an 80386).

A selector is really a memory handle, like the ones used in the Macintosh, defined as a pointer to a pointer (if you're ready for that). The operating system can change the pointer that points directly to memory, without having to change what the program uses—the pointer to the pointer.

If the memory is available, OS/2 is a wizard at it; up to 16 M of it in the machine. And, as if that weren't enough, you can use what is called *virtual memory*. What this means is that if OS/2 runs out of memory in the machine, it will take the least-frequently used sections of memory and send them out to the disk. There they will wait until there is either room for them again, or they are specifically referenced by a program then running.

When a section of memory is sent out to the disk, it is *swapped out*—a common occurrence in mainframe machines. In the PS/2, however, the disk-acccess time is pretty slow (compared with mainframe hard disks), so it will be noticeable if your program starts to swap out very much. What this means, in practice, is that the 16 M limit is not truly exceeded by using virtual (disk) memory but just softened.

Besides selectors and virtual memory, the 80286 uses almost all the normal tools for multitasking; and a complete description of them is beyond this book (a complete description is beyond almost *any* book). But we can mention a few more things that will be important.

## Gates

The 80286 uses hardware *gates* in protected mode. When we call a far location, control has to go through a gate before we can access memory in that location. The 80286 maintains a table that tells it whether we are qualified to pass through that gate, and, if not, access is denied. All this is done on a hardware level. This means that each program will stay in its own area of memory, although it can ask for more or even set up memory to share with other programs.

What is important for us is that if a program attempts to go through an illegal gate by making a memory access outside its own memory space, OS/2 terminates the program. A screen will come up, telling us why the program was terminated and what all the registers were set to.

## Rings

In addition, there are *rings* of protection. Ring 0 is the highest priority ring, and the innermost OS/2 procedures (the OS/2 kernel) run there. We progress outward to I/O handlers in ring 2 and then to normal application programs, which are always in ring 3, the ring with the least priority. Depending on which ring our process is in, we will be granted denied access to certain parts of memory.

Time-sharing depends on the rings. Inside the same ring, time is allocated equally. However, a program with a lower ring number (and therefore higher priority) will always get time before a program with a higher number (that is, lower priority).

# Multitasking Software Concepts

Now that we have seen a little of the chip, we can see that it was built with multitasking in mind. And OS/2 exploits that capability. To make a machine truly multitasking is a demanding problem, and it brings with it new conceptions of how programs will run. Central to multitasking are what OS/2 calls *threads*.

## Threads

A thread is an important concept in OS/2—it is what runs through programs that are active. For example, let's say that you have a notepad popup program under DOS and are running an editor. The notepad isn't running, because it has no *thread*. Under DOS there is only a single thread, and, here, the editor has it. When you pop up the notepad, then it gets the thread.

In OS/2, you can have multiple threads running at once, like voices in a speaker system. If the speaker has only one voice, like the PC or PS/2 speaker, then even if you emulate a fine instrument, you can play only one at a time. Multiple voices mean that multiple instruments can play at the same time, as in an orchestra. What voices are to a symphony, threads are to OS/2. Saying that OS/2 supports multiple threads means that many programs can be active at once.

## I/O Under OS/2

Also, to multitask, the computer can no longer let programs take over I/O devices, as happens under DOS. This is why many modem programs or some editors (which write directly to the screen controller chip registers) won't work even under OS/2's DOS compatibility mode. If you want direct access to an I/O device, instead of using the OS/2 services, you must ask OS/2 for permission.

## Communication Between Programs

OS/2 allows programs to pass data and signals back and forth. Although we aren't going to dig into those services here (they are far too complicated for this treatment: See my book *OS/2 Assembly Language* also by Brady Books), you can allocate shared segments. This segment can then be reached by multiple programs. In addition, you can ask the system to put aside an open segment that all programs can access.

Besides shared segments, *semaphores* communicate between programs. A semaphore is used by two programs as a flag. With it, one can tell the other that it is using, for example, a certain part of memory, and that the other shouldn't use it also until the semaphore is *cleared*.

Other types of communication can take place through OS/2 constructions like queues and pipes. You are probably familiar with queues from the PRINT command in DOS. When you queue a number of files to print, PRINT takes the one that was first and starts to print it. The next one in line has to wait (in the queue) until the first one is finished. In the same way, programs in OS/2 can set up queues for use between themselves.

Pipes work in a similar way—data can be put into a pipe from the output of one program and read as the input of another. Pipes can accept data from one program perhaps faster than the rate at which the other program can accept it. In this way, they can act as a buffer between programs. Even so, pipes aren't inexhaustible. When a pipe fills up, then OS/2 blocks the program that fills it until it is at least partially drained.

With these tools built into it, OS/2 has good support for interprogram (or intraprogram) communication. What we've said here only serves as the briefest of introductions to them; for more details, consult an OS/2 book.

## Files

The way we handle files is also going to need rethinking under multitasking. The OS/2 services that will deal with files work in similar ways to their DOS counterparts. The OS/2 services use file handles, just as DOS does (File Control Blocks are not supported any longer). One thing that will be different is the stress put on the *way* that the files are opened—do you want to read from the file? Or both read and write? Do you want to deny access to the files by other programs? If so, do you want to deny only programs that will write to the file or all other programs?

The program that first opens a file can write its own ticket in a number of ways. If it opens the file for both reading and writing and sets access from other programs to DENY_ALL, then it just about owns the file. On the other hand, a more benign program might open the file for READ_ONLY, and DENY_NONE. Then a second file might open the file for READ_ONLY and yet DENY_WRITE. If a third program tries to open the program for READ_WRITE, it won't be able to, since program 2 has opened it with a DENY_WRITE. Program 3 is out of luck in this case.

When a file is open, there is a file pointer—actually a *logical file pointer*, which operates just as the file pointer we already know about does. When we read or write, the file pointer is automatically advanced.

Now we've got a pretty good idea of what multitasking will mean to us. Let's jump in and see how to program in OS/2.

# Writing an OS/2 Program

Here's where we start to write code and put what we've learned to work. To use OS/2 services instead of the DOS and BIOS ones, we have to know how to reach them.

There are six major groups of OS/2 services that we can call from our assembly language programs—that is, link to—and each of them starts with a particular three-letter combination.

## The OS/2 Services

Vio, which means video Input/Output, is the way that you will write to the screen. It replaces BIOS INT 10H. Examples of the Vio services are VioWrtTTY, VioWrtCharStr, and VioScrollUp. You can get an idea of what they do just from their names.

Mou is the prefix for services that deal with the mouse. An example is MouGetPtrPos.

Kbd means Keyboard. These services are used for reading what has been typed. Two examples of Kbd services are KbdPeek and KbdCharIn. Dos may be a prefix that you were not expecting. In fact, the commands prefixed with Dos make up most of OS/2. All memory-management services—and this is a big consideration under a multitasking operating system—begin with Dos. The file-management services begin with Dos. In fact, everything not I/O-related begins with Dos. Some examples are DosWrite, DosRead, DosOpen, DosMKDir, and DosGetMachineMode.

The Win group of services is the foundation of the Presentation Manager, which we'll investigate in the next chapter. There services let you display and manage windows on the screen. Finally, the Gpi services make up the Presentation Manager Graphics Interface. These services let you write or draw in windows (including some services that rival Pascal's abilities). In many cases, the use of named procedures makes code easier to read. After all, what is INT 21H service 3FH? It is better to call the similar OS/2 service DosRead.

Also, the calling procedure makes it easier for high level languages to use OS/2. Under DOS, using assembly language routines was not very easy for users of Pascal. Now it will be much easier. The way you used to interact with assembly language from Pascal was to push parameters onto the stack, as we've seen, and worry about the interface. Now, because services are called, you can just call the routines directly.

As we'll see later, the way OS/2 returns errors is similar to the DOS interrupts too—it uses the AX register. Before, we could check AX for an error code. If AX was zero, this meant there was no error (although some services returned data in AX or some value that was not zero was returned to indicate no error). Under OS/2, the error code will also be returned in AX, and if it is zero, there was no error. If it was not zero, we will have to track down the error.

When we've filled our program with the Vio, Mou, Dos, Win, Gpi, and Kbd services, we can link your .OBJ files to OS/2 libraries to make a running .EXE file. As noted, however, this doesn't link in the routines right there.

## Dynamic Linking

This new aspect of OS/2 is called *dynamic linking*. What we have developed so far in this book, OS/2 calls *static linking*. In static linking, the .EXE or .COM file is complete. Everything that is necessary to run it is in it. All the code that needs to do the job is there.

Dynamic linking is different. Here is how it works: You run your .ASM file through MASM as you used to do under DOS. Then you use the OS/2 linker, LINK (which can also be run under DOS if you wish). LINK will ask for the name of the .OBJ file, and the names of any libraries you want to give it. One such library—the library we'll use—is called DOSCALLS.LIB. Under Presentation Manager, we'll have to use a new library, called OS2.LIB, which is available only from certain software programming toolkits.

The DOSCALLS.LIB library (supplied on the OS/2 disks) is set up to satisfy references to external calls to the OS/2 services. What usually happens at this point is that the procedure that satisfies the external call in the .ASM file is read in from the library and included in the .EXE file. Here, however, is where the difference comes in.

Instead of procedures, what is in OS/2 .LIB files are the names of *dynamic link library files*, and the locations in those dynamic link library files of the called procedure. The dynamic link library files have the extension .DLL.

Let's take an example. One OS/2 service, named DosOpen, is used to open or create files. If we were linking in a call to DosOpen, there would be a reference in DOSCALLS.LIB for DosOpen. It would indicate that DosOpen exists in a .DLL file (actually DOSCALL1.DLL) and give its location there.

When the .EXE file was loaded into memory to run, the loader would see that DosRead is indicated as being found in a .DLL file, and the appropriate .DLL file is read in. The procedure is placed in memory, and its address is placed into the call instruction in the program being loaded.

> If DosRead had already been installed in memory by another program, it isn't read in again.

This is what is meant by dynamic linking—the actual linking of the call to the called procedure isn't done until the program is loaded in and run.

## OS/2 EXE File Shell with DosExit

Now we know something about the OS/2 services, we can see how to create an .EXE file by using LINK under OS/2. We're ready to see what an .EXE file will look like.

Our OS/2 .EXE file shell isn't so different from what we are used to with .COM files—in fact, it's quite similar:

```
        .286
        .MODEL  SMALL
        .STACK  200H

        .DATA

        .CODE
        EXTRN   DOSEXIT:FAR

ENTRY:  ;Program goes here.


EXIT:   PUSH    1               ;A Normal Exit.
        PUSH    0
        CALL    DOSEXIT

        END     ENTRY
```

At the top, there is a directive .286, which begins the .ASM file. This enables the assembler to assemble instructions for the 80286 chip. Next, note that we have included a .STACK 200H directive.

```
        .286
        .MODEL   SMALL
        .STACK   200H     ←

        .DATA

        .CODE
        EXTRN    DOSEXIT:FAR

ENTRY:  ;Program goes here.


EXIT:   PUSH     1                    ;A Normal Exit.
        PUSH     0
        CALL     DOSEXIT

        END      ENTRY
```

This is necessary for .EXE files—in .COM files, DOS set a stack up for us at the end of the segment, but we are responsible for it in .EXE files. Under OS/2, all you have to do is include the line .STACK 200H; the 200H indicates the size of the stack (in bytes). This size is OK for most OS/2 programs; under the Presentation Manager, however, we will have to use a larger stack.

We have also set aside a .DATA area, although we don't use any data here. We saw the .DATA directive in Chapter 6, when we linked Pascal and assembly language together.

At the end of the program, we use the DosExit call. This is how you end a program under OS/2. To use it, you have to push two words, and then CALL DosExit.

```
        .286
        .MODEL   SMALL
        .STACK   200H

        .DATA

        .CODE
        EXTRN    DOSEXIT:FAR

ENTRY:  ;Program goes here.

EXIT:   PUSH     1                    ;A Normal Exit.
        PUSH     0
        CALL     DOSEXIT  ←

        END      ENTRY
```

The first word pushed is either 0 or 1 and indicates whether you want to terminate all threads. If you recall what a thread means, then you can see what this does—it is possible for a program to have many threads executing at the same time. A 0 here means that DosExit should terminate *only* the current thread; a 1 means that *all* threads should be terminated. We will always set this word to 1, since we aren't going to deal with multithreaded processes.

The second word pushed is a "termination code," which can be passed back to a program that started the current one. Since we aren't going to get that fancy here, we'll always use a "code" of 0:

```
        .286
        .MODEL   SMALL
        .STACK   200H

        .DATA

        .CODE
        EXTRN    DOSEXIT:FAR

ENTRY:  ;Program goes here.


EXIT:   PUSH     1         ←
        PUSH     0         ←
        CALL     DOSEXIT

        END      ENTRY
```

DosExit is also declared as EXTRN FAR in the beginning of the program, as all service calls will have to be from now on.

## Stack Preparation Under OS/2

Now that we are familiar with the stack-loading (as opposed to register-loading) calls of OS/2, we have to look at the *type* of items that can be loaded onto the stack. There are three such types:

| *Type* | *Means* |
|---|---|
| WORD | Just a 16-bit value. |
| DWORD | A value held in two words, like DX:AX. The high word of a register pair (DX here) is pushed first. |
| PTR | An address pointer. Here you just push values like DS:BX or ES:DI onto the stack. The *selector* value is pushed first, followed by the offset (like DS and then BX). |

Because of the nature of the OS/2 Applications Programming Interface (API) and its heavy reliance on pushing values on the stack, we will become quite familiar with these types.

## Defaults When Loading

When the .EXE file is first loaded, the registers are set to specific values. CS:IP is set to the entry point of the program, as expected. SS:SP is pointed to the top of the stack. DS holds the selector for the data segment. But AX holds something a little new—the selector for the *environment*. This is much like the PSP (Program Segment Prefix) under DOS in that we will be able to find all the characters typed after the program's name on the command line in the environment.

If you are going to use information from the environment, it is usual to move AX into DS (having preserved the data segment's selector, usually in ES). Then DS:0000 is the beginning of the environment. At this location, you will find an ASCIIZ string (ASCII terminated with a 0 byte) that gives the current program's full name, including path. For example, if you started a program named GO.EXE in C:\SUB like this:

```
C\SUB>GO
```

then the characters appearing at the beginning of the environment would be "C:\SUB\GO.EXE",0.

The BX register holds the offset, in the environment, of the string of characters typed after the program's name on the command line. If we had typed:

```
C\SUB>GO HI THERE!
```

(and had moved the environment selector into DS), we would find this at DS:BX—"HI THERE!",0.

In addition, when the .EXE file is first loaded, DX holds the size of the stack, and CX holds the actual length of the data segment. This information can be useful to a program as it is running. To produce the .EXE file GO.EXE from the file GO.ASM, we will use MASM:

```
MASM GO;
```

and then LINK. When we link, we'll have to use OS/2's linker and include the library that will resolve the EXTRN references for us, DOSCALLS.LIB. Here is the LINK command for GO.OBJ:

```
C>LINK GO          ← Type this
IBM Linker/2  Version 1.00
Copyright (C) IBM Corporation 1987
Copyright (C) Microsoft Corp 1983-1987.  All rights reserved.

Run File [GO.EXE]:
List File [NUL.MAP]:
Libraries [.LIB]: DOSCALLS       ← And this
Definitions File [NUL .DEF]:
```

That's our OS/2 .EXE file shell. It's not much different than a DOS .COM file shell. In fact, almost everything we examine will have some close DOS or BIOS counterpart, beginning with the first OS/2 programming topic we take up: OS/2 Output.

# OS/2 Output (Vio and DosWrite)

We took up the topic of output when we started programming in this book, and it makes sense to do so again. Although the OS/2 services match BIOS INT 10H, they have a flavor all their own.

Character output is always done in strings in OS/2. If you just want to type out one character, that's a string of length 1. Also, you pass the length of strings to OS/2—you don't terminate them, as you do under DOS (with $).

You may recall that the BIOS treatment of the cursor when typing out characters was sometimes disappointing because the cursor wasn't updated. OS/2 is even worse than that (unfortunately) in most of its string-printing services. It ignores the cursor altogether—you have to specify a row and column at which printout will start. This awkward method takes some getting used to in your programs.

## The DosWrite Service

```
PUSH    WORD    A file or device handle (=1 to print on screen)
PUSH    PTR     Address of data to be printed
PUSH    WORD    Number of bytes to print
PUSH    PTR     Address at which OS/2 is to return the number of bytes
                        it actually wrote (more useful for files than
                        typing on to the screen)
CALL    DOSWRITE
```

Before we get into the Vio services, let's look at DosWrite, similar to the all-purpose DOS INT 21H output service (40H). You simply give DosWrite a handle to write to, the location of the data, the length of the data, and you're off. This handle could be a handle to a file, which you got when opening or creating a file (we'll cover the OS/2 versions of this next chapter), or it could be one of the predefined handles.

In OS/2, the predefined handles are: Standard Input (STDIN = keyboard for all our purposes) = 0; Standard Output (STDOUT = the screen for us) = 1; and Standard Error (STDERR) = 2. These handles are always available (unless you are running under OS/2 detached mode—see the end of this chapter); they don't have to be opened with DosOpen, as for files.

To send output to the screen, we select a handle of 1 (STDOUT). We also have to give DosWrite these things on the stack, in order:

| | |
|---|---|
| WORD | A file or device handle (=1 to print on screen) |
| PTR | Address of data to be printed |
| WORD | Number of bytes to print |
| PTR | Address at which OS/2 is to return the number of bytes it actually wrote (more useful for files than typing on the screen) |

Let's make this clear with an example. Here is a small program, DOSWRITE.ASM, from beginning to end. All it does is print out the message "No Worries.":

```
        .286
        .MODEL  SMALL
        .STACK  200H

        .DATA
MESSAGE         DB      "No Worries."
MESSAGELEN      EQU     $-MESSAGE
NUMBER_BYTES    DW      0

        .CODE
        EXTRN   DOSWRITE:FAR, DOSEXIT:FAR

ENTRY:  PUSH    1
        PUSH    DS
        PUSH    OFFSET  MESSAGE
        PUSH    MESSAGELEN
        PUSH    DS
        PUSH    OFFSET NUMBER_BYTES
        CALL    DOSWRITE

        PUSH    1                   ;Exit normally.
        PUSH    0
        CALL    DOSEXIT


        END     ENTRY
```

Note that we put the message into the .DATA segment. Since this is our first OS/2 functioning program, let's take a look at it. We simply set up the message in the data segment:

```
        .DATA
MESSAGE         DB      "No Worries."   ←
MESSAGELEN      EQU     $-MESSAGE       ←
NUMBER_BYTES    DW      0
```

Note also that since we will require the length of the message, we find it with MESSAGELEN EQU $-MESSAGE, right after the definition of MESSAGE. We've used this method before—this just fills MESSAGELEN with the length of message. Now we add these instructions to the .EXE file shell:

```
        .286
        .MODEL  SMALL
        .STACK  200H

        .DATA
MESSAGE         DB      "No Worries."
MESSAGELEN      EQU     $-MESSAGE
NUMBER_BYTES    DW      0

        .CODE
        EXTRN   DOSWRITE:FAR, DOSEXIT:FAR

ENTRY:  PUSH    1
        PUSH    DS
        PUSH    OFFSET  MESSAGE
        PUSH    MESSAGELEN
        PUSH    DS
        PUSH    OFFSET NUMBER_BYTES
        CALL    DOSWRITE

        PUSH    1               ;Exit normally.
        PUSH    0
        CALL    DOSEXIT

        END     ENTRY
```

(Having carefully declared DosWrite EXTRN). In particular, note that we are now pushing immediate values, such as:

```
→       PUSH    1
                :
        PUSH    OFFSET  MESSAGE
        PUSH    MESSAGELEN
```

This is the first time we have seen this immediate method of pushing values, and it will come in handy with the enormous number of pushes you have to do in the average OS/2 program. Immediate pushing will not work on the 8088 or 8086 chips. To push values there, you must first load them into registers (of course, OS/2 will not work with 8088s or 8086s either).

In our program, we push the video handle (1), the address of MESSAGE, the length of MESSAGE, and the address of the location where OS/2 will return the number of bytes actually typed to the screen.

```
        .286
        .MODEL  SMALL
        .STACK  200H

        .DATA
MESSAGE         DB      "No Worries."
MESSAGELEN      EQU     $-MESSAGE
NUMBER_BYTES    DW      0
```

```
         .CODE
         EXTRN   DOSWRITE:FAR, DOSEXIT:FAR
ENTRY:   PUSH    1
         PUSH    DS
         PUSH    OFFSET  MESSAGE
         PUSH    MESSAGELEN
         PUSH    DS
         PUSH    OFFSET NUMBER_BYTES
         CALL    DOSWRITE
         :
         :
```

And then end with DosExit:

```
         .286
         .MODEL  SMALL
         .STACK  200H

         .DATA
MESSAGE          DB      "No Worries."
MESSAGELEN       EQU     $-MESSAGE
NUMBER_BYTES     DW      0

         .CODE
         EXTRN   DOSWRITE:FAR, DOSEXIT:FAR

ENTRY:   PUSH    1
         PUSH    DS
         PUSH    OFFSET  MESSAGE
         PUSH    MESSAGELEN
         PUSH    DS
         PUSH    OFFSET NUMBER_BYTES
         CALL    DOSWRITE

→        PUSH    1                   ;Exit normally.
→        PUSH    0
→        CALL    DOSEXIT

         END     ENTRY
```

Give this little program a try if you want to see our "No Worries." message appear under OS/2. Our first OS/2 program works and wasn't so hard to write.

DosWrite types out the bytes that you have selected starting at the current cursor position—as does the next OS/2 service, VioWrtTTY.

## VioWrtTTY—TTY Output to Screen (Uses and Updates Cursor)

```
PUSH     PTR      Pointer to the ASCII string to print on the screen.
PUSH     WORD     Length of the string.
PUSH     WORD     The VIO handle (must be 0).
CALL     VIOWRTTTY
```

The first of the Vio services we will work on is VioWrtTTY, which is close to its INT 10H teletype counterpart. Again, you pass the address of the data to be printed, then the number of bytes to print. The Vio handle for the screen, however, isn't 1, but 0. We'll see that you have to pass the Vio handle for virtually every Vio service, and it will always be 0. Perhaps in some future version of OS/2, multiple physical screens will be allowed, giving you non-zero Vio handles.

VioWrtTTY starts printing at the cursor location, unlike all the following Vio services. It treats screen control characters like carriage returns (ASCII 13) or linefeeds (ASCII 10) as control characters—it doesn't print them out as funny symbols as some of the BIOS services do. Instead, ASCII 13 generates a carriage return, ASCII 10 will generate a line feed, and so forth.

Also, the string to be printed is only ASCII; no screen display attributes are included. You may recall that characters typed to the screen can sometimes be specified as ASCII with a particular attribute under BIOS. This same thing can be done a number of ways under OS/2.

## VioWrtCellStr—Write a Cell String

```
PUSH     PTR      Address of cell string (attribute, character,
                  attribute, character...) to be printed.
PUSH     WORD     The number of bytes to be printed
PUSH     WORD     Screen Row where the string will be printed
PUSH     WORD     Screen Column where the string will be printed
PUSH     WORD     Vio Handle (must be 0).
CALL     VIOWRTCELLSTR
```

This is the first of the normal Vio printing services. VioWrtCellStr improves on its BIOS counterpart in that you can specify different attributes for each character to be printed. To make the Vio Services that print out at a specifed row, column print out at the cursor position, use the cursor position returned by VioGetCursor-Pos, covered below.

The combination of screen attribute and ASCII character (two bytes) is referred to as a character *cell*. This Vio service will let you print out a whole string of such cells.

The screen attributes that can be used in the Vio services that print attributes work like this:

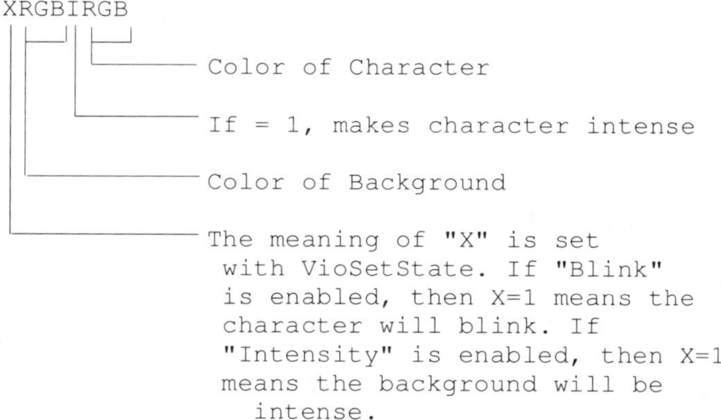


An example would be 01110100B = 74H, red on a white background, or 00001111 = FH, high intensity white on a black background.

For example, if you wanted to print out four red A's (ASCII 41H) on a white background (attribute 74H), followed by three blue B's (ASCII 42H) on a white background (attribute 71H), then you could define a *cell string* like this (with attribute first, then ASCII, attribute, ASCII, and so on):

```
CELL_STRING     DB 74H, 41H, 74H, 41H, 74H, 41H, 74H, 41H, 74H, 41H
                DB 71H, 42H, 71H, 42H, 71H, 42H, 71H, 42H
```

This service is one of the ones where you have to specify row and column at which your cell string will be printed.

| Remember that (0,0) is the upper left-hand corner of the screen.

If we wanted to use a service more like the old BIOS, where we specify what to type and and give only one attribute, the next service, VioWrtCharStrAtt, will let us do so.

## VioWrtCharStrAttr—Write Character String With Attribute

```
PUSH    PTR     Address of the character string to print on screen.
PUSH    WORD    The length in bytes of the character string.
PUSH    WORD    Screen Row at which printout will start.
PUSH    WORD    Screen Column at which printout will start.
PUSH    PTR     Address of the attribute byte.
PUSH    WORD    The Vio handle (must be 0).
CALL    VIOWRTCHARSTRATTR
```

This service prints out a character string (specified as a string of ASCII bytes) with a single attribute. It is what you'd expect from seeing the previous services, except that the way you pass the attribute byte to OS/2 seems like overkill. Instead of loading the attribute byte into a word (in, say, the lower byte) and pushing that, you pass the *address* (two words) of the attribute byte as stored in memory.

Let's give VioWrtStrAttr a try ourselves. Let's print out the "No Worries." message with some dramatic attribute—say blue on black, attribute 1. First, we'd start with the .EXE file shell:

```
        .286
        .MODEL  SMALL
        .STACK  200H

        .DATA

        .CODE
        EXTRN   DosExit:FAR

ENTRY:

        PUSH    1                   ;Exit normally.
        PUSH    0
        CALL    DOSEXIT

        END     ENTRY
```

Then we can add the data we'll need—the string itself, the string's length, and the attribute byte (which we'll call ATTRIBYTE):

```
          .286
          .MODEL  SMALL
          .STACK  200H

          .DATA
MESSAGE         DB      "No Worries."                        ←
MESSAGELEN      EQU     $-MESSAGE                            ←
ATTRIBYTE       DB      1       ;Use a blue-on-black attribute. ←

          .CODE
          EXTRN   DosExit:FAR

ENTRY:

          PUSH    1                   ;Exit normally.
          PUSH    0
          CALL    DOSEXIT

          END     ENTRY
```

Now we have to set up for VioWrtCharStrAtt. To begin, we have to push a pointer to MESSAGE. Pointers are pushed with the selector register first, so here goes:

```
        .286
        .MODEL  SMALL
        .STACK  200H

        .DATA
MESSAGE         DB      "No Worries."
MESSAGELEN      EQU     $-MESSAGE
ATTRIBYTE       DB      1       ;Use a blue-on-black attribute.

        .CODE
        EXTRN   VioWrtCharStrAtt:FAR, DosExit:FAR

ENTRY:  PUSH    DS              ←
        PUSH    OFFSET  MESSAGE ←
        PUSH    MESSAGELEN      ←

        PUSH    1               ;Exit normally.
        PUSH    0
        CALL    DOSEXIT

        END     ENTRY
```

Here we have followed it with the message's length, as required. Next, we have to select the row and column location of our message on the screen. Let's choose row 10, column 30—near the middle of the screen:

```
        .286
        .MODEL  SMALL
        .STACK  200H

        .DATA
MESSAGE         DB      "No Worries."
MESSAGELEN      EQU     $-MESSAGE
ATTRIBYTE       DB      1       ;Use a blue-on-black attribute.

        .CODE
        EXTRN   VioWrtCharStrAtt:FAR, DosExit:FAR

ENTRY:  PUSH    DS
        PUSH    OFFSET  MESSAGE
        PUSH    MESSAGELEN
        PUSH    10              ←
        PUSH    30              ←

        PUSH    1               ;Exit normally.
        PUSH    0
        CALL    DOSEXIT

        END     ENTRY
```

Finally, we push a pointer to the attribute byte ATTRIBYTE and the Vio handle (0). Here's the whole program:

```
        .286
        .MODEL  SMALL
        .STACK  200H

        .DATA
MESSAGE         DB      "No Worries."
MESSAGELEN      EQU     $-MESSAGE
ATTRIBYTE       DB      1         ;Use a blue-on-black attribute.

        .CODE
        EXTRN   VioWrtCharStrAtt:FAR, DosExit:FAR

ENTRY:  PUSH    DS
        PUSH    OFFSET  MESSAGE
        PUSH    MESSAGELEN
        PUSH    10
        PUSH    30
        PUSH    DS                        ←
        PUSH    OFFSET ATTRIBYTE          ←
        PUSH    0                         ←
        CALL    VioWrtCharStrAtt          ←

        PUSH    1                 ;Exit normally.
        PUSH    0
        CALL    DOSEXIT

        END     ENTRY
```

Another thing you could do under BIOS was simply to print out characters without changing the underlying attributes for those screen positions, and you can do that here too, with VioWrtCharStr.

## VioWrtCharStr

```
PUSH    PTR     Address of the character string to print.
PUSH    WORD    Length in bytes of the character string.
PUSH    WORD    Screen Row at which printout will start.
PUSH    WORD    Screen Column at which printout will start.
PUSH    WORD    Vio handle (must be 0).
CALL            VIOWRTCHARSTR
```

VioWrtCharStr prints a string of ASCII characters. When the string is printed on the screen, the existing attributes for each screen location aren't changed. If VioWrtCharStr is writing over a blue patch, through a red patch, and into a green patch, these attributes will be maintained.

You can use this simple service when you've set up the screen in some way that you want to maintain, instead of having to select some different attribute.

# The Cursor

As we've seen, many Vio services act independently of the cursor. If you want to coordinate what you are typing on the screen with the cursor, you'll have to find the cursor position (row, column) and pass it as the row, column at which printout is to begin.

To find the location of the cursor, use VioGetCursorPos.

## VioGetCursorPos—Get Cursor Position

```
PUSH    PTR     Address at which OS/2 will return current cursor row
PUSH    PTR     Address at which OS/2 will return current cursor col
PUSH    WORD    Vio handle (must be 0)
CALL    VIOGETCURSORPOS
```

This service is pretty self-explanatory. All VioGetCursorPos does is to get the cursor's position on the screen.

You may recall that in BIOS this information could be returned in one register (row and column number each taking up one byte). Here, you have to pass an *address* at which OS/2 will store the row and column numbers.

```
→      PUSH    PTR     Address at which OS/2 will return current cursor row
→      PUSH    PTR     Address at which OS/2 will return current cursor col
       PUSH    WORD    Vio handle (must be 0)
       CALL    VIOGETCURSORPOS
```

Other than that, this service is easy to use. The next service is the natural counterpart to this one: VioSetCursorPos.

## VioSetCursorPos—Set Cursor Position

```
PUSH    WORD    New Cursor Row Number
PUSH    WORD    New Cursor Column Number
PUSH    WORD    Vio handle (must be 0)
CALL    VIOSETCURSORPOS
```

With this service, you can set the cursor position. The parameters you pass are simple: a word that specifies the new cursor row, a word that specifies the new cursor column, and the omnipresent Vio handle (0). To set the cursor to screen position 10,20 (row, column), do this:

```
PUSH    10
PUSH    20
PUSH    0
CALL    VIOSETCURSORPOS
```

If you have to do a lot of screen work, especially if you're accepting typed input, you'll find this service useful.

## Scrolling

In BIOS, there are two ways to scroll (up and down); in OS/2, there are four (up, down, left, and right).

The four services are: VioScrollUp, VioScrollDn, VioScrollLe, and VioScrollRi. You pass the stack parameters to them in the same way:

```
PUSH    WORD    Top row of scroll area
PUSH    WORD    Left column of scroll area
PUSH    WORD    Bottom row of scroll area
PUSH    WORD    Right column of scroll area
PUSH    WORD    Number of rows or columns to scroll (FFFF → Clear
                the scroll area)
PUSH    PTR     Pointer to a two-byte cell (attribute, cell) that will
                fill the scrolled row or column.
PUSH    WORD    Vio handle (must be 0).
CALL    VIOSCROLLUP/VIOSCROLLDN/VIOSCROLLLE/VIOSCROLLRI
```

With these services, like their BIOS counterparts, you can scroll windows on the screen or the whole screen. Here, if you indicate that the number of rows or columns that is to be scrolled as FFFFH, the scroll area will be cleared.

Also, you can specify a "fill cell" that will be used to fill the newly blank row or column that has just been scrolled. This way you can make sure that a red window stays red as you are scrolling it, for example.

## VioSetMode—Set Video Mode

```
PUSH    PTR     Address of video mode data (see below).
PUSH    WORD    Vio handle (must be 0).
CALL    VIOSETMODE
```

You can set the screen mode under OS/2, just as you could under DOS. The allowed screen modes are in Table 9.1.

Table 9.1 OS/2 Screen Modes

| *Type* | *Colors* | *Cols* | *Rows* | | *Res* |
|---|---|---|---|---|---|
| B&W Text | 16 | 40 | 25 | CGA,EGA,VGA | 320x200 |
| | | | 43 | EGA,VGA | 320x350 |
| | | | 50 | VGA | 360x400 |
| Text | 16 | 40 | 25 | CGA,EGA,VGA | 320x200 |
| | | | 43 | EGA,VGA | 320x350 |

*Table 9.1, continued*

| | | | | | |
|---|---|---|---|---|---|
| | | | 50 | VGA | 360x400 |
| B&W Text | 16 | 80 | 25 | CGA,EGA,VGA | 640x200 |
| | | | 43 | EGA,VGA | 640x350 |
| | | | 50 | VGA | 720x400 |
| Text | 16 | 80 | 25 | CGA,EGA,VGA | 640x200 |
| | | | 43 | EGA,VGA | 640x350 |
| | | | 50 | VGA | 720x400 |
| Graphics | 4 | – | – | CGA,EGA,VGA | 320x200 |
| Graphics | 2 | – | – | CGA,EGA,VGA | 320x200 |
| Graphics | 2 | – | – | CGA,EGA,VGA | 640x200 |
| Mono Text | – | 80 | 25 | Mono,EGA,VGA | 720x350 |
| Graphics | 16 | – | – | EGA,VGA | 320x200 |
| Graphics | 4 | – | – | EGA,VGA | 640x200 |
| Graphics | 2 | – | – | EGA,VGA | 640x350 |
| Graphics | 16 | – | – | EGA,VGA | 640x350 |
| Graphics | 2 | – | – | VGA | 640x480 |
| Graphics | 16 | – | – | VGA | 640x480 |
| Graphics | 256 | – | – | VGA | 320x200 |

In BIOS, each of these modes had a number associated with it—in OS/2 that is not the case. Instead, you explicitly list all the parameters that make up the display mode you want, like number of pixels horizontally and vertically, or number of rows and columns, and so on.

You have to pass VioSetMode the address of a data area that holds this information in memory. That data area is set up like this:

```
DW      length of this data area (including this word).
DB      "Mode Characteristics"
        xxxxxxx0 → Monochrome printer adapter
        xxxxxxx1 → All others
        xxxxxx0x → Text mode
        xxxxxx1x → Graphics mode
        xxxxx0xx → Screen is color (color burst enable)
        xxxxx1xx → Screen is B&W (color burst disable)
DB      Number of colors in this video mode:
        1 → 2 colors (pixels are on or off)
        2 → 4 colors
        4 → 16 colors
DW      Number of text columns
DW      Number of text rows
DW      Horizontal resolution in pixels
DW      Vertical resolution in pixels
DD      A reserved double word. Make these words 0 when you push them.
```

Once you set up the address of this data area on the stack and push the Vio handle (as usual, 0), you can call VioSetMode. If the video mode was set correctly, AX will hold 0 on return. If there has been an error, AX will hold 255, which simply means that that display doesn't support the mode requested.

You can also get the current video mode, with VioGetMode. This service, which we'll cover next, is much like VioSetMode.

## VioGetMode—Get Video Mode

```
PUSH    PTR     Address of video mode data (see VioSetMode).
PUSH    WORD    Vio handle (must be 0).
```

This service will get the current video mode. You first set aside an area in memory that OS/2 will fill and push its address onto the stack, followed by the Vio handle. Upon return, the data area will be filled out with the values that we already defined in VioSetMode.

## VioPopUp

One additional Vio call deserves discussion here—and that is VioPopUp. VioPopUp is not to be used in the way that you might think—it is not to be used for normal pop-up utilities. Instead, it is to be used by programs that are normally cut off from using the screen when they need to grab screen control to report some sort of problem or emergency.

Under OS/2, you can *DETACH* a program, and it will continue to run. DETACH is a common mainframe command; however, the program can no longer accept input from the keyboard or print out to the screen unless it takes special action—and that action is calling VioPopUp.

The parameters you push are like this for VioPopUp:

```
PUSH    PTR     Address of a one-word option field:
                rrrrrrrr rrrrrrXW   (r = reserved)

                X = 0 → Nontransparent popup (screen cleared)
                  = 1 → Transparent popup

                W = 0 → Return with error if popup cannot be made.
                  = 1 → Wait for popup
PUSH    WORD    Vio handle (must be 0).
CALL    VIOPOPUP
```

Selecting a nontransparent pop-up means that the screen will be cleared before your program starts to print on it. If you were in graphics mode, the screen is reset to text mode. If you ask for a transparent popup, the screen isn't reset, and the call will fail if the screen is currently in graphics mode.

# The WAIT5 Program

Let's write a little program called WAIT5 that you can DETACH, and that will grab the screen and clear it after five minutes are up, with the message: "Time Is Up!." It will wait until you type a key and then reliniquish the screen.

To run WAIT5 after making WAIT5.EXE, just type DETACH WAIT5 at the OS/2 command prompt or run it from the File System. In a way, this is like the earlier DOS memory-resident programs but only slightly. WAIT5 cannot read what is being typed in the main session; it cannot print on the screen (except via VioPopUp), and it is isolated from everyone else.

You can write what are called *device monitors* that can monitor what is being typed, to pick out hot keys and the like. Using device monitors, you can make your own OS/2 popup programs or keyboard macros (see the OS/2 Assembly Language book where we develop many such programs).

In WAIT5, we'll use a service called DosSleep. If you pass DosSleep a number of milliseconds as a double word like DX:AX (push high word first, then low word), it will suspend the program for that long.

Since we want to suspend WAIT5 for five minutes, we need to know how many milliseconds there are in those five minutes. That is 5 (minutes) x 60 (seconds/minute) x 1000 (milliseconds/second) = 300,000 milliseconds. In hex, this is 493E0H. If we put this into the register pair DX:AX, DX would hold 4 and AX would hold 93E0H.

This means that we execute these instructions and then call DosSleep:

```
                          ;493E0H = 300,000 = no. of millisec.s in 5 minutes.
ENTRY:  PUSH     4        ;Push high word          ←
        PUSH     93E0H    ;Push low word           ←
        CALL     DosSleep                          ←
          :
          :
        END      ENTRY
```

After we return, we have to grab the screen with VioPopUp. To do that, we add this code:

```
        .286
        .MODEL  SMALL
        .STACK  200H

        .DATA

        .CODE
        EXTRN    DOSEXIT:FAR
                          ;493E0H = 300,000 = no. of millisec.s in 5 minutes.
ENTRY:  PUSH     4        ;Push high word
        PUSH     93E0H    ;Push low word
        CALL     DosSleep
```

```
        PUSH    DS                          ←
        PUSH    OFFSET POPUP_OPTIONS        ←
        PUSH    0                           ←
        CALL    VioPopUp                    ←
         :
         :
        END     ENTRY
```

Where POPUP_OPTIONS is defined in the data area to request a nontransparent pop-up that will wait:

```
        .286
        .MODEL  SMALL
        .STACK  200H

        .DATA
        POPUP_OPTIONS    DB 1     ←

        .CODE
        EXTRN   DOSEXIT:FAR
                        ;493E0H = 300,000 = no. of millisec.s in 5 minutes.
ENTRY:  PUSH    4       ;Push high word
        PUSH    93E0H   ;Push low word
        CALL    DosSleep

        PUSH    DS
        PUSH    OFFSET POPUP_OPTIONS
        PUSH    0
        CALL    VioPopUp
         :
         :
        END     ENTRY
```

After we have control of the screen, we have to print out our message. We can put the message into the data segment like this:

| VioPopUp gives a program control of the screen, keyboard, and mouse.

```
        .286
        .MODEL  SMALL
        .STACK  200H

        .DATA
        MESSAGE DB "Time Is Up!"            ←
        MESSAGELEN EQU $ - MESSAGE          ←
        POPUP_OPTIONS    DB 1

        .CODE
        EXTRN   DOSEXIT:FAR
                        ;493E0H = 300,000 = no. of millisec.s in 5 minutes.
ENTRY:  PUSH    4       ;Push high word
        PUSH    93E0H   ;Push low word
```

```
        CALL    DosSleep

        PUSH    DS
        PUSH    OFFSET POPUP_OPTIONS
        PUSH    0
        CALL    VioPopUp
         :
         :
        END     ENTRY
```

And print it out like this:

```
        .286
        .MODEL  SMALL
        .STACK  200H

        .DATA
        MESSAGE DB "Time Is Up!"
        MESSAGELEN EQU $ - MESSAGE
        POPUP_OPTIONS   DB 1

        .CODE
        EXTRN   DOSEXIT:FAR
                        ;493E0H = 300,000 = no. of millisec.s in 5 minutes.
ENTRY:  PUSH    4       ;Push high word
        PUSH    93E0H   ;Push low word
        CALL    DosSleep

        PUSH    DS
        PUSH    OFFSET POPUP_OPTIONS
        PUSH    0
        CALL    VioPopUp

        PUSH    DS                  ←
        PUSH    OFFSET MESSAGE      ←
        PUSH    MESSAGELEN          ←
        PUSH    0                   ←
        CALL    VioWrtTTY           ←
         :
         :
        END     ENTRY
```

Next we will wait for a key to be struck with the Kbd service KbdCharIn. Here, we are instructing OS/2 to read a key and if no keys are ready, to wait for one:

```
        .286
        .MODEL  SMALL
        .STACK  200H

        .DATA
        MESSAGE DB "Time Is Up!"
        MESSAGELEN EQU $ - MESSAGE
```

```
        POPUP_OPTIONS   DB 1
        CHAR_DATA       DB 0
                SCAN    DB 0
                STATUS  DB 0
                NSHIFT  DB 0
                SHIFT   DW 0
                TSTAMP  DD 0

        .CODE
        EXTRN   DOSEXIT:FAR
                        ;493E0H = 300,000 = no. of millisec.s in 5 minutes.
                        ;493E0H = 300,000 = no. of millisec.s in 5 minutes.
ENTRY:  PUSH    4       ;Push high word
        PUSH    93E0H   ;Push low word
        CALL    DosSleep

        PUSH    DS
        PUSH    OFFSET POPUP_OPTIONS
        PUSH    0
        CALL    VioPopUp

        PUSH    DS
        PUSH    OFFSET MESSAGE
        PUSH    MESSAGELEN
        PUSH    0
        CALL    VioWrtTTY

        PUSH    DS                        ←
        PUSH    OFFSET CHAR_DATA          ←
        PUSH    0                         ←
        PUSH    0                         ←
        CALL    KbdCharIn                 ←
          :
          :
        END     ENTRY
```

For more information about KbdCharIn, see Appendix 2. You might note in passing the data area we had to set up for KbdCharIn, just to read in a single key. After we receive a key, we just end the popup with VioEndPopUp:

```
        .286
        .MODEL  SMALL
        .STACK  200H

        .DATA
        MESSAGE DB "Time Is Up!"
        MESSAGELEN EQU $-MESSAGE
        POPUP_OPTIONS   DB 1
        CHAR_DATA       DB 0
                SCAN    DB 0
                STATUS  DB 0
                NSHIFT  DB 0
```

```
            SHIFT    DW 0
            TSTAMP   DD 0

        .CODE
        EXTRN     DOSEXIT:FAR
                          ;493E0H = 300,000 = no. of millisec.s in 5 minutes.
                          ;493E0H = 300,000 = no. of millisec.s in 5 minutes.
ENTRY:  PUSH      4       ;Push high word
        PUSH      93E0H   ;Push low word
        CALL      DosSleep

        PUSH      DS
        PUSH      OFFSET POPUP_OPTIONS
        PUSH      0
        CALL      VioPopUp

        PUSH      DS
        PUSH      OFFSET MESSAGE
        PUSH      MESSAGELEN
        PUSH      0
        CALL      VioWrtTTY

        PUSH      DS
        PUSH      OFFSET CHAR_DATA
        PUSH      0
        PUSH      0
        CALL      KbdCharIn

        PUSH      0                  ←
        CALL      VioEndPopUp        ←
          :
          :
        END       ENTRY
```

Now we're ready to exit with DosExit. Here's the whole WAIT5.ASM program, including all the EXTRNs:

```
        .286
        .MODEL  SMALL
        .STACK  200H

        .DATA
        MESSAGE DB "Time Is Up!"
        MESSAGELEN EQU $-MESSAGE
        POPUP_OPTIONS    DB 1
        CHAR_DATA        DB 0
                SCAN     DB 0
                STATUS   DB 0
                NSHIFT   DB 0
                SHIFT    DW 0
                TSTAMP   DD 0

        .CODE
```

```
        EXTRN   DosExit:FAR,DosSleep:FAR,VioPopUp:FAR,
        EXTRN   VioEndPopUp:FAR,VioWrtTTY:FAR,KbdCharIn:FAR

                        ;493E0H = 300,000 = no. of millisec.s in 5 minutes.
ENTRY:  PUSH    4       ;Push high word
        PUSH    93E0H   ;Push low word
        CALL    DosSleep

        PUSH    DS
        PUSH    OFFSET POPUP_OPTIONS
        PUSH    0
        CALL    VioPopUp

        PUSH    DS
        PUSH    OFFSET MESSAGE
        PUSH    MESSAGELEN
        PUSH    0
        CALL    VioWrtTTY

        PUSH    DS
        PUSH    OFFSET CHAR_DATA
        PUSH    0
        PUSH    0
        CALL    KbdCharIn

        PUSH    0
        CALL    VioEndPopUp

EXIT:   PUSH    1               ;A Normal Exit.
        PUSH    0
        CALL    DosExit

        END     ENTRY
```

Give it a try—just type DETACH WAIT5. Five minutes later, WAIT5 will let you know that the time's up, stopping the program that is running. This is our first multitasking example!

# 10

# Welcome to the OS/2 Presentation Manager

## Welcome to the Presentation Manager

The big news when OS/2 1.1 was released was Presentation Manager, a long-awaited event in PC-PS/2 history. For the first time, the primary interface with the machine made use of windows and the mouse.

This chapter is about Presentation Manager, which is an advanced topic. Programming the Presentation Manager isn't a simple task, nor can we hope to cover very much in one chapter. For a more thorough treatment, see a book devoted to Presentation Manager.

When we boot up under OS/2, we are faced with the Presentation Manager screen, which is a collection of icons and windows. Although it is possible to use the keyboard with Presentation Manager, it is uncompromisingly awkward. Similiar actions can require very different keystrokes, and the use of non-intuitive keycodes (like Alt-F4 or Ctrl-F5) make them hard to remember. To use the Presentation Manager fully, you must have a mouse.

### Using the Mouse

This was a big switch, but a big improvement. The Presentation Manager is a graphical interface, designed for easy screen manipulation (on the user's part, anyway). You just point and shoot. Windows open, scroll, or shrink into icons at the click of the mouse. Using the mouse has allowed the introduction of the desktop metaphor to the IBM line. The Macintosh has used the desktop metaphor from the beginning, and its introduction by IBM is a measure of its success. The idea is to think of computer tasks as being represented on pieces of paper on a desktop; papers can overlap, be moved, or even be thrown out. It is a very effective way to handle multiple tasks.

Presentation Manager (PM) programs simply open another window on the display and the user interacts with them primarily through the use of the mouse. Occasionally, you may have to type text commands (to name files, for example); for this purpose you can open *dialog boxes*, which accept keystrokes. The use of the mouse was also made easier by introducing *buttons* (actually a special type of window), which allow you to make easy choices on the screen. Another concept we will meet is the *menu*. If you've used PM, you're familiar with menus; you can click the mouse on the menu bar at the top of most windows, and various options appear, allowing you to select them.

The last new item on our screen is the *icon*. This is an easy handle representing a program or file, ready to spring into action as soon as it's clicked or selected. When you *minimize* a program's window, it becomes an icon on the lower part of the screen—to open that window up again, all you have to do is select it with mouse or keyboard.

With all these improvements, using Presentation Manager programs is easy. From the programmer's point of view, however, writing them has become more difficult.

## Programming PM

The number of functions available in the Win group of function calls—the central functions of PM programs—is enormous. That doesn't simply mean that the programmer has the luxury of choosing among hundreds of options—it means that he or she will have to be conversant with many functions before even starting. Programming PM is not easy; it is a whole world by itself. As we progress through this chapter, you'll get an indication of the complexity involved. When the Macintosh was introduced and became popular, programmers were dismayed with the extraordinary amount of material they had to learn to put together even the most rudimentary program. If you have any familiarity with the Macintosh Toolbox or have programmed in the Windows environment, you already know what's coming.

Presentation Manager programs are supposed to adhere to the basic PM philosophy: use the mouse, icons, and buttons—and avoid excessive use of the keyboard. PM program windows should look much like other PM program windows. If you've programmed on the Mac, you know that heavy stress is laid on making programs conform to the norm. That means that the programmer has to supply code to handle many tasks that the user expects, from the ability to import "clipboard" graphics from other programs to making sure your window has and can use scroll bars.

## Some Unpleasant Surprises

Non-amateur programming is so heavily emphasized that you can't even write Presentation Manager programs without purchasing either the expensive OS/2 Software Developer's Kit or the OS/2 Presentation Manager Toolkit.

Until now, all the programs we have written could be compiled under simple OS/2 1.0. To create links to the OS/2 functions in the dynamic-link libraries, we have linked in the DOSCALLS.LIB library when we have used LINK. DOSCALLS.LIB comes with OS/2, so there is no problem.

On the other hand, you cannot include any Win or Gpi functions in your programs if you have only DOSCALLS.LIB. All Presentation Manager functions are in a library named OS2.LIB. This library also includes all the functions we have been using up to now—that is, it includes all that DOSCALLS.LIB has and more. However, simple OS/2 itself does *not* include OS2.LIB. You have to buy this library in one of the two software packages listed above (the Software Developer's Kit or the PM Toolkit). In this chapter, we will be using OS/2.LIB when we link, not DOSCALLS:

```
D:\>LINK PROG,,,OS2;      ←
```

There's more bad news. The Presentation Manager is a graphical interface, and, until now, we've been dealing only with text I/O. That means that the Vio functions will no longer work (except some of them, and under certain circumstances). In addition, PM programs receive input through *messages*. Neither the Kbd nor the Mou functions will work here. Instead, we'll see how to process messages (which include keystrokes and mouse movements) sent to our particular window. Of course, the Mou, Kbd, and Vio functions aren't useless—PM is only one OS/2 session. In all the other sessions, they will work as expected. However, if you want to produce PM programs, you'll have to learn a new way of accepting input and displaying output. The Dos group, however, is unaffected.

However, the advantages of PM clearly outweigh the disadvantages. In this chapter, we're going to develop a Presentation Manager progam named WIN.ASM. When you run WIN, the screen snaps to the Presentation Manager display, and a window will appear that you can shrink, enlarge, maximize, or minimize (i.e., make into an icon).

# Getting Started

We can start with the usual OS/2 .EXE file skeleton:

```
.MODEL  SMALL
.286
.STACK  20000
.DATA
```

```
        .CODE
ENTRY:

        END         ENTRY
```

One thing you might notice immediately is that the stack is larger here—20,000 bytes. This size is more than ample; however, Presentation Manager programs are fond of using the stack, and you should not go below 4K of stack space.

The first thing we must do is initialize the window system with a call to WinInitialize. We pass a value of 0 to that function call like this:

```
        .MODEL  SMALL
        .286
        .STACK  20000
        .DATA

        .CODE
        EXTRN   WinInitialize:FAR

ENTRY   PROC FAR

→       PUSH    0                           ;Get Anchor Block Handle
→       CALL    WinInitialize
                 :
                 :
```

This function returns a 32-bit handle to something called an *anchor block*, an area of memory where OS/2 keeps track of much of the information associated with the window we are going to produce. The handle is returned in the register pair DX:AX.

| If the handle was a 16-bit one, it would have been returned in AX alone.

We have to put aside storage for the full 32-bit handle, which we can do with two words, ANCHOR_LOW and ANCHOR_HIGH, like this:

```
        .MODEL  SMALL
        .286
        .STACK  20000

        .DATA
→       ANCHOR_LOW      DW 0                ;Anchor block handle
→       ANCHOR_HIGH     DW 0

        .CODE
        EXTRN   WinInitialize:FAR

ENTRY   PROC FAR

        PUSH    0                           ;Get Anchor Block Handle
        CALL    WinInitialize
```

```
→       MOV     ANCHOR_LOW,AX
→       MOV     ANCHOR_HIGH,DX
                  :
                  :
```

We now have the 32-bit anchor block handle in custody. The next step is to set up a *message queue*. It is during this step that the screen switches to the Presentation Manager display (and graphics mode). All input to our program (like keyboard or mouse input) will be handled through this queue, so you can see that it is important. We can set it up using WinCreateMsgQueue. First, we have to push the anchor block handle. To push a 32-bit value, we first push the high word and then the low word—since these numbers are still in DX and AX respectively, we can push those like this:

```
        .MODEL  SMALL
        .286
        .STACK  20000

        .DATA
        ANCHOR_LOW      DW 0            ;Anchor block handle
        ANCHOR_HIGH     DW 0

        .CODE
        EXTRN   WinInitialize:FAR, WinCreateMsgQueue:FAR

ENTRY   PROC FAR

        PUSH    0                       ;Get Anchor Block Handle
        CALL    WinInitialize
        MOV     ANCHOR_LOW,AX
        MOV     ANCHOR_HIGH,DX

→       PUSH    DX   ;Set up message queue — Anchor high
→       PUSH    AX   ;Anchor low
                :
                :
```

Next we have to push the size of the message queue in bytes and then call WinCreateMsgQueue. If we push a value of 0, OS/2 will use the default size, which is fine for us:

```
        .MODEL  SMALL
        .286
        .STACK  20000

        .DATA
        ANCHOR_LOW      DW 0            ;Anchor block handle
        ANCHOR_HIGH     DW 0

        .CODE
        EXTRN   WinInitialize:FAR, WinCreateMsgQueue:FAR
```

```
ENTRY   PROC FAR

        PUSH    0                           ;Get Anchor Block Handle
        CALL    WinInitialize
        MOV     ANCHOR_LOW,AX
        MOV     ANCHOR_HIGH,DX

        PUSH    DX   ;Set up message queue—Anchor high
        PUSH    AX   ;Anchor low
→       PUSH    0    ;Use default size
→       CALL    WinCreateMsgQueue
                :
                :
```

WinCreateMsgQueue returns a 32-bit message queue handle that we'll need later. This handle is also returned in DX:AX. We can store it in the two words QUEUE_LOW and QUEUE_HIGH:

```
        .MODEL  SMALL
        .286

        .STACK  20000

        .DATA
        ANCHOR_LOW      DW 0                ;Anchor block handle
        ANCHOR_HIGH     DW 0
→       QUEUE_LOW       DW 0                ;Queue handle
→       QUEUE_HIGH      DW 0

        .CODE
        EXTRN   WinInitialize:FAR, WinCreateMsgQueue:FAR

ENTRY   PROC FAR

        PUSH    0                           ;Get Anchor Block Handle
        CALL    WinInitialize
        MOV     ANCHOR_LOW,AX
        MOV     ANCHOR_HIGH,DX

        PUSH    DX   ;Set up message queue – Anchor high
        PUSH    AX   ;Anchor low
        PUSH    0    ;Use default size
        CALL    WinCreateMsgQueue
→       MOV     QUEUE_LOW,AX
→       MOV     QUEUE_HIGH,DX
                :
                :
```

The message queue has been set up. The following step is to do some window work. We need to *register* the kind of window we will produce before we create it.

The main purpose of registering a window is to set up a *window function*, which answers any questions OS/2 has about the window and handles keyboard and mouse messages. When an action occurs (e.g., the mouse was moved or your window was covered up), OS/2 uses the window function to query your program about what it should do. The window function that we will write checks the message sent to it and returns appropriate values to OS/2. Our window function will be called (with complete lack of originality) WINDOW_FUNC.

To use the function WinRegisterClass and register our window, we have to push the anchor block handle:

```
        .MODEL   SMALL
        .286

        .STACK   20000

        .DATA
        ANCHOR_LOW       DW 0              ;Anchor block handle
        ANCHOR_HIGH      DW 0
        QUEUE_LOW        DW 0              ;Queue handle
        QUEUE_HIGH       DW 0

        .CODE
        EXTRN    WinInitialize:FAR, WinCreateMsgQueue:FAR

ENTRY   PROC FAR

        PUSH     0                         ;Get Anchor Block Handle
        CALL     WinInitialize
        MOV      ANCHOR_LOW,AX
        MOV      ANCHOR_HIGH,DX

        PUSH     DX    ;Set up message queue — Anchor high
        PUSH     AX    ;Anchor low
        PUSH     0     ;Use default size
        CALL     WinCreateMsgQueue
        MOV      QUEUE_LOW,AX
        MOV      QUEUE_HIGH,DX

→       PUSH     ANCHOR_HIGH       ;Register class so we can get messages
→       PUSH     ANCHOR_LOW
                 :
                 :
```

Next, we must name the class of windows we are registering. We don't need to name the class if we don't want to register the window—but to receive messages, we have to register it (unregistered windows exits, but they can't accept messages). We'll call the class of windows FRANK. We set up a string in memory, and push the address onto the stack in preparation for WinRegisterClass:

```
        .MODEL  SMALL
        .286

        .STACK  20000

        .DATA
        ANCHOR_LOW      DW 0            ;Anchor block handle
        ANCHOR_HIGH     DW 0
        QUEUE_LOW       DW 0            ;Queue handle
        QUEUE_HIGH      DW 0
→       CLASS_NAME      DB 'FRANK',0    ;Private window class name

        .CODE
        EXTRN   WinInitialize:FAR, WinCreateMsgQueue:FAR, DosExit:FAR

ENTRY   PROC FAR

        PUSH    0  ;Get Anchor Block Handle
        CALL    WinInitialize
        MOV     ANCHOR_LOW,AX
        MOV     ANCHOR_HIGH,DX

        PUSH    DX   ;Set up message queue — Anchor high
        PUSH    AX   ;Anchor low
        PUSH    0    ;Use default size
        CALL    WinCreateMsgQueue
        MOV     QUEUE_LOW,AX
        MOV     QUEUE_HIGH,DX

        PUSH    ANCHOR_HIGH     ;Register class so we can get messages
        PUSH    ANCHOR_LOW
→       PUSH    DS;Register this name for class
→       PUSH    OFFSET CLASS_NAME
                :
                :
```

Next we have to specify the class of window. We will use the most common user window: style 4. This style specifies that the window be redrawn when it is moved. The style is a doubleword, so we push the high word first, followed by the low word. The final parameter is the amount of extra storage we are requesting in bytes. We won't take advantage of that extra memory here, so we set that value to 0 and call WinRegisterClass:

```
        .MODEL  SMALL
        .286

        .STACK  20000

        .DATA
        ANCHOR_LOW      DW 0      ;Anchor block handle
        ANCHOR_HIGH     DW 0
        QUEUE_LOWDW 0     ;Queue handle
```

```
        QUEUE_HIGH       DW 0
        CLASS_NAME       DB 'FRANK',0     ;Private window class name

        .CODE
        EXTRN    WinInitialize:FAR, WinCreateMsgQueue:FAR, DosExit:FAR
        EXTRN    WinRegisterClass:FAR

ENTRY   PROC FAR

        PUSH     0  ;Get Anchor Block Handle
        CALL     WinInitialize
        MOV      ANCHOR_LOW,AX
        MOV      ANCHOR_HIGH,DX

        PUSH     DX    ;Set up message queue — Anchor high
        PUSH     AX    ;Anchor low
        PUSH     0     ;Use default size
        CALL     WinCreateMsgQueue
        MOV      QUEUE_LOW,AX
        MOV      QUEUE_HIGH,DX

        PUSH     ANCHOR_HIGH      ;Register class so we can get messages
        PUSH     ANCHOR_LOWPUSH     DS;Register this name for class
        PUSH     OFFSET CLASS_NAME
        PUSH     CS ;Set up window function
        PUSH     OFFSET CS:WINDOW_FUNC
→       PUSH     0;High style — use style 00000004H
→       PUSH     4;Low style
→       PUSH     0;No additional storage space
→       CALL     WinRegisterClass
                 :
                 :
```

Now when we start to request messages, OS/2 will know that WINDOW_FUNC is our message handler.

So far, nothing has appeared on the screen. We have gone to graphics mode, and the Presentation Manager desktop has appeared, but there is no window yet. The next call, WinCreateStdWindow, will make the window visible. We have to begin by pushing the handle of the parent window. In practice, the parent window is treated as the screen itself for a user window like ours, with a 32-bit handle of 1. You can also pass 0 here for the same effect. Here we push the parent handle (high word followed by low word), which means that our window will appear as a PM window.

Next, we push the style of the window. In our case, we want to make the window visible, so we push the corresponding value, 800000000H. That is pushed high word first, low word second. Then we have to specify what type of window we want. You can do that by pushing the address of a doubleword of window flags, which we'll call FLAGS:

```
        .MODEL   SMALL
        .286

        .STACK   20000

        .DATA
        ANCHOR_LOW       DW 0              ;Anchor block handle
        ANCHOR_HIGH      DW 0
        QUEUE_LOW        DW 0              ;Queue handle
        QUEUE_HIGH       DW 0
→       FLAGS     DW 0C3BH                 ;Window flags
→                 DW 8000H
        CLASS_NAME       DB 'FRANK',0      ;Private window class name

        .CODE
        EXTRN    WinInitialize:FAR, WinCreateMsgQueue:FAR, DosExit:FAR
        EXTRN    WinRegisterClass:FAR

ENTRY   PROC FAR

        PUSH     0  ;Get Anchor Block Handle
        CALL     WinInitialize
        MOV      ANCHOR_LOW,AX
        MOV      ANCHOR_HIGH,DX

        PUSH     DX   ;Set up message queue - Anchor high
        PUSH     AX   ;Anchor low
        PUSH     0    ;Use default size
        CALL     WinCreateMsgQueue
        MOV      QUEUE_LOW,AX
        MOV      QUEUE_HIGH,DX

        PUSH     ANCHOR_HIGH     ;Register class so we can get messages
        PUSH     ANCHOR_LOW
        PUSH     DS              ;Register this name for class
        PUSH     OFFSET CLASS_NAME
        PUSH     CS                      ;Set up window function
        PUSH     OFFSET CS:WINDOW_FUNC
        PUSH     0        ;High style - use style 00000004H
        PUSH     4        ;Low style
        PUSH     0        ;No additional storage space
        CALL     WinRegisterClass

→       PUSH     0        ;Parent window handle
→       PUSH     1
→       PUSH     8000H    ;Make window visible - Style high
→       PUSH     0000H    ;Style low
→       PUSH     DS       ;Point to window flags
→       PUSH     OFFSET FLAGS
                 :
                 :
```

Here are some of the flags you can use, specifying the types of windows you want to use:

| | |
|---|---|
| Visible | 80000000H |
| Minimized | 01000000H |
| Maximixed | 00800000H |
| Titlebar | 00000001H |
| SysMenu | 00000002H |
| Vert. scroll | 00000010H |
| Horiz. scroll | 00000020H |
| Side border | 00000040H |
| Border | 00000200H |
| Minbutton | 00001000H |
| Maxbutton | 00002000H |
| Minmax | 00003000H |

You can OR these together to form a window that you like. In our case, we will include a title bar, the system menu, and a minmax button in our window. We take the individual values from the list above, OR these options together ourselves, and place the result (low word first) at FLAGS, then pass the address to WinCreateStd-Window:

```
        .MODEL   SMALL
        .286

        .STACK   20000

        .DATA
        ANCHOR_LOW       DW 0              ;Anchor block handle
        ANCHOR_HIGH      DW 0
        QUEUE_LOW        DW 0              ;Queue handle
        QUEUE_HIGH       DW 0
→       FLAGS            DW 0C3BH          ;Window flags
→                        DW 8000H
        CLASS_NAME       DB 'FRANK',0      ;Private window class name

        .CODE
        EXTRN    WinInitialize:FAR, WinCreateMsgQueue:FAR, DosExit:FAR
        EXTRN    WinRegisterClass:FAR

ENTRY   PROC FAR

        PUSH     0                         ;Get Anchor Block Handle
        CALL     WinInitialize
        MOV      ANCHOR_LOW,AX
        MOV      ANCHOR_HIGH,DX

        PUSH     DX    ;Set up message queue - Anchor high
        PUSH     AX    ;Anchor low
```

```
        PUSH    0     ;Use default size
        CALL    WinCreateMsgQueue
        MOV     QUEUE_LOW,AX
        MOV     QUEUE_HIGH,DX

        PUSH    ANCHOR_HIGH     ;Register class so we can get messages
        PUSH    ANCHOR_LOW
        PUSH    DS              ;Register this name for class
        PUSH    OFFSET CLASS_NAME
        PUSH    CS                      ;Set up window function
        PUSH    OFFSET CS:WINDOW_FUNC
        PUSH    0       ;High style — use style 00000004H
        PUSH    4       ;Low style
        PUSH    0       ;No additional storage space
        CALL    WinRegisterClass

        PUSH    0       ;Parent window handle
        PUSH    1
        PUSH    8000H   ;Make window visible — Style high
        PUSH    0000H   ;Style low
→       PUSH    DS      ;Point to window flags
→       PUSH    OFFSET FLAGS
                :
                :
```

Next we push the address of the class name. This allows OS/2 to call our function WINDOW_FUNC since we registered WINDOW_FUNC under a specific class name ("FRANK") before. To specify the window class, and therefore WINDOW_FUNC, we point to the class name in memory:

```
        .MODEL  SMALL
        .286

        .STACK  20000

        .DATA
        ANCHOR_LOW      DW 0            ;Anchor block handle
        ANCHOR_HIGH     DW 0
        QUEUE_LOW       DW 0            ;Queue handle
        QUEUE_HIGH      DW 0
        FLAGS           DW 0C3BH        ;Window flags
                        DW 8000H
        CLASS_NAME      DB 'FRANK',0    ;Private window class name


        .CODE
        EXTRN   WinInitialize:FAR, WinCreateMsgQueue:FAR, DosExit:FAR
        EXTRN   WinRegisterClass:FAR

ENTRY   PROC FAR

        PUSH    0                       ;Get Anchor Block Handle
```

```
        CALL    WinInitialize
        MOV     ANCHOR_LOW,AX
        MOV     ANCHOR_HIGH,DX

        PUSH    DX    ;Set up message queue - Anchor high
        PUSH    AX    ;Anchor low
        PUSH    0     ;Use default size
        CALL    WinCreateMsgQueue
        MOV     QUEUE_LOW,AX
        MOV     QUEUE_HIGH,DX

        PUSH    ANCHOR_HIGH      ;Register class so we can get messages
        PUSH    ANCHOR_LOW
        PUSH    DS               ;Register this name for class
        PUSH    OFFSET CLASS_NAME
        PUSH    CS                       ;Set up window function
        PUSH    OFFSET CS:WINDOW_FUNC
        PUSH    0        ;High style - use style 00000004H
        PUSH    4        ;Low style
        PUSH    0        ;No additional storage space
        CALL    WinRegisterClass

        PUSH    0        ;Parent window handle
        PUSH    1
        PUSH    8000H    ;Make window visible - Style high
        PUSH    0000H    ;Style low
        PUSH    DS       ;Point to window flags
        PUSH    OFFSET FLAGS
→       PUSH    DS                 ;← make 0 for default window
→       PUSH    OFFSET CLASS_NAME ;← make 0 for default window
                :
                :
```

If we had passed a NULL address—that is, if both words were zero— we would have gotten the default window. However, we could not receive messages then, since we need a registered window class to receive messages; there is no way of setting up a window function for an unregistered window.

Now we have the option of giving our window a title. We need to pass the address of an ASCIIZ string here—if we pass 0000:0000, the default title will hold only the name of the program (WIN.EXE). We can add our own string here, however, like this:

```
.MODEL  SMALL
.286

.STACK  20000

.DATA
ANCHOR_LOW       DW 0              ;Anchor block handle
ANCHOR_HIGH      DW 0
QUEUE_LOW        DW 0              ;Queue handle
```

```
        QUEUE_HIGH      DW 0
        FLAGS           DW 0C3BH        ;Window flags
                        DW 8000H
        CLASS_NAME      DB 'FRANK',0    ;Private window class name
→       TITLE_BAR       DB 'Welcome to PM',0    ;Window title bar

        .CODE
        EXTRN   WinInitialize:FAR, WinCreateMsgQueue:FAR, DosExit:FAR
        EXTRN   WinRegisterClass:FAR

ENTRY   PROC FAR

        PUSH    0                       ;Get Anchor Block Handle
        CALL    WinInitialize
        MOV     ANCHOR_LOW,AX
        MOV     ANCHOR_HIGH,DX

        PUSH    DX   ;Set up message queue - Anchor high
        PUSH    AX   ;Anchor low
        PUSH    0    ;Use default size
        CALL    WinCreateMsgQueue
        MOV     QUEUE_LOW,AX
        MOV     QUEUE_HIGH,DX

        PUSH    ANCHOR_HIGH     ;Register class so we can get messages
        PUSH    ANCHOR_LOW
        PUSH    DS              ;Register this name for class
        PUSH    OFFSET CLASS_NAME
        PUSH    CS                      ;Set up window function
        PUSH    OFFSET CS:WINDOW_FUNC
        PUSH    0       ;High style - use style 00000004H
        PUSH    4       ;Low style
        PUSH    0       ;No additional storage space
        CALL    WinRegisterClass

        PUSH    0       ;Parent window handle
        PUSH    1
        PUSH    8000H   ;Make window visible - Style high
        PUSH    0000H   ;Style low
        PUSH    DS      ;Point to window flags
        PUSH    OFFSET FLAGS
        PUSH    DS                 ;← make 0 for default window
        PUSH    OFFSET CLASS_NAME ;← make 0 for default window
→       PUSH    DS      ;Point to title bar text
→       PUSH    OFFSET TITLE_BAR
                :
                :
```

Next, we have to push the style of the client window, which we will make 0, a "module handle," which we will also leave at zero (you can specify additional *resources* in a module, which we won't do here), and a resource ID, which we will also leave at 0. WinCreateStdWindow returns a handle to the client window—the space we will draw on, which makes up the center of the window (excluding scroll bars and title bar). We have to push the address of a double word to receive that handle:

```
        .MODEL   SMALL
        .286

        .STACK   20000

        .DATA
        ANCHOR_LOW       DW 0            ;Anchor block handle
        ANCHOR_HIGH      DW 0
        QUEUE_LOW        DW 0            ;Queue handle
        QUEUE_HIGH       DW 0
        FLAGS            DW 0C3BH        ;Window flags
                         DW 8000H
        CLASS_NAME       DB 'FRANK',0    ;Private window class name
        TITLE_BAR        DB 'Welcome to PM',0    ;Window title bar
→       CLIENT_LOW             DW 0            ;Client window handle
→       CLIENT_HIGH            DW 0

        .CODE
        EXTRN    WinInitialize:FAR, WinCreateMsgQueue:FAR, DosExit:FAR
        EXTRN    WinRegisterClass:FAR, WinCreateStdWindow:FAR

ENTRY   PROC FAR

        PUSH     0                        ;Get Anchor Block Handle
        CALL     WinInitialize
        MOV      ANCHOR_LOW,AX
        MOV      ANCHOR_HIGH,DX

        PUSH     DX    ;Set up message queue — Anchor high
        PUSH     AX    ;Anchor low
        PUSH     0     ;Use default size
        CALL     WinCreateMsgQueue
        MOV      QUEUE_LOW,AX
        MOV      QUEUE_HIGH,DX

        PUSH     ANCHOR_HIGH      ;Register class so we can get messages
        PUSH     ANCHOR_LOW
        PUSH     DS               ;Register this name for class
        PUSH     OFFSET CLASS_NAME
        PUSH     CS                       ;Set up window function
        PUSH     OFFSET CS:WINDOW_FUNC
        PUSH     0       ;High style — use style 00000004H
        PUSH     4       ;Low style
        PUSH     0       ;No additional storage space
        CALL     WinRegisterClass

        PUSH     0       ;Parent window handle
        PUSH     1
```

```
        PUSH     8000H    ;Make window visible — Style high
        PUSH     0000H    ;Style low
        PUSH     DS       ;Point to window flags
        PUSH     OFFSET FLAGS
        PUSH     DS                ;← make 0 for default window
        PUSH     OFFSET CLASS_NAME ;← make 0 for default window
        PUSH     DS       ;Point to title bar text
        PUSH     OFFSET TITLE_BAR
→       PUSH     0
→       PUSH     0
→       PUSH     0
→       PUSH     0
→       PUSH     DS       ;Get client handle
→       PUSH     OFFSET CLIENT_LOW
→       CALL     WinCreateStdWindow
                 :
                 :
```

And the window appears on the screen at this point. WinCreateStdWindow returns a handle to the main window in DX:AX, and we will store that handle in FRAME_HIGH and FRAME_LOW for later use. Already, WINDOW_FUNC (which we have yet to write) has been called five times by OS/2. In it, we have specified that our window should be solid, and then let OS/2 itself handle most of the defaults. Next, we have to set up a loop that continually receives messages from the message queue. We start by setting up a message area to receive message *packets* from the queue. That format looks like this (see QUEUE_MSG):

```
.DATA
ANCHOR_LOW      DW 0              ;Anchor block handle
ANCHOR_HIGH     DW 0
QUEUE_LOW       DW 0              ;Queue handle
QUEUE_HIGH      DW 0
FLAGS           DW 0C3BH          ;Window flags
                DW 8000H
CLASS_NAME      DB 'FRANK',0      ;Private window class name
TITLE_BAR       DB 'Welcome to PM',0     ;Window title bar
CLIENT_LOW      DW 0              ;Client window handle
CLIENT_HIGH     DW 0
FRAME_LOW       DW 0              ;Main window handle
FRAME_HIGH      DW 0
QUEUE_MSG         DW 0            ;Queue Message will go here
                  DW 0
  MSG             DW 0
  MP1             DW 0
                  DW 0
  MP2             DW 0
                  DW 0
  TIME            DW 0
                  DW 0
```

```
MOUSE_LOW_X       DW 0
MOUSE_HIGH_X      DW 0
MOUSE_LOW_Y       DW 0
MOUSE_HIGH_Y      DW 0
```

To fill this data area, we have to call WinGetMsg. We'll continually loop, waiting for messages. When one comes, we'll check to see if WinGetMsg returned 0—if it did, we should exit. Otherwise, here are the common messages, returned in MSG in QUEUE_MSG:

| | |
|---|---|
| Refresh window request | 0023H |
| Button 1 down | 0071H |
| Button 1 up | 0072H |
| Button 1 double click | 0073H |
| Button 2 down | 0074H |
| Button 2 up | 0075H |
| Button 2 double click | 0076H |
| Key was hit | 007AH |
| Window was created | 0001H |
| Window destroyed | 0002H |
| OK to erase background? | 004FH |
| Horizontal scroll | 0032H |
| Mouse moved | 0070H |
| Vertical scroll | 0031H |
| Window terminated | 002AH |

To use WinGetMsg, we have to push, in order: the handle of the anchor block; the address of the QUEUE_MSG data area; a window handle (NULL—that is, zero—specifies that we should receive all messages); and two parameters that specify how many messages we can accept (specifying 0 for both means we'll get all messages). Here's what it looks like:

```
.MODEL  SMALL
.286

.STACK  20000

.DATA
ANCHOR_LOW       DW 0              ;Anchor block handle
ANCHOR_HIGH      DW 0
QUEUE_LOW        DW 0              ;Queue handle
QUEUE_HIGH       DW 0
FLAGS            DW 0C3BH          ;Window flags
                 DW 8000H
CLASS_NAME       DB 'FRANK',0      ;Private window class name
TITLE_BAR        DB 'Welcome to PM',0     ;Window title bar
CLIENT_LOW       DW 0              ;Client window handle
CLIENT_HIGH      DW 0
```

```
        FRAME_LOW       DW 0            ;Main window handle
        FRAME_HIGH      DW 0
        QUEUE_MSG         DW 0          ;Queue Message will go here
                          DW 0
          MSG             DW 0
          MP1             DW 0
                          DW 0
          MP2             DW 0
                          DW 0
          TIME            DW 0
                          DW 0
   MOUSE_LOW_X            DW 0
   MOUSE_HIGH_X           DW 0
   MOUSE_LOW_Y            DW 0
   MOUSE_HIGH_Y           DW 0

        .CODE
        EXTRN   WinInitialize:FAR, WinCreateMsgQueue:FAR, DosExit:FAR
        EXTRN   WinRegisterClass:FAR, WinCreateStdWindow:FAR

ENTRY   PROC FAR

        PUSH    0                       ;Get Anchor Block Handle
        CALL    WinInitialize
        MOV     ANCHOR_LOW,AX
        MOV     ANCHOR_HIGH,DX

        PUSH    DX    ;Set up message queue — Anchor high
        PUSH    AX    ;Anchor low
        PUSH    0     ;Use default size
        CALL    WinCreateMsgQueue
        MOV     QUEUE_LOW,AX
        MOV     QUEUE_HIGH,DX

        PUSH    ANCHOR_HIGH     ;Register class so we can get messages
        PUSH    ANCHOR_LOW
        PUSH    DS              ;Register this name for class
        PUSH    OFFSET CLASS_NAME
        PUSH    CS                      ;Set up window function
        PUSH    OFFSET CS:WINDOW_FUNC
        PUSH    0       ;High style — use style 00000004H
        PUSH    4       ;Low style
        PUSH    0       ;No additional storage space
        CALL    WinRegisterClass

        PUSH    0       ;Parent window handle
        PUSH    1
        PUSH    8000H   ;Make window visible — Style high
        PUSH    0000H   ;Style low
        PUSH    DS      ;Point to window flags
        PUSH    OFFSET FLAGS
        PUSH    DS                 ;← make 0 for default window
        PUSH    OFFSET CLASS_NAME  ;← make 0 for default window
```

```
        PUSH    DS      ;Point to title bar text
        PUSH    OFFSET TITLE_BAR
        PUSH    0
        PUSH    0
        PUSH    0
        PUSH    0
        PUSH    DS      ;Get client handle
        PUSH    OFFSET CLIENT_LOW
        CALL    WinCreateStdWindow

        MOV     FRAME_HIGH,DX   ;Save main handle
        MOV     FRAME_LOW,AX

GET_MSG:        ;Main message loop
→       PUSH    ANCHOR_HIGH     ;Push anchor block handle
→       PUSH    ANCHOR_LOW
→       PUSH    DS              ;Push our data area for queue messages
→       PUSH    OFFSET QUEUE_MSG
→       PUSH    0
→       PUSH    0
→       PUSH    0
→       PUSH    0
→       CALL    WinGetMsg
                :
                :
```

When control returns from WinGetMsg, QUEUE_MSG has been filled. Some of those messages are intended for OS/2, some for us; we'll see how to handle messages later. The next step is to send the messages off to a dispatcher named WinDispatchMsg. This function call interprets the message and calls our WINDOW_FUNC to handle it if needed. To use WinDispatchMsg, push the anchor block handle, the address of QUEUE_MSG, and call it:

```
.MODEL  SMALL
.286

.STACK  20000

.DATA
ANCHOR_LOW      DW 0            ;Anchor block handle
ANCHOR_HIGH     DW 0
QUEUE_LOW       DW 0            ;Queue handle
QUEUE_HIGH      DW 0
FLAGS           DW 0C3BH        ;Window flags
                DW 8000H
CLASS_NAME      DB 'FRANK',0    ;Private window class name
TITLE_BAR       DB 'Welcome to PM',0    ;Window title bar
CLIENT_LOW      DW 0            ;Client window handle
CLIENT_HIGH     DW 0
FRAME_LOW       DW 0             ;Main window handle
FRAME_HIGH      DW 0
QUEUE_MSG         DW 0           ;Queue Message will go here
```

```
                        DW 0
    MSG                 DW 0
    MP1                 DW 0
                        DW 0
    MP2                 DW 0
                        DW 0
    TIME                DW 0
                        DW 0
    MOUSE_LOW_X         DW 0
    MOUSE_HIGH_X        DW 0
    MOUSE_LOW_Y         DW 0
    MOUSE_HIGH_Y        DW 0

        .CODE
        EXTRN   WinInitialize:FAR, WinCreateMsgQueue:FAR, DosExit:FAR
        EXTRN   WinRegisterClass:FAR, WinCreateStdWindow:FAR, WinGetMsg:FAR

ENTRY   PROC FAR

        PUSH    0                       ;Get Anchor Block Handle
        CALL    WinInitialize
        MOV     ANCHOR_LOW,AX
        MOV     ANCHOR_HIGH,DX

        PUSH    DX   ;Set up message queue - Anchor high
        PUSH    AX   ;Anchor low
        PUSH    0    ;Use default size
        CALL    WinCreateMsgQueue
        MOV     QUEUE_LOW,AX
        MOV     QUEUE_HIGH,DX

        PUSH    ANCHOR_HIGH     ;Register class so we can get messages
        PUSH    ANCHOR_LOW
        PUSH    DS              ;Register this name for class
        PUSH    OFFSET CLASS_NAME
        PUSH    CS                      ;Set up window function
        PUSH    OFFSET CS:WINDOW_FUNC
        PUSH    0       ;High style - use style 00000004H
        PUSH    4       ;Low style
        PUSH    0       ;No additional storage space
        CALL    WinRegisterClass

        PUSH    0       ;Parent window handle
        PUSH    1
        PUSH    8000H   ;Make window visible - Style high
        PUSH    0000H   ;Style low
        PUSH    DS      ;Point to window flags
        PUSH    OFFSET FLAGS
        PUSH    DS                 ; ← make 0 for default window
        PUSH    OFFSET CLASS_NAME ; ← make 0 for default window
        PUSH    DS      ;Point to title bar text
        PUSH    OFFSET TITLE_BAR
        PUSH    0
```

```
        PUSH    0
        PUSH    0
        PUSH    0
        PUSH    DS          ;Get client handle
        PUSH    OFFSET CLIENT_LOW
        CALL    WinCreateStdWindow

        MOV     FRAME_HIGH,DX    ;Save main handle
        MOV     FRAME_LOW,AX

GET_MSG:                ;Main message loop
        PUSH    ANCHOR_HIGH      ;Push anchor block handle
        PUSH    ANCHOR_LOW
        PUSH    DS               ;Push our data area for queue messages
        PUSH    OFFSET QUEUE_MSG
        PUSH    0
        PUSH    0
        PUSH    0
        PUSH    0
        CALL    WinGetMsg

→       CMP     AX,0             ;If null received, Exit has been selected
→       JE      FINISH

→       PUSH    ANCHOR_HIGH      ;No exit message recieved - dispatch message
→       PUSH    ANCHOR_LOW
→       PUSH    DS               ;Point to message itself
→       PUSH    OFFSET QUEUE_MSG
→       CALL    WinDispatchMsg

        JMP     GET_MSG          ;Loop again for another message
                :
                :
```

The message has been handled now—all that remains is to loop and wait for another message from WinGetMsg. Note that the first thing we did after getting the message was to check AX—if it was zero, the Close option was selected with the mouse from the system menu in our window. If it was selected, we jump to the label FINISH. At FINISH, we handle the process of shutting down the window. To begin, we call WinDestroyWindow and WinDestroyMsgQueue. To call those functions, you need only pass the correct handles, like this:

```
        .MODEL  SMALL
        .286

        .STACK  20000

        .DATA
        ANCHOR_LOW      DW 0            ;Anchor block handle
        ANCHOR_HIGH     DW 0
        QUEUE_LOW       DW 0            ;Queue handle
        QUEUE_HIGH      DW 0
```

```
FLAGS           DW 0C3BH        ;Window flags
                DW 8000H
CLASS_NAME      DB "FRANK",0    ;Private window class name
TITLE_BAR       DB "Welcome to PM",0    ;Window title bar
CLIENT_LOW      DW 0            ;Client window handle
CLIENT_HIGH     DW 0
FRAME_LOW       DW 0            ;Main window handle
FRAME_HIGH      DW 0
QUEUE_MSG       DW 0            ;Queue Message will go here
                  DW 0
  MSG             DW 0
  MP1             DW 0
                  DW 0
  MP2             DW 0
                  DW 0
  TIME            DW 0
                  DW 0
  MOUSE_LOW_X     DW 0
  MOUSE_HIGH_X    DW 0
  MOUSE_LOW_Y     DW 0
  MOUSE_HIGH_Y    DW 0

.CODE
EXTRN   WinInitialize:FAR, WinCreateMsgQueue:FAR, DosExit:FAR
EXTRN   WinRegisterClass:FAR, WinCreateStdWindow:FAR, WinGetMsg:FAR
EXTRN   WinDispatchMsg:FAR, WinDestroyWindow:FAR
EXTRN   WinDestroyMsgQueue:FAR

ENTRY   PROC FAR

PUSH    0                       ;Get Anchor Block Handle
CALL    WinInitialize
MOV     ANCHOR_LOW,AX
MOV     ANCHOR_HIGH,DX

PUSH    DX   ;Set up message queue — Anchor high
PUSH    AX   ;Anchor low
PUSH    0    ;Use default size
CALL    WinCreateMsgQueue
MOV     QUEUE_LOW,AX
MOV     QUEUE_HIGH,DX

PUSH    ANCHOR_HIGH     ;Register class so we can get messages
PUSH    ANCHOR_LOW
PUSH    DS              ;Register this name for class
PUSH    OFFSET CLASS_NAME
PUSH    CS                      ;Set up window function
PUSH    OFFSET CS:WINDOW_FUNC
PUSH    0       ;High style — use style 00000004H
PUSH    4       ;Low style
PUSH    0       ;No additional storage space
CALL    WinRegisterClass
```

```
        PUSH    0       ;Parent window handle
        PUSH    1
        PUSH    8000H   ;Make window visible — Style high
        PUSH    0000H   ;Style low
        PUSH    DS      ;Point to window flags
        PUSH    OFFSET FLAGS
        PUSH    DS                  ; ← make 0 for default window
        PUSH    OFFSET CLASS_NAME ; ← make 0 for default window
        PUSH    DS      ;Point to title bar text
        PUSH    OFFSET TITLE_BAR
        PUSH    0
        PUSH    0
        PUSH    0
        PUSH    0
        PUSH    DS      ;Get client handle
        PUSH    OFFSET CLIENT_LOW
        CALL    WinCreateStdWindow

        MOV     FRAME_HIGH,DX   ;Save main handle
        MOV     FRAME_LOW,AX

GET_MSG:        ;Main message loop
        PUSH    ANCHOR_HIGH     ;Push anchor block handle
        PUSH    ANCHOR_LOW
        PUSH    DS              ;Push our data area for queue messages
        PUSH    OFFSET QUEUE_MSG
        PUSH    0
        PUSH    0
        PUSH    0
        PUSH    0
        CALL    WinGetMsg

        CMP     AX,0             ;If null recieved, Exit has been selected
        JE      FINISH

        PUSH    ANCHOR_HIGH     ;No exit message received — dispatch message
        PUSH    ANCHOR_LOW
        PUSH    DS              ;Point to message itself
        PUSH    OFFSET QUEUE_MSG
        CALL    WinDispatchMsg

        JMP    GET_MSG          ;Loop again for another message

FINISH:
→       PUSH    FRAME_HIGH      ;Exit here — get rid of window
→       PUSH    FRAME_LOW
→       CALL    WinDestroyWindow

→       PUSH    QUEUE_HIGH      ;Get rid of message queue
→       PUSH    QUEUE_LOW
→       CALL    WinDestroyMsgQueue
                :
                :
```

Finally, we call the final function, WinTerminate, passing it the window handle, and use DosExit to end the procedure ENTRY:

```
        .MODEL   SMALL
        .286
        :
        :
FINISH:
        PUSH     FRAME_HIGH       ;Exit here — get rid of window
        PUSH     FRAME_LOW
        CALL     WinDestroyWindow

        PUSH     QUEUE_HIGH       ;Get rid of message queue
        PUSH     QUEUE_LOW
        CALL     WinDestroyMsgQueue

→       PUSH     ANCHOR_HIGH      ;Finish up with window
→       PUSH     ANCHOR_LOW
→       CALL     WinTerminate

EXIT:   PUSH     1 ;A Normal Exit.
→       PUSH     0
→       CALL     DosExit
ENTRY   ENDP
```

Everything is ready now, except the window function that handles messages from OS/2, WINDOW_FUNC, and we'll put that together next.

# The Window Function

As mentioned, the window function handles messages passed to us from OS/2. We will receive different codes depending on what action has occurred. It's up to us to tell OS/2 what to do when it asks. We can begin with a normal outline for a FAR procedure:

```
WINDOW_FUNC      PROC FAR
        :
        :
        RET
WINDOW_FUNC      ENDP

→       END      ENTRY
```

Because this procedure finishes off our file WIN.ASM, we have placed the line END ENTRY at the end to let the assembler know what our intended entry point is.

When OS/2 calls our function, it will have pushed these parameters:

| | |
|---|---|
| Double Word | Handle of window message is for |
| Word | The message itself |
| Far Address | Address of first message parameter |
| Far Address | Address of second message parameter |

Some messages come with extra parameters, and the final two addresses point to them; we won't use those extra parameters. After those seven words, OS/2 has pushed the two-word return address normal to any call. It is our responsibility to read the data from the stack and act accordingly.

Our first impulse might be to pop the words off the stack and store them in memory. Already, we're in trouble if we do that. WINDOW_FUNC has to be *reentrant*, and our program will crash unless we write it in a certain way.

## Re-entrant Code

One facet of multitasking is reentrant code. For example, imagine that we are just setting up our window. WINDOW_FUNC is called for the first time, and we pop the parameters off the stack and into memory locations to work with them. Most of the time, we will pass control on to PM's default message handler, WinDefWindow-Proc. While we're still waiting for control to return from WinDefWindowProc, it won't hesitate to call WINDOW_PROC again to learn another piece of information:

```
WINDOW_PROC   PROC FAR  <-----------------+
        :                                 |
[Store parameters from stack]             |
        :                                 |
CALL    WinDefWindowProc  -> WinDefWindowProc
        :
        :
        RET
WINDOW_PROC     ENDP
```

When this happens, the first thing that we do with the new call is to pick parameters off the stack as before and store them in memory—overwriting what was stored from the first call, which is still being processed. In this case, WinDef-WindowProc has called WINDOW_FUNC again while we are still waiting inside WINDOW_FUNC for it to return the first time.

Not only are the parameters (like the message itself) overwritten when we start to process the second call, but the original return address is also overwritten. When the second call finishes and WinDefWindowProc returns, we have lost the original parameters and return address. Our program will stop.

To handle this problem, let's take a look at what the stack holds when we get it:

| HANDLE1 |
|---|
| HANDLE2 |
| MESSAGE |
| PARM1HI |
| PARM1LO |
| PARM2HI |
| PARM2LO |
| PMRETHI |
| PMRETLO |

Where PMRETHI and PMRETLO stand for PM's return address. The trouble comes when we call WinDefWindowProc. Since we have to pass the same parameters to it that we have received, the stack would look like this:

| | |
|---|---|
| | HANDLE1 |
| | HANDLE2 |
| | MESSAGE |
| | PARM1HI |
| | PARM1LO |
| | PARM2HI |
| | PARM2LO |
| → | WPRETHI |
| → | WPRETLO |

Where WPRETHI and WPRETLO are *our* return address (so control returns to us) and we have stored PMRETHI and PMRETLO. If WinDefWindowProc calls WINDOW_FUNC again, PMRETHI and PMRETLO, the original return address, will be destroyed. The trick is to store them on the stack, not in memory. When we call WinDefWindowProc, we will have set the stack up this way:

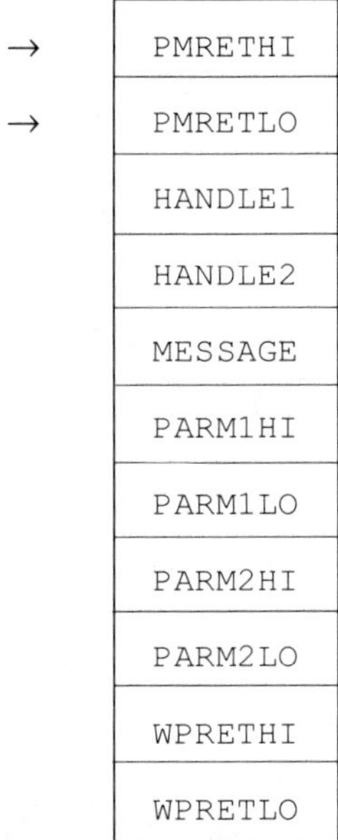


WinDefWindowProc will pop off our return address and the parameters, but no more than that. When we return from WinDefWindowProc, everything will be popped, except for the two words we need most: the orignal return address:

| PMRETHI |
|---|
| PMRETLO |

Now that the call to WinDefWindowProc has returned, these words are next on the stack, so we can just execute a RET ourselves and return from WINDOW_FUNC.

In WINDOW_FUNC, we can't even assume that DS is set correctly when we get control, so we first set it to our data segment (note the use of @DATA):

```
WINDOW_FUNC      PROC FAR

→       PUSH     @DATA    ;Set DS to our data segment
→       POP      DS
                 :
                 :
        RET
WINDOW_FUNC      ENDP

        END      ENTRY
```

Now we will store the parameters from the stack in memory. If we have to call WinDefWindowProc, we will push them back on the stack, so they will not be damaged—the important thing is to preserve the return address. Here's how we pop the values:

```
WINDOW_FUNC      PROC FAR

        PUSH     @DATA    ;Set DS to our data segment
        POP      DS
        POP      RET1     ;Save return values
        POP      RET2
        POP      P1       ;Get all parameters
        POP      P2
        POP      P3
        POP      P4
        POP      P5
        POP      P6
        POP      P7
        PUSH     RET2     ;Put return values back on stack for return
        PUSH     RET1
                 :
                 :
        RET
WINDOW_FUNC      ENDP

        END      ENTRY
```

Note that we put the two return words PMRETHI and PMRETLO back on the stack. We must add all those words to the data segment, starting with RET1:

```
        .MODEL  SMALL
        .286
        .STACK  20000

        .DATA
        ANCHOR_LOW       DW 0              ;Anchor block handle
        ANCHOR_HIGH      DW 0
        QUEUE_LOW        DW 0              ;Queue handle
        QUEUE_HIGH       DW 0
        FLAGS            DW 0C3BH          ;Window flags
                         DW 8000H
        CLASS_NAME       DB "FRANK",0      ;Private window class name
        TITLE_BAR        DB "Welcome to PM" ,0     ;Window title bar
        CLIENT_LOW       DW 0              ;Client window handle
        CLIENT_HIGH      DW 0
        FRAME_LOW        DW 0              ;Main window handle
        FRAME_HIGH       DW 0
        QUEUE_MSG          DW 0            ;Queue Message will go here
                           DW 0
          MSG              DW 0
          MP1              DW 0
                           DW 0
          MP2              DW 0
                           DW 0
          TIME             DW 0
                           DW 0
          MOUSE_LOW_X      DW 0
```

```
    MOUSE_HIGH_X     DW 0
    MOUSE_LOW_Y      DW 0
    MOUSE_HIGH_Y     DW 0
  RET1      DW 0                ;Return values on stack in WINDOW_FUNC
  RET2      DW 0
  P1        DW 0                ;Parameters on stack in WINDOW_FUNC
  P2        DW 0
  P3        DW 0
  P4        DW 0
  P5        DW 0
  P6        DW 0
  P7        DW 0
```

The stack looks like this now:

| PMRETHI |
|---|
| PMRETLO |

all set for a return from WINDOW_PROC to Presentation Manager. If we have to call WinDefWindowProc (which takes the same parameters in the same order as WINDOW_FUNC), we will push the parameters on the stack again, and the CALL instruction will push our return address, leaving the stack like this:

| PMRETHI |
|---|
| PMRETLO |
| HANDLE1 |
| HANDLE2 |
| MESSAGE |
| PARM1HI |
| PARM1LO |
| PARM2HI |
| PARM2LO |
| WPRETHI |
| WPRETLO |

When we return from WinDefWindowProc, everything will be cleared from the stack but the top two words, the return address we need to return to OS/2, so we can just execute a RET.

We also make a copy of the stack pointer in BP, the stack base pointer. As we know, this pointer can be used for stack manipulations just like BX can be used for data manipulations. We can pick parameters off the stack like this: MOV AX,[BP+14], where the offset is in bytes. Using BP provides an easy way of picking values from the stack, and although we won't use BP here, we include it because it frequently appears in window functions.

Now we have to check for various mesages from Presentation Manager. Let's start off by checking for a keystroke. With the way we've stored the parameters, the message is in P5, so we can check that against 7AH (the message meaning that a key was pushed). Let's have the program beep if a key was typed. We can do that with the function DosBeep:

```
WINDOW_FUNC       PROC FAR

          PUSH     @DATA    ;Set DS to our data segment
          POP      DS
          POP      RET1     ;Save return values
          POP      RET2
          POP      P1       ;Get all parameters
          POP      P2
          POP      P3
          POP      P4
          POP      P5
          POP      P6
          POP      P7
          PUSH     RET2     ;Put return values back on stack for return
          PUSH     RET1
          PUSH     BP       ;Save stack base pointer
          PUSH     SP
          POP      BP       ;Can use for stack manipulations
KEY:
→         CMP      P5,7AH   ;Keystroke?
→         JNE      NOT_KEY  ;No
→         PUSH     1500     ;Yes — beep
→         PUSH     1
→         CALL     DOSBEEP
→         JMP      RET_0    ;Return 0

NOT_KEY:
                   :
                   :
RET_0:    MOV      AX,0     ;Return 0 for OK
          MOV      DX,0
OVER:     POP      BP
          RET
WINDOW_FUNC        ENDP

          END      ENTRY
```

If it was a key, we call DosBeep and then exit. We can push the frequency of the tone, the duration in milliseconds, and call DosBeep. Before we exit, we must fill DX and AX with 0 for OS/2—the most common return value for us will be 0. This value is returned if we don't want to indicate an error or ask OS/2 to take any action.

We can cover other possibilities besides just a struck key; one important case is the erase background request from OS/2, message 4FH. If we see this message, PM is asking whether it's OK to erase the background behind the window—until now, our window has been a transparent box with borders. In this case, we return TRUE (DX=0, AX=1), and our window becomes solid (white):

```
WINDOW_FUNC      PROC FAR

        PUSH     @DATA   ;Set DS to our data segment
        POP      DS
        POP      RET1    ;Save return values
        POP      RET2
        POP      P1      ;Get all parameters
        POP      P2
        POP      P3
        POP      P4
        POP      P5
        POP      P6
        POP      P7
        PUSH     RET2    ;Put return values back on stack for return
        PUSH     RET1
        PUSH     BP      ;Save stack base pointer
        PUSH     SP
        POP      BP      ;Can use for stack manipulations
KEY:
        CMP      P5,7AH  ;Keystroke?
        JNE      NOT_KEY ;No
        PUSH     1500    ;Yes - beep
        PUSH     1
        CALL     DOSBEEP
        JMP      RET_0   ;Return 0

NOT_KEY:
        CMP      P5,1    ;Window created?
        JNE      NOT_CREATE       ;No
                                  ;Yes - do initialization
        JMP      RET_0
NOT_CREATE:
        CMP      P5,23H  ;Have to paint?
        JNE      NOT_PAINT        ;No
                                  ;Yes - do paint here
        JMP      RET_0            ;Return 0
NOT_PAINT:
        CMP      P5,71H  ;Button 1 pushed?
        JNE      NOT_BUTTON_1     ;No
                                  ;Yes - handle button 1
        JMP      RET_0            ;Return 0
```

```
NOT_BUTTON_1:
        CMP     P5,70H  ;Did the mouse move?
        JNE     NOT_MOUSE_MOVE  ;No
                                ;Yes - handle new mouse position
        JMP     RET_0           ;Return 0
NOT_MOUSE_MOVE:
        CMP     P5,31H  ;Vertical scroll?
        JNE     NOT_VSCROLL     ;No
                                ;Yes - scroll window
        JMP     RET_0           ;Return 0
NOT_VSCROLL:
        CMP     P5,32H          ;Horizontal scroll?
        JNE     NOT_HSCROLL     ;No
                                ;Yes - scroll window
NOT_HSCROLL:
→       CMP     P5,4FH          ;Make window solid?
→       JNE     NOT_ERASE_BKGND ;Not this time
→       MOV     DX,0            ;Yes - return 1 for true
→       MOV     AX,1
→       JMP     OVER
                :
                :
RET_0:  MOV     AX,0    ;Return 0 for OK
        MOV     DX,0
OVER:   POP     BP
        RET
WINDOW_FUNC     ENDP

        END     ENTRY
```

We'll pass any other case on to OS/2 for default handling by WinDefWindow-Proc. We do that by pushing the parameters again, and calling WinDefWindowP-roc. After the call, we simply return:

```
WINDOW_FUNC     PROC FAR

        PUSH    @DATA   ;Set DS to our data segment
        POP     DS
        POP     RET1    ;Save return values
        POP     RET2
        POP     P1      ;Get all parameters
        POP     P2
        POP     P3
        POP     P4
        POP     P5
        POP     P6
        POP     P7
        PUSH    RET2    ;Put return values back on stack for return
        PUSH    RET1
        PUSH    BP      ;Save stack base pointer
        PUSH    SP
        POP     BP      ;Can use for stack manipulations
```

```
KEY:
        CMP     P5,7AH  ;Keystroke?
        JNE     NOT_KEY ;No
        PUSH    1500    ;Yes - beep
        PUSH    1
        CALL    DOSBEEP
        JMP     RET_0   ;Return 0

NOT_KEY:
        CMP     P5,1    ;Window created?
        JNE     NOT_CREATE        ;No
                                  ;Yes - do initialization
        JMP     RET_0
NOT_CREATE:
        CMP     P5,23H  ;Have to paint?
        JNE     NOT_PAINT         ;No
                                  ;Yes - do paint here
        JMP     RET_0             ;Return 0
NOT_PAINT:
        CMP     P5,71H  ;Button 1 pushed?
        JNE     NOT_BUTTON_1      ;No
                                  ;Yes - handle button 1
        JMP     RET_0             ;Return 0
NOT_BUTTON_1:
        CMP     P5,70H  ;Did the mouse move?
        JNE     NOT_MOUSE_MOVE    ;No
                                  ;Yes - handle new mouse position
        JMP     RET_0             ;Return 0
NOT_MOUSE_MOVE:
        CMP     P5,31H  ;Vertical scroll?
        JNE     NOT_VSCROLL       ;No
                                  ;Yes - scroll window
        JMP     RET_0             ;Return 0
NOT_VSCROLL:
        CMP     P5,32H            ;Horizontal scroll?
        JNE     NOT_HSCROLL       ;No
                                  ;Yes - scroll window
NOT_HSCROLL:
        CMP     P5,4FH            ;Make window solid?
        JNE     NOT_ERASE_BKGND   ;Not this time
        MOV     DX,0              ;Yes - return 1 for true
        MOV     AX,1
        JMP     OVER
NOT_ERASE_BKGND:
                                  ;Handle other cases here
DEFAULT:
        POP     BP                ;Let WinDefWindowProc handle defaults
        PUSH    P7                ;Push parameters back on stack
        PUSH    P6
        PUSH    P5
        PUSH    P4
        PUSH    P3
        PUSH    P2
```

```
        PUSH    P1

        CALL    WinDefWindowProc        ;Call for default handling

        RET

RET_0:  MOV     AX,0    ;Return 0 for OK
        MOV     DX,0
OVER:   POP     BP
        RET
WINDOW_FUNC     ENDP

        END     ENTRY
```

That's it. When you assemble and run WIN.ASM, the screen will snap to the Presentation Manager display, and our window will appear. You can move the window around the screen, maximize or minimize it, switch to other windows, and close it using the system menu. And when you type a key, WINDOW_FUNC will process the keystroke and beep. So far, we have put a window on the screen. You can resize that window, open and close it, and move it around. But you can't type characters and watch them appear, or draw points, lines, and boxes, or resize the window and have the program react accordingly. We'll do that now.

We are going to explore the graphical interface function group—the Gpi group. By using these functions, you will be able to draw on the screen. We'll also start dissecting message packets from the keyboard to place typed keys in our particular window.

# The Gpi Functions

Unfortunately, you can't use the Vio functions (except for a small subgroup) here. Those functions are text-based, and the screen is in graphics mode when you are using windows. Instead, a whole new function group was written for Presentation Manager use: the Gpi functions. The ones we'll see here include: GpiCharStringAt, GpiSetBackColor, GpiSetColor, GpiSetCurrentPosition, GpiSetPel, and GpiPolyLine, among others. There are some strengths to the Gpi functions (graphics) and some weaknesses (cursor control). We'll see both aspects. To begin, let's send a character string that says "This is it!" to our window. To do that, we'll need GpiCharStringAt.

## GpiCharStringAt

This function is the primary string-printing function, but it has a number of prominent problems. Like almost all Vio functions, it doesn't advance the cursor (in fact, there is no cursor). Here, however, that is a much more significant problem because in graphics mode, we are dealing with individual dots on the screen, called *pels* (for picture elements), not orderly columns of text—and the font used by PM varies in width character by character. When we are done printing our string, we don't know exactly where to start printing again since the length of the string depends on the widths of the characters we've used.

However, GpiCharStringAt does print on the screen, and we'll use it here. If you have been following our progress so far, you are probably heartily sick of handles, but there is one more we need before we can actually print, and that is a presentation space, or PS, handle.

The presentation space need not be the screen (although for us it always is). Three kinds of presentation spaces are normal, micro, and cached micro. The first two can send output to any device (actually referred to as a device context), and the last one, which is much simpler to use, can send output only to the screen. We will restrict ourselves to cached micro presentation spaces. We need a handle to a cached micro PS, and we can get it with WinBeginPaint. We have to push the handle of the current window (which is passed to us as parameters six and seven when WINDOW_FUNC is called), a preexisting PS handle if we have one (if NULL—two words of zeros—the function will return one), and the address of a structure detailing the region in the window we want to update. If that last address is NULL, as it will be for us, it means we will be updating the whole window. The handle to the PS is returned, as usual, in DX:AX. Here's what it looks like so far:

```
WINDOW_FUNC       PROC FAR
                  :
                  :
NOT_CREATE:
        CMP       P5,23H
        JNE       NOT_PAINT
→       PUSH     P7
→       PUSH     P6
→       PUSH     0
→       PUSH     0
→       PUSH     0
→       PUSH     0
→       CALL     WinBeginPaint

→       MOV      PS_HANDLE_HIGH,DX
→       MOV      PS_HANDLE_LOW,AX
                  :
                  :
        JMP      RET_0
NOT_PAINT:
                  :
                  :
WINDOW_FUNC       ENDP
```

Now that we have the PS handle, we are free to print on the screen with GpiCharStringAt. First, we set up screen coordinates and a message in our data segment:

```
.DATA
ANCHOR_LOW        DW 0
ANCHOR_HIGH       DW 0
QUEUE_LOW         DW 0
QUEUE_HIGH        DW 0
FLAGS  DW 0C3BH
                  DW 8000H
CLASS_NAME        DB "FRANK",0
TITLE_BAR         DB "Welcome to PM",0
CLIENT_LOW        DW 0
CLIENT_HIGH       DW 0
FRAME_LOW         DW 0
FRAME_HIGH        DW 0
QUEUE_MSG         DW 0
                    DW 0
  MSG               DW 0
  MP1               DW 0
                    DW 0
  MP2               DW 0
                    DW 0
  TIME              DW 0
                    DW 0
  MOUSE_LOW_X       DW 0
  MOUSE_HIGH_X      DW 0
  MOUSE_LOW_Y       DW 0
  MOUSE_HIGH_Y      DW 0
HANDLE_LOW        DW 0
HANDLE_HIGH       DW 0
MESSAGE           DW 0
PARM1_LOW         DW 0
PARM1_HIGH        DW 0
PARM2_LOW         DW 0
PARM2_HIGH        DW 0
RET1     DW 0
RET2     DW 0
OLD_DS   DW 0
P1       DW 0
P2       DW 0
P3       DW 0
P4       DW 0
P5       DW 0
P6       DW 0
P7       DW 0
PS_HANDLE_LOW     DW 0
PS_HANDLE_HIGH    DW 0
→ SCREEN_COORDS   DW 0
→                 DW 0
→ Y               DW 0
```

```
→                       DW 0
→        MSSG        DB "This is it!",0
→        MSSG_LEN    DW $ - MSSG
```

Note that each of the screen coordinates (X first, then Y) is made up of a double-word—the low word is stored first. To use GpiCharStringAt, we have to push the handle of the PS, the address of the screen coordinates, the message length (a double-word value), and then the address of the message itself.

The window coordinates work like this: The bottom left corner of the window is defined as (0,0), and the coordinates then increase pel by pel as we move up or to the right:

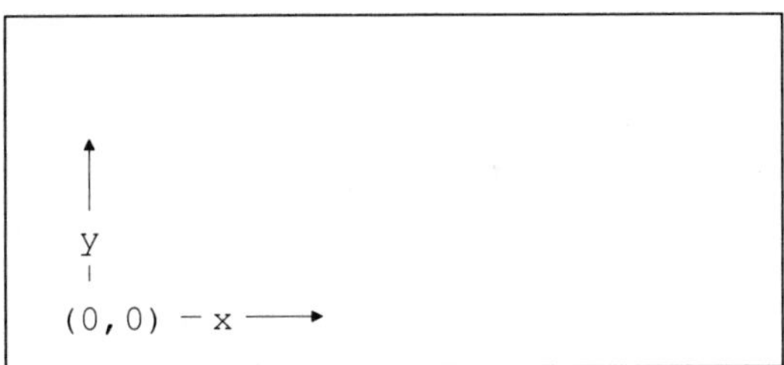


We will leave the coordinates at (0,0), so the message will be printed out in the lower left-hand corner of our window. Here's what it looks like in code:

```
WINDOW_FUNC     PROC FAR
                :
                :
NOT_CREATE:
        CMP     P5,23H
        JNE     NOT_PAINT
        PUSH    P7
        PUSH    P6
        PUSH    0
        PUSH    0
        PUSH    0
        PUSH    0
        CALL    WinBeginPaint

        MOV     PS_HANDLE_HIGH,DX
        MOV     PS_HANDLE_LOW,AX

        PUSH    PS_HANDLE_HIGH
        PUSH    PS_HANDLE_LOW
        PUSH    DS
        PUSH    OFFSET SCREEN_COORDS
        PUSH    0
        PUSH    MSSG_LEN
        PUSH    DS
        PUSH    OFFSET MSSG
        CALL    GpiCharStringAt
```

```
                    :
                    :
        JMP         RET_0
NOT_PAINT:
                    :
                    :
WINDOW_FUNC         ENDP
```

Finally, we have to close the PS handle, and we do that with WinEndPaint. All we have to do is to push the PS handle, and call it:

```
WINDOW_FUNC         PROC FAR
                    :
                    :
NOT_CREATE:
        CMP         P5,23H
        JNE         NOT_PAINT
        PUSH        P7
        PUSH        P6
        PUSH        0
        PUSH        0
        PUSH        0
        PUSH        0
        CALL        WinBeginPaint

        MOV         PS_HANDLE_HIGH,DX
        MOV         PS_HANDLE_LOW,AX

        PUSH        PS_HANDLE_HIGH
        PUSH        PS_HANDLE_LOW
        PUSH        DS
        PUSH        OFFSET SCREEN_COORDS
        PUSH        0
        PUSH        MSSG_LEN
        PUSH        DS
        PUSH        OFFSET MSSG
        CALL        GpiCharStringAt

→       PUSH        PS_HANDLE_HIGH
→       PUSH        PS_HANDLE_LOW
→       CALL        WinEndPaint

        JMP         RET_0
NOT_PAINT:
                    :
                    :
WINDOW_FUNC         ENDP
```

That's it: Our WINDOW_FUNC is ready. If you execute the complete program, the window will appear and "This is it!" will be printed at the lower left. Now we've sent output to our window. Of course, there are other options as well—we can print out in color.

# GpiSetColor

We can set the foreground (drawing) color, as well as the background color. Here is a list of colors that we can use with the functions GpiSetColor and GpiSetBackC-olor:

| | |
|---|---|
| Default | –3 |
| White | –2 |
| Black | –1 |
| Background | 0 |
| Blue | 1 |
| Red | 2 |
| Pink | 3 |
| Green | 4 |
| Cyan | 5 |
| Yellow | 6 |
| Neutral grey | 7 |
| Dark grey | 8 |
| Dark blue | 9 |
| Dark red | 10 |
| Dark pink | 11 |
| Dark green | 12 |
| Dark cyan | 13 |
| Brown | 14 |
| Light grey | 15 |

Each of these colors is passed as a double-word value, which means the high word is 0 for positive numbers and 0FFFFH for negative ones. Let's print out our message in yellow letters on a blue background. We begin by setting the background to blue by pushing the PS handle and the code for blue, which is 00000001H, and calling GpiSetBackColor:

```
WINDOW_FUNC     PROC FAR
                :
                :
NOT_CREATE:
        CMP     P5,23H
        JNE     NOT_PAINT
        PUSH    P7
        PUSH    P6
        PUSH    0
        PUSH    0
        PUSH    0
        PUSH    0
        CALL    WinBeginPaint

        MOV     PS_HANDLE_HIGH,DX
```

```
         MOV      PS_HANDLE_LOW,AX

→        PUSH     PS_HANDLE_HIGH
→        PUSH     PS_HANDLE_LOW
→        PUSH     0       ;Blue background
→        PUSH     1
→        CALL     GpiSetBackColor
                  :
                  :
         PUSH     PS_HANDLE_HIGH
         PUSH     PS_HANDLE_LOW
         PUSH     DS
         PUSH     OFFSET SCREEN_COORDS
         PUSH     0
         PUSH     MSSG_LEN
         PUSH     DS
         PUSH     OFFSET MSSG
         CALL     GpiCharStringAt

         PUSH     PS_HANDLE_HIGH
         PUSH     PS_HANDLE_LOW
         CALL     WinEndPaint

         JMP      RET_0
NOT_PAINT:
                  :
                  :
WINDOW_FUNC       ENDP
```

Next, we specify *overwrite* mode. When we do so, our text overwrites what is there already. To do that, we pass the PS handle and an option to the function GpiSetBackMix. That option is 00000000H to use the system default, 00000002H to overwrite the current color, and 00000005H to leave the current background color untouched:

```
WINDOW_FUNC       PROC FAR
                  :
                  :
NOT_CREATE:
         CMP      P5,23H
         JNE      NOT_PAINT
         PUSH     P7
         PUSH     P6
         PUSH     0
         PUSH     0
         PUSH     0
         PUSH     0
         CALL     WinBeginPaint

         MOV      PS_HANDLE_HIGH,DX
         MOV      PS_HANDLE_LOW,AX
```

```
        PUSH    PS_HANDLE_HIGH
        PUSH    PS_HANDLE_LOW
        PUSH    0       ;Blue background
        PUSH    1
        CALL    GpiSetBackColor

→       PUSH    PS_HANDLE_HIGH
→       PUSH    PS_HANDLE_LOW
→       PUSH    0       ;Overwrite current bkgnd color
→       PUSH    2
→       CALL    GpiSetBackMix
                :
                :
        PUSH    PS_HANDLE_HIGH
        PUSH    PS_HANDLE_LOW
        PUSH    DS
        PUSH    OFFSET SCREEN_COORDS
        PUSH    0
        PUSH    MSSG_LEN
        PUSH    DS
        PUSH    OFFSET MSSG
        CALL    GpiCharStringAt

        PUSH    PS_HANDLE_HIGH
        PUSH    PS_HANDLE_LOW
        CALL    WinEndPaint

        JMP     RET_0
NOT_PAINT:
                :
                :
WINDOW_FUNC     ENDP
```

Finally, we call GpiSetColor, specifying yellow for our text, and that's it:

```
WINDOW_FUNC     PROC FAR
                :
                :
NOT_CREATE:

        CMP     P5,23H
        JNE     NOT_PAINT
        PUSH    P7
        PUSH    P6
        PUSH    0
        PUSH    0
        PUSH    0
        PUSH    0
        CALL    WinBeginPaint

        MOV     PS_HANDLE_HIGH,DX
        MOV     PS_HANDLE_LOW,AX
```

```
        PUSH    PS_HANDLE_HIGH
        PUSH    PS_HANDLE_LOW
        PUSH    0       ;Blue background
        PUSH    1
        CALL    GpiSetBackColor

        PUSH    PS_HANDLE_HIGH
        PUSH    PS_HANDLE_LOW
        PUSH    0       ;Overwrite current bkgnd color
        PUSH    2
        CALL    GpiSetBackMix

→       PUSH    PS_HANDLE_HIGH
→       PUSH    PS_HANDLE_LOW
→       PUSH    0       ;Yellow letters
→       PUSH    6
→       CALL    GpiSetColor

        PUSH    PS_HANDLE_HIGH
        PUSH    PS_HANDLE_LOW
        PUSH    DS
        PUSH    OFFSET SCREEN_COORDS
        PUSH    0
        PUSH    MSSG_LEN
        PUSH    DS
        PUSH    OFFSET MSSG
        CALL    GpiCharStringAt

        PUSH    PS_HANDLE_HIGH
        PUSH    PS_HANDLE_LOW
        CALL    WinEndPaint

        JMP     RET_0
NOT_PAINT:
                :
                :
WINDOW_FUNC     ENDP
```

Now our message appears in yellow letters on a blue background.

Our next improvement has to do with reading keys. For the first time, we'll start accepting input to our Presentation Manager program.

# Reading Keys

As you know, we receive a variety of messages from OS/2 in WINDOW_FUNC. One of them, 7AH, has to do with keystrokes. Now that we can display output on the screen, let's see if we can't read a typed key and display that.

When we receive a keystroke message (the message parameter passed to WINDOW_FUNC, P5, will equal 7AH), a number of things may have happened. The key may have been pressed or released (we get messages for both). It may be a control key or a character. We have to find out what happened.

If a key has been typed, the lower word of MP1 in our message queue (as defined in our data segment) will hold information about the struck key. Bits will be set according to what type of key it was:

| | | |
|---|---|---|
| Character | Bit 0 | (1) |
| Special key | Bit 1 | (2) |
| Scan code | Bit 2 | (4) |
| Shift key | Bit 3 | (8) |
| Control key | Bit 4 | (16) |
| Alt key | Bit 5 | (32) |
| Key up | Bit 6 | (64) |
| Key was down | Bit 7 | (128) |
| Single key | Bit 8 | (256) |
| Unused key | Bit 9 | (512) |
| Composite key | Bit 10 | (1024) |
| Invalid | Bit 11 | (2048) |
| Toggle key | Bit 12 | (4096) |

In our case, we are looking for a character (bit 0 set), and we want to read the character only when the key was released (bit 6 set also). Under the key case in WINDOW_FUNC, we check bit 6 first to make sure a character was typed:

```
        WINDOW_FUNC     PROC FAR
                :
                :
KEY:
        CMP     P5,7AH
        JE      POSS_KEY
        JMP     NOT_KEY

POSS_KEY:
        MOV     AX,MP1    ←
        AND     AX,64     ←
        JZ      KEY_IN    ←
        JMP     RET_0     ←

KEY_IN:
                :
                :
        JMP     RET_0

NOT_KEY:
                :
                :
WINDOW_FUNC     ENDP
```

Next we make sure the key is being released:

```
        WINDOW_FUNC       PROC FAR
                    :
                    :
KEY:
        CMP         P5,7AH
        JE          POSS_KEY
        JMP         NOT_KEY

POSS_KEY:
        MOV         AX,MP1
        AND         AX,64
        JZ          KEY_IN
        JMP         RET_0

KEY_IN: MOV         AX,MP1      ←
        AND         AX,1        ←
        JNZ         CHAR_IN     ←
        JMP         RET_0       ←

CHAR_IN:
                    :
                    :
        JMP         RET_0

NOT_KEY:
                    :
                    :
WINDOW_FUNC         ENDP
```

Now we know that a key has been typed. The ASCII code itself is in the low word of MP2. To print it out, we will use GpiCharStringAt as before. First, we have to get a PS handle. It turns out that we don't have to use WinBeginPaint, although we could, to get a PS handle. There is a quicker function named WinGetPS, and we have only to push the window's handle that has already been passed to us in WINDOW_FUNC. We get the handle, save it, and also set overstrike mode like this:

```
        WINDOW_FUNC       PROC FAR
                    :
                    :
KEY:
        CMP         P5,7AH
        JE          POSS_KEY
        JMP         NOT_KEY

POSS_KEY:
        MOV         AX,MP1
        AND         AX,64
        JZ          KEY_IN
        JMP         RET_0
```

```
KEY_IN: MOV      AX,MP1
        AND      AX,1
        JNZ      CHAR_IN
        JMP      RET_0

CHAR_IN:
→       PUSH     P7
→       PUSH     P6
→       CALL     WinGetPS

→       MOV      PS_HANDLE_HIGH,DX
→       MOV      PS_HANDLE_LOW,AX

→       PUSH     PS_HANDLE_HIGH
→       PUSH     PS_HANDLE_LOW
→       PUSH     0
→       PUSH     2
→       CALL     GpiSetBackMix
                 :
                 :
        JMP      RET_0

NOT_KEY:
                 :
                 :
WINDOW_FUNC      ENDP
```

The next step is to get the character and print it. Since it is just the bottom 16 bits of MP2, we can load those bits into a word named CHAR_1 and print them with GpiCharStringAt:

```
        WINDOW_FUNC     PROC FAR
                 :
                 :
KEY:
        CMP      P5,7AH
        JE       POSS_KEY
        JMP      NOT_KEY

POSS_KEY:
        MOV      AX,MP1
        AND      AX,64
        JZ       KEY_IN
        JMP      RET_0

KEY_IN: MOV      AX,MP1
        AND      AX,1
        JNZ      CHAR_IN
        JMP      RET_0

CHAR_IN:
        PUSH     P7
```

```
            PUSH     P6
            CALL     WinGetPS

            MOV      PS_HANDLE_HIGH,DX
            MOV      PS_HANDLE_LOW,AX

            PUSH     PS_HANDLE_HIGH
            PUSH     PS_HANDLE_LOW
            PUSH     0
            PUSH     2
            CALL     GpiSetBackMix

→           MOV      AX, MP2
→           MOV      CHAR_1, AX

→           PUSH     PS_HANDLE_HIGH
→           PUSH     PS_HANDLE_LOW
→           PUSH     DS
→           PUSH     OFFSET SCREEN_COORDS
→           PUSH     0
→           PUSH     1
→           PUSH     DS
→           PUSH     OFFSET CHAR_1
→           CALL     GpiCharStringAt
                     :
                     :
            JMP      RET_0

NOT_KEY:
                     :
                     :
WINDOW_FUNC          ENDP
```

Now we still have to release the PS handle, which we can do with WinReleasePS (not WinEndPaint), like this:

```
            WINDOW_FUNC       PROC FAR
                     :
                     :
KEY:
            CMP      P5,7AH
            JE       POSS_KEY
            JMP      NOT_KEY

POSS_KEY:
            MOV      AX,MP1
            AND      AX,64
            JZ       KEY_IN
            JMP      RET_0

KEY_IN:     MOV      AX,MP1
            AND      AX,1
            JNZ      CHAR_IN
```

```
        JMP     RET_0

CHAR_IN:
        PUSH    P7
        PUSH    P6
        CALL    WinGetPS

        MOV     PS_HANDLE_HIGH,DX
        MOV     PS_HANDLE_LOW,AX

        PUSH    PS_HANDLE_HIGH
        PUSH    PS_HANDLE_LOW
        PUSH    0
        PUSH    2
        CALL    GpiSetBackMix

        MOV     AX, MP2
        MOV     CHAR_1, AX

        PUSH    PS_HANDLE_HIGH
        PUSH    PS_HANDLE_LOW
        PUSH    DS
        PUSH    OFFSET SCREEN_COORDS
        PUSH    0
        PUSH    1
        PUSH    DS
        PUSH    OFFSET CHAR_1
        CALL    GpiCharStringAt

→       PUSH    PS_HANDLE_HIGH
→       PUSH    PS_HANDLE_LOW
→       CALL    WinReleasePS

        JMP     RET_0

NOT_KEY:
                :
                :
WINDOW_FUNC     ENDP
```

And that's all there is to it: We have read a character and printed it on the screen. Now our PM program can both accept input and display output—the fundamentals of any real program. You can see that it took much preparation before we were able to reach this point.

Although this program prints out the character in the lower left-hand corner of the window, you can specify the location for text output yourself with GpiCharStringAt. You can also accept a number of characters and make up a string before printing them out all at once. The next step is graphics. Presentation Manager is the first part of the operating system to support graphics—OS/2 1.0 couldn't do graphics, and neither could the system services under DOS or BIOS. However, PM certainly can.

# Graphics

A number of graphics functions are supported; we will see that the graphics tools in PM rival those in Pascal. We will draw in our window when we get a repaint message. As before, this message means that we have to refresh the window or draw it for the first time. Let's start off by getting a PS handle and setting the drawing colors to yellow on blue:

```
WINDOW_FUNC         PROC FAR
                    :
                    :
PAINT:   PUSH       P7
         PUSH       P6
         PUSH       0
         PUSH       0
         PUSH       0
         PUSH       0
         CALL       WinBeginPaint

         MOV        PS_HANDLE_HIGH,DX
         MOV        PS_HANDLE_LOW,AX

         PUSH       PS_HANDLE_HIGH
         PUSH       PS_HANDLE_LOW
         PUSH       0         ;Blue background
         PUSH       1
         CALL       GpiSetBackColor

         PUSH       PS_HANDLE_HIGH
         PUSH       PS_HANDLE_LOW
         PUSH       0         ;Overwrite current bkgnd color
         PUSH       2
         CALL       GpiSetBackMix

         PUSH       PS_HANDLE_HIGH
         PUSH       PS_HANDLE_LOW
         PUSH       0         ;Yellow letters
         PUSH       6
         CALL       GpiSetColor
                    :
                    :
         JMP        RET_0
NOT_PAINT:
                    :
                    :
WINDOW_FUNC         ENDP
```

Our first action will be to draw a line from (0,0) to (30,30). The GpiLine function draws lines from the *current graphics position* to a specified point. To set that current graphics position to (0,0), we need only to set the location in SCREEN_COORDS, push the PS handle, point to SCREEN_COORDS, and call GpiSetCurrentPosition. GpiLine will then draw a line from there to a specified new set of coordinates, which we set to (30,30), which is measured in pels from the lower left-hand corner of our window. To use GpiLine, we just push the PS handle and the address of the new screen coordinates:

```
WINDOW_FUNC      PROC FAR
                 :
                 :
PAINT:  PUSH     P7
        PUSH     P6
        PUSH     0
        PUSH     0
        PUSH     0
        PUSH     0
        CALL     WinBeginPaint

        MOV      PS_HANDLE_HIGH,DX
        MOV      PS_HANDLE_LOW,AX

        PUSH     PS_HANDLE_HIGH
        PUSH     PS_HANDLE_LOW
        PUSH     0         ;Blue background
        PUSH     1
        CALL     GpiSetBackColor

        PUSH     PS_HANDLE_HIGH
        PUSH     PS_HANDLE_LOW
        PUSH     0         ;Overwrite current bkgnd color
        PUSH     2
→       CALL     GpiSetBackMix

        PUSH     PS_HANDLE_HIGH
        PUSH     PS_HANDLE_LOW
        PUSH     0         ;Yellow letters
        PUSH     6
        CALL     GpiSetColor

        PUSH     PS_HANDLE_HIGH
        PUSH     PS_HANDLE_LOW
        PUSH     DS
        PUSH     OFFSET SCREEN_COORDS
→       CALL     GpiSetCurrentPosition

        MOV      SCREEN_COORDS,30
        MOV      Y,30

        PUSH     PS_HANDLE_HIGH
        PUSH     PS_HANDLE_LOW
        PUSH     DS
        PUSH     OFFSET SCREEN_COORDS
→       CALL     GpiLine
```

```
                :
                :
        JMP     RET_0
NOT_PAINT:
                :
                :
WINDOW_FUNC     ENDP
```

At this point, a line has been drawn on the window—it was that easy. We can also set pels on the screen with GpiSetPel. We need only to push the PS handle and set SCREEN_COORDS like this:

```
WINDOW_FUNC     PROC FAR
                :
                :
PAINT:  PUSH    P7
        PUSH    P6
        PUSH    0
        PUSH    0
        PUSH    0
        PUSH    0
        CALL    WinBeginPaint

        MOV     PS_HANDLE_HIGH,DX
        MOV     PS_HANDLE_LOW,AX

        PUSH    PS_HANDLE_HIGH
        PUSH    PS_HANDLE_LOW
        PUSH    0       ;Blue background
        PUSH    1
        CALL    GpiSetBackColor

        PUSH    PS_HANDLE_HIGH
        PUSH    PS_HANDLE_LOW
        PUSH    0       ;Overwrite current bkgnd color
        PUSH    2
        CALL    GpiSetBackMix

        PUSH    PS_HANDLE_HIGH
        PUSH    PS_HANDLE_LOW
        PUSH    0       ;Yellow letters
        PUSH    6
        CALL    GpiSetColor

        PUSH    PS_HANDLE_HIGH
        PUSH    PS_HANDLE_LOW
        PUSH    DS
        PUSH    OFFSET SCREEN_COORDS
        CALL    GpiSetCurrentPosition

        MOV     SCREEN_COORDS,30
        MOV     Y,30
```

```
        PUSH    PS_HANDLE_HIGH
        PUSH    PS_HANDLE_LOW
        PUSH    DS
        PUSH    OFFSET SCREEN_COORDS
        CALL    GpiLine

        MOV     Screen_Coords, 50
        MOV     Y, 50

        PUSH    PS_HANDLE_HIGH
        PUSH    PS_HANDLE_LOW
        PUSH    DS
        PUSH    OFFSET SCREEN_COORDS
→       CALL    GpiSetPel
                :
                :
        JMP     RET_0
NOT_PAINT:
                :
                :
WINDOW_FUNC     ENDP
```

Here, the dot at (50,50) is turned on and becomes the current drawing color. Now that you have control over the individual pels, you can (in theory) draw any figure you require.

We can draw boxes too. To do that, set the current position, specify new screen coordinates, and call GpiBox. You push the PS handle, a doubleword style, the address of the new screen coordinates, and two doublewords having to do with rounding the corners (that we will set to 0 for sharp corners). The style parameter can be 1 to fill the box, 2 to outline the box, and 3 to do both. Here's how it would look to draw a box from (200,200) to (300,300):

```
WINDOW_FUNC     PROC FAR
                :
                :
PAINT:  PUSH    P7
        PUSH    P6
        PUSH    0
        PUSH    0
        PUSH    0
        PUSH    0
        CALL    WinBeginPaint

        MOV     PS_HANDLE_HIGH,DX
        MOV     PS_HANDLE_LOW,AX

        PUSH    PS_HANDLE_HIGH
        PUSH    PS_HANDLE_LOW
        PUSH    0           ;Blue background
        PUSH    1
```

```
        CALL    GpiSetBackColor

        PUSH    PS_HANDLE_HIGH
        PUSH    PS_HANDLE_LOW
        PUSH    0        ;Overwrite current bkgnd color
        PUSH    2
        CALL    GpiSetBackMix

        PUSH    PS_HANDLE_HIGH
        PUSH    PS_HANDLE_LOW
        PUSH    0        ;Yellow letters
        PUSH    6
        CALL    GpiSetColor

        PUSH    PS_HANDLE_HIGH
        PUSH    PS_HANDLE_LOW
        PUSH    DS
        PUSH    OFFSET SCREEN_COORDS
        CALL    GpiSetCurrentPosition

        MOV     SCREEN_COORDS,30
        MOV     Y,30

        PUSH    PS_HANDLE_HIGH
        PUSH    PS_HANDLE_LOW
        PUSH    DS
        PUSH    OFFSET SCREEN_COORDS
        CALL    GpiLine

        MOV     Screen_Coords, 50
        MOV     Y, 50

        PUSH    PS_HANDLE_HIGH
        PUSH    PS_HANDLE_LOW
        PUSH    DS
        PUSH    OFFSET SCREEN_COORDS
        CALL    GpiSetPel

→       MOV     Screen_Coords, 200
→       MOV     Y, 200

        PUSH    PS_HANDLE_HIGH
        PUSH    PS_HANDLE_LOW
        PUSH    DS
        PUSH    OFFSET SCREEN_COORDS
        CALL    GpiSetCurrentPosition

→       MOV     Screen_Coords, 300
→       MOV     Y, 300

        PUSH    PS_HANDLE_HIGH
        PUSH    PS_HANDLE_LOW
        PUSH    0
```

```
        PUSH    2
        PUSH    DS
        PUSH    OFFSET SCREEN_COORDS
        PUSH    0
        PUSH    0
        PUSH    0
        PUSH    0
        CALL    GpiBox

        PUSH    PS_HANDLE_HIGH
        PUSH    PS_HANDLE_LOW
        CALL    WinEndPaint

        JMP     RET_0
NOT_PAINT:
                :
                :
WINDOW_FUNC     ENDP
```

Note at the end that we used WinEndPaint to release the PS handle. To produce these graphics figures, you have to put WinEndPaint into the whole program and run it.

# Resizing the Window

It turns out that there is even a resizing message sent to WINDOW_FUNC when the window is resized. In that case, the resizing message number (in P5) is 7, so we can put it to use immediately by adding another case to WINDOW_FUNC. The new size of the window is in the parameters passed to WINDOW_FUNC. The new height (in pels) is in P2, and the new width is in P1.

It is important to respond to such a message—if the window is resized, programs should adjust their output accordingly, perhaps shrinking their displays to fit into the new window.

Let's write an example program to print an X in the center of the window and keep it there, even as the window is being resized. This way, as the window shrinks or enlarges, the X will stay in the center. We start off by checking for message 7:

```
WINDOW_FUNC     PROC FAR
                :
                :
NOT_PAINT:
→       CMP     P5,7            ;Resized window
→       JE      SIZED
→       JMP     NOT_SIZE

SIZED:
                :
                :
        JMP     RET_0
```

```
NOT_SIZE:
                    :
                    :
WINDOW_FUNC         ENDP
```

If the window is indeed being resized, we will first get a PS handle:

```
WINDOW_FUNC         PROC FAR
                    :
                    :
NOT_PAINT:
          CMP       P5,7                ;Resized window
          JE        SIZED
          JMP       NOT_SIZE

SIZED:    PUSH      P7                              ←
          PUSH      P6                              ←
          CALL      WinGetPS                        ←

          MOV       PS_HANDLE_HIGH,DX               ←
          MOV       PS_HANDLE_LOW,AX                ←
                    :
                    :
          JMP       RET_0
NOT_SIZE:
                    :
                    :
WINDOW_FUNC         ENDP
```

Next we want to set up the SCREEN_COORDS to point to the center of the window. If the vertical height is H and the horizontal width is W, then the center of the window is at (H/2,W/2).

Let's put our X there by setting up SCREEN_COORDS to match. First we get the x position by dividing P1 by 2 (using SHR):

```
WINDOW_FUNC         PROC FAR
                    :
                    :
NOT_PAINT:
          CMP       P5,7                ;Resized window
          JE        SIZED
          JMP       NOT_SIZE

SIZED:    PUSH      P7
          PUSH      P6
          CALL      WinGetPS

          MOV       PS_HANDLE_HIGH,DX
          MOV       PS_HANDLE_LOW,AX

→         MOV       AX,P1
→         SHR       AX,1
```

```
→       MOV     SCREEN_COORDS,AX
                :
                :
        JMP     RET_0
NOT_SIZE:
                :
                :
WINDOW_FUNC     ENDP
```

And then the y coordinates by doing the same to P2:

```
WINDOW_FUNC     PROC FAR
                :
                :
NOT_PAINT:
        CMP     P5,7            ;Resized window
        JE      SIZED
        JMP     NOT_SIZE

SIZED:  PUSH    P7
        PUSH    P6
        CALL    WinGetPS

        MOV     PS_HANDLE_HIGH,DX
        MOV     PS_HANDLE_LOW,AX

        MOV     AX,P1   ;MP2
        SHR     AX,1
        MOV     SCREEN_COORDS,AX

→       MOV     AX,P2   ;MP2_HIGH
→       SHR     AX,1
→       MOV     Y,AX
                :
                :
        JMP     RET_0
NOT_SIZE:
                :
                :
WINDOW_FUNC     ENDP
```

All that remains now is to print out the X with GpiCharStringAt and quit:

```
WINDOW_FUNC     PROC FAR
                :
                :
NOT_PAINT:
        CMP     P5,7            ;Resized window
        JE      SIZED
        JMP     NOT_SIZE

SIZED:  PUSH    P7
        PUSH    P6
```

```
            CALL    WinGetPS

            MOV     PS_HANDLE_HIGH,DX
            MOV     PS_HANDLE_LOW,AX

            MOV     AX,P1   ;MP2
            SHR     AX,1
            MOV     SCREEN_COORDS,AX

            MOV     AX,P2   ;MP2_HIGH
            SHR     AX,1
            MOV     Y,AX

→           PUSH    PS_HANDLE_HIGH
→           PUSH    PS_HANDLE_LOW
→           PUSH    DS
→           PUSH    OFFSET SCREEN_COORDS
→           PUSH    0
→           PUSH    1
→           PUSH    DS
→           PUSH    OFFSET XCHAR
→           CALL    GpiCharStringAt

→           PUSH    PS_HANDLE_HIGH
→           PUSH    PS_HANDLE_LOW
→           CALL    WinReleasePS

            JMP     RET_0
NOT_SIZE:
                    :
                    :
WINDOW_FUNC         ENDP
```

That's it for our demonstration programs and for our coverage of Presentation Manager. As you can see, it's not a terribly simple programming environment—and there are still hundreds of functions we did not cover. With care PM's rich resources can be an extremely powerful tool.

# Appendix 1

# BIOS and DOS Reference

This appendix is intended to be a reference. We will work through all the available interrupts, from 0 to FFH, reviewing useful ones. We also include the book's OS/2 functions.

## Interrupt 0 Divide By 0

This is the first of the BIOS interrupts—BIOS uses interrupts 0 to 1FH, and DOS continues from 20H upward. Interrupt 0 is the divide by zero routine; if a divide by zero occurs, then this interrupt is called. It prints out its message, "Divide Overflow," and usually stops program execution.

## Interrupt 1 Single Step

No one, except a debugger, uses this interrupt. It is used to single-step through code, with a call to this interrupt between executed instructions.

## Interrupt 2 Non-Maskable Interrupt (NMI)

This is a hardware interrupt. This interrupt cannot be blocked off by using STI and CLI; it is always executed when called.

## Interrupt 3 Breakpoint

This is another debugger interrupt. DEBUG uses this interrupt with the Go command. If you want to execute all the code up to a particular address and then stop,

DEBUG inserts an INT 3 into the code at that point and then gives control to the program. When the INT 3 is reached, DEBUG can take control again.

## Interrupt 4 Overflow

This is similar to INT 0. If there is an overflow condition, this interrupt is called. Usually, though, no action is called for, and BIOS simply returns.

## Interrupt 5 Print Screen

This interrupt was chosen by BIOS to print out the screen. If you use the PrtSc key on the keyboard, this interrupt gets called. Needless to say, your program can also issue an INT 5 by just including that instruction in the program. There are no arguments to be passed.

## Interrupts 6 and 7 Reserved

## Interrupt 8 Time of Day

This is another hardware interrupt. This interrupt is called to update the internal time of day (stored in the BIOS data area) 18.2 times a second. If the date needs to be changed, this interrupt will handle that too.

This interrupt calls INT 1CH as well. If you want to intercept the timer and do something 18.2 times a second, it is recommended you intercept INT 1CH instead of this one.

## Interrupt 9 Keyboard

This hardware interrupt may be intercepted by memory-resident programs.

## Interrupt 0AH Reserved

## Interrupts 0BH-0FH

These interrupts point to the BIOS routine D_EOI, which is BIOS' End of Interrupt routine. All this routine does is reset the interrupt handler at port 20H and return.

# INT 10H Service 0 Set Screen Mode

Input

AH=0
AL=Mode

| *Mode (in AL)* | *Display Lines* | *Number of Colors* | *Adapters* | *Maximum Pages* |
|---|---|---|---|---|
| 0 | 40x25 | B&W text | CGA, EGA, VGA | 8 |
| 1 | 40x25 | Color text | CGA, EGA, VGA | 8 |
| 2 | 80x25 | B&W text | CGA, EGA, VGA | 4 (CGA) 8 (EGA, VGA) |
| 3 | 80x25 | Color text | CGA, EGA, VGA | 4 (CGA) 8 (EGA, VGA) |
| 4 | 320x200 | 4 | CGA, EGA, VGA | 1 |
| 5 | 320x200 | B&W | CGA, EGA, VGA | 1 |
| 6 | 640x200 | 2 (on or off) | CGA, EGA, VGA | 1 |
| 7 | 80x25 | Monochrome | MDA, EGA, VGA | 1 (MDA) 8 (EGA, VGA) |
| 8 | 160x200 | 16 | PCjr | 1 |
| 9 | 320x200 | 16 | PCjr | 1 |
| A | 640x200 | 1 | PCjr | 1 |
| B | Reserved for future use. | | | |
| C | Reserved for future use. | | | |
| D | 320x200 | 16 | EGA, VGA | 8 |
| E | 640x200 | 16 | EGA, VGA | 4 |
| F | 640x350 | monochrome | EGA, VGA | 2 |
| 10H | 640x350 | 16 | EGA, VGA | 2 |
| 11H | 640x480 | 2 | VGA | 1 |
| 12H | 640x480 | 16 | VGA | 1 |
| 13H | 320x200 | 256 | VGA | 1 |

# INT 10H Service 1 Set Cursor Type

| *Input* | *Output* |
|---|---|
| AH=1 | New Cursor |
| CH = Cursor Start Line | |
| CL = Cursor End Line | |

# INT 10H Service 2 Set Cursor Position

| *Input* | *Output* |
|---|---|
| DH,DL = Row, Column | Cursor position changed |
| BH = Page Number | |
| AH=2 | |
| Note DH,DL = 0,0 = Upper Left | |

## INT 10H Service 3 Find Cursor Position

| *Input* | *Output* |
|---|---|
| BH=Page Number<br>AH=3 | DH,DL=Row, Column of Cursor<br>CH,CL=Cursor Mode currently Set |

## INT 10H Service 4 Read Light Pen Position

| *Input* | *Output* |
|---|---|
| AH=4 | AH=0→ Light pen switch not down<br>AL=1→ DH, DL=Row, Column of Light Pen position<br>CH Raster line (Vertical) 0-199<br>BX Pixel Column (Horizontal) 0-319, 639 |

## INT 10H Service 5 Set Active Display Page

| *Input* | *Output* |
|---|---|
| AL=0–7 (Screen Modes 0, 1)<br>0–3 (Screen modes 2, 3)<br>AH=5 | Active Page Changed |

Different Pages Available in Alphanumeric Modes Only (Graphics Adapters)

## INT 10H Service 6 Scroll Active Page Up

*Input*

AL=#Lines blanked at bottom (0→Blank whole area)
CH, CL=Upper Left Row,Column of area to scroll
DH, DL=Lower Right Row,Column of area to scroll
BH=Attribute used on blank line
AH=6

## INT 10H Service 7 Scroll Active Page Down

*Input*

AL=#Lines blanked at bottom (0→Blank whole area)
CH, CL=Upper Left Row, Column of area to scroll
DH, DL=Lower Right Row, Column of area to scroll
BH=Attribute used on blank line
AH=7

## INT 10H Service 8 Read Attribute and Character at Cursor Position

| *Input* | *Output* |
|---|---|
| BH = Page Number | AL=Character read (ASCII) |
| AH=8 | AH=Attribute of character (Alphanumerics only) |

## INT 10H Service 9 Write Attribute and Character at Cursor Position

| *Input* | *Output* |
|---|---|
| BH=Page Number | Character written on screen at Cursor Position |
| BL→Alpha Modes=Attribute | |
| Graphics Modes=Color | |
| CX=Count of characters to write | |
| AL=IBM ASCII code | |
| AH=9 | |

## INT 10H Service A Write Character ONLY at Cursor Position

| *Input* | *Output* |
|---|---|
| BH=Page Number | Character written on screen at Cursor Position |
| CX=Count of characters to write | |
| AL=IBM ASCII code | |
| AH=0AH | |

## INT 10H Service B Set Color Palette

*Input*

BH=Palette Color ID
BL BH=0→BL=Background Color
BH=1→BL=Palette Number
(0=Green/Red/Yellow)
(1=Cyan/Magenta/White)
AH=11

## INT 10H Service C Write Dot

*Input*

DX=Row Number(0–199)   (0, 0) is upper left
CX=Column Number(0–319, 639)
AL=Color Value (0–3)
AH=12

If bit 7 of AL is 1, the color value is XORed with the current value of the dot.

## INT 10H Service D Read Dot

| *Input* | *Output* |
|---|---|
| DX=Row Number(0–199) | AL=Color Value (0–3) |
| CX=Column Number(0–319, 639) | |
| AH=13 | |

(0, 0) is upper left

If bit 7 of AL is 1, the color value is XORed with the current value of the dot.

## INT 10H Service E Teletype Write to Active Page

*Input*

AL=IBM ASCII code
BL=Foreground Color
(Graphics mode)
AH=14

## INT 10H Service FH Return Video State

| *Input* | *Output* |
|---|---|
| AH=15 | AH=Number of alphanumeric columns on screen |
| | AL=Current mode (See INT 10H Service 0) |
| | BH=Active display page |

## INT 10H Service 10H Set Palette Registers

Default Palette Colors (0–15) on EGA

| *Color Value* | *Color* | *rgbRGB* |
|---|---|---|
| 0 | Black | 000000 |
| 1 | Blue | 000001 |
| 2 | Green | 000010 |
| 3 | Cyan | 000011 |
| 4 | Red | 000100 |
| 5 | Magenta | 000101 |
| 6 | Brown | 010100 |
| 7 | White | 000111 |
| 8 | Dark Gray | 111000 |
| 9 | Light Blue | 111001 |
| 10 | Light Green | 111010 |
| 11 | Light Cyan | 111011 |
| 12 | Light Red | 111100 |
| 13 | Light Magenta | 111101 |
| 14 | Yellow | 111110 |
| 15 | Intense White | 111111 |

## INT 10H Service 10H Function 0—Set Individual Palette Register

*Input*

AH = 10H
AL = 0
BL = Palette register to set (0–15)
BH = value to set (0–63)

## INT 10H Service 10H Function 1—Set Overscan (Border) Register

*Input*

AH = 10H
BH = Value to set (0–63)

## INT 10H Service 10H Function 2—Set All Palette Registers

*Input*

AH = 10H
AL = 2
ES:BX = Address of a 17-byte table holding color selections (0–63)

| | |
|---|---|
| Bytes 0–15 | hold color selections for palette registers 0–15 |
| Byte 16 | holds the new overscan (border) color |

## INT 10H Service 10H Function 7—Read Individual Palette Register

| *Input* | *Output* |
|---|---|
| AH = 10H | BH = Register setting |
| AL = 7 | |
| BL = Register to read (color value) | |

## INT 10H Service 10H Function 8—Read Overscan (Border) Register

| *Input* | *Output* |
|---|---|
| AH = 10H | BH = Overscan setting |
| AL = 8 | |

## INT 10H Service 10H Function 10H—Set DAC Register

*Input*

AH = 10H
AL = 10H
BX = register to set (0–255)
CH = Green Intensity
CL = Blue Intensity
DH = Red Intensity

## INT 10H Service 10H Function 12H—Set DAC Registers

*Input*

AH = 10H

AL = 12H

BX = first register to set (0–255)

CX = Number of registers to set (1–256)

ES:DX = Address of a table of color intensities. Three bytes are used for each DAC register (use only lower 6 bits of each byte). Table is set up: red, green, blue, red, green, blue...

## INT 10H Service 10H Function 13H—Select Color Page Mode

*Input*

AH = 10H

AL = 13H

BL = 0 Select Color Paging Mode

  BH = 0 Selects 4 DAC register pages of 64 registers each.

  BH = 1 Selects 16 DAC register pages of 16 registers each.

BL = 1 Select Active Color Page

 For use with 4 page mode:

  BH = 0 Selects the first block of 64 DAC registers

  BH = 1 Selects the second block of 64 DAC registers

  BH = 2 Selects the third block of 64 DAC registers

  BH = 3 Selects the fourth block of 64 DAC registers

 For use with 16 page setting:

  BH = 0 Selects the first block of 16 DAC registers

  BH = 1 Selects the second block of 16 DAC registers

  :

  :

  BH = 2 Selects the 15th block of 16 DAC registers

  BH = 3 Selects the 16th block of 16 DAC registers

## INT 10H Service 11H—Character Generator

## INT 10H Service 12H—Alternate Select

*Input*

AH = 12H
BL = 30H
AL = 0 → 200 screen scan lines
 = 1 → 350 screen scan lines
 = 2 → 400 screen scan lines

## INT 11H Equipment Determination

*Output*

Bits of AX
 15, 14 = Number of Printers
 13 Not used
 12 Game Adapter attached
 11, 10, 9 Number of RS232 cards installed
 8 Unused
 7, 6 Number of Diskette drives
  (00→1;01→2;10→3;11→4 If Bit 0 = 1)
 5, 4 Video Mode
  (00 Unused, 01=40x25 Color Card
  10=80x25 Color Card, 11=80x25 Monochrome)
 3, 2 Motherboard RAM
  (00=16K, 01=32K, 10=48K, 11=64K)
 1 Not used
 0 = 1 if there are diskette drives attached

## INT 12H Determine Memory Size

*Output*

AX=Number of Contiguous 1K Memory Blocks

## INT 13H Service 0 Reset Disk

| *Input* | *Output* |
|---|---|
| AH=0 | No Carry → AH=0, Success<br>Carry → AH=Error Code (See Service 1) |

Hard disk systems: DL=80H→reset diskette(s)
DL=81H→reset hard disk

## INT 13H Service 1 Read Status of Last Operation

| *Input* | *Output* | |
|---|---|---|
| AH=1 | Disk Error Codes: | |
| | AL=00 | No Error |
| | AL=01 | Bad Command passed to controller |
| | AL=02 | Address Mark not found |
| | AL=03 | Diskette is Write Protected |
| | AL=04 | Sector not found |
| | AL=05 | Reset failed |
| | AL=07 | Drive parameters wrong |
| | AL=09 | DMA across segment end |
| | AL=0BH | Bad track flag seen |
| | AL=10H | Bad error check seen |
| | AL=11H | Data is error corrected |
| | AL=20H | Controller failure |
| | AL=40H | Seek operation has failed |
| | AL=80H | No response from disk |
| | AL=0BBH | Undefined error |
| | AL=0FFH | Sense operation failed |

DL = Drive number; set bit 7 to 1 for hard disks.
For hard disks, drive number in DL can range from 80H to 87H.

## INT 13H Service 2 Read Sectors into Memory

| *Input* | *Output* |
|---|---|
| AH=2 | No Carry→ AL = no. sectors read (diskette) |
| DL=Drive Number | Carry→AH=Disk Error Code (See Service 1) |
| DH=Head Number | |
| CH=Cylinder or Track (Floppies) Number | |
| CL=bits 7, 6 high 2 bits of 10-bit cylinder number | |
| CL=Sector Number (bit 0-5) | |
| AL=Number of Sectors to Read | (Floppies 1-8<br>Hard Disks 1-80H<br>Hard Disks Read/Write Long 1-79H) |
| ES:BX=Address of buffer for reads and writes | |

DL = Drive number; set bit 7 to 1 for hard disks.
For hard disks, drive number in DL can range from 80H to 87H.

## INT 13H Service 3 Write Sectors to Disk

| *Input* | *Output* |
|---|---|
| AH=3 | No Carry→AL = no. sectors written (diskette) |
| DL=Drive Number | Carry→AH=Disk Error Code. (See Service 1) |
| DH=Head Number | |
| CH=Cylinder or Track (Floppies) Number | |
| CL=bits 7,6 high 2 bits of 10-bit cylinder number | |
| CL=Sector Number (bits 0-5) | |
| AL=Number of Sectors to Write | (Floppies 1-8<br>Hard Disks 1-80H<br>Hard Disks Read/Write Long 1-79H) |
| ES:BX=Address of buffer for reads and writes | |

DL = Drive number; set bit 7 to 1 for hard disks.
For hard disks, drive number in DL can range from 80H to 87H.

## INT 13H Service 4 Verify Sectors

| *Input* | *Output* |
|---|---|
| AH=4 | No Carry→AH=0, Success |
| DL=Drive Number | Carry→AH=Disk Error Code (See Service 1) |
| DH=Head Number | |
| CH=Cylinder or Track (Floppies) Number | |
| CL=bits 7, 6 high 2 bits of 10-bit cylinder number | |
| CL=Sector Number (bits 0–5) | |
| AL=Number of Sectors | (Floppies 1–8<br>Hard Disks 1–80H<br>Hard Disks Read/Write Long 1–79H) |

DL = Drive number; set bit 7 to 1 for hard disks.
For hard disks, drive number in DL can range from 80H to 87H.

## INT 13H Service 8 Return Drive Parameters

This service works *only* on hard disks and PS/2s.

| *Input* | *Output* |
|---|---|
| AH=8 | DL=Number of drives attached to controller |
| DL=Drive No (0 based) | DH=Maximum value for Head Number |
| | CH=Maximum cylinder value |

CL=bits 7,6 high 2 bits of 10-bit cylinder no
CL=Maximum value for sector number (bits 0–5)
BL (For PS/2 diskettes only)
= 1 → 360K drive
= 2 → 1.2 Mbyte drive
= 3 → 720K drive
= 4 → 1.44 Mbyte drive

DL = Drive number; set bit 7 to 1 for hard disks.
For hard disks, drive number in DL can range from 80H to 87H.

## INT 13H Services 0AH and 0BH Reserved

## INT 13H Service 0CH Seek

This service works *only* on hard disks.

| *Input* | *Output* |
|---|---|
| AH=0CH | No Carry→AH=0, Success |
| DH=Head Number | Carry→AH=Disk Error Code (See Service 1) |
| DL=Drive Number (80H–87H allowed) | |
| CH=Cylinder Number | |
| CL=Sector Number; bits 7,6 of CL = high 2 bits of 10-bit cylinder no | |

DL = Drive number; set bit 7 to 1 for hard disks.
For hard disks, drive number in DL can range from 80H to 87H.

## INT 13H Service 0DH Alternate Disk Reset

## INT 13H Services 0EH and 0FH Reserved

## INT 13H Service 10H Test Drive Ready

## INT 13H Service 11H Recalibrate Hard Drive

This service works *only* on hard disks.

| *Input* | *Output* |
|---|---|
| AH=11H (Read) | No Carry→AH=0 |
| | Carry→AH=Disk Error Code (See Service 1) |

DL=Drive Number. (80H-87H allowed)

DL = Drive number; set bit 7 to 1 for hard disks.
For hard disks, drive number in DL can range from 80H to 87H.

## INT 13H Diagnostic Services

These services work *only* on hard disks.

| *Input* | *Output* |
|---|---|
| AH=12H (RAM Diagnostic) | No Carry→AH=0 |
| AH=13H (Drive Diagnostic) | Carry→AH=Disk Error Code (See Service 1) |
| AH=14H (Controller Diagnostic) | |
| DL=Drive Number (80H-87H allowed) | |

DL = Drive number; set bit 7 to 1 for hard disks.
For hard disks, drive number in DL can range from 80H to 87H.

## INT 13H Service 19H Park Heads PS/2 Only

| *Input* (PS/2) | *Output* |
|---|---|
| DL = Drive Number | Carry = 1 → Error, AH = Error Code |
| | = 0 → Success |

DL = Drive number; set bit 7 to 1 for hard disks.
For hard disks, drive number in DL can range from 80H to 87H.

## INT 14H, AH=0 Initialize RS232 Port

| *Input* | | | *Output* |
|---|---|---|---|
| AH=0 | | | |
| Bits of AL: | | | |
| 0,1 | | | |
| 2 | | | |
| 3,4 | Parity. 00→None, 01→Odd, 11→Even | | |
| 5,6,7 | Baud Rate. | 000→110 | |
| | | 001→150 | |
| | | 010→300 | |
| | | 011→600 | |

100→1200
101→2400
110→4800
111→9600

## INT 14H, AH=1 Send Character Through Serial Port

| *Input* | *Output* |
|---|---|
| AH=1 | If Bit 7 of AH is set, failure. |
| AL=Character to send | If Bit 7 is not set, bits 0-6 hold status (see INT 14H |

## INT 14H, AH=2 Receive Character From Serial Port

| *Input* | *Output* |
|---|---|
| AH=2 | AL=Character Received<br>AH=0, success<br>Otherwise, AH holds an error code (see INT 14H, AH=3). |

## INT 14H, AH=3 Return Serial Port's Status

| *Input* | *Output* |
|---|---|
| AH=3 | AH Bits Set:<br>7→Time Out<br>6→Shift Register Empty<br>5→Holding Register Empty<br>4→Break detected<br>3→Framing Error<br>2→Parity Error<br>1→Overrun Error<br>0→Data Ready<br>AL Bits Set:<br>7→Received Line Signal Detect<br>6→Ring Indicator<br>5→Data Set Ready<br>4→Clear to Send<br>3→Delta Receive Line Signal Detect<br>2→Trailing Edge Ring Detector<br>1→Delta Data Set Ready<br>0→Delta Clear to Send |

## INT 15H Cassette I/O

| *Input* | | *Output* |
|---|---|---|
| AH=0 → | Turn Cassette Motor On. | |
| AH=1 → | Turn Cassette Motor Off. | |
| AH=2 → | Read one or more 256 byte blocks. Store data at ES:BX. CX=Count of Bytes to read. | DX=Number of bytes actually read. Carry flag set if error. If Carry, AH =01→CRC Error =02→Data transitions lost =04→No Data Found |
| AH=3 → | Write one or more 256 byte blocks from ES:BX. Count of bytes to write in CX. | |

In recent BIOS versions, new items have been added to this interrupt, such as joystick support, the ability to switch processor mode (protected or not), mouse support, and some BIOS parameters.

## INT 16H, Service 0 Read Key from Keyboard

| *Input* | *Output* |
|---|---|
| AH = 0 | AH=Scan Code AL=ASCII code |

## INT 16H, Service 1 Check if Key Ready to be Read

| *Input* | *Output* | |
|---|---|---|
| AH = 1 | Zero Flag=1 → | Buffer Empty |
| | Zero Flag=0 → | AH=Scan Code<br>AL=ASCII Code |

## INT 16H, Service 2 Find Keyboard Status

| *Input* | *Output* |
|---|---|
| AH = 2 | AL=Keyboard Status byte |

## INT 17H Service 0 Print character in AL

| *Input* | *Output* |
|---|---|
| AH=0<br>AL=Character to be printed.<br>DX=Printer Number (0,1,2) | AH=1→ Printer Time Out |

## INT 17H Service 1 Initialize Printer Port

| *Input* | *Output* |
|---|---|
| AH=1 | AH=Printer Status: |
| DX=Printer Number (0,1,2) | Bits Set of AH: |
| | 7→Printer Not Busy |
| | 6→Acknowledge |
| | 5→Out of Paper |
| | 4→Selected |
| | 3→I/O Error |
| | 2→Unused |
| | 1→Also Unused |
| | 0→Time Out |

## INT 17H Service 2 Read Printer Status into AH

| *Input* | *Output* |
|---|---|
| AH=2 | AH Set to Status Byte as in INT 17H |
| DX=Printer Number (0,1,2) | |

## INT 18H Resident BASIC

This interrupt starts up ROM-resident BASIC in the PC.

## INT 19H Bootstrap

This interrupt is the one that boots the machine (try it with DEBUG).

## INT 1AH Service 0 Read Time of Day

| *Input* | *Output* |
|---|---|
| AH=0 | CX=High Word of Timer Count |
| | DX=Low Word of Timer Count |
| | AL=0 If timer has not passed 24 hours since last read. |

Timer count increments by 65536 in one hour.

## INT 1AH Service 1 Set Time of Day

*Input*

AH=1
CX=High Word of Timer Count
DX=Low Word of Timer Count

Timer count increments by 65536 in one hour.

## INT 1BH Keyboard Break Address

## INT 1CH Timer Tick Interrupt

## INT 1DH Video Parameter Tables

## INT 1EH Diskette Parameters

## INT 1FH Graphics Character Definitions

## DOS Interrupts

Interrupt 1FH is the last BIOS Interrupt, and DOS starts with INT 20H.

## INT 20H Terminate

Programs are usually ended with an INT 20H.

## Interrupt 21H

Interrupt 21H is the DOS service interrupt. To call one of these services, load AH with the service number, and the other registers as shown.

## INT 21H Service 0 Program Terminate

*Input*

AH = 0

## INT 21H Service 1 Keyboard Input

| *Input* | *Output* |
|---|---|
| AH = 1 | AL = ASCII code of struck key<br>Does Echo on screen |

Checks for ^C or ^Break

## INT 21H Service 2 Character Output on Screen

*Input*

DL=IBM ASCII character
AH=2

## INT 21H Service 3 Standard Auxiliary Device Input

| *Input* | *Output* |
|---|---|
| AH=3 | Character in AL |

## INT 21H Service 4 Standard Auxiliary Device Output

*Input*

AH=4
DL=Character to output

## INT 21H Service 5 Printer Output

*Input*

AH=5
DL=Character to output

## INT 21H Service 6 Console I/O

| *Input* | | *Output* |
|---|---|---|
| AH = 6 | | |
| DL = FF | → | AL holds character if one ready |

| | | |
|---|---|---|
| DL < FF | → | Type ASCII code in DL out<br>Does *not* Echo on screen |

Does *not* check for ^C or ^Break

## INT 21H Service 7 Console Input Without Echo

| *Input* | *Output* |
|---|---|
| AH = 7 | AL = ASCII code of struck key<br>No echo on screen. |

Does *not* check for ^C or ^Break

## INT 21H Service 8 Console Input w/o Echo with ^C Check

| *Input* | *Output* |
|---|---|
| AH = 8 | AL = ASCII code of struck key.<br>Does NOT echo the typed key. |

Checks for ^C or ^Break

## DOS INT 21H Service 9 String Print

*Input*

DS:DX point to a string that ends in '$'.
AH=9

## INT 21H Service A String Input

| *Input* | *Output* |
|---|---|
| AH = 0AH<br>(DS:DX)=Length of buffer | Buffer at DS:DX filled.<br>Echo the typed keys. |

Checks for ^C or ^Break

## INT 21H Service 0BH Check Input Status

| *Input* | *Output* |
|---|---|
| AH = 0BH | AL = FF → Character ready<br>AL = 00 → Nothing to read in |

^Break is checked for

## INT 21H Service 0CH Clear Keyboard Buffer and Invoke Service

| *Input* | *Output* |
|---|---|
| AH = 0CH<br>AL = Keyboard Function # | Standard Output from the selected Service. |

^Break is checked for

## INT 21H Service 0DH Disk Reset

*Input*

AH=0DH

## INT 21H Service 0EH Select Disk

*Input*

AH=0EH
DL=Drive Number
(DL=0→A
DL=1→B
and so on).

## INT 21H Service 0FH Open Pre-Existing File

| *Input* | *Output* |
|---|---|
| DS:DX points to an FCB.<br>AH=0FH | AL=0 → Success<br>AL=FF → Failure |

## INT 21H Service 10H Close File

| *Input* | *Output* |
|---|---|
| DS:DX points to an FCB. | AL=0 → Success |
| AH=10H | AL=FF → Failure |

## INT 21H Service 11H Search for First Matching File

| *Input* | *Output* |
|---|---|
| DS:DX points to an unopened FCB. | AL=FF → Failure |
| AH=11H | AL=0 → Success<br>DTA holds FCB for match. |

Note: DTA is at CS:0080 in .COM files on startup.

## INT 21H Service 12H Search for Next Matching File

| *Input* | *Output* |
|---|---|
| DS:DX points to an unopened FCB. | AL=FF → Failure |
| AH=12H | AL=0 → Success<br>DTA holds FCB for match. |

Use this Service after Service 11H.

## INT 21H Service 13H Delete Files

| *Input* | *Output* |
|---|---|
| DS:DX points to an unopened FCB. | AL=FF → Failure |
| AH=13H | AL=0 → Success |

## INT 21H Service 14H Sequential Read

| *Input* | *Output* |
|---|---|
| DS:DX points to an opened FCB. | Requested Record put in DTA |
| AH=14H | AL=0 Success |
| Current Block and Record Set in FCB. | 1 End of File |

| | |
|---|---|
| | 2 DTA Segment too small for record. |
| | 3 End of File; record padded with 0. |

Record address incremented.

## INT 21H Service 15H Sequential Write

| *Input* | *Output* |
|---|---|
| DS:DX points to an opened FCB. | One record read from DTA and written. |
| AH=15H | AL=0 Success |
| Current Block & Record Set in FCB. | 1 Disk full |
| | 2 DTA Segment too small for record |
| | Record Address Incremented |

## INT 21H Service 16H Create File

| *Input* | *Output* |
|---|---|
| DS:DX points to an unopened FCB. | AL=0 Success |
| AH=16H | =FF Directory Full |

## INT 21H Service 17H Rename File

| *Input* | *Output* |
|---|---|
| DS:DX points to a MODIFIED FCB. | AL=0 Success |
| AH=17H | =FF Failure |

Modified FCB → Second file name starts six bytes after the end of the first file name, at DS:DX+11H.

## INT 21H Service 18H Internal to DOS

## INT 21H Service 19H Find Current Disk

| *Input* | *Output* |
|---|---|
| AH=19H | AL=Current Disk (0=A) |

## INT 21H Service 1AH Set the DTA Location

| *Input* | *Output* |
|---|---|
| DS:DX points to new DTA address<br>AH=1AH | None |

Note: DTA= Disk Transfer Address, the data area used with FCB services
Note: Default DTA is 128 bytes long, starting at CS:0080 in the PSP.

## INT 21H Service 1BH FAT Information for Default Drive

| *Input* | *Output* |
|---|---|
| AH=1BH | DS:BX points to the "FAT Byte"<br>DX=Number of Clusters<br>AL=Number of Sectors/Cluster<br>CX=Size of a Sector (512 bytes) |

Note: Files are stored in clusters—the smallest allocatable unit on a disk.

## INT 21H Service 1CH FAT Information for Specified Drive

| *Input* | *Output* |
|---|---|
| AH=1CH<br>DL=Drive Number (0=Default<br>1=A...) | DS:BX points to the "FAT Byte"<br>DX=Number of Clusters<br>AL=Number of Sectors/Cluster<br>CX=Size of a Sector (512) |

Note: Files are stored in clusters—the smallest allocatable unit on a disk.

## INT 21H Services 1DH - 20H Internal to DOS

## INT 21H Service 21H Random Read

| *Input* | *Output* |
|---|---|
| DS:DX points to an opened FCB.<br>Set FCB's Random Record field<br>at DS:DX+33 and DS:DX+35<br>AH=21H | AL=00 Success<br>=01 end of file<br>=02 not enough space in DTA segment<br>=03 end of file<br>padded with 0s |

## INT 21H Service 22H Random Write

| *Input* | *Output* |
|---|---|
| DS:DX points to an opened FCB.<br>Set FCB's Random Record field<br>at DS:DX+33 and DS:DX+35<br>AH=21H | AL=00 Success<br>=01 Disk is full<br>=02 not enough space in DTA segment |

## INT 21H Service 23H File Size

| *Input* | *Output* |
|---|---|
| DS:DX points to an unopened FCB.<br>AH=23H | AL=00 Success<br>=FF No file found that matched FCB<br>Random Record Field set to file length in records, rounded up |

## INT 21H Service 24H Set Random Record Field

| *Input* | *Output* |
|---|---|
| DS:DX points to an opened FCB.<br>AH=24H | Random Record Field set to match Current Record and Current Block. |

## INT 21H Service 25H Set Interrupt Vector

*Input*

AH=25H
AL = Interrupt Number
DS:DX = New Address

Note: This service can help you intercept an interrupt vector

## INT 21H Service 26H Create a New Program Segment (PSP)

## INT 21H Service 27H Random Block Read

| *Input* | *Output* |
|---|---|
| DS:DX points to an opened FCB. | AL=00 Success |
| Set FCB's Random Record field | =01 end of file |
| at DS:DX+33 and DS:DX+35 | =02 not enough space in DTA segment |
| AH=27H | =03 end of file, partial record padded with 0s. |
| | CX=Number of records read |
| | Random Record Fields set to access next record. |

Note: The data buffer used in FCB services is the DTA, or Disk Transfer Area

## INT 21H Service 28H Random Block Write

| *Input* | *Output* |
|---|---|
| DS:DX points to an opened FCB. | AL=00 Success |
| Set FCB's Random Record field | =01 Disk is full |
| at DS:DX+33 and DS:DX+35 | =02 not enough space in DTA segment |
| CX=number of records to write | |
| AH=28H | Random Record Fields set to access next record. |

CX=0 → file set to the size indicated by the Random Record field
The data buffer used in FCB services is the DTA, or Disk Transfer Area

## INT 21H Service 29H Parse Filename

| *Input* | *Output* |
|---|---|
| DS:SI = Command line to parse. | DS:SI = 1st character after filename |
| ES:DI = Address to put FCB at | ES:DI = Valid FCB |

AL = Bit 0=1 → Leading separators are scanned off command line.
Bit 1=1 → Drive ID in final FCB will be changed ONLY if a drive was specified.
Bit 2=1 → Filename in FCB changed ONLY if command line includes filename.

Bit 3=1 → Filename extension in FCB will be changed ONLY if command line contains a filename extension.

AH=29H

If the command line doesn't contain a valid filename, ES:[DI+1] will be a blank.

## INT 21H Service 2AH Get Date

| *Input* | *Output* |
|---|---|
| AH=2AH | CX = Year - 1980 |
| | DH = Month (1=January, etc.) |
| | DL = Day of the month |

## INT 21H Service 2BH Set Date

| *Input* | *Output* |
|---|---|
| CX = Year - 1980 | AL = 0 Success |
| DH = Month (1=January, etc.) | AL = FF Date not valid |
| DL = Day of the month | |
| AH=2BH | |

## INT 21H Service 2CH Get Time

| *Input* | *Output* |
|---|---|
| AH=2CH | CH = Hours (0-23) |
| | CL = Minutes (0-59) |
| | DH = Seconds (0-59) |
| | DL = Hundredths of Seconds (0-99) |

## INT 21H Service 2DH Set Time

| *Input* | *Output* |
|---|---|
| AH=2DH | AL = 0 Success |
| CH = Hours (0-23) | AL = FF Time is Invalid |
| CL = Minutes (0-59) | |
| DH = Seconds (0-59) | |
| DL = Hundreds of Seconds (0-99) | |

## INT 21H Service 2EH Set or Reset Verify Switch

*Input*

AH=2EH
DL=0
AL=1 → Turn Verify On.
  =0 → Turn Verify Off.

## INT 21H Service 2FH Get Current DTA

| *Input* | *Output* |
|---|---|
| AH=2FH | ES:BX = Current DTA address |

The data buffer used in FCB services is the DTA, or Disk Transfer Area

## INT 21H Service 30H Get DOS Version Number

| *Input* | *Output* |
|---|---|
| AH=30H | AL=Major Version Number (3 in DOS 3.10)<br>AH=Minor Version Number (10 in DOS 3.10)<br>BX=0<br>CX=0 |

If AL returns 0, you are working with a version of DOS before 2.0

## INT 21H Service 31H Terminate Process and Keep Resident

*Input*

AH=31H
AL=Binary Exit Code
DX=Size of memory request in paragraphs.

Exit code can be read by a parent program with Service 4DH. It can also be tested by ERRORLEVEL commands in batch files.

## INT 21H Service 32H Internal to DOS

## INT 21H Service 33H Control-Break Check

| *Input* | | *Output* |
|---|---|---|
| AH=33H | | |
| AL=0 → | Check state of ^Break Checking. | DL=0 → Off<br>DL=1 → On |
| =1 → | Set the state of ^Break Checking.<br>(DL=0→ Turn it Off.<br>DL=1→ Turn it On.) | |

## INT 21H Service 34H Internal to DOS

## INT 21H Service 35H Get Interrupt Vector

| *Input* | *Output* |
|---|---|
| AH=35H<br>AL=Interrupt Number | ES:BX = Interrupt's Vector |

## INT 21H Service 36H Get Free Disk Space

| *Input* | *Output* |
|---|---|
| AH=36H<br>DL=Drive Number (0=Default<br>1=A...) | AX=0FFFH→Drive Number Invalid<br>AX=Number of Sectors/Cluster<br>BX=Number of available Clusters<br>CX=Size of a Sector (512)<br>DX=Number of Clusters |

Note: Files are stored in clusters—the smallest allocatable unit on a disk.

## INT 21H Service 37H Internal to DOS

## INT 21H Service 38H Returns Country Dependent Information

| *Input* | *Output* |
|---|---|
| AH=38H<br>DS:DX = address of 32-byte block<br>AL=0 | Filled in 32-byte block (see below) |

The 32-byte block looks like this:

2 Bytes DATE/TIME Format
1 Byte of currency symbol (ASCII)
1 Byte set to 0
1 Byte thousands separator (ASCII)
1 Byte set to 0
1 Byte decimal separator (ASCII)
1 Byte set to 0
24 Bytes used internally

The DATE/TIME format has these values:
0 = USA (H:M:S M/D/Y)
1 = EUROPE (H:M:S D/M/Y)
2 = JAPAN (H:M:S D:M:Y)

In DOS 3+ you can set, as well as read, these values.

## INT 21H Service 39H Create a Subdirectory

| *Input* | *Output* |
|---|---|
| AH=39H<br>DS:DX point to ASCIIZ string<br>with directory name | No Carry→ Success<br>Carry→ AH has error value<br>AH=3 Path Not Found<br>AH=5 Access Denied |

## INT 21H Service 3AH Delete a Subdirectory

| *Input* | *Output* |
|---|---|
| AH=3AH<br>DS:DX point to ASCIIZ string<br>with directory name. | No Carry→ Success<br>Carry→ AH has error value<br>AH=3 Path Not Found<br>AH=5 Access Denied or<br>Subdirectory not empty |

# INT 21H Service 3BH Change Current Directory

| *Input* | *Output* |
|---|---|
| AH=3BH | No Carry→ Success |
| DS:DX point to ASCIIZ string with directory name. | Carry→ AH has error value<br>AH=3 Path Not Found |

# INT 21H Service 3CH Create a File

| *Input* | *Output* |
|---|---|
| DS:DX points to ASCIIZ filename. | No Carry → AX=File Handle |
| CX=Attribute of File | Carry → AL=3 Path not found |
| AH=3CH | =4 Too many files open |
| | =5 Dir full |

# INT 21H Service 3DH Open a File

| *Input* | *Output* |
|---|---|
| DS:DX points to ASCIIZ filename. | No Carry → AX=File Handle |
| AL=Access Code | Carry → AL=Error Code |
| AH=3DH | (Check Error Table) |

Access Codes:
- AL=0 File Opened for Reading
- AL=1 File Opened for Writing
- AL=2 File Opened for Reading and Writing

Access Code DOS 3+: isssraaa
- i = 1 → file is not to be inherited by child processes
- i = 0 → file handle will be inherited
- sss = 000 → Compatibility Mode
- sss = 001 → Deny All
- sss = 010 → Deny Write
- sss = 011 → Deny Read
- sss = 100 → Deny None
- r = reserved
- aaa = 000 → Read Access
- aaa = 001 → Write Access
- aaa = 010 → Read/Write Access

## INT 21H Service 3EH Close a File Handle

| *Input* | *Output* |
|---|---|
| BX holds a valid File Handle | Carry → AL=6 → Invalid handle |
| AH=3EH | |

## INT 21H Service 3FH Read from File or Device

| *Input* | *Output* |
|---|---|
| DS:DX = Data Buffer Address | No Carry→ AX=Number of bytes read |
| CX=Number of bytes to read | Carry→ AL=5 Access Denied |
| BX=File Handle | AL=6 Invalid Handle |
| AH=3FH | |

## INT 21H Service 40H Write to File or Device

| *Input* | *Output* |
|---|---|
| DS:DX = Data Buffer Address | No Carry→ AX=Number of bytes written |
| CX=Number of bytes to write | Carry→ AL=5 Access Denied |
| BX=File Handle | AL=6 Invalid Handle |
| AH=40H | |

Full disk is *not* considered an error: Check the number of bytes you wanted to write (CX) against the number actually written (returned in AX). If they do not match, the disk is probably full.

## INT 21H Service 41H Delete a File

| *Input* | *Output* |
|---|---|
| DS:DX = ASCIIZ filename | No Carry→ Success |
| AH=41H | Carry→ AL=2 File Not Found |
| | AL=5 Access Denied |

No wildcards allowed in filename.

## INT 21H Service 42H Move Read/Write Pointer

| *Input* | *Output* |
|---|---|
| BX=File Handle | No Carry→DX:AX=New Location of Pointer |
| CX:DX=Desired offset | Carry→AL=1 Illegal Function Number |
| AL=Method Value | AL=6 Invalid Handle |
| AH=42H | |

Method Values (AL):

| | |
|---|---|
| AL=0 | Read/Write Pointer moved to CX:DX from the start of the file. |
| AL=1 | Pointer incremented CX:DX bytes. |
| AL=2 | Pointer moved to end-of-file plus offset (CX:DX). |

## INT 21H Service 43H Change File's Attribute

| *Input* | | *Output* |
|---|---|---|
| DS:DX = | ASCIIZ Filestring | No Carry→Success |
| AL=1→ | File attrib. changed | Carry→AL=2 File Not Found |
| | CX holds new attribute | AL=3 Path Not Found |
| AL=0→ | File's current attribute | AL=5 Access Denied |
| | returned in CX | If AL was 0, CX returns the attribute. |
| AH=43H | | |

## INT 21H Service 44H I/O Control

## INT 21H Service 45H Duplicate a File Handle

| *Input* | *Output* |
|---|---|
| BX=File handle to duplicate | No Carry→AX=New |
| AH=45H | Carry→AL=4 Too many files open |
| | AL=6 Invalid handle |

## INT 21H Service 46H Force Duplication of a File Handle

| *Input* | *Output* |
|---|---|
| BX=File handle to duplicate | No Carry→Handles refer to same "stream" |
| CX=Second File handle | Carry→AL=6 Invalid Handle |
| AH=46H | |

## INT 21H Service 47H Get Current Directory on Specified Drive

| *Input* | *Output* |
|---|---|
| AH=47H<br>DS:SI point to 64 byte buffer.<br>DL=Drive Number | No Carry→ Success<br>Carry→AH=15 Invalid Drive Specified |

Drive letter is *not* included in returned ASCIIZ string.

## INT 21H Service 48H Allocate Memory

| *Input* | *Output* |
|---|---|
| AH=48H<br>BX=Number of paragraphs requested | No Carry→AX:0000 memory block address.<br>Carry→AL=7 Memory control blocks destroyed.<br>AL=8 Insufficient Memory contains maximum allowable request. |

## INT 21H Service 49H Free Allocated Memory

| *Input* | *Output* |
|---|---|
| AH=49H<br>ES=Segment of block being freed. | No Carry → Success<br>Carry → AL =7 Memory Control Blocks Destroyed.<br>=9 Incorrect Memory Block Address. |

## INT 21H Service 4AH SETBLOCK

| *Input* | *Output* |
|---|---|
| AH=4AH<br>ES=Segment of block to modify.<br>BX=Requested size in paragraphs. | No Carry → Success.<br>Carry → AL = 7 Memory Control Blocks Destroyed.<br>= 8 Insufficient Memory; BX holds maximum possible request.<br>= 9 Invalid Memory Block Address. |

## INT 21H Service 4BH Load or Execute a program — EXEC

| *Input* | *Output* |
|---|---|
| AH=4BH | See Below. |
| DS:DX=ASCIIZ string with drive, pathname, filename. | |
| ES:BX=Parameter Block Address (See Below). | |
| AL=0 → Load and execute the program. | |
| 3 → Load but create no PSP, don't run. (Overlay) | |

Parameter Block for AL = 0:

Segment Address of environment to pass. (Word)
Address of command to put at PSP+80H (DWord)
Address of default FCB to put at PSP+5CH (DWord)
Address of 2nd default FCB to put at PSP+6CH (DWord)

Parameter Block for AL = 3:

Segment Address to load file at (Word).
Relocation Factor for image (Word).

Output:
No Carry → Success
Carry:
AL=1 Invalid Function Number
2 File Not Found on Disk
5 Access Denied
8 Insufficient Memory for requested operation
10 Invalid Environment
11 Invalid Format

## INT 21H Service 4CH Exit

*Input*

AH=4CH
AL=Binary Return Code

This service can end a program.

## INT 21H Service 4DH Get Return Code of Subprocess

| *Input* | *Output* |
|---|---|
| AH=4DH | AL=Binary Return Code from Subprocess<br>AH=0 If subprocess ended normally.<br>1 If subprocess ended with a ^Break.<br>2 If it ended with a critical device error.<br>3 If it ended with Service 31H. |

## INT 21H Service 4EH Find First Matching File

| *Input* | *Output* |
|---|---|
| DS:DX→ASCIIZ filestring.<br>CX=Attribute to match.<br>AH=4EH | Carry→ AL=2 No Match Found.<br>AL=18 No More Files.<br>No Carry→DTA filled as follows:<br>21 Bytes reserved.<br>1 Byte Found Attribute.<br>2 Bytes File's Time.<br>2 Bytes File's Date.<br>2 Bytes Low Word of Size.<br>2 Bytes High Word of Size.<br>13 Bytes Name and Extension of found file in ASCIIZ form (no pathname). |

Note: The data buffer used in FCB services is the DTA, or Disk Transfer Area. See earlier services.

## INT 21H Service 4FH Find Next Matching File

| *Input* | *Output* |
|---|---|
| Use Service 4EH BEFORE 4FH.<br>AH=4FH | Carry→ AL=18 No More Files.<br>No Carry→DTA filled as follows:<br>21 Bytes reserved.<br>1 Byte Found Attribute.<br>2 Bytes File's Time.<br>2 Bytes File's Date.<br>2 Bytes Low Word of Size.<br>2 Bytes High Word of Size.<br>13 Bytes Name and Extension of found file in ASCIIZ form (no pathname). |

The data buffer used in FCB services is the DTA, or Disk Transfer Area. See earlier services.

## INT 21H Services 50H-53H Internal to DOS

## INT 21H Service 54H Get Verify State

| *Input* | *Output* |
|---|---|
| AH=54H | AL=0→ Verify is OFF.<br>1→ Verify is ON. |

## INT 21H Service 55H Internal to DOS

## INT 21H Service 56H Rename File

| *Input* | *Output* |
|---|---|
| DS:DX=ASCIIZ filestring to be renamed.<br>ES:DI=ASCIIZ filestring that holds the new name.<br>AH=56H | No Carry→Success.<br>Carry→ AL=3 Path Not Found.<br>AL=5 Access Denied.<br>AL=17 Not Same Device. |

File *cannot* be renamed to another drive.

## INT 21H Service 57H Get or Set a File's Date & Time.

| *Input* | *Output* |
|---|---|
| BX=File Handle. | No Carry: |
| AL=0→ Get Date & Time . . . . . . . . . . . . . . . . . . . . | CX returns Time.<br>DX returns Date. |
| AL=1→ Set Time to CX . . . . . . . . . . . . . . . . . . . . . .<br>Set Date to DX. | File's date and time set. |
| | Carry→AL=1 Invalid Function Number.<br>6 Invalid Handle. |

The time and date of a file are stored like this:

Time = 2048xHours + 32xMinutes +Seconds/2

Date = 512x(Year-1980) + 32xMonth + Day

## INT 21H Service 58H Internal to DOS

## INT 21H Service 59H Get Extended Error DOS 3+

| *Input* | *Output* |
|---|---|
| AH = 59H | AX = Extended Error |
| BX = 0 | BH = Error Class |
| | BL = Suggested Action |
| | CH = Locus |

This error handling service is very lengthy, and involves the many DOS 3+ extended errors.

## INT 21H Service 5AH Create Unique File DOS 3+

| *Input* | *Output* |
|---|---|
| AH = 5AH | AX = Error if Carry is set |
| DS:DX = Address of an ASCIIZ path (ending with "\") | DS:DX = ASCIIZ path and filename |
| CX = File's Attribute | |

## INT 21H Service 5BH Create a New File DOS 3+

| *Input* | *Output* |
|---|---|
| AH = 5BH | AX = Error if Carry is set |
| DS:DX = Address of an ASCIIZ path (ending with "\") | = Handle if Carry is not set |
| CX = File's Attribute | |

## INT 21H Service 5CH Lock and Unlock Access to a File DOS 3+

| *Input* | *Output* |
|---|---|
| AH = 5CH | If Carry = 1, AX = Error |
| AL = 0 → lock byte range<br>1 → Unlock byte range | |
| BX = File handle | |
| CX = byte range start (high word) | |
| DX = byte range start (low word) | |
| SI = No. bytes to (un)lock (high word) | |
| DI = No. bytes to (un)lock (low word) | |

## INT 21H Service 5E00H Get Machine Name DOS 3+

| *Input* | *Output* |
|---|---|
| AX = 5E00H | DS:DX = ASCIIZ computer name |
| DS:DX = Buffer for computer name | CH = 0 → Name not defined |
| | CL = NETBIOS number |
| | AX = Error if Carry set |

## INT 21H Service 5E02 Set Printer Setup DOS 3+

| *Input* | *Output* |
|---|---|
| AX = 5E02H | AX = Error if Carry is set |
| BX = Redirection list index | |
| CX = Length of Setup String | |
| DS:DI = Pointer to printer setup buffer | |

## INT 21H Service 5E03 Get Printer Setup DOS 3+

| *Input* | *Output* |
|---|---|
| AX = 5E03H | AX = Error if Carry is set |
| BX = Redirection list index | CX = Length of data returned |
| ES:DI = Pointer to printer setup buffer | ES:DI = Filled with printer setup string |

## INT 21H Service 5F03 Redirect Device DOS 3+

| *Input* | *Output* |
|---|---|
| AX = 5F03H | AX = Error if Carry is set |
| BL = Device Type<br>= 3 → Printer Device<br>= 4 → File Device | |
| CX = Value to save for caller | |
| DS:SI = Source ASCIIZ device name | |
| ES:DI = Destination ASCIIZ network path with password | |

## INT 21H Service 5F04H Cancel Redirection DOS 3+

| *Input* | *Output* |
|---|---|
| AX = 5F04H<br>DS:SI = ASCIIZ device name or path | AX = Error if Carry is set |

## INT 21H Service 62H Get Program Segment Prefix DOS 3+

| *Input* | *Output* |
|---|---|
| AX = 62H | BX = Segment of currently executing program. |

## INT 21H Service 67H Set Handle Count DOS 3.30

| *Input* | *Output* |
|---|---|
| AX = 67H<br>BX = Number of allowed open handles (up to 255) | AX = Error if Carry is set |

## INT 21H Service 68H Commit File (Write Buffers) DOS 3.30

| *Input* | *Output* |
|---|---|
| AX = 68H | BX = File Handle |

68H is the last of the DOS 3.3 INT 21H services.

## INT 22H Terminate Address

## INT 23H Control Break Exit Address

## INT 24H Critical Error Handler

*Input*

AH filled this way:

0 Diskette is write protected
1 Unknown Unit
2 The requested drive is not ready

3 Unknown command
4 Cyclic Redundancy Check error in the data
5 Bad request structure length
6 Seek Error
7 Media Type Unknown
8 Sector not found
9 The printer is out of paper
A Write Fault
B Read Fault
C General Failure

If you just execute an IRET, DOS will take an action based on the contents of AL. If AL=0, the error will be ignored. If AL=1, the operation will be retried. If AL=2, the program will be terminated through INT 23H.

## INT 25H Absolute Disk Read

| *Input* | *Output* |
|---|---|
| AL=Drive Number. | No Carry→ Success. |
| CX=Number of Sectors to Read. | Carry→AH=80H Disk didn't respond. |
| DX=First Logical Sector. | AH=40H Seek failed. |
| DS:BX=Buffer address. | AH=20H Controller failure. |
| | AH=10H Bad CRC error check. |
| | AH=08 DMA overrun. |
| | AH=04 Sector not found. |
| | AH=03 Write protect error. |
| | AH=02 Address Mark missing. |
| | AH=00 Error unknown. |

Flags left on stack after this INT call because information is returned in current flags. After you check the flags that were returned, make sure you do a POPF. Also, this INT destroys the contents of ALL registers.

## INT 26H Absolute Disk Write

| *Input* | *Output* |
|---|---|
| AL=Drive Number. | No Carry→ Success. |
| CX=Number of Sectors to Write. | Carry→AH=80H Disk didn't respond. |
| DX=First Logical Sector. | AH=40H Seek failed. |
| DS:BX=Buffer address. | AH=20H Controller failure. |
| | AH=10H Bad CRC error check. |
| | AH=08 DMA overrun. |

AH=04 Sector not found.
AH=03 Write protect error.
AH=02 Address Mark missing.
AH=00 Error unknown.

Flags left on stack after this INT call because information is returned in current flags. After you check the flags that were returned, make sure you do a POPF. Also, this INT destroys the contents of ALL registers.

## INT 27H Terminate and Stay Resident

*Input*

DS:DX = point directly after end of code which is to stay resident.

## INTs 28H-2EH Internal to DOS

## INT 2FH Multiplex Interrupt

## INT 30H-3FH DOS Reserved

## INT 40H-5FH Reserved

## INT 60H-67H Reserved for User Software

## INTs 68H-7FH Not Used

## INTs 80H-85H Reserved by BASIC

## INTs 86H-F0H Used by BASIC Interpreter

## INTs F1H-FFH Not Used

# Appendix 2

# OS/2 Reference

Push address pointers (PTR) selector first, followed by offset. Push DWORDs high word first. Doubleword values are returned with high word in DX, low word in AX; addresses are returned with selector in DX, offset in AX.

## DosAllocHuge

```
PUSH    WORD    Number of whole segments to allocate
PUSH    WORD    Length of the last segment
PUSH    PTR     Address of memory word to receive allocated
                        memory selector
PUSH    WORD    Maximum number of segments to which allocated
PUSH    WORD    OR these values: 1 → Shareable with DosGiveSeg
                                 2 → Shareable with DosGetSeg
                                 4 → Segment may be discarded
```

## DosAllocShrSeg

```
PUSH    WORD    Size of the segment requested
PUSH    PTR     Pointer to the ASCIIZ name of the shared memory
PUSH    PTR     Pointer to memory word for returned memory selector
```

## DosBeep

```
PUSH    WORD    Frequency (25 to 32K)
PUSH    WORD    Duration (milliseconds)
```

## DosChgFilePtr

```
PUSH    WORD     Open file handle
PUSH    DWORD    Distance to move file pointer
PUSH    WORD     Method: 0 → move from start of file
                         1 → move from current location
                         2 → move from end of file
PUSH    PTR      Address of memory dword to recieve new
                         file pointer location in file
```

## DosClose

```
PUSH    WORD     File handle to close
```

## DosCloseSem

```
PUSH    DWORD    Semaphore handle returned by DosOpenSem or
                         DosCreateSem
```

## DosCreateSem

```
PUSH    WORD     Type of semaphore: 0 → not shared
                                    1 → shared
PUSH    PTR      Pointer to dword field to receive semaphore handle
PUSH    PTR      Pointer to ASCIIZ name of sem, must begin with
                         "\SEM\"
```

## DosCreateThread

```
PUSH    PTR      Pointer to thread procedure
PUSH    PTR      Pointer to dword field to recieve thread ID
PUSH    PTR      Pointer to top of stack set aside for thread
```

## DosEnterCritSec

```
(No PUSHes)
```

## DosExecPgm

```
PUSH    PTR      Address of fail buffer (128 or so bytes long)
PUSH    WORD     Length of fail buffer
PUSH    WORD     Flags: 0 → synchronous execution
                        1 → Asynchronous execution (don't save
                                    child's result)
```

```
                         2 → Asynchronous execution (save child's
                                 result)
                         3 → Run program in debug mode
                         4 → Detached - use different session
PUSH      PTR      Address of two ASCIIZ strings, one after the other
                           First is program name (omitting extension),
                           next is command line input.
PUSH      PTR      ASCIIZ environment block. May be a NULL string
PUSH      PTR      Address of a dword area for termination information
                          Asynchronous execution → first word is
                                 process ID of terminating process
                          Synchronous Execution → first word is:
                                 0 → normal
                                 1 → hard error exit
                                 2 → trap
                                 3 → DosKillProcess used
                           Second word is always child's termination code
PUSH      PTR      Address of full ASCIIZ filename to execute (include
                          file's extension)
```

## DosExit

```
PUSH      WORD     Action code: 0 → stop this thread only
                                1 → stop all threads
PUSH      WORD     Termination code, passed to parent
```

## DosExitCritSec

```
(No PUSHes)
```

## DosGetHugeShift

```
PUSH      PTR      Address of word to receive huge shift count
```

## DosGetInfoSeg

```
PUSH      PTR      Pointer to word to receive selector of global
                          informatin segment
PUSH      PTR      Pointer to word to receive selector of local
                          informatin segment
```

## DosGetPrty

```
PUSH    WORD    Scope of request: 0 → priority of first thread
                                  2 → priority of specified thread
PUSH    PTR     Address of word that will receive the priority value
PUSH    WORD    ID of process (if scope is 0) or thread (if scope is
                        2) that priority is requested for
```

## DosGetShrSeg

```
PUSH    PTR     Address of ASCIIZ string holding the name of the
                        segment
PUSH    PTR     Address of memory word to receive segment selector
```

## DosKillProcess

```
PUSH    WORD    Action code: 0 → kill specified process and
                                 its descendants
                             1 → kill only indicated process
PUSH    WORD    Process ID of process to kill
```

## DosMakePipe

```
PUSH    PTR     Address of word to receive pipe read handle
PUSH    PTR     Address of word to receive pipe write handle
PUSH    WORD    Size of pipe in bytes
```

## DosMonClose

```
PUSH    WORD    Device monitor handle to close
```

## DosMonOpen

```
PUSH    PTR     Address of ASCIIZ device name
PUSH    PTR     Address of memory word to recieve monitor handle
```

## DosMonRead

```
PUSH    PTR     Address of monitor input buffer (set up with
                        DosMonReg)
PUSH    WORD    0 → wait for data
                1 → do not wait for data
```

```
PUSH     PTR      Address of data buffer for monitor input record
PUSH     PTR      Address of word to receive size of read bytes in data
                          record
```

## DosMonReg

```
PUSH     WORD     Device monitor handle
PUSH     PTR      Address of input buffer to register
PUSH     PTR      Address of output buffer to register
PUSH     WORD     I/O chain location: 0 → no preference
                                      1 → install at head of chain
                                      2 → install at end of chain
PUSH     WORD     Depends on device
```

## DosMonWrite

```
PUSH     PTR      Address of monitor output buffer (set up with
                          DosMonReg)
PUSH     PTR      Address of buffer that will hold monitor output record
PUSH     WORD     Length of data record in output buffer
```

## DosOpen

```
PUSH     PTR      Address of ASCIIZ filename
PUSH     PTR      Address of word to receive the file handle
PUSH     PTR      Address of word to receive action code:
                          1 → file existed
                          2 → was created
                          3 → was replaced
PUSH     DWORD    Initial file size (valid only when file is opened
                          or created)
PUSH     WORD     File attribute
PUSH     WORD     Open flag
                          If file does not already exist:
                                  0000 nnnn fail
                                  0001 nnnn create file
                          If file does exist already:
                                  nnnn 0000 fail
                                  nnnn 0001 open file
                                  nnnn 0010 create file
PUSH     WORD     Open mode: dwfrrrrrisssraaa (see file handling
                          chapter)
PUSH     DWORD    Both words must be 0
```

## DosOpenSem

```
PUSH     PTR      Address of dword to receive semaphore handle
PUSH     PTR      Address of ASCIIZ semaphore name (begin with "\SEM\")
```

## DosRead

```
PUSH     WORD     File handle
PUSH     PTR      Address of input buffer to use
PUSH     WORD     Length of input buffer
PUSH     PTR      Address of word to receive number of bytes read
```

## DosSemClear

```
PUSH     DWORD    Semaphore handle
```

## DosSemRequest

```
PUSH     DWORD    Semaphore handle
PUSH     DWORD    Timeout value:
                          0FFFFH → wait forever
                          00000H → return immediately if cannot get
                                   semaphore
                          nnnnnH → milliseconds to timeout
```

## DosSemSet

```
PUSH     DWORD    Semaphore handle
```

## DosSetPrty

```
PUSH     WORD     Scope:
                          0 → the process and all threads
                          1 → process and all decendants
                          2 → single thread in current process
PUSH     WORD     New priority class:
                          0 → do not change class
                          1 → idle
                          2 → regular
                          3 → time-critical
PUSH     WORD     Change in priority (-31 to 31)
PUSH     WORD     (scope = 0 or 1) ID of process; (scope = 2) ID of
                          thread
```

## DosSleep

```
PUSH     DWORD    Number of milliseconds to suspend execution
```

## DosStartSession

```
PUSH     PTR      Address of start session record:
                           DW 24
                           DW relation: 0 → new session is independent
                                        1 → new session is child
                           DW 0 → start session in foreground
                              1 → start session in background
                           DW 0 → session is not traceable
                              1 → session is traceable
                           DD address of ASCIIZ session title
                           DD address of program to run
                           DD address of parameter list passed to program
                           DD address of termination queue (can be NULL)
PUSH     PTR      Address of word to receive new session ID
PUSH     PTR      Address of word to receive ID of process in new
                           session
```

## DosSuspendThread

```
PUSH     WORD     Thread ID
```

## DosWrite

```
PUSH     WORD     File handle
PUSH     PTR      Address of output buffer to use
PUSH     WORD     Length of output buffer
PUSH     PTR      Address of word to receive number of bytes written
```

## GpiBox

```
PUSH     DWORD    Presentation space handle
PUSH     DWORD    Style:  0 → fill box
                          1 → outline box
                          2 → fill and outline
PUSH     PTR      Address of screen coordinates for one corner
PUSH     DWORD    Horizontal rounding (0 in this book)
PUSH     DWORD    Vertical rounding (0 in this book)
```

## GpiCharStringAt

```
PUSH     DWORD    Presentation space handle
PUSH     PTR      Address of screen coordinates
PUSH     DWORD    Length of string
PUSH     PTR      Address of the string
```

## GpiLine

```
PUSH    DWORD   Presentation space handle
PUSH    PTR     Address of screen coordinates to draw to
```

## GpiPolyLine

```
PUSH    DWORD   Presentation space handle
PUSH    DWORD   Number of coordinates to connect on screen
PUSH    PTR     Address of first pair of screen coordinates
```

## GpiSetBackColor

```
PUSH    DWORD   Presentation space handle
PUSH    DWORD   Color:
```

| | |
|---|---|
| Default | -3 |
| White | -2 |
| Black | -1 |
| Background | 0 |
| Blue | 1 |
| Red | 2 |
| Pink | 3 |
| Green | 4 |
| Cyan | 5 |
| Yellow | 6 |
| Neutral gray | 7 |
| Dark gray | 8 |
| Dark blue | 9 |
| Dark red | 10 |
| Dark pink | 11 |
| Dark green | 12 |
| Dark cyan | 13 |
| Brown | 14 |
| Light gray | 15 |

## GpiSetBackMix

```
PUSH    DWORD   Presentation space handle
PUSH    DWORD   Option: 0 → Default
                        1 → Overwrite current color
                        2 → Leave curent background unchanged
```

## GpiSetColor

```
PUSH    DWORD   Presentation space handle
PUSH    DWORD   Color:
```

| | |
|---|---|
| Default | -3 |
| White | -2 |
| Black | -1 |

| | |
|---|---|
| Background | 0 |
| Blue | 1 |
| Red | 2 |
| Pink | 3 |
| Green | 4 |
| Cyan | 5 |
| Yellow | 6 |
| Neutral gray | 7 |
| Dark gray | 8 |
| Dark blue | 9 |
| Dark red | 10 |
| Dark pink | 11 |
| Dark green | 12 |
| Dark cyan | 13 |
| Brown | 14 |
| Light grey | 15 |

## GpiSetCurrentPosition

```
PUSH    DWORD   Presentation space handle
PUSH    PTR     Address of screen coordinates
```

## GpiSetPel

```
PUSH    DWORD   Presentation space handle
PUSH    PTR     Address of screen coordinates
```

## KbdCharIn

```
PUSH    PTR     Address of kbd input structure:
                        DB ASCII character code
                        DB scan code
                        DB character status
                        DB NLS shift status
                        DW Shift state
                        DD Time stamp (milliseconds)
PUSH    WORD    0 → wait for character
                1 → do not wait
PUSH    WORD    Kbd handle (default = 0)
```

## KbdStringIn

```
PUSH    PTR     Address of input buffer
PUSH    PTR     Address of structure: DW Input buffer length
                                      DW Returned data length
```

```
PUSH    WORD    0 → wait until buffer is full
                1 → return immediately
PUSH    WORD    Kbd handle (default = 0)
```

## MouClose

```
PUSH    WORD    Mouse handle
```

## MouDrawPtr

```
PUSH    WORD    Mouse handle
```

## MouGetPtrPos

```
PUSH    PTR     Pointer to structure to return data:
                        DW row
                        DW column
PUSH    WORD    Mouse handle
```

## MouOpen

```
PUSH    PTR     Address of ASCIIZ name of mouse
PUSH    PTR     Address of word to receive mouse handle
```

## MouReadEventQueue

```
PUSH    PTR     Address of structure for returned data:
                        DW mouse state (see input chapter)
                        DD time tamp (milliseconds)
                        DW absolute or relative row
                        DW absolute or relative column
PUSH    PTR     Address of word which holds: 0 → do not wait
                                             1 → wait for data
PUSH    WORD    Mouse handle
```

## VioEndPopUp

```
PUSH    WORD    Vio handle (0)
```

## VioPopUp

```
PUSH     PTR      Option flags, OR these: 2 → transparent
                                          1 → wait for popup
PUSH     WORD     Vio handle (0)
```

## VioWrtCellStr

```
PUSH     PTR      Address of cell string (attribute, character)
PUSH     WORD     Length of string
PUSH     WORD     Row on screen
PUSH     WORD     Column on screen
PUSH     WORD     Vio handle (0)
```

## VioWrtCharStr

```
PUSH     PTR      Address of character string
PUSH     WORD     Length of string
PUSH     WORD     Row on screen
PUSH     WORD     Column on screen
PUSH     WORD     Vio handle (0)
```

## VioWrtCharStrAtt

```
PUSH     PTR      Address of character string
PUSH     WORD     Length of string
PUSH     WORD     Row on screen
PUSH     WORD     Column on screen
PUSH     PTR      Address of attribute byte to use
PUSH     WORD     Vio handle (0)
```

## VioWrtTTY

```
PUSH     PTR      Address of character string
PUSH     WORD     Length of string
PUSH     WORD     Vio handle (0)
```

## WinBeginPaint

```
PUSH     DWORD    Window handle (passed to window function)
PUSH     DWORD    If NULL, returns a Presentation Space handle
PUSH     PTR      Address of a region structure (left NULL in this book)
RETURNS: 32-bit Presentation space handle
```

## WinCreateMsgQueue

```
PUSH     DWORD    Anchor block handle
PUSH     WORD     Size (0 = default)
RETURNS: Queue handle
```

## WinCreateStdWindow

```
PUSH     DWORD    Parent window handle (0000 0001)
PUSH     DWORD    Style: 8000 000H to make visible)
PUSH     PTR      Address of window flags (see window chapter)
PUSH     PTR      Address of class name (set up with WinRegisterClass)
PUSH     PTR      Address of title bar text
PUSH     DWORD    Resource handle (set to 0 in this book)
PUSH     DWORD    Resource ID (set to 0 in this book)
PUSH     PTR      Address of dword to receive client window handle
RETURNS: 32-bit Frame handle
```

## WinDefWindowProc

```
PUSH     7 WORDS PASSED WINDOW FUNCTION
```

## WinDestroyMsgQueue

```
PUSH     DWORD    Queue handle
```

## WinDestroyWindow

```
PUSH     DWORD    Frame handle (returned by WinCreateStdWindow)
```

## WinDispatchMsg

```
PUSH     DWORD    Anchor block handle
PUSH     PTR      Address of queue buffer
```

## WinEndPaint

```
PUSH     DWORD    Presentation space handle
```

## WinGetMsg

```
PUSH     DWORD    Anchor block handle
PUSH     PTR      Address of queue buffer
```

```
PUSH     DWORD    Handle of window that you want to get messages for
                           (NULL → receive all messages)
PUSH     WORD     Set to 0
PUSH     WORD     Set to 0
```

## WinGetPS

```
PUSH     DWORD    Window handle (passed to window function)
RETURNS: 32-bit Presentation space handle
```

## WinInitialize

```
PUSH     WORD     Set to 0
RETURNS: 32-bit Anchor block handle
```

## WinRegisterClass

```
PUSH     DWORD    Anchor block handle
PUSH     PTR      Address of ASCIIZ window class name to register
PUSH     PTR      Address of window function
PUSH     DWORD    Set to 4 to have window redrawn when resized
PUSH     WORD     Extra memory requested (default = 0)
```

## WinReleasePS

```
PUSH     DWORD    Presentation space handle
```

## WinTerminate

```
PUSH     DWORD    Anchor block handle
```

# Index

# D

# E



# F

# G



# H



# I

# J



# K



# L



# M

# N



# O



# P

# Q



# R



# S

# T



# U

## V



## W



## X

# Turbo Pascal® Express

## Revised

250+ Ready-To-Run Assembly Language Routines that make Turbo Pascal Faster, More Powerful, and Easier to Use

By Robert Jourdain

---

*". . a huge volume of excellent Turbo Pascal Routines with source code. If you program in Turbo Pascal, you really should have this book."*

*Jerry Pournelle*
Byte Magazine

---

At last! This "worth its weight in gold" favorite among Pascal programmers has been revised for version 4.0 of Turbo Pascal.

The two diskettes contain more than 250 ready-to-use assembly language subroutines with source code. A few keystrokes put them to work in your Turbo Pascal programs, saving endless hours of labor. The book provides extensive documentation for each routine, including Pascal code examples.

ISBN 0-13-933193-X
$39.95

Among the contents you'll find:

- Equipment determination routines and access to expanded memory;
- Routines for bit operations and data compression;
- Extremely fast video facilities, including text-graphics routines for fancy menus and windows;
- Routines for elaborate printer control, formatting, and error recovery; and
- Powerful routines for searching and displaying directory trees.

Look for this and other Brady titles at your local book or computer store. To order directly call 1 (800) 624-0023, in New Jersey 1 (800) 624-0024
Visa/MC accepted

# Get Faster, More Powerful Programs in Assembler

*PS/2-PC Assembly Language* is designed for PC/PS/2 users with some high-level programming experience. If you want to speed up key sections of your C, Pascal, or BASIC programs, it's the book for you. Learn how to control this powerful language to create truly professional programs. Containing hundred of programs examples and routines, *PS/2-PC Assembly Language* also covers:

- OS/2 and DOS 4
- All of the PC microprocessors
- Screen handling and fast graphics
- Pop-up windows and linking files

Learn the ins and outs of assembly language with tip boxes and margin notes that provide special hints and approaches to coding. *PS/PS2 -PC Assembly Language* is the only guide you'll need.

ISBN: 0-13-731878-2
Price: $24.95

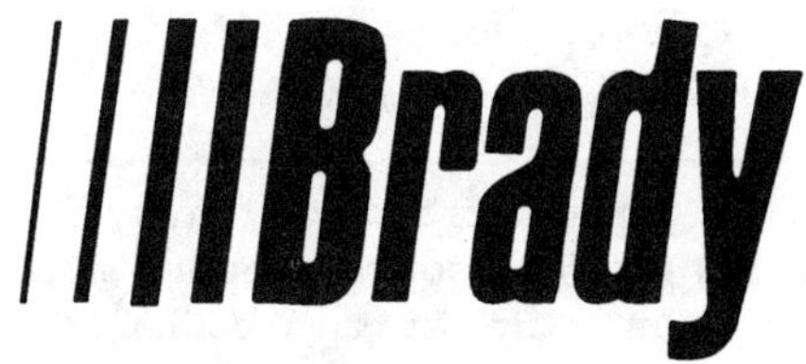


**Look for this and other Brady titles at your local book or computer store. To order directly: call 1 (800) 624-0023, Visa/MC accepted**

# Peter Norton's Assembly Language Book

## Revised and Expanded

by Peter Norton and John Socha

Learn Assembly Language with Software Tools from Peter Norton!

Speak to your IBM PC or PS/2 in the language it knows best—assembly language—with this unique software package from two master programmers: Peter Norton and John Socha. This easy-to-use guide, with its powerful disk, gives you hands-on experience with assembly language. Gain a throrough understanding of the fundamentals of 8088 and 80286 hardware, high-level languages, and how to write full-scale assembly language programs of your own! The disk contains an advanced version of "Dskpatch"—the program developed throughout the book—in addition to the chapter examples.

You can use this book and disk with an IBM PC, XT, AT, PS/2, or compatible, with a minimum of 256K, one disk drive, PC or MS-DOS Version 2.0 or higher, and Microssoft's MASM (version 5.0 or later, the Turbo Assembler from Borland, or .OPTSAM from SLR systems.

All the chapter examples are included (from chapters 9 through 27, 30, and 32). Appendix A provides a complete list of the files and their revisions. Appendix B provides the program listings.

Now, let your adventure in assembly language begin. . .

With the expertise of Peter Norton and John Socha, you're guaranteed an experience that's both informative and practical.

The Peter Norton Foundation Series
ISBN: 0-13-662479-0 $44.95 book/disk
(also available in paper ISBN: 0-13-662453-7 $24.95 )

Look for this and other Brady titles at your local book or computer store. To order directly call 1 (800) 624-0023
Visa/MC accepted

# About the Author

Steven Holzner earned his BS degree at MIT and a Ph.D. at Cornell, where he was a lecturer in physics. He has travelled to over 30 countries, lived for a year each in Hong Kong and Hawaii, and spends summers in Austria. Steven is now moving to Santa Cruz, California.